Todd,
Hope it's to your
liking.
Troy Parfitt

April 5th, 2011

D1473831

Troy Parfitt

Why China Will Never Rule the World

Travels in the Two Chinas

First Edition

**Western
Hemisphere
Press**

Saint John, New Brunswick

WHY CHINA WILL NEVER RULE THE WORLD
TRAVELS IN THE TWO CHINAS
by Troy Parfitt

Western Hemisphere Press
125 Rothesay Avenue, PO Box 1401
Saint John, New Brunswick, Canada
E2L 4H8
Orders: west.hem.press@gmail.com

Soft cover ISBN: 978-0-9868035-0-5

First Edition 2011

Printed and bound in the United States.

Library and Archives Canada Cataloguing in Publication

Parfitt, Troy, 1972-
  Why China will never rule the world : travels in the two Chinas / Troy Parfitt.

Includes bibliographical references.
Includes some text in Chinese characters and Romanized Chinese.
ISBN 978-0-9868035-0-5

  1. Parfitt, Troy, 1972- --Travel--China. 2. Parfitt, Troy, 1972- --Travel--Taiwan. 3. China--Description and travel. 4. Taiwan--Description and travel. 5. China--Civilization--21st century. I. Title.

DS712.P368 2011   951.06092   C2010-907784-9

DEDICATION

In loving memory of my mother and father.

Acknowledgements

I would like to thank my editor Steven Crook, my proofreader John Ross, and my translator Emma Chou for all their patience, hard work, and encouragement.

Notes on spelling, currency, names and Romanization

The text of this book utilizes Canadian spelling, which is more British than American. 'Dollars' and the dollar sign refer to US dollars, unless otherwise stated, e.g. Hong Kong dollars (HK$) or New Taiwan dollars (NT$). Names of Chinese people have been rendered in the form most familiar to English speakers. For example, China's most famous leader is best-known as Mao Zedong not Mao Tse-tung. When it comes to the Romanization of place names in China, I have used the *hanyu pinyin* system, which is all but ubiquitous in that country. There are still a few place names in China that don't always appear in *hanyu pinyin*, such as Harbin, Turpan, and Tibet. The only one of these I have converted to *hanyu pinyin* is Harbin, which appears in these pages as Haerbin. Romanization in Taiwan is something of a mixed bag with *hanyu pinyin* now competing against Wade-Giles, or a somewhat corrupted version of Wade-Giles. I've simply written place names in the latest preferred spelling. One exception is Jinmen, which in Taiwan is usually spelled Kinmen.

TABLE OF CONTENTS

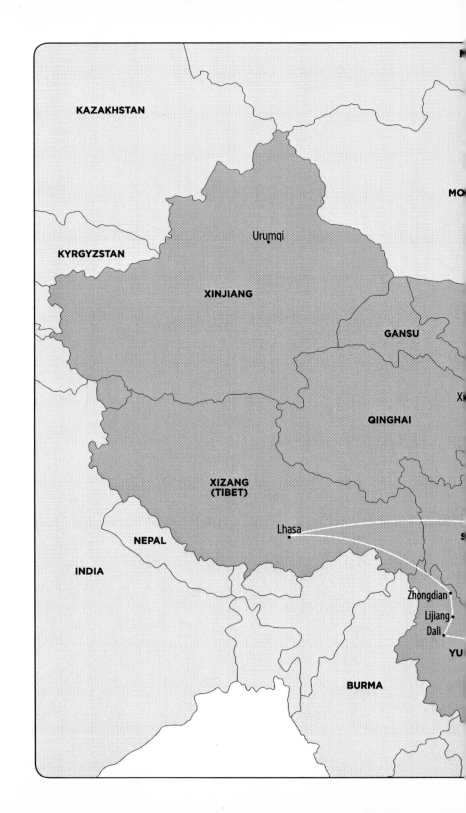

KAZAKHSTAN

KYRGYZSTAN

XINJIANG

Urumqi

GANSU

QINGHAI

Xi

XIZANG
(TIBET)

NEPAL

Lhasa

S

INDIA

Zhongdian

Lijiang

Dali

YU

BURMA

MO

MO

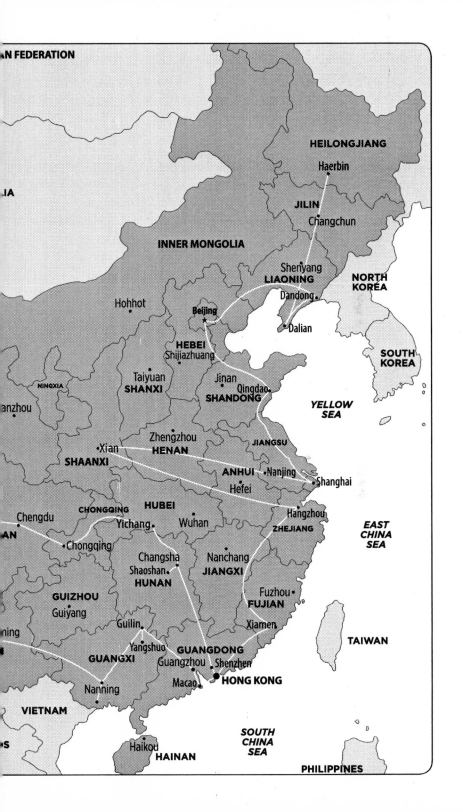

"From now on, there are two totally different states in the territory of China. One is the so-called Republic of China, which is a tool of imperialism…. The other is the Chinese Soviet Republic, the state of the broad masses of exploited and oppressed workers, peasants, and toilers."

- Mao Zedong

That which is united will eventually separate, and that which is separated will eventually reunite.

- A Chinese proverb

"Orthodoxy means not thinking – not needing to think. Orthodoxy is unconsciousness."

- George Orwell

"Next to the right to create, the right to criticize is the richest gift that liberty of thought and speech can offer."

- Vladimir Nabokov

WHY CHINA
WILL NEVER
RULE THE WORLD

PROLOGUE

'China, China, China.' It seems it's all you ever hear these days. At least it seems it's all *I* ever hear these days. I live in Taiwan, Republic of China, the island Beijing regards as a renegade province, so all the hubbub is a little hard to ignore. 'People in China are well educated, highly skilled, inordinately industrious, exceedingly clever, English-speaking, shrewd at business, and generally not to be messed with,' my adult students had routinely informed me over the years. "*Tamen dou hen lihai*," or so went the common refrain: "They're all so very formidable." 'Soon, we won't be able to compete with them,' the sentiment usually continued. 'No one will. It's just a matter of time before they start to shape the world.'

I used to chalk up all this adulation to cultural bias. However, I couldn't help notice that attitudes in the West tended to mimic this outlook. From the concerned parent's, "Gosh, they make *everything* over there now, don't they?" to the businessperson's inspection of China book titles (*When China Rules the World, China Shakes the World, The China Road: A Journey into the Future of a Rising Power*) to the university student's enrolment in Mandarin classes, it seemed as if Westerners were finally starting to sit up and take notice, and not solely owing to the country's impressive economic performance, although that certainly was a large part of it.

Since having joined the World Trade Organization in 2001, China had doubled its share of global manufacturing output, had seen its annual trade surplus reach as high as $218 billion, had enjoyed an average annual growth of more than 10 percent in all but three years, and had amassed foreign-exchange reserves in excess of $2.4 trillion; half invested in US Treasury bonds (China is now the world's largest holder of US Treasury bonds) and half invested in notes. Not only had the country experienced a colossal commodity boom fuelled by rising incomes and the emergence of a *bona fide* middle class, but there had been minimal inflation, nominal unemployment (if official reports are to be believed), a colossal sum of direct foreign investment (in 2003, China became the world's chief recipient of direct foreign investment), and – most significantly – no real sign of things slowing down, at least until the global recession came along, but even that wasn't enough to stagger the leviathan. In 2009, China's economy reportedly grew by 8.3 percent, surpassing World Bank expectations by nearly 2 percentage points. Even if it wasn't the double-digit growth the country had become used to, China could always console itself with the trillion or so dollars it held in US debt. It could also take comfort in its currency, the *yuan* or *renminbi* or RMB, a non-tradable unit not subject to speculation or volatility. China's cheap and seemingly bottomless labour pool was something else it could be chuffed about.

In mid-2010, China surpassed Japan to become the world's second largest economy. Goldman Sachs has predicted it will outstrip the United States economy by the year 2027.

By 2020, or so pundits were predicting, the Middle Kingdom was slated to become the world's foremost tourist destination, evidence to suggest that, for the first time, large numbers of non-Chinese were taking more than just a casual interest in China's history and culture. Indeed, Chinese culture was finally beginning to make inroads abroad, or at least beyond the superficialities of takeaway, tattoos, and *The Tao of Pooh*. In the West, Mandarin had made great strides in the realm of second-language study. China's Ministry of Education estimated that there would be 100 million learners of the language outside of Greater China by 2010. A portion of this cohort would take classes in both Mandarin and Chinese culture at one of the Chinese-government-established Confucius Institutes, of which there are more than 145 spread over some 50 countries. In addition to language, educated and progressive people everywhere have shown an interest in Chinese calligraphy, Traditional Chinese Medicine (TCM), Tai Chi, and even *fengshui*. There was just something so very intriguing, so very Eastern about it all.

Of course, not everyone was besotted by China and its media-touted meteoric rise. To be certain, something of a pitched battle had begun between a wide range of individuals and interest groups essentially over whether China was friend or foe. Politicians, Sinologists, other academics, journalists, authors, businesspeople, talk-show hosts, and casual observers were all weighing in on the matter, and, consequently, were facing off against one another in the rough capacity of Sinophile vs. Sinophobe, or panda hugger vs. dragon slayer, as they had contemporarily become known.

At the time of writing, it should have been obvious to most observers that China had more than its fair share of problems. The once steady stream of sanguine fiscal projections, accompanied by snapshots of happy shoppers and glittering skylines, had failed to stem a recurring tide of negative press. Human rights abuses, peasant revolts, pollution horror stories, tainted exports, natural disasters, corrupt officials, growing concerns over an expanding military, unrest in Tibet and Xinjiang, the Taiwan issue, and friction with the United States clearly indicated a nation under strain. Yet, in spite of the rather ominous shadow that such reports regularly cast, the prevailing sentiment seemed to be that China either *was* the future or that it was scheduled to be an integral part of the future. It was a forgone conclusion. The Chinese themselves were claiming that the twenty-first century was going to be theirs, and panda huggers and dragon slayers were nodding their heads in either joyous or reluctant agreement.

But if China was rising, where exactly was it rising to? This seemed to be the question on many people's minds.

I found it odd that the focus was on what China might one day become and not on what it is at present and what it had been in the past. Although definitely important to keep an eye on the future, it occurred to me that predictions weren't one of mankind's strong suits. It also occurred to me that commentators preferred to focus on the theoretical because they often possessed only a notional understanding of China in the now and a fundamentally formless one of it in history.

I suppose I had become tired of hearing about how wonderful China's economy was. I was equally weary of hearing China being labelled a superpower or a great nation, with those terms seldom being qualified. I was unimpressed with the bulk of opinion piece forecasts I read in newspapers ('Five reasons why China will collapse,' 'China's inevitable path to democracy,' etc.). I remained especially unmoved by China writers and watchers who had, for one reason or another, become smitten with the Middle Kingdom, believing it to be a land of immeasurable achievement and boundless opportunity; a nation that deserved its place in the sun by virtue of its antiquity and what it had endured. To my way of thinking, this equated to a near total refutation of its history. "China's future is bright. So is its past," or so went an optimistic blurb I read in a Western news magazine. But that was only true if you'd never studied China's past. Anyway, with well over 800 Chinese missiles pointed my way, there was never much chance of a conversion. Truly, I failed to see any of the People's Republic's charms, although it has been said I lack imagination.

But then, I wasn't an enormous admirer of Taiwan, Republic of China, either – or at least its particular take on what a nation and society ought to resemble. I mention this because long-term foreign residents of

Taiwan are often intensely pro-ROC and, by extension, deliriously anti-PRC. As a comparative model, I believe Taiwan to be superior in nearly every respect, and, admittedly, I sympathize with its plight, yet I feel it possesses a broad spectrum of conspicuous deficiencies which never seem to get acknowledged, let alone addressed. Taiwan, Republic of China is out of sync with the Western world, a world it often claims to be a part of.

I figured that I could bring a unique perspective to the table. I had no vested interest save for a bookish one and was without professional affiliation of any kind. I wasn't a journalist, so I couldn't embarrass my publication. I wasn't an academic, so I needn't censor myself for fear of being barred from conferences, university lectures, and wine-and-cheeses in, say, Shanghai. Neither did I have to fret about corporate funding being cut off from my think tank should I happen to come to a supremely negative conclusion. In America, China experts are often hired by the government to produce reports advocating "engagement" while they go about beefing up their investment portfolios with Chinese shipping and coal companies. But that wasn't me. I wasn't a Sinophile, but I wasn't a Sinophobe. I was merely an English teacher who had taken an interest. I had spent most of my adult life in a Chinese society, and during that time I had read up on Chinese history, studied the language, read the literature, and spent an immoderate to unhealthy amount of time observing the people and contemplating the national psyche, as it were. I figured I had as much to say as anyone.

I surmised that if China really were going to take its place as a nation among nations, then Western people were going to have to learn something about it; about its people, its culture, its history, and what it felt like to live and travel there. And if Westerners were ever going to do that, they would need to cease exoticizing China and be more discriminating when told what it was. Not that this was entirely their fault, mind you. Thanks to the press and certain writers, China was habitually depicted as alien and unfathomable to the point where it seemed more another planet than another nation-state, and casual observers had been habituated to believe that this perennially recycled perception was the reality. But China *is* a nation-state and the Chinese themselves are entirely knowable and frequently predictable, despite what all the mythomaniacs would have you believe.

Also inherent in the standard analysis was the implication that the China observer or visitor ought to suspend his or her judgment as China was just, in some undefined way, different. But surely suspending one's judgment wasn't the answer. After all, the entire point of investigation is to arrive at a conclusion, not to merely regurgitate the same old stilted phrases ('the dragon awakes') or dredge up exhausted imagery (the skyscrapers of Pudong). That's what Western philosophy teaches us: to continually investigate and scrutinize, and to do so with total intellectual freedom. Many so-called China experts had forgotten this. I thought that China was long overdue for a reassessment.

I felt compelled to see if there were anything to it all; if there were anything I might have missed. I wanted to know what lay behind the headlines and images. Was China really and finally on its way to becoming a modern state, or was it simply undergoing a belated industrial revolution and a period of economic liberalization? Was the modernization pervasive, or was it merely window-dressing; something grafted on to an ancient society and mindset? And what about political liberalization? Chinese democracy was frequently portrayed as something that was just around the corner. Was there any evidence to support this? Did the people even want it? I needed to know. I needed to know the truth. More precisely, I needed to know *my own* truth.

To do this, I would have to explore China in its entirety, something I had always wanted to do anyway. I would follow the tourist path when it suited me or stray far from the beaten track. I would comment on aspects of culture, history, and politics, and I would report on what I saw. I would talk to the people. I would observe them. I would note down what they said and did. I would speak Mandarin when it was called for and English when it wasn't. So as not to draw attention, I would dress and act like a tourist and pretend to know next to nothing. At the same time, I would try not to take it all too seriously. The quirkiness of the Chinese world had not eluded me, and I wasn't without a sense of humour.

I had been living in the shadow of the red giant for some 12 years, watching as it had begun to warp and distend, as its sway and pull had begun to influence the trajectory of its satellites. And yet, besides a stopover in Hong Kong and a month-long study sojourn in Beijing, I had never *really* been there. I decided that this had to change. So, blowing the dust off my Mandarin textbooks, I enrolled in language classes in Taipei, dialed up my travel agent, and set aside three months to complete my journey. As Allan Bloom once wrote, "The mind that has no prejudices at the outset is empty." Absolutely. But in spite of my prejudices, I honestly tried to approach the experience with as open a mind as possible. And I must admit that things certainly started off well enough.

PART ONE

To and from the Western Treasure House

Chapter One

It felt as though I had been submerged in an ocean of tar. Peering through the smallish square, my eye was met with a pitch black void. For quite some time, there existed only this bordered onyx constant along with the familiar and reassuring hum. I was about to nod off when suddenly – startlingly – a phosphorescent streak shot forth, mutely bursting into a tangle of jubilant purple and glittering green before cascading soundlessly into the abyss below. Fireworks. This was the first image I got of China. Other fragments came into view: myriad dots of light, silhouettes of mountains, miniaturized skyscrapers, Victoria Harbour…. It was Hong Kong, and within minutes my plane would be touching down and I would be looking for transport to whisk me into neon-bejewelled Kowloon.

Emerging into an airless night, I boarded a double-decker bus and watched as the impossible hills of Lantau Island gave way to tenement blocks, which duly succumbed to the shops, hotels, and brilliant lights of Nathan Road, Kowloon's so-called Golden Mile. It was a Saturday evening in June and the street lamps were busy bathing the sidewalks and pedestrians in a soft, mustard-coloured glow. Overhead, incandescent signs alternated between splotchy Chinese characters and upper-case English letters: 永隆銀行, YUE HWA CHINESE PRODUCTS, 大久保日本料理, WANG FAT PAWN SHOP, 信和大藥房, XXX KARAOKE NIGHT CLUB. At Tsim Sha Tsui, the bus doors hissed open and I crossed the street and made my way past an ensemble of Africans, South Asians, and Middle Easterners. "Hey boss! Hash? Rolex? Girl?" Entering a doorway, I was met with an edifice of stale air before finally squeezing into a slow moving lift that took me to one of the 90 or so low-rent, no-frills guest houses located above. This was Chungking Mansions, Hong Kong's most notorious building.

A 17-storey labyrinth of small apartments and small enterprises (curry joints, money exchanges, luggage kiosks, mahjong parlours, sweat shops), Chungking Mansions has served as a haunt for foreign backpackers, foreign labourers, and foreign "businessmen" for decades owing to its budget rooms and prime location. With its monstrous veneer of moss green tiles and obtruding air conditioners, the building sticks out like a bad simile when viewed from without, but is infinitely worse when examined from within. Floors are awash with litter and spittle, and stairwells have been tattooed with cigarette burns. Smoke and a host of nameless odours mingle about your nostrils while surveillance cameras record the movements of the multinational clientele. There is a decidedly illicit air about the place and not much in the way of conversation or even eye contact. Police raids are not infrequent.

I eventually settled on Tom's Guest House. It wasn't the Ritz, but it was an improvement over the other two places I'd looked at. An aging Filipino woman with thick glasses and a gold cross around her neck was the acting receptionist. She smelled of booze and the counter behind her was a glass menagerie of rum bottles. When I asked after the price, she said that she didn't know and would have to telephone the owner.

"Papa!" she screamed down the receiver. "There is man here who wants room. What price I should speak to heem? I *said*, 'What price I should speak to heem!?' No, papa. He's European. *Eur-o-pee-an*. No… not *Indian*, papa. From *Europe*. I don't know, maybe England. Okay. Okay, Papa. You get some rest. I *said*, 'You get some rest, papa!'" And then she placed the phone back in its cradle. "That'll be a hundred and thirty Hong Kong dollars, sir." I paid, and she handed me the key.

In the room, there were perhaps two and a half square metres of floor space. I sent a cockroach scurrying for cover when I turned on the bathroom light and a switch caused the air conditioner to cough and sputter to life. It grumbled thereafter in muffled imitation of a prop plane. Whenever I activated the ceiling fan, the room would suddenly begin to smell of fried noodles. I switched it on and off trying to determine which was worse: suffering from the heat or suffering from the stench. I took an abridged shower and then lay down with a book, careful not to move lest I disturb anything that might have considered the space beneath the bed to be its home. My final thought before falling into a fitful slumber was, 'If there's a fire, I'm finished.'

I woke to a stunningly beautiful day and sauntered along store-filled streets and past buildings ribbed with bamboo scaffolding. I headed to Salisbury Road and the Star Ferry Pier. Besides a few text-messaging Filipinos, some camera-clicking tourists, and the odd leaflet-dispensing Mormon, the city was sleeping in and therefore curiously quiet. Purchasing a ticket, I traversed a gangway and plunked myself down on one of the long wooden benches. The pong of diesel fumes hung thickly in the air.

With its unassuming flotilla of rotund boats, Hong Kong's Star Ferry has been chugging between Kowloon and Hong Kong Island for more than a century, having been conceived of by a Parsee gentleman with the wonderfully melodic name of Dorabjee Nowrojee, who christened his service in an allusion to an Alfred Lord Tennyson poem entitled 'Crossing the Bar.' Supposedly, the alternating length of its lines was meant to lend it a wave-like quality.

Sunset and the evening star,
And one clear call for me!
And may there be no moaning at the bar,
When I put out to sea,

It is fitting that the ferry's origin should be imbued with a tinge of romantic legend as there is something inexplicably enchanting about riding it and observing Hong Kong Island as it travels steadily toward you. Here, the eye is met with one marvel of modern architecture after another in a skyline that has been described as "a dream of Manhattan arising from the South China Sea."

After alighting, I strolled past the stately neoclassical Legislative Council Building, in front of which sat throngs of chatting Filipinos, who were ignoring police requests to move along. Coming to a main thoroughfare, I jumped on a tramcar uncertain of exactly where I was headed, but this hardly seemed to matter.

Although Hong Kong has both a first-rate bus and excellent metro system, the city's 163 double-deck tramcars are still immensely popular with residents and tourists, seeing nearly a quarter million passengers daily. It was definitely popular with me, and even though I was only being shuttled through a corridor of department stores and glass towers, it wasn't hard to conjure a vignette-like image of yesteryear, one replete with imposing colonial structures, darting coolies and rickshaws, occasional stout automobiles, overhanging wooden signs, and clattering vehicles identical to the one I was on now. From St. John's Cathedral, I bought a ticket and boarded another type of tram. As is the norm on one's first day in Hong Kong, I was "goin' up the Peak."

It used to be that Victoria Peak was the place to reside if you were non-Chinese and filthy rich. Nowadays, you only have to be filthy rich. About $12 million is what you will need for a triplex, although you can spend many times that if you require space in addition to opulence. An infinity pool or tennis court might be included, but, like anywhere, the obligatory sports car is sold separately.

In the past, the Peak's inhabitants were actually carried to and from their breezy mansions in sedan chairs, an endeavour typically involving an hour of gruelling work. The construction of the Peak Tram in 1888 converted this tortuous slog into a ten-minute jaunt, albeit one that was at a severe angle. Whenever I had seen a snapshot of the vehicle, it was invariably a postcard-like image of it arriving at the summit. I hadn't been aware that its trajectory was closer to that of an elevator than the sort of leisurely ride one normally associates with the word 'tram.'

Up through swaying trees and spastic shadows, I peered to my right to note that tenement buildings were jutting straight out of people's throats. In front of me, an elderly Japanese couple clung to each other for dear life. But it wasn't so bad; not once you got used to it. In fact, it was quite agreeable. Any one of them – the Star Ferry, the double-deck tramcars, the Peak Tram – was a treat in and of itself. When ridden in succession, the experience was nothing short of superb and had the irrepressible side effect of making you feel awake and alive.

The first order of business was to examine the mesmerizing skyline, which I did under a pagoda with the aid of a chart. This done, I gazed toward the wake-streaked harbour and then to Kowloon and the mountainous New Territories beyond. It was all very impressive, especially when you consider the city's humble origins. Hong Kong, which means "Fragrant Harbour," was little more than a listless fishing village until the sixteenth century, when foreign powers began trading here after having set up shop in nearby Macau. As is well known, the territory was ceded to the British, and this occurred in a piecemeal fashion during a period of nearly 58 years. And this, as is also well known, was the result of the Opium Wars, a series of defining events in Chinese history, critical to understanding the Chinese mindset of today.

In attempting to trade with the Chinese, the British were faced with a couple of considerable obstacles. For one, the Chinese didn't trade, at least not officially. Unofficially, the country had benefited from barter for nearly a century; whole regions prospered from it and the government relied on taxing it. But it could never be sanctioned. Trade entailed a partnership between equals, and China was the greatest civilization on Earth. Hence, the government would only accept "tribute" and "gifts" from vassal states.

There was also the matter of the Chinese not wanting anything. As Emperor Qianlong famously put it to King George III, "We possess all things. I set no value on objects strange or ingenious and have no use for your country's manufactures."[1]

During the eighteenth century, this niggling dilemma became more pronounced when tea became Britain's national drink. The British were forced to import the stuff, thus putting a severe strain on the national treasury. Eventually, Britain hit on the only thing the Chinese did want: opium, and lots of it. For the British, this turned out to be a catholicon, but for the Chinese it proved to be an unmitigated disaster. The gummy narcotic had a devastating effect socially, economically, and politically. Addiction spread like wildfire and silver exited the country by the boatload. An already feeble and fraudulent Qing government tottered and swayed under the strain.[2]

After a prolonged period of inaction followed by a lengthy episode of moral exhortation, the Chinese finally concretized their objections with a blockade, the imprisonment of foreign merchants, and the confiscation and destruction of 3 million pounds of the drug. But one thing (among the many) that the Chinese failed to comprehend was that the seized chests of opium constituted Crown property as they had been handed over by the superintendent of foreign trade. Rather than take a sabbatical and reflect upon the ethical implications of running drugs and ruining a nation, as the Chinese had hoped, the foreign devils simply petitioned the Crown for compensation, hence rattling the queen's jewels and inflaming public opinion.

An armed flotilla was dispatched to put things right, and the Chinese soon found themselves signing the Treaty of Nanjing, whereby Hong Kong Island was ceded to Britain "in perpetuity" to be governed "as was seen fit." The ports of Shanghai, Ningbo, Fuzhou, and Xiamen were pried open to foreign trade and settlement as well. Up until then, only Guangzhou (Canton) had been officially open for business. Taking their cue from the British, the Americans and French promptly drew up their own treaties with even more demands (and the British had quite a few demands) and asked that the Chinese kindly sign them.

---

1   The message to the British monarch, communicated by letter through Earl Macartney, was actually much longer not to mention patronizing in tone. It praised England for having sought out civilization before outlining just why trade wasn't possible. It concluded with a warning: "You, O King, should simply act in conformity with our wishes by strengthening your loyalty and swearing perpetual obedience to ensure that your country may share the blessings of peace."

2   The Qing Dynasty (1644–1912) was China's final dynasty. The Qing were ethnically Manchu and therefore considered by the Han Chinese to be outsiders. The Manchus had managed to mollify all of China by 1683 and their stability stemmed from a high degree of integration with Chinese culture along with brutal repression. In the late nineteenth century, the dynasty became increasingly corrupt and inefficient and was destabilized by revolts and dissent.

As for the original treaty, the Chinese were reluctant to comply with its many clauses. They had, after all, signed it at gunpoint. Their intransigence brought about the Second Opium War, which saw another military walkover followed by the signing of another treaty, one which stipulated that foreigners would have the right to establish permanent diplomatic residence in Beijing. However, before the agreement could be ratified, a local army attacked a British one, killing hundreds and sinking several ships. The British responded by allying with the French and invading Beijing, whereupon troops looted the city and set fire to both the new and old Summer Palaces. The second treaty, known as the Treaty of Tianjin (1858, 1859), saw the opium trade, partially banned in 1729 and totally banned in 1799, legalized.

Westerners sometimes take the view that what happened to the Chinese was regrettable but necessary, as if China was somehow done a favour by being woken from its torpor. That the Middle Kingdom needed to realize there were technologically superior societies all around it, there is no question, but lending legitimacy to bald-faced aggression and interference is another matter entirely. That isn't to say the Chinese didn't handle the situation badly, though. That the Western powers felt it necessary to exercise the military option strongly suggests that they did.

In their book, *Narcotic Culture: A History of Drugs in China*, authors Frank Dikötter, Lars Laamann, and Zhou Xun offer up a spirited challenge to the standard perception that China was, in fact, enslaved by imperialism or that it was a casualty of opium addiction. According to their research, Sinologists are guilty of reproducing an excessively simplistic history of China's opium years, one formed in the late nineteenth century by prohibitionist missionaries who dealt in the currency of "narcophobic discourse," as well as foreign journalists and Chinese nationalists keen to broadcast the evils of Occidental intrusion. In solidifying their claims, the writers make some interesting observations. For example, they point out that China itself had a very healthy opium industry of its own; the drug wasn't always imported. Furthermore, opium is not a single or even uniform substance, so it's difficult to determine precisely what commentators mean when they refer to it and its usage. The conception of China having become a nation of drug fiends is also deconstructed; most consumption was "light and moderate" without any "serious loss of control." Like nicotine, opium is a psychotropic substance, meaning it's taken in determined amounts, not ever-increasing ones. The image of the opium den as a breeding ground for depravity also comes under fire. The writers remind us that W. Somerset Maugham was astonished to note that the opium house he

visited was "neat and bright, with clean matting in every room." Even
the League of Nations conceded that opium houses were clean and tidy
more often than not. Ultimately, say the authors, academics have spent far
too much time focusing on the pharmacological effects of the substance
when they ought to be examining its cultural context.

However, by deemphasizing opium's pharmacological effects, not
to mention the topics of addiction and abuse, the arguments in *Narcotic
Culture* quickly lose much of their steam. Opium smoking constituted
a highly intricate and complex ritual in which nearly everyone partook,
the authors claim. It was a collective experience. But what they fail
to mention is that almost everything in Chinese culture is a collective
experience. Besides, the complexity or collectiveness involved in
consumption is irrelevant, as are many other of the book's arguments.
For example, it is noted that opium was widely available in other parts
of the world. It even provided "an escape from the strains of working-
class life in Victorian England." An opium house was akin to a pub, and
the taking of opium could be compared to the taking of tea, and so on
and so forth. That's all fine and well, but opium is not tea and China
is not England. The tome goes on to state that opium was widely used
as a palliative against a broad spectrum of maladies and conditions in
China, but so was the eating of ash from incense and the powder from
"dragon bones." As late as 2007, residents of a village in the province
of Henan were found peddling powdered dinosaur femurs and declaring
their product medicine. It ought to go without saying that just because
someone believes something to be good for them, it doesn't necessarily
mean that it is, and just because a practice is widespread doesn't signify
that it's valid. Dikötter and company aver that opium had no "serious
consequences for the health or life expectancy of the vast majority of its
users," but of course such a claim is impossible to substantiate. Besides,
just one page previous, they state that retailers often cut the stuff with
tobacco, arsenic, mercury, turpentine, sand, clay, and lead.

Opium is a sedative. It makes you stoned, it makes you lethargic, and
it temporarily erodes your linear thinking. I should know. I've smoked it
on two occasions. These days, the BBC reports on "opium addiction"
in poverty-stricken Afghanistan. I wonder how the authors of this book
would explain away the term as it relates to the cultural context of that
unfortunate nation. The book succeeds only partially in illustrating what
the opium era wasn't, but it is unconvincing in its description of what it
was.

Incidentally, what the opium era really was is a matter of interest only
to non-Chinese. The Chinese themselves already understand the issue

very well, it having been part of the educational pablum they have been fed since childhood. In the Pearl River town of Humen, officials have built a giant pair of hands rising out of the soil snapping an opium pipe in two. At the town's Sandy Point Fortress, where the British fired the first shots of the Opium Wars, there is a museum where visitors can partake in mock search-and-destroy missions against smugglers. This involves shooting laser guns at grinning, red-haired automatons that shuttle along on tracks saying, "Bastard! I'll chop you!" Down the coast, there is the Lin Zexu Memorial Hall, where guests can visit the pits where the first chests of seized opium were destroyed. Then, they can fire rubber balls from cannons at images of British vessels painted on a wall.

It's difficult to find a book about China that doesn't offer a summary of the Opium Wars, so I apologize for the repetition. Having said that, it's difficult to understate the significance of the events; the Opium Wars and the shame that they brought may as well have occurred yesterday. Mainly owing to the efforts of the Chinese Communist Party, which spends an overgenerous amount of time educating and reminding its citizenry (and military) about this disgraceful episode, the Opium Wars are now portrayed as the starting point of modern Chinese history. A grade-school primer in China called *Ten Must-Knows for Elementary School Students*, disseminated to celebrate the 50th anniversary of the People's Republic of China, cites "one hundred years of Chinese people opposing foreign aggression" as the state's *raison d'être*. China refers to the hundred years between 1849 and 1949 as its "century of shame," and the Opium Wars constitute the basis of that shame and the basis of all anti-foreigner sentiment, things you don't have to search very hard to find. But clearly, here, I'm getting ahead of myself.

I decided to walk around the Peak and was soon sauntering along a welcoming path walled by a dense array of subtropical foliage. The walk was lovely and the views fetching. The trees and bushes were buzzing with insects and fidgeting with birds and butterflies. The pathways were nicely built and featured distance markers and interesting bits of information on the island's history, geology, flora, and fauna. The trail bypassed several mansions with fences either topped with barbed wire or jagged bits of broken glass. An old couple stood near one such barrier selling grass grasshoppers that they had apparently made. I wound my way back to the tram and used my return ticket to descend and view the crooked skyscrapers in reverse.

Thinking I might spend the afternoon doing a walking tour suggested in my guidebook,[3] I got on yet another tramcar and asked the

---

3   The Lonely Planet. On the whole, I found it to be excellent.

driver how many stops it was until Sutherland Road. "I don't know," he said smilingly. "I don't know English street name." This is something that quickly hits you in Hong Kong: despite having been a Crown colony for nearly 140 years, neither English culture nor the English language really ever took hold.

With a population density of roughly 6,300/km² there isn't much in Hong Kong you can expect to have to yourself, so you can imagine my surprise upon discovering that I was pretty much the only soul out of doors in a district known as Sheung Wan. It was baking-hot and I doused myself in sunscreen and craned my neck around at the sights and sounds. I ambled down Chinese Medicine Street, where I peered in at the apothecaries and sacks of foodstuffs, and noted a wonderful old corner store done up in Bruce Lee posters. On Possession Street, I took note of the spot where the Union Jack was first planted. Then I walked by a branch of the Hong Kong Jockey Club, the territory's foremost taxpayer. A collection of men congregated about the entrance and adjacent alleyway where they smoked and silently scrutinized information sheets, each formulating his own winning strategy.

I ended up at Man Mo Temple, located on Hollywood Road. It possessed wax red pillars, hanging incense coils, blackened ceiling fans, and students who had come to pray for good exam results. A sign on the wall advertised fortune telling. It read:

'PEOPLE ALWAYS THINK ABOUT WHAT TO BE IN FUTURE. WHAT'S THE PLAN. OR IMAGINE ABOUT HIS/ HER FUTURE GOOD OR BAD. COME IN DON'T LOSE THIS CHANCE TO KNOW YOUR FUTURE DON'T GUESS WHAT IT WILL BE……….. PLEASE COME IN I CAN TELL YOU EVERYTHING YOU WANT TO KNOW…..'

As I stood there jotting this down, I heard a voice addressing me. "You want your fortune told?" It belonged to a robed, middle-aged man sitting behind a desk piled high with books and papers.

"That depends on how much it costs," I replied. He then showed me a chart with various prices and corresponding degrees of divination.

"How about you go for the twenty-dollar one?" he suggested. "It's cheap and only takes two minutes." Twenty Hong Kong dollars was about three bucks. I agreed.

"Good, now pick a piece of bamboo," he instructed, and thrust a jar at me. I picked a piece with the number eight.

"Okay, number eight. That's a lucky number," he said. "What year were you born?"

"Nineteen seventy-two."

"Okay, so that's 'the year of the rat.' Did you know that?"

"Yes."

"Well... "

"Well what?"

"Well... don't you have any questions?"

I hadn't thought that far ahead. Unimaginatively, I asked him what he saw in my future.

"I get the sense that you are making something – creating something. So, slowly – you're a step by step kind of guy – slowly, next year, or the year after, whatever it is you are making or creating now, that will bring you success."

"What kind of success?"

"Well, if you wanna know that," he replied wryly. "You gotta pay another hundred."

I told him that that wouldn't be necessary, thanked him, and took my leave. He was pretty slick, I have to admit. If the Man Mo Temple ever becomes a Starbucks (a fate that befalls many buildings in Chinese cities) there would surely be a career for him selling "Rolexes" in southern Kowloon.

Unlike southern Kowloon, with its darting-eyed Bangladeshi tailors ("Suit, sir? Tie? Just have a look, sir."), electronics shops ('Tax Free'), massage centres ('Special - $HK 99'), and probing tourists ("Are these ties real silk, do ya think?"), Hong Kong Island's Causeway Bay is where fashion-conscious locals go; to eat, to shop, to be entertained, and to see and be seen. The entire district resembled an indoor-outdoor shopping plaza. It was obscenely commercialized, with stores, ads, signs, cinemas, and sidewalk menus competing for each of your 360 degrees. Sinewy, tattooed men unloaded goods in the area's narrow, race-course-like streets. Old women sat fanning themselves as they sold tabloids, comic books, and soft porn from bulky newsstands capped by soft-drink-ad-adorned awnings, and brightly lit bistros with their back-wall shrines and plastic chairs hummed and sang with business and banter.

In Causeway Bay, it struck me that everything was either slightly too small or much too large; the sidewalks were too narrow, the signs too low, the delivery trucks undersized; yet there were jumbo TV screens, massive billboards, colossal apartment blocks, and the dark mass of Victoria Peak looming in the middle distance. People fiddled with their cell phones as they queued up for kebabs (intestine kebabs, fish-ball kebabs, tofu kebabs), and vendors sold junk jewellry and T-shirts late into the evening in the middle of the street from makeshift cardboard-box tables. In one of the pedestrian-only lanes, activists had hung a banner: 'HEAVEN WILL NOT FORGIVE THE CHINESE COMMUNIST PARTY. NEVER FORGET FALUN GONG.' The place pulsed with people, light, sound, energy, colour, commerce, and heat. It couldn't have been any more *Blade Runner*.

Back in my broom-closet room, I watched an interview on CNN with Jung Chang, author of the powerful and nicely written *Wild Swans: Three Daughters of China*. She had just co-authored a new book with her English husband, Jon Halliday, entitled *Mao: The Unknown Story* and was in the process of promoting it. Essentially, she was asking the viewers to consider the implications of an up-and-coming superpower that still feverishly revered a madman directly responsible for the deaths of 70 million of his own people. Westerners assumed that those days were long over, she said, yet the truth of the matter was that Mao's personality cult was still very much alive. His image could be seen everywhere, including on all of the banknotes. This, the author warned, was something we needed to think about. The phone lines, however, were soon lighting up in remonstration. "So he made a few mistakes," one man whined. "He was trying to help his country." I set the air conditioner on high, stuffed my ears with toilet paper, and fell asleep.

CHAPTER TWO

Hong Kong is a Special Administrative Region, or SAR, and is to remain one until 2047. Many nationalities don't require a visa for Hong Kong, but they do for the rest of China, so the next morning I went to the relevant office to apply for mine. This done, I went off in search of the Hong Kong Museum of History, which proved to be outstanding.

I knew from living in Taiwan that Chinese museums tended to be lacklustre affairs typified by the yawning security guard, the garbled English explanation, and people touching things they shouldn't, all the while pretending that examining rows of bronze pots was somehow enlightening. But that wasn't the case here. This museum featured unique and entirely unpredictable exhibits spanning a multitude of themes and several millennia. You could explore a Chinese junk, or a late-nineteenth-century street replete with mock shops, or take in a short film on the history of the local television and movie-making industries. And the staff was helpful and impeccably polite. After getting a better sense of the former colony's history (in a sentence: poverty and adversity overcome by the sheer determination of the Chinese people and the occasional shove in the right direction from their colonial overlords), it was sad to see the story end, so to speak, with the territory's return to China, especially without its citizens having been consulted on how they felt about the transfer. Conspicuously absent were exhibits dedicated to key events which had transpired since July 1, 1997; specifically public outcry over human rights abuses in China and Beijing's meddling in local affairs, that is: its slow strangulation of civil liberties.

Of vital concern to nearly 7 million Hong Kong residents is the issue of universal suffrage, expressly the right to elect their chief executive and all other members of their Legislative Council. After dragging their feet on the issue for decades, Britain finally made a real move toward making this a reality in 1985, the year after it was decided that China would take control of the territory in 1997. Britain's manoeuvrings prompted Beijing to establish a shadow government across the border in Shenzhen, and this was the body that took office in Hong Kong on the day of the handover. At its head as chief executive was the Beijing-backed Tung Chee Hwa, a Shanghai-born shipping magnate who had his business bailed out by cadres in the capital in the 1980s.

Despite this, and despite the fact that the People's Liberation Army (PLA) rumbled into the territory at dawn that day,[1] the people of Hong Kong remained hopeful as, according to the territory's governing law, democracy would have to be implemented in full after 2007. However, it has been ruled out for elections every year since by a standing committee in Beijing established to interpret Hong Kong law. This has led many to conclude that the Mandarin term for 'after 2007' is most closely approximated in Cantonese as 'never.' So said a pamphlet I was handed outside the museum: "Democracy deferred is democracy denied."

Writing in the 1820s, the German philosopher Georg Wilhelm Friedrich Hegel noted that the Chinese "cherish the meanest opinion of themselves, and believe that men are born only to drag the cart of Imperial Power." Hegel also noted how easily Chinese people bent to the whims of their rulers, as if they held slavery to be their destiny. Sir James Brooke, writing a couple of decades later, commented, "I know not whether most to admire the Chinese for their many virtues or to despise them for their glaring defects. Their industry exceeds that of any other people on the face of the Earth. They are labourious, patient, and cheerful. But on the other hand, they are corrupt, supple, and exacting, yielding to their superiors and tyrannical to those who fall into their power."

However, in the case of Hong Kong, perhaps there is still hope. Tung Chee Hwa stepped down during his second term due to "health reasons," brought on by a bout of extreme unpopularity manifesting itself in the form of incessant media attacks and massive street protests. Demonstrations are held on the anniversary of the handover in the former colony and have seen upwards of half a million people. Hong Kong also holds annual candle-light vigils in remembrance of the 1989 Tiananmen Square crackdown, making it, in a sense, China's conscience. Tung Chee Hwa was replaced by another Beijing appointee, the bowtie-wearing Donald Tsang, a man who has promised democracy even though he is in no position to provide it.

I made my way to the regal Kowloon Hotel, where two Sikhs greeted me and pulled open the doors. After dining on dim sum, I walked up

---

1   Deng Xiaoping had promised Hong Kong that the PLA would be kept out of the territory. When Hong Kong reporters reminded him of this, he shouted, "Bullshit!" before daring them to "go print it."

bustling Nathan Road, dodging Bangladeshi tailors as I went until I got
to the thoughtfully named Kowloon Park, a pleasant patch of greenery
that boasted no less than 35 varieties of trees. It used to be a slum. A
mustachioed man from Iran was sitting on a bench. After introducing
himself, he flashed me a salacious smile and asked that I join him, patting
the spot next to his lap. "You have a nice day, sir," I said, and carried on.

Having heard that the New Territories were quite striking, not to
mention refreshingly undeveloped, I decided to give the area a look.
Taking the metro north, I transferred to an ultrasleek and speedy new
railway that dashed between broccoli-like hills and clusters of gleaming
high-rises. Shortly, the latter yielded to the former and the view was one
of a cloudless sky resting atop long and liberally furrowed mountains of
deep green. At one point, an elderly man sitting across from me started
singing. This caused the woman next to him to fire off a reproachful
look. He shot her one back that said, 'What? I'm only singing.' He and I
then exchanged glances.

"Are you going to Yuen Long Station?" he asked politely.

"Yes, I am. Are you coming home from work?"

"No, I'm going *to* work. I'm an English teacher. My name is Henry
Lim."

Mr. Lim told me that he worked for a company that did business with
the United States and that they often required his services given that the
employees' English wasn't up to snuff.

"You know, in the old days," he explained, "we *had* to learn English.
It was an official language. It still is. But now, young people… they
don't care. They just want to own the latest shoes. Most of the people
I teach are university graduates, yet they can't even use English to fill in
a purchase order or write a simple e-mail. And their grammar is *terrible*.
That's where I come in. My job is to stamp out bad grammar. I guess you
could say that I'm a kind of fireman."

I confided that I was an English teacher too, and we chatted for a
while about the pros and cons of language teaching before arriving at
our destination, which, fittingly, was a shopping mall. None of the buses
would stop to pick me up, so I hailed a cab and indicated that I wanted to
go to a place called Kat Hing Wai.

Kat Hing Wai is a walled village dating from the sixteenth century.
Built by a clan with the surname Tang, 400 descendants still live there,
which must be something of a irritant for the mailman. Of course, all the
homes have been rebuilt, but the six-metre-thick brick walls, crumbling
cannon towers, and unassuming moat are all remnants of the originals
and serve as a reminder of China's turbulent and not-so-distant past, one

characterized by utter chaos and lawlessness, or in this case: marauding bandits, wild tigers, and rival clans. I passed between two banyan trees and entered the narrow gate. Immediately, I was set upon by two prune-faced ladies who began bleating, "Photo! Money! Photo! Money!"

"Okay, okay," I said to them in Mandarin. "Calm down. You can take my photo. Now, where's your money?"

"We don't understand Mandarin," one answered in Mandarin.

"Well, I'm sorry," I said sincerely. "I don't speak Hakka."

"We're not Hakka!" they cried.

"Really?" I answered. I had read that the Tangs were Hakka, which means "guest" and refers to a migratory and historically persecuted variety of Chinese comparable to the Jews.

"Of course not," they replied. "We're *Punti*!"

"*Punti?*" I had never heard of this group before, but discovered later that it meant "local" or "Cantonese-speaker." *Punti* and Hakka factions battled each other for years during the nineteenth century, which doubtlessly accounted for the women's emphatic correction. I gave them some change, but it mustn't have been enough because they started trailing me and demanding more. I lost them easily, though, and spent the next little while meandering about the warren of constricted alleys and poking my face into people's living rooms.

Finished comparing altars, doormats, cats, and clotheslines, I snuck past the two sentinels, who were by now fast asleep on their lawn chairs. I made my way to a store across the street in order to ask for directions to another village located about one kilometre north. Leading me outside, the smiling clerk pointed to an apartment block across the road and said, "Okay, you see that building there? You just walk along the front of it and then go around the corner. Then go straight and you'll find it." I walked around the corner and found myself standing in the middle of a vegetable garden, beyond which lay a brook. In a nearby lane, I found a store run by an Indian man and figured I should ask him. As I half expected, he gave me precise and correct directions. In this part of the world, if you want to know where something is, ask an outsider.

I nearly made it, but at some point on a lengthy stretch lined with large homes and wrought iron gates, my feet would carry me no further. The sun was rubbing against the horizon, and I thought it best to head back before dark. Eventually, I managed to catch a cab that took me to the train station. Back in Kowloon, I stumbled out of the subway and into a shabby diner called Hand-Stir Noodles and was directed to a table where a wool-capped man was already seated and embroiled in a heated debate with himself. I passed on the 'fried pork fat' and 'salted pig's trotters' and ordered some fried rice and crispy wontons, which tasted just like Western Chinese food. Sated, I went to the counter to pay. While waiting for my change, I noticed that the man I had dined with had found a conversation partner: his cigarette.

I walked to the Temple Street Night Market, with its multitude of Chinese-themed mementos and blinding, generator-powered lights. No matter where you go in China, souvenirs are essentially the same: paper cuts, imperial coins, jade bracelets, Buddha statuettes, chopsticks, silk pillows, silk dresses, fans, jewellry boxes, commemorative plates with images of various Communist Party figures, *The Thoughts of Chairman Mao*, and so on. This market also offered an assortment of toys: toys for kids, adult toys…. I bought a tacky sun hat adorned with a grinning orange squid and the phrase 'South of China.' My tourist disguise was now complete.

The following afternoon, I picked up my visa and headed back to Hong Kong Island. I was going there in search of prostitutes. Well, in point of fact, I was going there in search of the past.

One of the first glimpses the outside world got of Hong Kong was via the 1957 novel *The World of Suzie Wong* along with the subsequent film that it inspired. Penned by an Englishman named Richard Mason, the story depicts the life of a struggling painter named Robert Lomax, who heads to Hong Kong in order to concentrate on his craft. Shortly after his arrival, he finds himself on the Star Ferry where he meets a young and attractive woman named Suzie who passes herself off as the daughter of a wealthy Chinese businessman. In reality, she is a hooker working out of the Nam Kok Hotel, which, it just so happens, the artist ends up staying at, unaware that it's more brothel than lodge. Robert eventually falls in love with Suzie, but finds himself being pursued by a woman who really is the daughter of a wealthy businessman in addition to being English and very well connected. Within this dilemma, the reader is exposed to the dichotomous world of 1950s Hong Kong: life on the Peak, with its butlers, whiskey tumblers, and racist residents juxtaposed against the squalor and tragicomedy of Wan Chai, a district then teeming with Chinese refugees.

Richard Mason is no Emily Brontë, though his story is entertaining, and between the chance encounters and embroidered dialogue it offers some decent descriptions of what the city resembled in those days. Consider this sketch of the waterfront: "Further along the quay, shirtless, barefoot coolies were unloading junks, filing back and forth along the gangplanks like trails of ants. Sampans tied up amongst the junks tossed sickeningly in the wash of passing boats. Across from the quay were narrow open-fronted shops, between which, dark staircases led up to crowded tenement rooms; and along the pavement children played hopscotch whilst shovelling rice into their mouths from bowls, for all Chinese children seemed to eat on the move."

Suzie's world may have been consigned to history, but I was curious to know whether any of the modern-day "Wan Chai girls" were aware of it. Having read that the area featured a bar that had borrowed the novel's name, I went to see if I could find it. Not having an address, I stepped into a regular-looking bar to see if anyone could help me out. Affixing myself to stool, I ordered a beer and surveyed the handful of foreign patrons. Next to me sat a man fiddling with a very serious camera.

"Professional?" I inquired.

"Yes," he said.

"Do you sell to magazines?"

"Yes. I do portraits," he replied, revealing an English accent. He then showed me one of a stunning Asian model in a white, low-back dress peering back seductively over her shoulder.

"It's the kind of thing magazines want," he sighed. "Personally, I go in for things a little more real. Like that, for instance," he said, and nodded toward the open door. Outside, five men had begun to argue shrilly in Cantonese. We sat there for a minute watching them. "It'd be easy to get a good shot of two or three of them," the man explained as he wiped his camera. "But the trick is to get one of all of them; all of them wild-eyed and pointing their fingers in each other's faces. There we are," he said. "Something like… *that*." He was right. It would have made for a superb shot.

Mason's protagonist explains how when he used to visit the London art galleries as a boy, he found observing the spectators more absorbing than the "woodenly posed" subjects in the paintings. "Why on Earth… were all the portraits so stodgy? Why were they never caught in a moment of life? There was more character, more meaning, in one uncertainly peering spectator's face than in any dozen of the faces in frames."

I asked the man, whose name was Terrance, if he had heard of the bar, The World of Suzie Wong, and he gave me a searching look before saying that no such place existed. He then asked me why I wanted to find it, so I told him.

"No one knows about that book anymore," he warned me.

"Well, that's what I'm going to find out," I replied.

"And you say you want to interview prostitutes?"

"That's right. Why? What?" He was staring at me strangely.

"Well, it's just that I don't really think of them as prostitutes anymore…"

At Terrance's urging, we left and went to a quieter and nicer place. On the way, he pointed out the upscale Luk Kwok Hotel, the present incarnation of the one that inspired Mason's story. We sat on a veranda and Terrance started talking. After giving me a thorough – almost academic – overview of Hong Kong's prostitution scene, he admitted that he had once frequented pick-up joints. That is: until he fell in love with one of the girls. They had been together for a decade, and according to him were still very much in love. "There was just something about her," he said. "There was this incredible chemistry between us. I just knew she was the one." It appeared I had found Robert Lomax. Now if I could only find Suzie Wong.

But it wasn't to be. On Lockhart Road, a thuggish-looking man waved me indoors and I suddenly found myself sitting at a very different type of bar: one with Christmas lights pulsing against scarlet walls and black vinyl furniture. It was staffed by Filipinos. These days, the Chinese women are mostly illegals from China who are deported once officials become suspicious of all the stamps in their passports, or so Terrance told me. After making my intentions clear to the mama-san, I was told I could conduct an interview provided I purchase two exorbitantly priced cocktails. So I sat there, surrounded by four half-naked women and the aging mama-san. Only she was familiar with the story, having seen the film years before. "I remember that Nancy Kwan played Suzie," she said. "She was *very* beautiful. I wonder what she did after that."

"Suzie never sees what she does as being immoral," I explained. "She's just doing what she has to in order to survive and provide for her child." The women confided that they didn't wrestle with morality either and that they too had children to support. Most of them were married. Their spouses thought they were working as waitresses in Kowloon. They were quick to add that their job was legitimate and that the government provided monthly check-ups. None of them had had repeat customers, nor had there ever been any emotional involvement. One, however, said she would make an extra effort if the guy were good-looking. They claimed that they would like to read the novel, describing it as 'something they could relate to.' All of them were extraordinarily nice, which Filipinos customarily are. And this, of course, made it all the more depressing. I went back out into the heat and neon.

In Taiwan, virtually all I had ever heard from expatriates and locals alike was that people in Hong Kong were a strident lot of mean-spirited, scandal-obsessed, money-grubbing snobs, but I didn't find that to be necessarily so. I didn't speak to many of them, mind you, but, in my defence, they were often moving too quickly for me to corner them. It's certainly true that they are materialistic and infatuated with cash, and would like nothing more than for you to hand them a sizeable stack of the stuff, but that didn't make them exclusive. And besides, they were at least polite about it. Several people stopped to ask if I needed directions and a taxi driver wouldn't take a tip after he'd used his cell phone to locate an address for me. He did this because he didn't know the English street name, something he apologized for. Overall, I was fairly impressed and enjoyed my time in Hong Kong. The city exhibited a few shabby vestiges here and there, but just enough to counter the commercialism and lend it a sense of character.

CHAPTER THREE

The next morning, I caught a ferry to Macau and was accompanied by several hundred nattering retirees. I divided my time between dozing off and gazing out the window at the swirling fog and surfeit of boats. Visibility was abysmal. Vessels would materialize suddenly out of a sauna-room-like murk and shoot past us at alarming speed. This worried me because only one week earlier – in the same waters, at the same time of day, and in similar weather conditions – a ferry had collided with a high-speed passenger boat, causing the latter to sink. There were no fatalities, although people were injured. Luckily, on this day, the sun burrowed through and split up the haze.

After trundling past the hoary, gaping mouth of the Pearl River, China's southeastern extreme rose up to offer splendid coastal vistas. Enormous mountains of scrubby green pushed up into splotchy clouds of smudgy grey. Vehicles and buildings on the shoreline appeared as train-set models.

The terminal in Macau was impossibly crowded, and I faced a long wait to get my passport stamped. After exiting, I lined up again for a taxi and gave the driver the name and address of a guest house located down a narrow alley off of a major street. At the first red light, the man peered at my reflection in his rear-view mirror and confessed that he didn't know where the place was. This took me by surprise. Macau is, after all, an unpretentious 27.3 km² in size.

"Do you mean you don't know where that particular guest house is, or you don't know where the alley is?" I asked.

"I don't know the alley."

"Well, here. I have a map," I said helpfully, and pointed to the dot that I wanted to go to.

"This is in Portuguese," he declared disdainfully. "I don't understand Portuguese."

Again, this threw me. In a place as modestly proportioned and geographically distinct as Macau (it's little more than a miniature peninsula plus two tiny islands), it shouldn't have mattered if the map were marked with ancient runes.

"So, you don't know where, say, *this* street is, for example?" I probed, pointing to the closest of the three main arteries to span the peninsula.

"No," he replied.

"Right," I said. "And are you actually from Macau?"

"Yes, I'm from Macau!" he shot back moodily. "But nobody here understands Portuguese. *Nobody.*"

That was very nearly true. Although an official language, Portuguese is only spoken as a first language by 0.6 percent of Macau's population. About 87 percent of Macanese speak Cantonese as a first language, the territory's other official tongue. After Macau's handover in 1999, the government had probably decided to keep Portuguese on street signs and buildings as a sort of tourist decoration. In any event, Portuguese-language maps aren't much use in the territory.

Downtown Macau's soundtrack was a frenzied disharmony of car horns and jackhammers and the fumes were noxious; literally dizzying. I stumbled on a place I thought might be the guest house, but the woman behind the counter wasn't certain if it was or not. Neither the Portuguese name nor the map was of any help. I asked a man at a stationery store, but he didn't know. I went into a travel agency, but they didn't know either. Giving up, I decided to go to another hotel across town and hailed a cab, but unlike my first driver, this one didn't speak English.

"The Far East Hotel!" I yelled into the din.

Lowering his sunglasses, the man furrowed his forehead and said, "*Ee-ai-yo-hoke-lo?*"

"No, no. The Far East *Hotel.*" But, he didn't understand, so I showed him my map. He scrutinized it for some time before peering over his lenses again. "Macau?" he asked.

He then enlisted the help of a police officer and the two of them chattered, shrugged, and gesticulated for more than a minute, presumably attempting to determine just why a foreign tourist was asking after accommodation in Miami, Florida. Finally, I made myself understood by speaking Mandarin. In all the heat and clamour, I had temporarily forgotten that many Cantonese speakers can at least understand that language.

Both the Far East Hotel and its surroundings had clearly seen better days. The aging inn resembled a large daub of green positioned amidst a hodgepodge of horrid grey: apartment blocks divided by narrow, squalid, and impossibly cluttered alleys. I saw bicycles, stacks of dusty bricks, dismantled scaffolding, renegade plants, and a small community of skinny cats. It seemed there was no space between anything. Macau has a population of 540,000 and a population density of more than 18,500/km², which distinguishes it as the densest sovereign state and/or dependent territory in the entire world.

The aging male receptionist attempted to overcharge me, so I complained. On a bad day, it can seem that much in Chinese society revolves around the assumption you won't. The man feigned a miscalculation and adjusted my bill.

I set out on a walking tour from Largo do Senado, or Senate Square, a plaza of wavy black and gold lines flanked by rows of colonial edifices that have spent centuries staring at one another. A McDonalds, a Starbucks, and a Häagen Dazs each occupied one of the pastel-coloured buildings. I thought this was sad.

Under a cream-coloured brushstroke of a sky, I ambled contentedly around some bustling back alleys, where I inspected the interiors of old cathedrals and sampled some homemade almond cookies, a local specialty. Ultimately, I made my way up a cobblestone knoll in order to take in the incongruous-looking St. Paul's Cathedral. All that remains of the Jesuit-built structure is its enormous southern facade; the rest was destroyed by fire during a typhoon in 1835. The ruin constitutes a fitting symbol for Macau and its imperial past.

Macau has the distinction of having been the very first and very last European colony in China, having been run by the Portuguese under one arrangement or another for a total of 450 years. Not only did it serve as a major trading hub, but it was soon doing a brisk business in Christian conversions as well. Indeed, the proselytizing Portuguese viewed the outpost as a sort of spiritual gateway, but even with its initial promise, the settlement found itself outmoded as early as the mid-nineteenth century. The reason for this, and for the lengthy decline that followed, had to do with Portugal losing its 'most favoured nation' trading status to England. Also, Victoria Harbour offered a superior alternative. Macau, like Hong Kong, currently falls under the SAR or "one country, two systems" arrangement. Theoretically, it is to enjoy a large degree of autonomy until 2049, or 50 years after its handover.

After being sufficiently humbled by the Ruinas de São Paulo's dignified stone veneer, I climbed up to the Forteleza do Monte and surveyed the city in its entirety. Atop Victoria Peak, all I could think to say was, "Wow." Here, all I could think to say was, "Yeesh." It looked as though the entire peninsula were under construction, and what wasn't probably should have been. The skyline featured as many cranes as it did buildings, and nearly half of those were only partially complete. There was the odd glint of a glass tower; the occasional gleam of modernity, but in the main it was categorically repellent. The business district reminded me of pictures of Hong Kong taken around 1960. An even bigger eyesore could be found in the mishmash of structures that constituted the residential areas. Vast patches of corrugated roofs ornamented by thousands of silver water tanks lent the former enclave a fatigued, quilt-like appearance.

Chinese houses are akin to Chinese characters; they are fundamentally erect and possess a rough degree of uniformity, yet they are always unique; an infinite array of strokes and angles. Streets run like sentences; neighbourhoods like paragraphs. In the main, homes are dreary, utilitarian affairs, appearing to have been modelled after either the pillbox or the cinder block. They lack paint and possess windows that are entirely barred. Not surprisingly, when houses catch fire the inhabitants often perish as they can't escape for the metal contraptions they've affixed for their protection. Rarely, however, is a TV stolen. And if exterior walls aren't of the soot-stained, concrete variety, they are covered in thousands of usually off white tiles, thus causing entire communities to appear as collections of outsized maximum-security outhouses. If you ever wondered why you have never seen *Houses of China* alongside *Apartments of Berlin* or *English Cottage Homes* in the design section of your local bookstore, now you know. It's no accident that Chinese homes and businesses often look the way they do; there's a reason for it, and it's called the third generation curse.

Although merchants own a low rung on the Confucian ladder, China has always had its fair share of them, especially here in the south. Early on, such men noticed an incongruity in accumulating wealth. Once an enterprise (usually a family one) declared itself successful, the momentum would slow to the point of idleness. This seemed to follow a pattern whereby one generation sweated and toiled for the next, the next fiddled, fooled, and fumbled the ball, and the third squandered whatever was left. The way to overcome the curse, or so it was believed, was to treat success as something that was just over the horizon no matter how wealthy you got. Additionally, one should always appear to be extremely frugal. Being free with one's money would only draw undue attention to family and friends.

I walked down the other side of the hill and continued on. I sauntered around a large, leafy park filled with cane-clutching seniors, and then took a look at the Old Protestant Cemetery, interesting to me because it is the resting place of a man named Robert Morrison, the first Protestant missionary to China as well as the author of the first Chinese-

English dictionary.

After dark, I took in a couple of casinos. I had never been to a casino before, but it was exactly as I imagined: smoky, garish, and not at all to my liking. That said, I had been up for a bit of blackjack, but couldn't find anybody playing it. In fact, I didn't recognize any of the games. I ended up peering over people's shoulders and losing stacks of Macau patacas to a row of slot machines while under the tutelage of a kindly old man who couldn't have been any more sympathetic.

Casinos are big business in Macau. In 2006, they took in a whopping $7 billion, outstripping Las Vegas for the very first time. As of the same year, Macau boasted a total of twenty-two of the places, but by the time you read this they should have built twenty-five more on a piece of reclaimed land, hence putting them ahead of Las Vegas by a total of seven. I left and walked along an artery of jewellry stores and dazzling neon. The sidewalks were full of tuxedo-wearing casino employees finishing their shifts.

The next day, I awoke to the sound of grumbling thunder and emerged from the Far East Hotel to find rain falling in sheets from a leaden sky. Hailing a cab, I headed to the waterfront. In a quavering tributary of the Pearl River, flotsam and jetsam meandered about, garnishing an assemblage of empty, rusted tankers whose sterns sagged into the corridor of liquid brown. I bought a ticket for the Maritime Museum.

Small in scale, the place was nonetheless tastefully done. There was a fine aquarium and a salient collection of model boats. But I was more curious to see how the legendary admiral Zheng He was presented. I wanted to see if the Chinese had bought into the Gavin Menzies myth: that not only was Zheng He the first to circumnavigate the world, but that he discovered the Americas, Antarctica, Australia, Greenland, New Zealand, and the Northwest Passage in addition to having a go at the north and south poles while somehow managing to find the time to establish settlements pretty much everywhere along the way besides Europe – all in just two years. These fanciful notions were set forth in Mr. Menzies's book, *1421: The Year China Discovered the World*. The book was a hit and was followed by *1434: The Year a Magnificent Chinese Fleet Sailed to Italy and Ignited the Renaissance*. A retired British submarine commander, Gavin Menzies claimed his background provided him with unique insight into premodern naval exploration, but his theories have been unreservedly rejected by historians. One critic has wondered if his trilogy's coda might be entitled *1438: The Year China Launched the First Manned Rocket to Mars*. Judging from this museum, the Chinese hadn't subscribed to the Menzies myth, and this made me happy. The accepted history is interesting enough.

An explorer *cum* envoy, Zheng He embarked on seven voyages that saw China extend its cultural and commercial influence to a total of 37 countries. The first of these expeditions occurred in 1405. Most notably, the admiral explored India, the Persian Gulf, and East Africa – an extraordinary undertaking in those days – sailing with an armada of 317 vessels, including 62 enormous and precision-crafted treasure ships. Imperial records tell us that these nautical mastodons were an incredible 137 metres in length and 55 metres in width.[1] After the admiral's death in 1433, China reinstated its policy of isolationism and the giant-sized vessels were either burned by Confucian scholars or simply left to rot, or so it is said. There was nothing to be gained from consorting with the barbarians. The majority of Zheng He's meticulously drawn charts were destroyed as well.

Although ethnically Chinese, Zheng He was actually a Muslim whose original given name was Sanbao. One theory has it that he inspired the legend of *Sinbad the Sailor*, which, if true, almost certainly had to do with his physical stature. He was said to have stood over seven feet tall. And this almost certainly had to do with a hormonal imbalance resulting from having had his goolies cut off as a boy. Admiral Zheng He was a eunuch. Talk about an impediment to a Hollywood movie.

That the Chinese underwent any sort of age of exploration – let alone one so extensive – is truly amazing given their inward-looking nature. The period of seclusion that followed Zheng He's death lasted for the next five centuries. Even today, Chinese people remain little more than theoretically aware of countries offshore of their own and possess only the most inchoate knowledge as to where many of them might be or what might go on in them. When the taxi driver asked me if the map of Macau were a map of Macau, that wasn't an aberration; that is the norm.

One of the exhibits was set up to illustrate the voyages of eight Portuguese explorers, among them Vasco da Gama, Bartolomeu Dias, and Ferdinand de Magellan. Next to a biographical sketch and a photo of each was a corresponding button. Pressing it would plot that explorer's journey from Portugal on a large world map by utilizing a string of tiny lights. It was rudimentary, but amusing. I had just gotten to Dias when two stout and voluble women with northern accents padded over for an appraisal. "What's this thing!?" one bellowed. The other one shrugged and thundered, "I don't know!" They began thumping all the buttons

---

1   King Henry V's *Grace Dieu*, built in 1418, was 66 metres in length and 15 metres in width. It was the biggest ship in Europe.

at once. "Whoa!" they exclaimed in unison. "*Hao piaoliang*!" "So pretty!"
Then, satisfied that they'd lit up all the shiny lights on the otherwise drab,
blue and green abstract painting, they shuffled off, perchance to the
aquarium to have staring contests with the squid.

I had lunch back at the Far East Hotel's restaurant: a dim-sum diner
that also did seafood and duck. Frowning fish moped about murky
tanks while glazed fowl hung stiffly from metal bars. The corners of
faded paper menus (once red, now pink) had begun to curl away from
their peeling ochre walls, and fleshy women in rubber boots trundled
to and fro with metal trolleys, clapping down dishes in front of patrons
and bellowing orders to white-capped chefs in the steam-filled kitchen.
Greyish light forced its way through the grotty windows and everything
was coated in a layer of condensation. The chicken tarts were delicious.
This was authentic Cantonese dining.

The thing that surprised me the most about Macau was that I didn't
like it. I had never heard a bad word about the place, and had once met
an Italian man who insisted it was worth visiting for the Portuguese egg
tarts alone. I failed to see what he did. The tourists and casinos may have
provided it with a pulse, but the city had a neglected – nay, melancholic
– feel about it. In the rain, its monotonous buildings morphed perfectly
into the atmospheric gloom and not even its European influence could
detract from its general unsightliness. Perhaps it was just the weather, but
it seemed a forlorn little city and its denizens appeared rather cheerless.
It was a big step down from Hong Kong, but to that end, it was a perfect
transition for China proper.

CHAPTER FOUR

In the early afternoon, I took a bus through the drizzle to the border, where I had the privilege of standing in an enormous queue in a warehouse-like building specializing in enormous queues. After clearing customs, I got on another bus that set off on a long, straight, properly built highway. Soon, we were passing by neat little communities typified by modern apartment complexes, newly built and level sidewalks, and fine landscaping. But I suppose; you couldn't have everything go to seed the instant you crossed the border.

The planted palms and showcase neighbourhoods (satellite dishes, tennis courts) eventually dwindled, however; replaced by immense fields, legions of marching suspension towers, one-storey factories attached to menacingly corpulent smokestacks, and boat-strewn tentacles of the mighty Pearl River.

In Hong Kong and Macau, there had always been something occupying my peripheral vision, but for the next few hours that wasn't so; everything was extensive and level. It seemed odd, but of course it shouldn't have. China is, after all, a colossally huge place. But interestingly, just how colossally huge it is remains a point of considerable contention.

In actual fact, numbers on China's dimensions differ from one source to the next to the point where it is either listed as being slightly bigger than the United States, or smaller by a chunk of land larger than Great Britain, meaning that it is either the third largest country in the world or it is the fourth. According to both *National Geographic* and the CIA Fact Book, it is the fourth, with the latter putting it at very precise 9,596,960 km².[1] The CIA lists the United States as being 9,826,630 km². But even if America is slightly larger, with over nine and a half million square kilometres of territory, geographically, China is no slouch.

Stretched over 50 degrees of latitude, the country's vast landscape

---

1   This does not include Taiwan.

was shaped by the most remarkable tectonic collision in history. The meeting of the plates of India and Eurasia, some 35 million years ago, yielded the Himalayan Mountains and the Tibetan Plateau. Naturally, the resultant shift in elevation made for a dramatic change in climate patterns, creating deserts in the north and northwest (roughly 20 percent of China's land is desert) and monsoons in the southeast. From the great plateau's glaciers (the Tibetan Plateau comprises one third the width of the entire country), the Yangtze and Yellow rivers channelled through the mountainous regions of Sichuan and central China, thus spawning the generative lowlands that extend to the coast, of which China possesses 18,400 kilometres. Something like 18.2 percent of the land is forested whereas 13 percent is arable. Of further geographical note: the Middle Kingdom ranks first in terms of number of countries bordered, with 14; an honour it shares with Russia. A sort of who's who of developing nations, this list includes Afghanistan, Bhutan, Burma, India, Kazakhstan, North Korea, Kyrgyzstan, Laos, Mongolia, Nepal, Pakistan, Russia, Tajikistan, and Vietnam.

To the China traveller, it often appears as though the country's predominant physical feature is concrete, and this of course has to do with points of interest typically being situated within or nearby urban areas.[2] Although the country is still principally rural, at present it has something like 500 million people residing in 647 urban areas.[3] By 2015, the Chinese government projects that there will be 600 million people living in 1,000 urban areas. As has already been touched upon, Chinese urban areas are often stupendously unbeautiful places. The one I was about to enter, although nicer than most, was no exception.

Guangzhou, otherwise known as Canton (meaning 'piece or portion of a country'), is the capital of Guangdong province and one of China's oldest municipalities, having served as a key entryway to the nation for more than a millennium. Located on the Pearl River, and within easy reach of the South China Sea, the rambling metroplex acts as a major commercial and industrial hub, seeing something like 15 percent of all China's foreign trade. Foreign trade (or the exchange of tribute and gifts) is something that the city has been involved in since the second century CE, starting with ancient Rome and followed by ancient India. Subsequent centuries witnessed the arrival of the Persians and

---

2   The Chinese government defines an urban area as a zone or municipality containing 200,000 people or more.

3   At the time of writing, the official number of urban areas was 668. I arrived at 647 by excluding the cities on Taiwan that have a population of 200,000 or more. The PRC counts them as their own.

the Arabs, after which there appeared the Portuguese, the British, the French, and then the Dutch. In 1834, Guangzhou became the first port officially open to foreign trade, but tight restrictions on the movement and operations of foreign nationals remained in place until a sandbank in the Pearl River was ceded to France and Britain for the purpose of business and settlement. Through land reclamation and the planting of banyan trees, this sandbank was eventually built up into a small but sturdy island known as Shamian, or "Sandy Surface." It was my present destination.

Guangzhou appeared as a study in greys. Everything was grey: the sky, the roads, the buildings, the river, the people…. It all seemed so doleful. The volume of construction and development, however, was absolutely astonishing. According to *China Daily* (the Communist Party mouthpiece), there were more than 2,000 construction sites in the city (many of which were office towers) and 400,000 people working on them. Many of the buildings were ultramodern and slick-looking; a few were even aesthetically pleasing.

Entering the conurbation by way of a super-high viaduct, our bus rolled between a series of lofty apartment blocks that were so near that you felt you ought to nod to the people visible through their 15th-storey windows. We drove along the hazy river to the bus station, where three aggressive Africans suggested I buy some marijuana ("You buy it, man. You like it."). From here, I caught a cab to the verdant and tranquil Shamian. At the counter of the youth hostel I decided upon, I was met by a cordial though solemn pair of female receptionists. The room I got turned out to be excellent, and after a rejuvenating shower I headed out to explore.

Except for a handful of tourists and the odd sidewalk vendor, the streets of Shamian were vacant. Sounds from the surrounding city filtered through the banyans before reverberating gently off the old colonial walls. Once closed to the Chinese, apart from maids and servants, the island had served as more than just a place for British and French merchants to set up their "factories" for selling opium and buying Chinese porcelain, silk, and tea; it was meant as a sort of sanctuary, a role it appeared to be playing still.

I wandered about for a short time, astonished to note that vendors understood American tourists who addressed them in brisk, idiomatic English. I was equally surprised to find a replica of an American diner called Lucy's Bar and Restaurant with an interior decked out in US licence plates and pictures of Elvis Presley and Marilyn Monroe. To top it all off, it was filled with hamburger-eating, Budweiser-drinking Americans. One minute I was ambling along the Pearl River, and the next I was ordering a cheeseburger in a Midwestern greasy spoon.

As I discovered from my eavesdropping, the Americans were there to adopt children. Nearly all children adopted in Guangzhou are baby girls.

After a meal of *faux* fast food, I left the island and walked to a nearby neighbourhood. Chinese neighbourhoods are customarily engrossing places, particularly at night, and I figured that one located in the heart of Guangzhou couldn't possibly disappoint. A Frenchman writing in the early 1900s described the city's residential quarters as being "compressed so closely together that they give one the feeling of being indoors, and seem like an infinite number of corridors…." Things hadn't changed very much, evidently.

Situated within a muddled array of feeble-looking brick buildings there stood a host of ambitious clothing boutiques, crumbling corner stores, decaying black-windowed brothels, and brash eateries packed with yakking patrons and storm clouds of cigarette smoke. Lanterns, altars, rubbish, stray cats, and hanging laundry provided for visual detail, while clanging voices, clacking mahjong tiles, and tinny music supplied the audio. Arguments could occasionally be heard and foul kitchen odours emanated from ground-floor windows. Men in tank tops congregated under street lamps to play chess or cards while their wives popped out of dark doorways to dump buckets of sullied water onto grubby, crack-filled sidewalks. Chinese neighbourhoods are always the same and yet perpetually dissimilar: their disarray and disorder are forever arrayed and ordered dissimilarly.

The thing to do in Guangzhou at night is to take a stroll along the river, so that's what I did. The daylight greys had been swallowed by an inky blackness festooned with flickering neon, and the esplanade was overflowing with couples, hawkers, and Chinese tourists. Ramshackle tenement blocks peeked between flashy coffee shops and brilliant, tacky seafood restaurants staffed by shapely women dressed in red *cheongsams*. In the distance, skyscrapers flashed and pulsed, causing the otherwise tarry river to flash and pulse synchronously.

I walked until my feet hurt and then repaired to a beer garden to cool down and take notes. I was greeted by a mob of waitresses, each dressed in a colourful outfit representing a different beer brand. They were all rather gangly and caked with makeup. Like their attire, their smiles were synthetic.

At the imitation diner, my note-taking had aroused the suspicion of the manager, who actually came over to ask me what I was writing. The same thing happened here, as it would on innumerable occasions

on my journey. The sight of a foreigner taking notes was clearly a
cause for concern. To deal with this, I would prominently display my
guidebook and start to underline random sentences in it whenever I
spied anyone taking an interest. On this occasion, a female manager and
a pair of waitresses (Miss Carlsberg and Miss Heineken, both in white
with green trim) popped over for a look. Smiling, I pointed to the word
'China' on the cover and gave them a thumbs-up. The manager turned
to her underlings and asked them what the word meant. Both of them
shrugged.

Back on the street, a teenaged boy handed me a card with a picture of
a blond woman in a bikini frolicking about a swimming pool. The back
read, in English only, 'Do you like the sexy beautiful girl? Yes! That's what
we have! We guarantee delivery and satisfaction. Call this number for your
lovely pleasures.'

Back at the youth hostel, I nodded to the pair of dour-faced
receptionists before nearly being abducted by the resident hair stylist.
Latching onto my arm, she waved a list of services in my face and
implored me to let her give me a massage. One of the items read, 'Eyes
Wash.'

"Eye wash?" I asked in Mandarin. "As in, you wash my eyes with
soap?"

"Yes," she replied buoyantly.

"Maybe tomorrow," I lied, and attempted to squeeze past her.

"Room massage?" she asked, yanking at my arm again. "One hundred
and twenty *yuan*."

"No thanks," I said, but she was persistent. Following me to the
elevator, she bellowed, "Okay! Only one hundred!" I pressed the button.
"Ninety! Oh, all right. How much do you want to pay!?"

I could see the pair of receptionists still standing at attention and
staring blankly ahead. They had heard every word and yet hadn't moved a
muscle.

The next morning, I gave the island a good going-over. In addition
to the resplendent foliage and the brick and pie-crust buildings, Shamian
possessed the most bizarre bronze statues, usually grouped and arranged
in some sort of scene. One minute I was walking along thinking things
like, "That must be the Church of Our Lady of Lourdes," or "I wonder
how much opium *that* building held," only to round a corner and mentally
exclaim, "*What the bloody hell?*" In one such arrangement, a Western couple
in nineteenth-century garb stood examining a Chinese woman darning
socks. Its caption read, 'A gentleman, a lady and a darn woman.'

Meant to depict the co-operation that existed between the two cultures during the good old days of gunboat diplomacy and drug addiction, the scenes were, of course, little more than cant. An eighth-grade Chinese social science textbook opens with the line, "Our motherland in history was once an advanced and great nation… but after the invasions of the European and American capitalist Great Powers, a profound national crisis occurred."

Once again, I left the serenity of the island and walked toward the adjacent old neighbourhood, which in the daytime houses Guangzhou's renowned Qingping Market. It was everything you might expect of a Cantonese market: throngs of jostling people, the constant unloading of goods, sidewalks piled high with boxes, and shops crammed with sacks of foodstuffs, multihued herbs, and spices. I saw mint, cinnamon, ginseng, Chinese dates, walnuts, peppercorns, licorice, wolfberry, tangerine, garlic, and much else. Buckets of writhing snakes, eels, turtles, and star fish, along with hanging ducks, dangling dogs, and live bound alligator made up the bulk of the meat section. For the more adventurous, there were scorpion-kebabs, dung beetles, cicadas, silk worms, and other critters. Each store emitted its own distinct smell: a heady whiff of mould, meat, and spice.

I stumbled upon a raucous pedestrian-way lined with clothing stores often blaring Canto-pop. Here, I discovered more bronze statues. One of a strutting woman had been christened 'Swanky Lady' while another was entitled 'Funny Kid.' A boy wearing a watermelon as a hat had his private parts dangling out of a slit in his trousers. By the by, some children's pants really do have slits in them, making it easier to pee, which their parents allow them to do almost anywhere. Not only is peeing on the street more convenient, it is also more sanitary than most public toilets; at least for that child.

As a fiery orb began to sharpen the quarter's contours, I made my way to Sun Yat-sen Memorial Hall, located within one of China's largest parks and representing a tasteful example of traditional Chinese architecture – or so it's always described. It *was* nice, at least its exterior: octagonal in shape and done in Nationalist colours: pillars and walls of crimson topped by a tiled roof of cobalt.

A young man at the ticket counter asked if I needed a guided tour. I said 'no,' but he insisted, saying how he wanted to practise his English. I grudgingly accepted, but was soon wishing I hadn't. He was garrulous, denigrating, and full of patriotic zeal. Undeniably, he was full of something. Inside a dusty and wholly unremarkable domed theatre he launched into his shtick.

"The harmony dome of theatre is too high and too magnificent it

can almost touch the heaven and this room have no echo *that* is not easy
to achieve in nineteen twenty-three so you can see this is the splendid
example of graceful Chinese culture's architectures and histories and
perfect environment of deliberation of Dr. Sun Yat-sen father of
Chinese nation-state and father of Chinese democracies in near future
our government will surely to grant full democracies to Chinese people
everywhere in fulfilling the dreams of Dr. Sun Yat-sen no matter that
person is the proletariat or is the aristocrat is the man woman young
old all can vote I think you do not have any building like this in your
countries I think you only have McDonalds."

"Oh, that's not true," I corrected him. "There's actually much more to
Western culture than meets the eye."

"Oh?" he replied.

"Of course. We have Burger King, Dairy Queen, Wendy's..."

But it was lost upon him. He was a talker, not a listener. Besides,
even the most general cultural references would have been impossible
for him to process. He then asked if I knew who Sun Yat-sen was, and
I lied and said I didn't. This prompted him to furnish me with a thin
synopsis littered with trifling details and flowery language. Luckily, my
indoctrination was cut short by a smiling family that wanted to have their
picture taken with me.

The reason I told him I knew nothing about Sun Yat-sen was that I
didn't want to disappoint him. Generally speaking, and especially when
it comes to matters of history and politics, Chinese people consider
Westerners to be unsophisticated and naive in the extreme, so I played the
part and must have played it well, for I had him believing I didn't know
who Mao Zedong was either ("Is that the guy on the money?"). In any
event, there was little point in discussing the life of Sun Yat-sen, or any
other historical figure for that matter; he would have his history and I
would have mine.

Born into a peasant family in an impoverished village just southeast
of Guangzhou in 1866, Sun Yat-sen immigrated with his family to
Hawaii, where he received his education in mission schools and was
taught the merits of democracy, republican-style government, and
the teachings of Jesus Christ. Returning to Hong Kong, he converted
to Christianity and studied to be a surgeon at an institute that wasn't
recognized by British authorities. Consequently, he couldn't practise in the
then British territory or in any other foreign-controlled areas. Perturbed,
"Dr." Sun made an abrupt and lifelong career change: he became a
revolutionary.

His objective was to overthrow the tyrannical, ham-handed, and hopelessly unprincipled Qing government and to replace it with a republic based on his newly devised political philosophy, the Three Principles of the People, often translated as nationalism, democracy, and the people's welfare or livelihood. Originally penned in English, the Three Principles of the People traces its origins to Abraham Lincoln and his belief in a government "… of the people, by the people, and for the people…."

Largely owing to a near total inability to deal with foreign aggression, antipathy toward the Qing had become rife. Something of a reform movement sprang up, although it was hardly what you would call united. That simply wasn't possible under Qing rule, where treason was dealt with officially by the 'Death of a Thousand Cuts,' although, to be fair, government troops weren't above on-the-spot beheadings or long, drawn-out strangulations. Regardless of the very real dangers involved, a good many secret societies emerged, assessing correctly that if the Qing Dynasty weren't dismantled, and if China failed to embark on a program of rapid industrial modernization and militarization, the country would be "carved up like a melon," a process already well underway.

In Guangzhou, Dr. Sun enlisted the help of triad leaders in order to mobilize an army of bandits and smugglers (elements the area has never been short of) in an effort to wrest control of the city's imperial garrison. Once accomplished, or so he reckoned, an army could then be raised to take control of the entire nation. However, the *coup* was poorly organized and quickly discovered by court officials who promptly meted out the customary punishment. A reward for Sun's capture was then offered, so he snipped off his cue (the braid that the Qing forced all male citizens to wear; not wearing one was punishable by death), bought a Western-style suit, and caught the first boat to Hawaii. Although the *putsch* had been botched and Sun Yat-sen was to blame, the event catapulted him into the national spotlight and he was hailed as a national hero.

For the next 16 years, Sun Yat-sen would lead the life of a fugitive, going from one country to the next in order to make speeches and drum up financial support from triads and associations of overseas Chinese. In San Francisco, the new-look Sun foolishly posed for a photograph that was quickly sold and sent to Chinese embassies everywhere. He then sailed to England, where he was spotted the instant he disembarked by a detective hired by the Chinese government. Coincidentally, Sun's temporary residence was situated only a stone's throw from the Chinese embassy, a building he took to passing daily. Like with the photograph, Sun Yat-sen's ego got the better of him and he decided to pop in one afternoon for a spot of tea and a bit of banter. He figured that with his disguise no one would know who he was.

Sun Yat-sen spoke to an interpreter who noticed that the visitor's comments pertained solely to the present administration and its numberless inadequacies. More significantly, the caller's watch was inscribed with the surname Sun. Upon leaving, the staffer alerted his superiors, and the next day, he was placed outside the front gate as a lure. Incredibly, Sun returned and accepted an offer of lunch before being whisked away by two burly men and locked up in a small room. Here, the doctor spent an unhappy week while surreptitious arrangements were made for his extradition and execution. His saviour came in the form of an English housekeeper, who, out of pity, snuck a message to one of his associates. In turn, the press was contacted and a kind of media frenzy ensued. Officers from the Foreign Office and Scotland Yard were soon pushing their way through a crowd of journalists and spectators in order to claim the political exile. A truncated version of Sun's capture and release became a global, front-page story, and this translated into an international outpouring of sympathy and support for his cause. Once only a national hero, Sun Yat-sen became a universally recognized name.

Sun Yat-sen continued his international dog-and-pony-show ("from Singapore to Saskatoon," as author and historian Sterling Seagrave has put it) and orchestrated several more revolts, all of which failed; some spectacularly so. When the great revolution finally did occur, Dr. Sun was taken completely by surprise as it was achieved by an entourage of disgruntled soldiers that had no political affiliation with him or anyone else. Indeed, he learned of the event while reading the morning newspaper while on tour in Denver, Colorado.

As it happened, a military clique in the city of Wuhan had been planning an uprising of their own when one of their homemade bombs accidentally went off. Their scheme discovered, the police hurriedly surrounded their barracks. Knowing what surrender would mean, the men decided to fight their way out, although not without some hesitation. In fact, it took them two weeks to finally go through with it, and, according to one account, a colonel only agreed to take charge after being threatened at gunpoint by his men as he hid under his bed. The moment the rebels eventually chose happened to be a good one; the imperial soldiers were caught off guard. They retreated and quickly fled the city.

Not having counted on victory, the insurgents had no idea what to do with it. Luckily, that wouldn't matter. News of their act was enough to spark a chain reaction whereby one province after another declared itself free of Qing authority. And just like that, more than two millennia of dynastic rule came to an abrupt and bizarre end. The date of the so-called revolution was October 10, 1911, which would become known as Double Tenth, the most revered holiday in the Nationalist calendar. In Taiwan, it is celebrated with much fanfare, including a large military parade marked by columns of students who carry Sun Yat-sen's portrait. The doctor's portrait can also be found in Taiwanese classrooms and offices, while streets, parks, schools, districts, and so on throughout both the Republic of China and the People's Republic of China bear his name.

Rather than return to China directly, Sun Yat-sen went to Washington, London, and finally Paris in order to gain concessions. But since he held no official post, and foreign dignitaries and heads of state tended to regard him as a something of a windbag, he was politely ignored in each instance. By the time he finally did arrive in China, much had already transpired. Nevertheless, he was installed as "provisional president" of the new republic, the administration of which was located in Nanjing. Here, he managed to bring various squabbling republican factions together under the newly created Chinese Nationalist Party,[4] but he stepped down a mere 45 days after his inauguration having correctly assessed that he was entirely powerless. The real power, as everyone knew, still lay in Beijing, embodied in a rotund militarist with a walrus mustache whose name was Yuan Shikai. Without Yuan Shikai's assent, Sun Yat-sen's republic was stillborn.

After taking Sun Yat-sen's place, Yuan Shikai handed the doctor the position of 'director of national railroads,' a job that he took very seriously indeed as he believed the train to be the answer to many of China's problems. With a large retinue of foreign reporters, sycophants, and beautiful women[5] China's chief demagogue embarked on a domestic railway tour and was greeted by cheering crowds at every stop. As his train rattled its way around the nation, Sun Yat-sen put his national vision on paper, drawing a series of perfectly straight lines from one provincial capital to another. This done, he informed his Australian advisor, William

---

4   The Chinese Nationalist Party is often referred to as the Nationalists or the KMT. KMT is an abbreviation of the party's Chinese name: Kuomintang, sometimes written Guomindang. In Part One and Part Two, I usually refer to the organization as "the Nationalists." In Part Three, for contextual reasons, I usually refer to it as "the KMT."

5   Sun was a notorious womanizer. Even his closest supporters were abhorred by the way he caroused with prostitutes and frequented brothels. He fathered three children with his first wife who he left in Hawaii. His second wife, Soong Ching-ling, was the daughter of Charlie Soong, a friend who heavily bankrolled the doctor during his formative years as a revolutionary and wasn't at all pleased about Sun's feelings for his girl. Sun Yat-sen had another child with a Japanese woman. Sun's advisor, William Henry Donald, said of him, "That was the problem with the old boy. Couldn't keep him off the women." This side of Sun Yat-sen's character seems to have been erased from Chinese history; Chinese people aren't aware of it.

Henry Donald, that he wanted nearly 53,000 kilometres of track (or 1.2 times the circumference of the Earth) built within 10 years. When Donald opined that a task of that magnitude might be problematic, not least of all because the new government was penniless, he was ignored. He was ignored again when he tried to explain to Dr. Sun that the straight line he had drawn to Lhasa would have to traverse the Himalayas. Sun Yat-sen failed to fathom why this would pose a problem.

With the doctor tied up on his whistle-stop tour, Yuan Shikai began purging the government of Nationalists and replacing them with his own supporters. His plan was to make himself emperor. By the time the Nationalists realized what was afoot, it was too late. Sun Yat-sen denounced Yuan Shikai publicly and was promptly dismissed from his position. The warlord president followed up by ordering Sun's arrest and execution. Once again, Sun Yat-sen fled the country.

Sun Yat-sen returned to Guangzhou after Yuan Shikai's death, but was soon sent fleeing by another warlord. Finally realizing that his revolution needed teeth, as well as organization, the republican ideologue enlisted the help of the Russian Bolsheviks and the fledgling Chinese Communist Party. Just down the Pearl River at Huangpu, the Soviets paid for a military academy that came to be headed by an ambitious young military man named Chiang Kai-shek, a character who had firmly affixed himself to the coattails of Sun Yat-sen and his revolution.

China had never seen a modern military academy before, but ironically Guangzhou became the most unruly city in the entire country. It was bursting with brothels and opium dens, not to mention warlords and gangsters, most of whom were on the Nationalist payroll. After a lifetime of work, Sun Yat-sen held sway over little more than his residence, yet Guangzhou was dubbed 'the southern government' and the doctor was honoured with the title 'president extraordinaire.' The president extraordinaire's southern government was protected by mercenaries who looted shops, took hostages, engaged in piracy, collected "taxes," ran gambling and prostitution rings, and sold drugs. One outfit advertised narcotics in a local newspaper.

The situation became grave when Chiang Kai-shek decided to teach Guangzhou's merchant class a lesson after it took a stand against furnishing the government with any more "loans." Unleashing his fanatically loyal troops on them, Guangzhou was turned into a smouldering, corpse-filled rubble heap. Not long thereafter, Dr. Sun travelled to Beijing in order to negotiate with the northern warlords, but while there he developed liver cancer and died. Half a million people turned out to view his body, which was buried outside of Beijing, but later moved to a mausoleum outside of Nanjing.

There is no question that Sun Yat-sen's heart was in the right place. His chief criticism of Chinese society was that was it was "built upon a foundation of sand," and that is an apt description – one that still holds true today. However, characterizations from those who knew or worked with the doctor directly range between quixotic and simple-minded. Some of his closest associates nicknamed him Sun Dapao, or "Sun the Cannon," owing to his strong partiality to words over action. Chiang Kai-shek described him as "impractical" (the two often argued), whereas Lenin painted him as a person of "inimitable – one might say, 'virginal' – naivety." Yet, to Chinese people everywhere, Dr. Sun Yat-sen was and is nothing short of a saint. Mind you, this largely has to do with his cause having been usurped by both the Nationalists and the Communists in order to lend themselves legitimacy. Chiang Kai-shek went so far as to add two whole sections to Dr. Sun's Three Principles of the People while Mao Zedong rendered his petition for a parliament in Marxist terms.

In China, Sun Yat-sen's vision will apparently have to wait. In 2007, the Communist Party announced that the nation would not be ready for democracy for at least another one hundred years. One could argue that his dream has been realized in the Republic of China, though democracy there is hardly mature. Taiwan's Legislative Yuan, which features an enormous portrait of Sun Yat-sen staring down at proceedings, is the most disorderly national assembly in the world, known more for its punch-ups than its passing of bills.

Interestingly, Dr. Sun Yat-sen, Father of the Republic of China and Father of Chinese Democracy, wondered aloud more than once whether a democratic system was even viable in China. In his later years, he made statements to the effect that it might not suit the national character.

My tour culminated in an unassuming hallway with old photos of early-twentieth-century Guangzhou. There were also shots of dignitaries, both foreign and from the Nationalist Party (the bloated, medal-decorated Yuan Shikai, Chiang Kai-shek – white-gloved and atop a white horse) as well as old newspaper clippings.

"You look," commanded my guide. "Chinese word is so beautiful is like art is not like English word English word is too simple."

"Yes, but these are written in complex characters," I replied, abandoning my ignorance. "Nowadays, complex characters are only found in Hong Kong and Taiwan. In China, you use simplified characters." I paused for effect. "Can you even read this?"

"A little," he replied.

I spent the rest of the afternoon in another part of town visiting the very nice and very interesting Museum of the Southern Yue Royal Mausoleum before heading back to Shamian. Coincidentally, in the cab, an English news program proudly announced the opening of the Qinghai-Tibet railway. With it, the amount of track in China would exceed Dr. Sun's original proposal. It has been estimated that nearly 10 million people are riding China's train system at any given moment. Perhaps Dr. Sun Yat-sen wasn't such a dreamer after all. Perhaps he was merely ahead of his time.

CHAPTER FIVE

I had recently read Paul Theroux's lengthy but engaging *Riding the Iron Rooster: By Train Through China* (1988), and was looking forward to taking the Number 38 overnight train to Guilin, a city located in Guangxi. I was pleased to find that my soft-sleeper compartment was relatively clean. The station had been anything but.

What little space that existed between people in the station was occupied by an assortment of repugnant smells and cigarette smoke. Shrill, static-filled announcements pierced the air and the floor was a greasy mess of litter and spittle. It was your typical public scene, really: people pushed, shoved, elbowed, cut in line, argued, shouted, smoked, emptied their lungs, and dropped their trash and cigarette butts where they stood. Groups of slothful, expressionless police officers milled about whilst spiritless salesclerks in grey uniforms sold oily newspapers, bruised fruit, and glossy packages of cigarettes from booths of grimy glass. In all the commotion, it took me some time to find my waiting area, which may have had something to do with its having been labelled in both English and Chinese as 'Maternity Ward.'

I read for hours and then slept uneasily, but at least I slept. As I did, the train clacked its way northwest into Hunan before turning southwest and crossing into Guangxi. I woke early and sat in the corridor on a fold-down chair. We were rolling through some mesmeric scenery: unfurled fields of swaying jade adorned with brick homes and formations of karst, the craggy, luxuriant, limestone mountains that dominate much of the southeast.

Karst comes in a staggering variety of shapes and sizes, from the so-called stone forests to towering pinnacles of rock and leaf. The formations are fun to gaze at, and a bit of imagination can make them appear as something other; here, a collection of witches' hats; there, a marching column of trolls. Frequently, clusters of summits could be seen leaning in one direction, as if magnetized by some far-off force. Despite their range and diversity, karst formations are all the result of a single phenomenon, one that makes for a sort of optical illusion.

In this part of the world, the Earth's crust is comprised of an extraordinarily thick stratum of limestone formed from the fossilized sediment of an ancient seabed. Because limestone is soft, streams lose water to it via sinkholes, some of which are frighteningly large. One in Sichuan province has a diameter of 666 metres. After the water is drained off, it passes through an ever-expanding system of caves and the water table drops. In short, the land collapses imperceptibly. The bits of terrain that once constituted mounds or knolls develop into theatrical hills. As the land falls away all around them, one is left with the impression that they have burst forth from within the Earth.

After alighting, I made my way through a parking lot teeming with insistent touts. From the door of the station to the road in front of the station, I was addressed with a mocking or solicitous "Hawlo!" precisely 13 times. On the sidewalk, I got out my map. Vehicles honked and swerved; pedestrians and cyclists pointed and stared. As is well known, northern and southern China are dissimilar to the point where they could almost be considered two separate countries. The same principle applies to the nation's vast interior; municipalities along the coast seem almost sophisticated by comparison.

Bordering Vietnam and the Gulf of Tonkin, Guangxi, which means "Vast West" (Guangdong means "Vast East"), has traditionally been thought of as China's badlands, a coarse and impoverished place to which outlaws fled and officials were banished. My guidebook said, "Guangxi's historic backwater isolation has always, for the Chinese, impelled visions of rough hinterland, an uneasy buffer of sorts for more savage places." Only 25 percent of Guangxi's population is Han Chinese.

Guilin, the former capital, was described by a Chinese writer in the mid-seventeenth century as a town where one could find "all manner of betel-nut chewers and aborigine whorehouse owners." More recently, it was known for its calendar-photo topography and exotic food (Guidebook: armadillo, Asian deer, bamboo rat, gem-faced civet, horned pheasant, mini-turtle, monkey, oily tea, short-tailed monkey, snake-bile wine, and snake soup). I tried a cup of oily tea, but only one.

I ended up staying at a low-grade inn near the train station after discovering that accommodation downtown was scarce. The Guilin Train Station, as I knew from my reading, had been an evacuation point during the war with the Japanese (the Second Sino-Japanese War, 1937–1945), or at least theoretically. As the Japanese advanced, tens of thousands scrambled to leave. Railway employees closed their counters and auctioned off tickets out the back door. This exacerbated the mayhem and several hundred people were killed when a locomotive steamed into the station, as they'd desperately assembled on the tracks. As for the highest bidders, along with those who could bribe the Nationalist soldiers for a spot onboard, they never made it very far. The train would chug a few miles out of town and stop whereupon the passengers would be forced off at gunpoint. The train would then chug back to the station to pick up another load.

Guilin's main artery is Zhongshan (Sun Yat-sen) Road and it divides the diminutive metropolis into its eastern and western halves. I rode in a cab along it to Banyan Lake, so named because of the 800-year-old tree that drinks from its waters. I strolled along the subdued, café- and restaurant-dominated lakefront for a while and chatted with an elderly man who indicated that he liked my beard. "Var gude!" he yelled, pointing to his own beard and then at me. He wanted to know where I was from, so I told him. "Oh," he replied, and had nothing more to add, which was usually the case.

Chinese people have neat little answers ready for whenever foreign countries are mentioned. This partly stems from their penchant for slogans, fits in neatly with not having to think, and, if you will allow me to labour the point, owes an enormous amount to a near total lack of knowledge pertaining to the outside world. Commentary on America varies: it's "very big" or "very beautiful" ('America' in Chinese is literally "Beautiful Country"), "Americans like hamburgers," and so on. Everyone from England is a "gentleman" (even the ladies, apparently), France is hopelessly "romantic," the Germans have "good beer," and Italy possesses "old buildings" and is "good at soccer." Australia's got kangaroos, but Canada? What in the world went on there? In a way, it was the perfect conversation closer.

I went to a place called Solitary Beauty Peak, a 152-metre-high karst formation located next to a restored fourteenth-century walled fort. Stairs wound their way around the rock to the summit, so I clambered up to have a look. The view was otherworldly; an expanse of squat apartment blocks huddled within a giant ring of jutting hills, some of which appeared quite eerie. One was aptly named Old Man Mountain, and in the far distance a series of triangular forms resembled a tribe of fantasy-novel monsters moodily walking away from town.

I walked back down and made my way to another park that lay adjacent to the Li River. Along a grassy riverbank, I sat down to take in the view. A mountain shaped like an elephant appeared to be drinking from the river and a run of willows on the far bank dipped low in imitation. I found the scene so attractive that I attempted to sketch it, something I hadn't done in years.

As I sat there, a short, silver-haired man in a brown Mao suit (formerly known as a Sun Yat-sen suit) plunked himself down next to me and complimented me on my amateurish artwork. His name was Mr. Wei and we talked for some time, although it wasn't always easy to make out his accent. It was eighty-five kilometres down the river to Yangshuo, he said. I could take a boat there if I wanted. It was a pleasant journey. Not that he was trying to sell me anything, mind you; he was just saying it was nice. The river used to be filled with fish. Not so much now. It wasn't as deep as it used to be either. Nowadays, you could wade across it, etc.

As we talked, a doe-eyed girl barely out of her teens parked herself between us. She was from Changsha, the capital of Hunan. "Near Mao's birthplace," she boasted. "It's where he went to school." She announced that she wanted to treat me to some fish, at which point she sought out a vendor and picked out a greasy, skewered haddock. Mr. Wei used her departure to take his own. As we shook hands goodbye, he leaned close and whispered, "You be careful of her. She's from Hunan. She'll try and steal your wallet." Somehow, I doubted it. She struck me as a kind, curious, and uncomplicated sort, who just wanted to talk. She worked at the nearby military hospital as a nurse. She had to be back shortly, so I offered to escort her through the pleasant park. We must have gotten a dozen dirty looks. During our chat, she casually mentioned that her family had supported the Nationalists back in the day. There ensued a bit of a silence.

Saying your family supported the Nationalists was another way of saying, "Our lives became a living nightmare." Those not fortunate enough to escape to Taiwan were considered to be politically tainted, usually for life. Most were branded reactionaries or enemies of the people (or one of the many other labels) and promptly relieved of all property and possessions. Often, they lived out the remainder of their days as non-citizens and were deprived of all means of livelihood. It didn't matter that the Nationalists had been the lone legitimate government or that their goon squads press-ganged entire villages; any involvement with that organization whatsoever would affect one's clan for decades. Guilt by association has long been a powerful element in Chinese society. I mistook the hospital for a restaurant. It had been done up in Christmas lights and was identified by a large red neon sign. The nurse and I shook hands and parted ways.

That night, I retired to a café in a shopping district marked by cobblestone streets and stores with names like Solid Jeans, Coolala,

and Stunner. The World Cup was on and coffee shops and restaurants
had banners and TVs set up to attract customers. I engaged in the very
important cultural endeavour of watching Germany vs. Argentina while
cooling off with a couple of lukewarm Tsingtao beers. China wasn't
in the World Cup this year. In fact, its FIFA ranking was a dismal 89,
but you never would have known it from watching the China Central
Television (CCTV) coverage.

Each match featured a pre-game show from Beijing that opened
with slick footage of Chinese players performing various physics-defying
feats. This was always followed by a cultural production that was wholly
unconnected to soccer (e.g. traditional dancing from one province or
another), as well as regular updates from the national team's training
ground ("What drill are you running *now*, Trainer Chen?"). During the
match, the reception cut out 27 times. I counted. I didn't count the
number of times I was solicited for sex as I walked toward the taxi stand
at two in the morning, but it was a lot.

The next day, I happily left Guilin and its legions of peddlers, touts,
and gawking residents and made my way to Yangshuo on a rambling
back road by bus. I bought my ticket at a hole-in-the-wall agency in front
of the train station, mainly because the owner, a self-effacing Mr. Lin,
had granted me asylum from a souvenir-wielding mob. I decided against
the river cruise, knowing that I'd be informed of what every mound,
bend, and patch of trees had been named (Fish Tail Peak, Five Finger
Hill) and why. Also, Mr. Lin informed me that his brother-in-law could
pick me up in Yangshuo and take me to his hotel, and if I didn't like it, I
wouldn't be obliged to stay. That sounded fine by me.

Mr. Lin's brother-in-law's English name was Clint, although he didn't
speak English, or so he said. He was waiting for me at the bus station.
As we walked to his hotel in the sweltering heat (a half-hour task) he
asked me where I was from.

"*Janada*," I told him. Canada.

"Canada!?" he exclaimed. "Oh! I've heard you don't need a visa or
any special documents to live or work there. You can just show up, find a
job, and after two years you can apply for citizenship."

I intimated that that wasn't so.

"No, I'm sure of it," he insisted. "My cousin moved there. He said
the economy is booming, especially in the capital, Moscow." There was
a pause, and then he said, "Oh, wait. I'm thinking of Russia. Yes, Russia.
Is it easy to live and work in Russia?" When I told him I didn't know, his
aspect took on an incredulous look.

Whenever you check into a hotel in China, you're required to fill in a special form that is then faxed to the local police station. These are forever different and forever incorrectly labelled. One box required my 'Validity of Stay.' Another asked for my 'Certificate?' and, implausibly, 'Port of Entry' referred to the town of Yangshuo.

"What are you doing tomorrow?" Clint asked, as I scribbled some nonsense on the paper.

"I don't know yet," I said.

"Why don't we go have lunch and talk about it?"

"Talk about what?"

"What you are going to do tomorrow."

"Like I said, I don't know yet."

"Well, if you want, there's a school you can teach at in the morning, and then in the afternoon you can go with the children on a field trip and tell them what things are called in English. It's volunteer work, of course. You won't get paid. I'll tell you what. I'm going out now, but I'll be back in two hours and we can talk about it then. I'll knock on your door. Two hours."

"All right," I said, "but don't be late."

He said he wouldn't and I left the hotel an hour and a half later.

Until the late 1980s, Yangshuo was a hushed little village far out in the countryside, a place to sleep after an instructional float down the compliant Li River. Currently, it was a thriving tourist town made up of bars, restaurants, travel agencies, and billboards that said, 'What are You Waiting For? Open Your Business in Yangshuo Today.' West Street served as its focal point; (yet another) cobblestone walkway lined with magnificent timber buildings highlighted by splendid old doors and inviting wooden verandas bedecked with rotund, smudgy lanterns. It may have been overcrowded, but it wasn't too overdone. On the whole, I found it to be a convivial, relaxing place in addition to being a superb base from which to explore the countryside.

I walked the length of West Street and followed a winding road that mimicked the curve of the river. Charcoal-tinted, century-year-old houses with faded door-frame epigrams and silhouettes of people pottering about inside lined the way while struggling to stay upright, and the views of the river and beyond were faultless. Below billowing clouds and a serrated skyline, horses grazed along the riverbank and children swam and shrieked. At dusk, a breeze wandered out of the hills and waltzed through the town, and I saw a man on a sampan propelling himself with a bamboo pole. At the rear of his vessel sat a cormorant, which is tame and used to catch fish. This is an age-old practice in southern China and is only performed at night. The fisherman hangs a light from the front of his skiff and the bird swims alongside it, just below the surface and toward the light. When it catches a fish, the man pulls it up and retrieves it. The bird is fitted with a collar that prevents the catch from being swallowed. I spent the evening padding around and playing tourist before heading back to the hotel. A note on my room door read, 'Helo. I am Clint. Where are you go? You tomorrow morning is teaching book at the school.'

The next morning, I went downstairs to find that Clint's elderly mother was the only one on duty. She was wearing a pair of beclouded spectacles that still had the price tag on them. A white sticker saying, '150 *yuan*' was prominently affixed to the left lens. When I pointed this out to her, she took the glasses off and examined them. "What? Oh, that! That's just the tag!" she said. She then put them back on, obscuring her left eye.

I rented an electric scooter and headed out of town. Driving along the spindly Jade Dragon River, I passed through microscopic communities before crossing a bridge and continuing on. It was another cloudless, scorcher-of-a day and the karst-hill landscape was crisp and radiant. Often, I would just pull over and marvel – and listen. It was exquisitely quiet. The area, I determined, was a veritable paradise, or would have been if not for the manifest poverty.

I stopped at one of the ramshackle collections of houses to buy bottled water from a handful of peasants relaxing under an enormous banyan tree. They had a cooler and an English sign saying, 'Water & Ice Cream.'

"Hawlo! Hawlo!" they chirped as I pulled into the dusty driveway. "Buy water? Buy ice cream?" As it was, they were a curious lot. "How long have you been in China?" asked a man with a single corn-coloured tooth.

"About a week," I responded.

"A week! And your Chinese is already so good!" he shouted, revealing a hearing problem.

"I learned it all from a phrasebook on the airplane," I quipped.

"That's incredible!" he cried.

"Oh, he must have learned it before he got here," offered an old woman, and then, turning to me, she asked, "Are you a Chinese teacher?" This made me laugh. I most definitely wasn't, I told her.

"There's a Dutchman who lives nearby," said another man in a high-pitched, quivering tone. "He made that sign for us. He speaks Chinese better than you do."

"I don't doubt it," I said, and lingered to chat with them. They were kindly, simple folk and I allowed them to pepper me with their innocent questions. My answers failed to register.

The area's foremost attraction was a limestone formation called Moon Hill, so named because of the large, round, naturally formed hole that skewers its peak. I managed to locate it (it was the hill with the hole in it), but was disappointed to discover that a metal tower had been affixed to its summit. There were literally hundreds of other hills in the area, so there was no need to choose this one; except, of course, to show Mother Nature who the boss was.

While gazing up at this marred, geographical oddity, I was accosted by another faction of peasants. One woman handed me a piece of cardboard that read, 'Hello. I'm collecting nots stamp and coing from difficia countries if you have some I would appreciate it a lot.' I gave her some Hong Kong dollars and Macao patacas only for a band of women to try and rid her of them. They jostled until a skirmish broke out. I decided to leave.

Back in town that evening, I took a Mandarin class from a man who ran a guest house and restaurant. He spoke nice, natural-sounding English (which he had learned on his own) and wasn't a bad Chinese teacher, especially considering he'd had no formal training. He seemed incredibly bored, not just with the lesson, but with life. When I asked him questions, he would answer and then heave a weary sigh and stare at the table. Nevertheless, he kept betraying his intelligence. When I asked him what he had majored in, he said, "Financial management." When I asked him what that had been like, he shuddered and said, "It was (*sigh*)... extremely boring." When I told him I'd learned my Chinese in Taiwan, he mechanically replied, "Oh. Taiwan.... Taiwan is famous for tea." Sometimes I got tea; sometimes tofu or beef noodles, but it was always something you could ingest. Talking about anything more substantial – not that I wished to do so – was out of the question. Discussing Taiwanese independence in China can land you in hot water. Technically, it is punishable by death.

The following day, I did pretty much the same thing all over again: another long, relaxing, exploratory drive into the serene, lush, and completely surreal countryside followed by a language lesson with my bright but spiritless tutor. Afterward, I did a bit of reading and resting on one of West Street's agreeable verandas. I played ping pong at an outdoor table near the river and managed to hold my own. I poked my nose into shops and chatted with people. I walked down to the river to look at the horses. I enjoyed myself and felt at ease. Yangshuo may have been heavy on tourists and meretricious bric-a-brac, and it wasn't difficult to see that it was well on its way to becoming the proverbial parody of its former self, but I took pleasure in it nonetheless. It was attractive, relatively tranquil, and full of easygoing and gracious people. And in China, those qualities are hard to come by.

CHAPTER SIX

Back in Guilin, I boarded a train and spent the better part of the day reading and peering out the window. Once again, the views were captivating. Low abodes, minimal and medieval, stood among sweeping fields of rice and occasional clutches of maize. Bricks and tires were busy keeping jaundiced roof tiles from wandering off and ducks dotted scrap-filled yards of muck. There were turgid rivulets bordered with bamboo, dirt driveways lined with palms, and undulating hills decorated with jaunty bunches of eucalyptus trees. Dark-skinned farmers in conical hats hunched over their crops, cows sought out streams, and small factories gravitated toward the tracks. The arcing train was sucked into a tunnel so old that its entrance was crooked. It bathed us in its blackness and spit us out into a setting of mountains and four-storey houses, their red-and-gold, door-frame couplets brilliant in the glaring white light. A town emerged as a distant murmur. When it came into view, I saw kids playing soccer with an empty bleach bottle in front of disintegrating apartment blocks that had been bandaged together with laundry.

As I sat taking this in, a thin man with acid-washed jeans and a thread-bare dress shirt sat down across from me. He had so much purple dye and gel in his hair as to make it look plastic. Taking out a music player, he set it on the table between us and turned it on. Plainly, he wanted to share with me his love of boy bands. Someone in a nearby bunk heard it and turned on his own music: lutes and zithers meandering betwixt electronic drums. The two got into a duel, each frantically manipulating the volume. Neither, however, could compete with the piped-in pop music and squawking announcements indicating that the dining car was now open and that we ought to pay strict attention to public safety. I got up to explore the hard-sleeper class.

The soft-sleeper compartments contained four bunks and were mainly comprised of businessmen: men with briefcases, golf shirts, black dress pants, and slip-on shoes; men who intently sent text messages on their mobile phones and never smiled when they got

responses. The hard-sleeper compartments contained six bunks and
were packed with couples, families, babies, wandering toddlers, and men
who would slurp instant noodles, down cups of *baijiu*,[1] and then head
to the passageway to smoke and spit on the floor. People talked into
their phones as if they were on the Styrofoam-cup-and-string system.
The floor was littered with packaging and peanut shells and women
hung their bras and panties from bars above the windows. Many dozed,
more talked, and I saw a man on a middle bunk with his hand jammed
between a woman's legs. No one looked out the window for longer than
an instant and nobody read. A brief commotion in one compartment
caused representatives from four others to peek in and report on what
they saw ("It's a couple. They're arguing. About forty, I'd say."). Perhaps
it's because the Chinese lead lives of such great tedium that they are such
great busybodies.

In Guilin, I had picked up editions of yesterday's and today's *China
Daily* as I was curious to know what (the Communist mouthpiece said)
was going on. A front-page headline from yesterday's paper announced
that a new law had been passed banning members of the media from
reporting on accidents, natural disasters, and public health incidents
– unless they had express permission from the state. The article
maintained that this was solely for the purpose of maintaining accurate
information and ensuring social order. The law would apply to Hong
Kong as well, in spite of the "one party, two systems" arrangement.

In reality, the law was a backlash for the reporting of the 2002-2003 SARS
epidemic (severe acute respiratory syndrome) and the government's
bungled attempt to cover it up. The doctor who broke the story was
jailed as were several journalists. The media had managed to stay ahead
of the censors by simply publishing their articles before they could be
banned. This new law closed the loophole. Today's headlines stated
that an earthquake measuring 5.1 on the Richter scale had struck Hebei
province the previous day, but that "no casualties or property damage
had been reported." Parenthetically, China jails more journalists than any
other nation.

In 2009, the Paris-based media watchdog, Reporters Without
Borders, ranked China 168th out of a total of 175 countries in terms of
freedom of the press. The only nations to rank lower were Burma, Cuba,
Eritrea, Iran, Laos, North Korea, and Turkmenistan. Even weather

---

1   *Baijiu*, pronounced "Bye Joe" and meaning "white liquor," is usually distilled from
sorghum or rice. It is strong stuff: 80 to 120 proof, or 40 to 60 percent alcohol by volume.
The brand I saw most often in China, Red Star, utilized large lettering to boast of being 56
percent alcohol by volume.

reports are falsified in China. For decades, meteorologists have not been permitted to report temperatures exceeding 35 degrees Celsius (or 95 degrees Fahrenheit). Purportedly, if the temperature exceeds 37 degrees, workers across the nation are to be given the day off. As one of my students in Taiwan once told me, "The only thing in a Chinese newspaper you can know to be true is the date."

At around 5:00 p.m., I made my way to the dining car. It was ancient and begrimed with filth. There was no air conditioning, so all the windows were down making for fluttery curtains and warm currents of country air. Dining cars in China often seem to have more staff, police, and soldiers than actual diners and this was the case today. Ten uniforms – both male and female – were crowded around two tables. Half of them were eating and yakking with their mouths full while the rest cracked sunflower seeds between their teeth and spat the shells onto the table and floor. All of the men were smoking, even the chef, who was still on duty. One officer had gone so far as to construct a water pipe from a plastic bottle and was sucking smoke through it insatiably. Another was endeavouring to flirt with a female colleague by roughly grabbing at her arm. She put her chopsticks down and angrily swatted his hat off of his head. This caused everyone to howl, and then cough. He spent the next several minutes pouting, and smoking.

When this smoke-enshrouded entourage noticed me, they began to giggle and stare. I ordered the *qingjiao jirou*, or diced chicken with green pepper. The waitress did an impression of a chicken to make sure she had my order right. Again, everyone laughed. Just when I was about to leave, the only other passengers in the car extended a genuine invitation to join them, so I did. They were two men in their mid-twenties who were both very friendly. We chatted for an hour, sipping warm beer from oversized thimbles (there was no refrigerator) and toasting each other decorously. They were construction workers who had just helped complete a hotel in Yangshuo and were now headed home to Kunming. They missed their wives, they said, and home-cooked meals. Their skin was dark and leathery. Their eyes were sunken and their faces haggard and worn. They looked a decade older than they were. When the inevitable 'Where are you from?' ensued, one responded by saying that Canada was "very good" and "very developed." He then asked if it were located in the middle of the United States and famous for corn. I figured he was thinking of Kansas.

The limestone knolls surrendered to lazy hills, which slowly eroded into sloping fields of shimmering green. Belching smokestacks appeared more regularly, as did clusters of sooty brick homes and the muddy tracks that led to them. The buildings got bigger and changed from brown to grey. We arrived at Nanning, Guangxi's capital, at seven-thirty in the evening.

Her name was Meizhen and I had met her in Beijing. I had asked her where something was and she didn't know. I then asked, as I always did, whether she was a local. "No, I'm not," she said, shaking her head. "I'm from Nanning." She was visiting her aunt, who lived somewhere in the fringes of that never-ending city, and she was sightseeing. We got to talking; I offered to buy her lunch and we spent the afternoon together touring the *hutong*, the old grey neighbourhoods of incapacious alleys and courtyard homes. She was pretty and had a lovely smile. As I would discover, she was humourous, serious, stubborn, impatient, selfish, generous, contemptuous, kind, immature, austere, inquisitive, and self-governing. She saw all the same traits and contradictions in me. We held hands and kissed on a bridge spanning a frozen lake. We had kept in touch and she had invited me to come visit her – and her Chihuahua *Nunu* – in her hometown. So, here I was. But before we would meet, I had a day to myself.

Nanning was certainly rustic; intersections were treacle-flows of interweaving vehicles and jaywalkers, motorcyclists didn't wear helmets, cars parked and formed two lanes of traffic on the sidewalks, and city workers painted crosswalks with outsized calligraphy brushes. But it wasn't nearly as rustic as I had imagined.

It was Nanning's homogeny that I found irksome: a repetitive mass of five-storey manila buildings comprised of tiles and bars separated by gritty, tree-lined streets and grubby back lanes. Along its Yong River, there stood the light-adorned, skyscraper- and shopping-plaza district that you find in almost every Chinese city as well as a giant billboard of Mao Zedong, Deng Xiaoping, and Jiang Zemin smiling and applauding the town's development. They hovered above an aerial shot of Nanning like a triumvirate of archangels. Nanning has a mere 1.3 million people and is less than 150 kilometres from Vietnam. My Lonely Planet guidebook characterized it as "putting a dent in overgeneralized stereotypes of backwater capitals."

On Nanning's main street, I saw a public toilet with water gushing out the door and flooding the thoroughfare. City workers were blocking off the sidewalk with a pair of heavy barricades made of rusted pipe. These were about 18 metres long and were meant for cordoning off streets, not sidewalks. Instead of positioning them diagonally, however, the workers left them sticking straight out into the road, where they blocked off an entire lane of traffic. It was dark, the way was poorly lit (as usual), and the men put down no reflective signs or pylons. Their job done, they jumped into their little blue truck and sped away. They had barely gotten out of sight when a man on a motorbike drove straight into one of the barricades at full speed. He groaned, sat up, shook his head, and lit a cigarette – toilet water gurgling all around him.

The next evening, I met Meizhen for dinner. She wanted to have sushi, so we went to the "most famous sushi restaurant in town." Meizhen said it was a franchise based out of Guangzhou, but I knew better. They'd simply copied the design of a Japanese chain store and then done away with all the superfluous Japaneseness: civility, cleanliness, and excellence. The fish was rubbery, I heard a kimono-wearing waitress tell a customer how annoying he was, and the plastic lids that covered the plates were so dirty that you had to search for a clear spot to see what was under them. We left after only a couple of bites, at my urging. On the street, Meizhen asked me where I wanted to go. "I feel like Western food," I told her. "You choose the best Western restaurant you can think of and I'll treat. Money's no object."

At Café Lead-Land, my "American steak" was served with Thousand Island dressing. Under the Chinese characters for 'gravy,' the menu read, in English, 'Digs up a kind of optional juice, black pepper juice, onion juice, wild fungus juice, vanilla juice, red wine juice, garlic fragrant juice, fever juice, tomato sauce.' As Meizhen and I got caught up, the restaurant played songs by Lionel Richie, Barbara Streisand, and Paul McCartney – except they weren't actually sung by Lionel Richie, Barbara Streisand, or Paul McCartney, although they sounded awfully close. I had noticed this on my previous visit to Beijing; seldom were Western songs sung by the original artists, and no one knew the difference. China is a nation of much fakery; there's fake sushi, fake steak, fake gravy, fake music, fake goods, fake pharmaceuticals, fake news, fake weather reports, fake education, fake rights, fake laws, fake courts, fake judges, a fake congress, a fake constitution…. "Foreigners are easily fooled," or so the Chinese axiom goes, but I would posit that Chinese society has been assembled in such a fashion as to ensure that Chinese people perennially fool themselves, and without any means of comparison, most don't realize this is the case. In the distant past, surely there was a reason for all this pretending: it was too complicated or too expensive to do otherwise and the masses were too ignorant to know the difference. But largely due to the Chinese penchant for replication, this way of doing things – the way of doing just about everything – had become entrenched and ossified to the extent that it is seldom questioned. The utility of ignorance is the safeguarding of power, but ignorance eventually runs so deep that it devastates the very foundation of that which was meant to be safeguarded.

Meizhen took the following day off work to show me around. We ended up playing ping pong at some government-run "sports facility," a decrepit hall with a handful of table tennis and billiards tables. The walls were yellow, mildew-covered, and cracked. There was no air conditioning and the air was sour-smelling and damp. A limp, red, slogan-adorned banner hung on the far wall, its gusto mocked by neglect and rot. When we came in, the clerk was napping on a wooden bench behind the counter. After we woke her, she gave us two battered paddles and a pair of slightly egg-shaped balls and promptly went back to sleep. When the phone rang, it took her about 10 rings to answer it. After she finished talking, she disconnected it and lay down again. Between the ping pong tables there were metallic, cylindrical ashtrays like the kind you find (or used to find) in pool halls. They were filled with yellow butts, brown liquid, and black flies. Only two other people were there playing. In China, you practically never see anyone exercising or playing sports. The factories that manufacture all those Olympic gold-medal winners are not open to the general public.

The following afternoon, Meizhen introduced me to her female friend Xu Beiru and the three of us caught a cab to a bus station on the edge of town. 'Please be Civilized' announced a sign. 'Everyone has Responsibility,' read another. We took a minibus far out into the countryside. It began to pour and within minutes the road was inundated with rust-coloured water. In an hour, it was sunny again and the pillbox housing that lined the way cowered at the feet of startling hills. Attractive fields lay under skies of fresh blue streaked by bands of white and silver.

Beiru worked for a Canadian cosmetics company in Nanning and rented a room in the company dorm for eight dollars a month. She went home once every three or four weeks to see her family and had suggested to Meizhen that we join her. She was classically beautiful with a face that looked as though it belonged in a painting. She was also smartly dressed in black pumps, a back skirt, a white blouse, and a very visible black bra. She had large almond eyes, flowing hair, golden teeth, and the worst body odour I have ever smelled.

At the plywood terminus, we hopped in the back of an auto-rickshaw that grumbled down a bumpy lane. I saw a bullock tethered to a tree and a low, trembling field of green; a single straw hat decorated it like a cushion button. Suddenly, we pulled over and stopped and the driver shouted something in the local dialect.

"What did he say?" I asked.

"We've got to get out," Meizhen translated. "There's a traffic jam."

"A traffic jam?" I asked. "How can there be a traffic jam?"

Beiru explained. "It's watermelon season."

We walked past a row of vehicles and I saw what had caused the traffic jam. Farmers from Beiru's village had brought their watermelons on flatbeds hitched to tractors. Grinning, dark-complected peasants were loading them onto trucks that would haul them to market. Rather than just use half the road (or the empty parking lot near the bus station) they were using all of it. Those not working were drinking beer and gabbing. Hammocks had been set up. The road was full of crates and rubbish and bits of trampled watermelon. Everyone seemed cheerful, and 30 drivers (including a couple of police officers) waited patiently, but for what? It was impossible to pass. With Meizhen's Chihuahua nosing out of a shopping bag slung over my shoulder, I followed her and Beiru. We walked past this scene ("Hawlo! Hawlo!") before filing across fields, around cow paddies, over garbage-embedded tracks that ran between smelly duck ponds, past an aqueduct, and on to a village where the primary difference between people's homes and their pig pens was size. As anyone who has ever studied Chinese can tell you, the character for 'household' or 'home' is a pictograph of a boar under a roof.

The Xu family lived on the uppermost floor of a four-floor building at the edge of the village. They were better off than most. Situated on raised ground, the structure offered bewitching vistas of pure nature that stretched for eternity. Mr. Xu's brothers lived on the other floors with their families. Beiru's grandmother, 84 and deaf, sat on the front steps, a permanent fixture I imagined.

There was no air conditioning or fan in the house, so the windows had been thrown open. The outside world was a tangle of vegetation and a drone of insects interspersed by quacks and ribbits. That evening, we ate a large meal seated on plastic stools around a low table. Mrs. Xu had prepared garlic chicken, a plate of duck, water spinach, and a large pot of mutton soup with corn. The teenaged son asked me hesitant questions about America and showed me his hairdryer. Mr. Xu told me they had once had a man from Xinjiang stay with them. I asked where we were in relation to Nanning. After some debate, the collective response was, "South." "So, quite close to Vietnam, then," I offered, but they couldn't say. I asked them questions about their daily life and thanked them repeatedly for their hospitality. "No need to be polite," replied Mr. Xu, and poured me more beer. It was as warm as tea and he and I were the only ones allowed to drink it. For dessert, there was watermelon. When that was finished, everyone gathered up the rinds and chucked them out the window.

We went up to the roof to look around. Night had fallen and the village appeared as a sparse smattering of orange lights. Overhead, stars twinkled through a ribcage of clouds and I wished I had brought a tent. We moved to the living room to watch TV. The only reading material was a handbook from the local Communist Party headquarters; the only decoration a government calendar showing a buxom female military officer saluting in front of a mobile multiple rocket launcher in the midst of firing; streaks of orange and white ripping through a sky of software-generated blue.

To prevent any more bugs from flinging themselves at the room's only light, mosquito coils were lit. Mr. Xu squashed a centipede that he said was "quite venomous," and we sat there in the haze and television glow watching the Guangxi regional news. Everyone seemed wholly contented, even through the 'Guangxi premier congratulates Nanning No. 4 steelworks on record production,' type stories. I slept alone in the son's bed under a mosquito net. I was bitten several times during the night, but not by anything with wings.

The next day after lunch, during which a couple of villagers turned up to meet me, we gathered around the other family cynosure: the karaoke unit. Mr. and Mrs. Xu gave us two large sacks of watermelon to take back to Nanning and we walked back to the centre of the village where a truck was waiting to drive us to the bus station. It was an experience I won't soon forget: walking with two pretty women in the countryside in China somewhere near Vietnam with a bag of watermelon in one arm and a Mexican dog under the other.

I spent the next few days pottering around Guangxi's capital. I explored a scenic area with arresting views of the Yong River, strolled around a leafy university campus (where someone from the administration darted out of an office to offer me a teaching job), and went to see a couple of movies with Meizhen in a complex that was obviously brand-new. During both films, there were about a dozen other audience members who sat together; at times, chatting on their cell phones, and at other times talking about the characters and plot, even though it was clear they didn't know each other. "Who's the guy with the sword?" "Do they all have magical powers or just the children?" "Uh-oh, I don't think she should go inside that cave!"

I left one evening on the K230 bound for Kunming. On the platform, Meizhen and I said goodbye. She got a little emotional, and a pair of young soldiers began gawking at us. They gestured and giggled. I fixed them with a psychotic stare until they turned away, defeated. Trying her hand at English, Meizhen asked, "Am I a nice guy?" I told her she was a very nice guy and promised to call her the next day. I found my bunk and went to the dining car to relax. I ordered a beer and opened a book. A waitress ordered me back to my compartment, but I pretended not to understand her. There were other people there getting drunk and disorderly – their faces red as beets – and there I was: nursing a lager and reading.

Luckily, she gave up looking for someone who could say 'Please go to bed,' in English after she got a man's order wrong and he blew up at her. "Idiot!" he screamed. "I asked for fried *beef*, not fried *pork*! *Ai ya*!" Then, she billed a pair of men for nine bottles of beer when they'd only had eight (and a couple bottles of Red Star *baijiu*). What was she trying to do? Cheat them or something? A huge squabble broke out – purple faces, pointing fingers, foul language – and it spread until half the car was consumed by dispute. Just before I got to the passageway, I turned around to survey this scene and saw that the television set above everyone's head was showing a military parade from Beijing with hundreds of soldiers goose stepping in perfect unison.

There was a Danish couple in the next compartment and we got to talking. Yes, I told them, I had noticed that the train smelled. Eventually, they told me that they had their guidebook confiscated upon arrival in Beijing. I asked them why.

"They said it was politically incorrect," he replied. "It didn't include Thailand or something."

"Tai*wan*," his girlfriend corrected him.

"Oh, yeah. Tai*wan*. Anyway, we didn't even know what Taiwan was until some other travellers told us. I couldn't believe it. In Denmark, you could never confiscate a book, unless it was Nazi literature or something. It's really amazing."

Indeed. This was the second time I had heard this story. In Yangshuo, I had overheard a South African woman say the exact same thing. It reminded me of my own experience in Beijing when an immigration officer noticed that my passport had been issued in Taipei. As a prerequisite for leaving, he wanted me to declare that Taipei (and, by extension, Taiwan) was part of China. He put it in the form of a question. I answered him by saying Taipei was in Taiwan and that Taiwan was famous for beef noodles. I then suggested he try the beef noodles should he ever go there, something I knew was impossible. Finally, I asked him if he liked beef noodles, and I did so in the most serious of manners. Gauging that he wasn't dealing with an especially bright individual, he gave up and let me go. But I was worried about having my guidebook taken away. After all, I had the exact same book, three other China books, and a pair of rather thick, rather circumspect notebooks.

At 6:00 a.m., I was jolted awake by a shrieking announcement. Seconds later, the door flew open and an attendant appeared demanding my blankets. Another one entered and began to sweep the carpet with an old straw broom. "*Kuai dao le*!" she bellowed. "We're about to arrive!" That meant we had another two hours.

I was borne along a river of jostling, nattering people that surged from the platform through a dark underpass. I was carried beyond the turnstiles and deposited at a taxi stand. From there, I headed to the Camellia Hotel. After a nap and a shower, I made some arrangements at the in-house travel agency before setting out to explore. Hotels in China almost always have in-house travel agencies through which you can purchase almost any type of ticket. They are convenient and easy to find as they are customarily adjacent to the in-house massage parlour.

Kunming is the capital of Yunnan, the most physically and culturally diverse of China's provinces. Yunnan means "South of the Clouds" and it borders Vietnam, Laos, and Burma. It has a landmass slightly larger than that of Norway. Something like 38 percent of Yunnan's population are members of ethnic minority groups, of which there are at least 24.

The city of Kunming had an emphatically laid-back feel. People didn't appear to be travelling in seven directions at once, nor did they drive as though one or both of their feet were on fire. This may have had to do with the temperate climate. At an altitude of nearly 1,900 metres, Kunming, dubbed "The City of Eternal Spring," was reasonably and refreshingly cool.

Kunming's metamorphosis into anything that might be called a city is the result of the Second World War, when it was transformed by industry and refugees fleeing the Japanese. It also served as the terminus of the legendary Burma Road, the sole overland supply route through which Western provisions were shipped to the Chinese people and *matériel* was sent to Chiang Kai-shek and his army. Images of the tenacious Chinese chiselling a path over precipitous mountain passes (one section climbed around 22 hairpin loops) while stooped under loads nearly twice their weight as they skirted Japanese bombs left an indelible impression on the West. But what the sympathetic Occidentals could not have known was that most of the supplies would be easily captured, withheld from troops in the field, or sold outright to the enemy.

In 1979, Kunming acted in another military capacity: it was a major base of operations for the invasion of Vietnam, a punitive action arising from that country's courting of the Soviet Union, its expulsion of half a million Chinese "capitalists," and its war with Cambodia. With the stated aim of "teaching the Vietnamese a lesson," 80,000 PLA troops poured over the border. Seventeen days later, 20,000 of them were dead. The Chinese promptly withdrew and labelled the incursion "a great success," one which led directly to the massive military modernization efforts underway today.

Tellingly, Kunming's star attractions were two Tang Dynasty pagodas, and I started my tour there. They were unremarkable. I walked around a nearby park full of chess- and mahjong-playing seniors before strolling along a street of imitation cafés, the classiest of which featured a sign saying, 'STEAK PIZZA PASTA SALAD SANDWHICH CAKE ICE CREAM COFEE SMOOT.' Across the street was what appeared to be the city's South Gate, an imposing (if completely rebuilt) Ming-era edifice with a stately tower rising above tiled eaves and an enormous arched door. In front of it, a man was riding a bicycle that was built into a large grooved aluminum wheel, which was propelled by the bicycle's own wheels. "Whoohoo!" yelled the man as he did loop-dee-loos. "Whoohoo!" I reckoned that he had long since arrived at the conclusion I was only just nearing: there wasn't all that much to do in Kunming.

There was only one north-south road that spanned the entire city, and it was Beijing Road. I headed there next as I needed to do some banking. As a lark, I decided to ask ten people if they could tell me where Beijing Road was (we were on it), but only four could. One of those who couldn't was a security guard stationed in front of a government building. Yes, he had lived in Kunming all his life, he told me smilingly. This is all the more surprising when you consider that the centres of Chinese cities are typically grids that are laid out according to the points of a compass. Moreover, major arteries almost always contain bearings in their names, e.g. Nanjing East Road. Obviously, this doesn't preclude getting lost, but it does tend to make things fairly straightforward. I would wager that just about anyone could be randomly inserted into the heart of almost any Chinese city and be able to get their bearings at the first major intersection, without the aid of a map.

After exchanging dollars for *renminbi*, I encountered an extended family walking toward me. When the little boy at the forefront spotted me, he cried, "Mom! Look! A foreigner!" and began running my way. Unfortunately, he got caught up on a pant leg and fell, quite literally, flat on his face. As his mother wiped the tears away and checked for damage, his grandparents shot me homicidal looks. Only moments later, another odd thing happened. In an otherwise empty lane, a car was parked on the sidewalk. Its driver-side door was open and an arc of urine was emanating from within, splashing down on the street and footway. I made my own arc around this scene and saw that a child was standing on the seat peeing, encouraged by his mother. Incredibly, a stylishly dressed couple walking behind me hadn't noticed anything and just kept plodding along. They only missed getting hit because the boy had voided his bladder. They splashed through the puddle, though, oblivious to all but themselves.

It's difficult to know what it is Chinese people see. In Singapore, a five-year medical study was performed on more than 110,000 subjects in order to determine the prevalence of myopia among four different ethnic groups: Eurasians, Malays, Indians, and Chinese. As you will have guessed, incidence of short-sightedness was highest among the last group, at 48.5 percent. The Eurasians were second at 34.7 percent, followed by the Indians at 30.4 percent, and the Malays at 24.5 percent. The study concluded that racial and cultural differences appeared to be responsible for the discrepancy.

On my previous visit to Hong Kong, I rounded a corner one sunny afternoon to find an entire street flooded with human waste. A team of workers and two large trucks were in the process of cleaning it up. In addition to the smell, there were signs, pylons, and flashing lights, but that wasn't enough to deter dozens of people from sloshing 10, 20 and even 30 metres into the stuff. I watched as one man walked halfway down the street before realizing what he had done.

In Taipei, I was in a subway station once when I saw a well-dressed and well-groomed man sitting on top of a boxed computer printer vomiting all over the platform. Public drunkenness is not all that common in Taiwan (I figured he'd just come from a company party and had won the printer), but what made this so noteworthy was the *way* in which he failed to hold his drink; he wretched and bobbed simultaneously and so dramatically that his head nearly touched the floor repeatedly. It was nearly midnight and I joined a pack of staring people. A train arrived, and only four passengers alighted. They all walked directly toward this convulsing salary man and the puddle that extended away from his toes all the way to the track. Only at the last second did the first three see what they were headed for. They backtracked and made a detour around the staircase the man was leaning against. The fourth person, a businessman, walked – not without a certain swagger – straight through the mess before ascending the escalator and glaring back at the onlookers in a 'What are you lot staring at!?' manner. How he didn't hear the splashing sound, notice the smell, or see the man – whose bobbing head came within a hair of hitting his hip – was a miracle, especially when you consider that he had stridden straight toward him unobstructed for half the length of a soccer pitch. Other examples I have seen during my time in Taiwan could fill a whole other volume.

I came upon a diminutive Muslim quarter where I visited a mosque, its lonely minaret jutting above an uneven horizon of ebony tiled roofs. The area was a vibrant one, brimful with shops that were crammed with goods, and sidewalks that were dotted with grinning, shish-kebab-peddling Muslims.

Kunming may have been behind in the race for skyscrapers, but it was working to remedy that. Next to the tiny Muslim district, a neighbourhood of squat, wooden homes was being levelled to make way for Ronald, the Colonel, and Frapuccinos from Seattle. The fence surrounding the zone was decorated with artists' renditions of shiny buildings and tidy lawns. They looked like those perky illustrations of modern life in America in the 1950s. Accompanying them was an assortment of ponderous, justifying slogans written in Chinese and upper-case English lettering:

THE CULTURE IS RISING, POWER INEVITABLE

THE INHERITANCE MARKETPLACE COMMERCIAL CULTURE BRINGS HONOUR TO THE NATIONAL CULTURE TO BE SUCCINCT

KUNMING OLD STREET JEWELRY FLOWER AND BIRD MARKET POURS INTO THE NEW VIGOR FOR THE CITY NAMECARD

I made my way back to the hotel and went for an evening stroll. In front of an ambitious, Parthenon-inspired hotel, a wedding reception was being held. An entourage of wine-sipping guests was mingling about the sidewalk and snapping photos of one another. Suddenly, a scream pierced the air, silencing everyone.

In the middle of the street, and directly in front of the guests, a husband and wife were embroiled in a match of tug-of-war with their daughter; her arms representing opposite ends of the rope. After the man won, he heaved his prize over his shoulder and gambolled off. He was too inebriated to get very far, however, and crashed pathetically – headlong – into the curb. The daughter howled. The struggle resumed for what seemed an eternity, and nobody did the slightest thing about it. A policeman arrived on a motorbike whereupon he lit up a cigarette, pulled up his pant leg, scratched his shin, and watched. Drivers didn't even honk. In the end, the father wrestled his hysterical daughter into a cab that raced away. The mother hopped on her scooter and pursued them. Catching up at a red light, she delivered a series of determined kicks to one of the taxi's doors. The light turned green and they sped out of sight. The crowd dispersed. The guests returned to their wine and conversation.

Chapter Seven

The bus to Xiaguan reeked of oil. The recently mopped floor was covered with little ponds and brooks of dirty water and my seat refused to budge from the recline position. Because of construction, it took nearly an hour just to get out of Kunming. For miles, the road was no more than a collection of dirt, rocks, potholes, and idle heavy equipment. Nobody was working. This was the first of many times I would see this: lengthy stretches of torn-up or totally inadequate roadway with hardly any work being done. In a nation of 1.3 billion people, and one in which there was reportedly no shortage of capital, this made no sense to me.

After being thoroughly jolted and jarred, we reached actual asphalt and proceeded to drive past some pretty scenery. Dark brooding mountains towered above majestic forests, and timbered hills and dells were sliced by glinting rivulets. The sky opened up in a sweep of June-July blue and highway signs said things in English like, 'No Drunkenness Driving' and 'No Tiredness Driving.' We stopped at a canteen for lunch (instant noodles, packaged peanuts, Pepsi-Cola) purchased from wordless, frowning clerks. Nearly everyone littered. The canteen floor and parking lot were wild with refuse.

Four hundred kilometres later, we were at our destination. From Xiaguan to Dali Old Town it was another eighteen clicks, best to do by cab. A harassed-looking British couple spotted me negotiating with a driver in Mandarin and was quickly at my side. We picked up an effusive woman from New Zealand and set off.

China, the two women agreed, was ugly and awful. Where was all this history, culture, and scenery they'd heard of? If they didn't see something nice soon, they threatened, they were going somewhere else, maybe Hanoi.

"I was jus' sayin' ta John 'bout the pollution, we never seen anythin' like it. Isn't that right luv?"

"Eh?"

"I was jus' tellin' 'er – sorry whus your name, dear?"

"Lucy,"

"I was jus' tellin' Lucy 'ere 'bout the pollution, said we never seen anythin' like it."

"Aye."

"An' av ya seen the state of the toilets here? Did you see them at that roadside dump that we stopped at fer lunch? My god, they're absolutely disgraceful, are they not John?"

"Aye, that they are. They are despicable."

"Have they no standards, the Chinese?"

We had to pay the equivalent of $1.20 each for the ride, yet all they could think to do was to wonder whether we were being taken. I was more taken with the landscape.

A miniature walled town dating from the Ming Dynasty, Dali is a collection of cobbled streets, brooding willows, brooks that churn and bubble, and traditional-style houses constructed from stone and wood. It lies at the foot of the Green Jade Mountain Range, an immense procession of towering summits, the loftiest of which extends up to a very respectable 4,000 metres. In the winter, the chain's verdant crests and shadowy crevices are dusted with snow for effect, but in the summer they are obfuscated by bulging clouds, from which ethereal fingers of mist extend down, caressing the mass's furrows and folds. Surrounding the town, there are gardens, houses, pagodas, temples, and a great deal of wonderful nothingness. Although the township itself is fairly level, the land slopes steeply from its eastern gate. Thereafter, it angles down at a gallop for some distance until it vanishes into the Ear Shaped Lake, a powder blue body of water roughly 40 kilometres in length.

After finding a place to stay, I set out for a poke around. Next to my guest house was a row of stately white houses marked by grey tiled roofs. Their carved doors were open wide revealing carpenter shops and the pungent aroma of sawdust. Inside, craftsmen were whittling latticed windows and assembling traditional-style furniture.

Within the town walls, people were hawking maps, balloons, cotton candy, and donkey-cart rides. Packs of Bai women – the region's primary ethnic group – gathered together in their time-honoured dress drumming up business for one venture or another. Despite the town's charm, its main road was loud and obnoxious; a bevy of tourists bustling past kitsch, travel agencies, and ice-cream puddles. The side streets, however, as well as the northern section of the enclave, were more residential, more authentic in their commerciality, and much more to my liking.

Chinese people can finally afford to travel, but they tend to do so domestically as expensive and hard-to-obtain permits are required to venture abroad. In 2007, the last year for which data is available, there were only 55 million outbound tourists in China, or a scant 4.16 percent of the population. In the same year, there were 1.61 billion domestic tourists, making for an average of 1.21 in-country trips per citizen. Of the 4.16 percent, more than half (or so it is estimated) only made it to Hong Kong or Macau. And this, of course, is how the government likes it. Not only is massive domestic travel a boon to the economy, but, in a nation as ethnically and regionally fractured as China, it helps foster feelings of connectedness and nationalism. Along with whipping the national economy into shape, whipping up patriotic sentiment has been Beijing's chief aim ever since the crackdown at Tiananmen Square in 1989. Furthermore, with so few truly travelling abroad (and candidates would have to be considered safe in order to get approval) the outside world is whatever the authorities say it is.

For foreign tourists, domestic tourists can be rather curious, and by 'curious' I suppose I mean 'irritating.' They block up entire streets, vociferously commandeer restaurants and hotels, they point, they stare…. But they can also be amusing. They sport identical neon baseball caps and mutely shuffle behind flag-carrying leaders who assail them with such absorbing factoids as, "This banyan tree has a height of twenty-three point eight metres," and "Those buildings on your left are old and traditional in style." As I sat sipping tea outside a café, one tour guide pointed me out to her herd and raised the megaphone to her lips. "And, as you can see," she squawked, "foreigners appreciate the beauty of Dali Old Town, too." The pack of blinking individuals silently appraised me for a moment before simultaneously turning their attention back to their leader. I have seen brighter-looking ostriches.

The next morning, I bought a ticket for a boat tour and walked down to the lake. The boats were all identical with cabins built in the fashion of Chinese pavilions. We shuttled across the water until we came to a rocky protrusion ornamented with temples and stairs. We stopped by ramming into the pier. The driver had hardly even slowed down. Everyone scrambled off and then scrambled up several flights of concrete steps. It didn't appear that anyone lived on the outcrop, but the stairs were lined with nagging vendors, and unless you wanted to stay on the boat, there was no escaping them. The sight of the lake and mountain range beyond was quite extraordinary, however. Dali appeared as a thumbprint with the pagodas imitating toothpicks.

The second island we visited was inhabited by a thousand people employed in either fishing or tourism. While inspecting some ancient lanes, I was accosted by a girl who worked in the latter. Addressing me in broken English, she invited me to tea. "I don't want money," she insisted. "I just want let you understand Bai people hospitality." I accepted, and we switched to Mandarin. Past racks of drying fish, she led me up a rocky pathway and introduced me to a couple of wrinkly elders who were sitting in front of their humble, crumbling home.

"You seem different from most foreigners," she said. "You speak Chinese and were willing to talk to me. Most Westerners just ignore me."

"Well, I suppose they think that you only want their money," I replied.

"Oh, but when a Bai person invites you to tea, it is only to drink tea. Hospitality is part of our culture."

When we got to her home, we entered a room with a sofa and a coffee table and she went off to put the kettle on.

"When I give you this cup, you have to say, '*La wei ni*,'" she instructed courteously. "That means 'thank you' in the Bai dialect. This is *ku cha* ('bitter tea') but it doesn't taste bitter. We drink it whenever a Bai person leaves his family in search of work."

I had a few sips and she went off to prepare another cup. Bitter tea tasted no different from green tea.

"This one is *xingfu cha* ('happiness tea') because it's got walnuts and brown sugar and can make you happy," she explained with a laugh.

"*La wei ni*," I attempted.

"Good!" she exclaimed. "You have very good pronunciation." She then scurried away to prepare the third cup.

"This last one is called *sandao cha* ('third course tea'). It was the preferred drink of the emperor thirteen hundred years ago. He thought it could prevent colds. In those days, if a man wanted to introduce his sweetheart to his parents, the mother would approve by serving *sandao cha*. If she disapproved, she would serve fish."

Personally, I would have preferred some fish. *Sandao cha* tasted like warm cough syrup mixed with flat ginger ale.

"Which one do you like best?" she asked.

"The *xingfu cha*," I replied. "It's sweet and tastes good."

"Yes, it *is* good," she agreed. "And it can bring you happiness and wealth. And it's only fifteen *yuan*. I have change if you don't have any small bills."

It's rare in life that you are conned and yet pleased by it. I smilingly paid her and she swiftly showed me to the door. Sometimes, foreigners *are* easily fooled.

"Be sure to tell people in your country about the hospitality of the Bai people!" she called after me. I assured her I would.

The boat crashed into the jetty we had disembarked from and I took a malodorous ride via horse-drawn carriage back up the hill. I spent the remainder of the day wandering around, peering in people's doors, and doing nothing in particular. In a back alley, an old woman offered me both opium and marijuana, but I declined. Not only do recreational drugs not appeal to me, but there was my annual drug test to consider. In Taiwan, Republic of China, English teachers are required to undergo a yearly examination for AIDS, tuberculosis, barbiturates, and opium. Interestingly, if I were to give up language teaching and open a trading company that imported, say, whiskey and dildos, such a test would be waived, but as a member of a perceived subclass of alien residents, it was yearly X-rays, blood tests, and urine samples for me. While we're on the subject, foreign nationals wishing to marry in Taiwan are obliged to undergo a test for leprosy.

The following afternoon, I left the Old Town of Dali on a bus bound for the Old Town of Lijiang. After following the Ear Shaped Lake to its lobe, we rolled through a massive valley lined with cloud-draped massifs, cascading rice terraces, ribbed hillocks, and handsome villages. When we finally arrived, my first thought was, 'My god! Look at all the tourists!' The Chinese have a saying: *ren shan ren hai*, which means 'people mountain, people sea.' This sea was neon-capped and shark-finned with tour-leader flags. Proceeding down an alley, I checked into an antique guest house with a quaint little courtyard and then ventured out for a glance around.

Lijiang's Old Town was a little like a highly compressed version of Dali Old Town with the most noticeable differences being that it lay within a valley and lacked gates or walls. Also, nosing about its narrow lanes, it was impossible to get a sense of what it resembled overall. It was a cramped labyrinth of stony streets, weeping willow trees, sprightly canals, miniature arched bridges, hefty lanterns, and dark rustic buildings.

Lijiang has been in existence for more than eight centuries and was once part of the ancient Tea and Horse Caravan Trail, which saw tea transported from Sichuan to Tibet. The town briefly caught the world's attention in 1996 when an earthquake measuring 7.0 devastated more than a third of it. That catastrophe left over 300 people dead and another 16,000 injured. Painstakingly rebuilt, it went on to become a UNESCO World Heritage Site. Personally, I couldn't see what was so alluring about it until nightfall. It was then I realized that almost all of the buildings were wired up with lights. Peripheral sections of the village were silent with a kind of Christmas-time enchantment whereas others possessed a sort of Mardi-Gras charm. Bar and restaurant verandas were packed with alcohol-swilling twenty-somethings attempting to outsing and outchant their counterparts on rival verandas. It was all very lively and the temperature was mercifully cool. Lijiang rests at an altitude of 2,400 metres.

I was served by a rude waiter in a restaurant full of rude waiters before repairing to the upper deck of another restaurant to drink tea and take in the elevated view. It was perfect. A dazzling array of lights flickered and shone against the town's crimson walls and raven-hued roofs. As I sat there, a man in his fifties asked if he could join me. He was also from Canada and lived in Nunavut, one of that country's three northern territories. He was a teacher and explained that he had taken a year off to teach and travel in China. He had just finished a contract at a high school in Dalian, in the northeast. I asked him how he had liked it.

"Oh, it was *great*," he purred. "And the kids were so nice and so open to new ideas, especially about sex."

He confided that he had often given his students writing assignments like the following: 'You're in a room with a naked man and/or woman. What do you do?' and 'Your parents find out you're gay. What do you tell them?' He went on and on about all kinds of things he shouldn't have, but I sat there and listened nonetheless. Afterwards, I took notes. There are times when I feel like a magnet for sociopaths and degenerates, and this was one of them. For a final-day activity, the man explained, he took his students to the beach. "Some of the girls felt shy in their bathing suits, so I told them, 'Don't be ashamed of your bodies! Be proud!'" And with that he pumped two fists into the air. Then he spread his arms like wings and grinned. "Oh, that day was a lot of fun. I brought my video camera and we made a movie called *Broke Back Beach*." Later on, I searched for his name on INTERPOL, but didn't find anything.

I woke early and took a stroll atop the crest of a nearby hill. After being made fun of by three labourers who kept repeating, "Hawlo," "Shank you ferry muchee," and "I dung know," in between fits and starts of uproarious laughter, I ran into a young Australian fellow and we struck up a conversation. We had both been hoping to take in the 5,600-metre Jade Dragon Snow Mountain off in the distance, but it was wreathed in cloud. He told me that he was in China to meet his fiancée's parents and to travel. He spoke excellent Chinese and added that, so far, China hadn't been a very pleasant experience. I asked him why.

"Well, it all started with our hotel in Hong Kong. I booked it online, and it looked fine in the pictures, but when we got there..."

"Chungking Mansions?" I ventured.

"Yeah, that's the one!"

He described how when he opened his door the morning after he arrived he discovered a line of police officers standing there. He didn't understand their presence until he noticed the blood-soaked floor behind them. A "foreign businessman" had been fatally stabbed after having been chased through a number of "business establishments."

I left Old Town and walked to the nearby Black Dragon Pool Park. Stretched across a silvery pond was an arched bridge of stone and marble connected to a tiered structure with upturned eaves. The foot of a luxuriant hill angled into the picture while the backdrop was governed by the Jade Dragon Snow Mountain, which surged from dark green to grey to white, or would have if I had been able to see it. Bougainvillea completed the scene, which has graced the cover of at least one guidebook. Admission to the park was an ambitious eight dollars, although a portion of this went to the funding of a research centre meant to preserve Naxi culture. As this was also in the park, I decided to stop in and have a look.

The Naxi (pronounced *na-shee*) are one of China's 54 officially recognized ethnic minorities.[1] Descendents of nomadic Tibetans, they reside among the foothills of the Himalayas with Lijiang representing their quote-unquote spiritual capital. What sets the Naxi apart from other groups is that their society is a matriarchal one. While the blue-robed, Quaker-looking women oversee work and finance, the men are encouraged to spend their days gardening or learning a musical instrument. Additionally, the Naxi employ their own unique form of writing, the only one in existence that still utilizes hieroglyphics.

Upon first glance, the script brings to mind Egyptian, but a closer look reveals something far less profound; something slightly comical, even. On pieces of tawny parchment you see boxed scenes like those found in a comic strip. This is fitting, as some of the pictographs look like mid-twentieth-century cartoons. You see a man carrying a sack and walking toward a giant cat. The sky is filled with birds and objects that call to mind flying breasts. Beyond the cat there stands a tree and an oversized winged mouse which bears a resemblance to an early version of Mickey Mouse. Your reaction is to stifle a giggle.

Far from being child's play, however, the pictographs are in fact excruciatingly complex, and this of course renders them almost completely useless. Add to this the fact that the language is going the way of many minority languages and you are left with a situation where only a handful of scholars are actually capable of employing it, and even they

---

1   In fact, China recognizes 55 ethnic minorities, 54 on the mainland and 1 in Taiwan. China refers to the Taiwanese minority as "the mountain people." In point of fact, there are 14 such groups in Taiwan and although a similar blanket term is sometimes used to describe them there, that is now considered to be inappropriate.

use a simplified version and are hardly what you might call prolific. In the past, the Naxi produced literature by the ream; nowadays only a scant few texts are drawn up, usually for funerals or blessings.

Much of what we know about these pantheistic people and their unique script comes from a hefty bundle of manuscripts procured by an intriguing character named Joseph Rock (1884–1962), an Austrian-American explorer and self-taught linguist, geographer, and botanist, who lived in Lijiang for 24 years. In addition to the manuscripts, Rock penned two histories of the Naxi people while still managing to find the time to compile a 1,094-page dictionary of their language. His manuscripts were eventually sold to the Library of Congress, where they remain and are scrutinized today. From them, we know that the Naxi were a shamanistic tribe obsessed with demons, exorcisms, funerals, and ritual suicides. They suffered tremendously during the Cultural Revolution.

As I made my way up the path that led to the institute, a man in his twenties intercepted me and welcomed me inside. After attempting to explain some writing samples, he led me into a wooden school house where a class was just finishing. The man was Han Chinese, but was studying the Naxi language out of linguistic interest, or so he said. He attributed the medium's decline not to its complexity or impracticality, but rather to the corrosive influence of Western culture, specifically fast food and blue jeans, yet he was wearing blue jeans. Like the guide at Sun Yat-sen Memorial Hall, he was overconfident and very bad at masking an air of cultural superiority. He was also tactless and extremely pushy, repeating that I should make a donation in order to "protect world culture for the noble benefit of all mankind." I had bought a ticket and put change into a donation plate, but plainly that wasn't enough. "You could have your name translated onto a scroll for twenty American dollars," he urged. Somehow, I had trouble imagining what Troy Parfitt would appear as in hieroglyphs. "Or you could pose for a photograph with a priest-scholar for fifteen American dollars," he pressed, pointing to the corner. I turned to find a man in an ornate chair. I hadn't seen him in the dim light, but I saw him plainly now. He was wrapped up in some type of thunder-and-lightning outfit, a blinding assemblage of sapphire and gold. A giant feather soared out of his ceremonial cap. He smiled at me. I smiled back. "No thanks," I said, and turned to go. I went out the door, and the young man hounded me all the way down the path.

That evening, I returned to the restaurant with the view and sat in the same seat. I ordered the same pot of tea and read the same book. At a nearby table, an American couple was discussing politics – American foreign policy, actually, and rather heatedly. It quickly became an argument and she got up and announced she was going back to the room. He stayed and stared at the wall. After a minute, he stood up and asked if he could join me. I was beginning to feel like a priest.

This was Jerome Philip Austen of Frankfort, Kentucky. He had spiky blond hair and piercing blue eyes. His name card, in both English and Chinese, told me that he was a major in the United States Army in addition to being a defense attaché officer and something called a foreign area officer. He confessed, without any prompting whatsoever, that he was in China on an errand of sanctioned spying. "Major Major," I quipped as I examined the card, but he didn't get the reference. Major Austen explained how he was part of an exchange program. "We send our people over here, and the Chinese, well, they send their people back to the States," he said. "Hell, we just gave the Chinese a tour of one our aircraft carriers."

I had read about this in *The Christian Science Monitor.* The Pentagon believed that allowing a Chinese reporter on the USS *Kitty Hawk* might make for a powerful deterrent. The article noted, however, that while Chinese officers had inspected nuclear submarines and sat in on classes at West Point, their American counterparts were often treated to tours of vacant bases and military parades.

The major divided his time between studying Mandarin in Beijing and travelling around the country on weekends to places of "historical interest." This meant places of Communist Party historical association – to better understand the "national mindset," which is to say the government's mindset. It was then that I mentioned I lived in the other China.

"Oh, you mean the Precious Island," he corrected me, earnestly. That's what Beijing calls Taiwan when it's not calling it the renegade province. I didn't rise to the bait. I didn't even answer. "How long would it take to travel around the island?" he asked, changing tack.

I said, "Maybe a couple of weeks. You would start in Taipei and go clockwise. The east coast is quite dramatic and you could go to a couple of the outlying islands. The Western portion is where all the major cities are – Kaohsiung, Tainan, Taichung, and then back up around to Taipei again. It wouldn't take long to do. It's a pretty small country, really."

This did not sit well.

"Don't call it a country!" ordered the major.

"Why not?" I honestly hadn't meant anything by it.

"Cuz people 'round here don't like it. *That's* why not." He eyed me suspiciously. I looked at him blankly. He asked what my 'take on the whole thing' was.

"I don't know," I replied. "What's yours?"

"Well, I think the Taiwanese ought to be careful," he opined, narrowing his eyes. "That foolish President Chen Shui-bian goes and declares independence and – *hell* – that'll cause a right ol' mess. China," he added smugly, "wouldn't hesitate for a second."

"What about the Taiwan Relations Act?" I asked.

"Oh, that's just a piece of paper," the major scoffed.

"It doesn't mean anything?"

"Of course not."

The Taiwan Relations Act declares that a threat to Taiwan would constitute "a threat to the peace of the Western Pacific area and (be) of grave concern to the United States," and that normal China-US relations are based on "the expectation that the future of Taiwan will be determined by peaceful means." The act also obliges America to provide Taiwan with the weaponry required to make it defence-ready, although this largely equates to Washington selling Taipei multi-billion-dollar packages of outdated equipment. Even though the Taiwan Relations Act stops short of mandating direct intervention, it is law in the United States.

"Can you think of any reason why Taiwan wouldn't want to unite with China?" I prodded. Notice I didn't say "reunite."

"Not really," he replied dimly.

"And what about the eight hundred or so missiles China has aimed at the place?" I asked. "Or the thirty billion it spent on its military last year? I read that its military spending has increased by more than ten percent for the past thirteen or fourteen years. What do you think they're planning to do with all that manpower and equipment?"

"Oh, they're just trying to modernize. Hey, you're not a journalist are you?"

I assured him I wasn't and he admitted that he hadn't known China had eight hundred missiles aimed across the strait. What was more, he didn't have any "hard numbers" when it came to military spending. I found that utterly astonishing. Surely, it was his job to know a whole list of hard numbers and much else.

That same year, China would allocate a record-high $45 billion for national defence, and in doing so would heighten global suspicion. Adding to this was the widely held belief that China was only reporting on a fraction of its actual spending; its official budget is thought to cover only basic training, troop pay, and what is known as operations and readiness. Additional expenditures, which include everything from nuclear weapons programs to weapons procurement to research and development, are hidden away in various slots of the state and provincial budgets. The United States Defense Intelligence Agency has calculated that the PRC's actual military expenditures for that year were anywhere between $85 million and $1.25 billion. In all likelihood, China's military spending is second only to that of the United States, and with more than 3 million members (2.25 million of which make up its standing army), China's military is the largest in the world. It appeared that in between briefings, language lessons, and weekend vacations to Yanan, Major Jerome Philip Austen of the US Army had failed to read the morning paper.

Three months after our discussion, a Chinese submarine surfaced within eight kilometres (firing range) of the *Kitty Hawk* battle group while it was on routine manoeuvres off of Okinawa. It appeared as though the sub had been stalking the carrier, although the US denied this. Tom Clancy once likened tracking a Chinese submarine to pursuing a blind man through an empty parking lot on a sunny Sunday afternoon; no longer, apparently. And only a short distance from where the major and I had had our talk, China fired a missile that successfully knocked out one of its own satellites. American spy satellites help monitor the Taiwan Strait, and it has been estimated that if they were to become inoperable, repelling an invasion would become a difficult business indeed. I had noticed that CCTV was overflowing with clips of frigates and tanks blasting away at some indeterminate enemy. These images were shown so often that the Chinese people considered them to be entirely normal, which, of course, was the whole idea.

The major retired and I stayed up until four in the morning watching the World Cup final. The tenacious Italian side won. The old man in Joseph Heller's *Catch-22* might have predicted it: "You see, Italy is really a very poor and weak country, and that's what makes us so strong."

CHAPTER EIGHT

I slept for an hour, got up before sunup, and trudged through the slumbering town. A slash of violet hovered above the horizon and the stillness was almost intimidating. The rosy-fingered dawn emerged tepidly, after which it yellowed and melted away the shadows. I took a seat in the far back corner of the bus, where I fruitlessly attempted to fall asleep.

On my map, the road north looked to be a major artery, but it was, once again, in a serious state of disrepair. Infinitely worse than this, however, was the discovery that I was now part of a guided tour, something I hadn't been informed of when I purchased my ticket.

At eight o'clock, the festivities began. With the aid of a microphone, the tour guide introduced himself, blathered for an hour, and then led the passengers through a lively repertory of songs, mostly of the 'You Are My Sunshine' variety. Afterward, the microphone was passed around so that everyone could introduce themselves. I pretended to be asleep, but of course I was sitting beside the only other passenger who knew how to speak English.

"Excuse me," said the woman, tapping me on the arm. She was from Shanghai and was travelling with her husband and son.

"Yes?" I said, opening an eye. Every one of the 38 other passengers was turned around and smiling at me.

"Now, we are a big group," she explained cheerily, "and we are so happy and want to know something about you."

"Like what?"

"Like where you are from."

I mumbled the answer, which she translated. There was collective "*Oooooh!*" and then a lengthy round of hellos. One small boy yelled out in English, "Hawlo foreigner!"

Introductions out of the way, the guide resumed talking. And talking. And talking. And everyone sat, merrily enraptured by his incessant prattling. We began to pass through some hypnotic scenery, but no one noticed except for me. The pack-mentality-minded tourists only appreciated the view when told to.

"Look at that little farm!" yelled the guide. "Is it pretty or not!?"

"It's pretty!" answered the passengers in unison and I saw what I had seen in Dali: everyone swivelled around to gaze out the window and then they swivelled back toward the man with the microphone.

Having lived in Chinese society for as long as I have, there are quite a few things I've gotten entirely used to and don't find at all alien anymore. Pliability isn't one of them. It never ceases to amaze me, especially in light of the fact there is so little trust in the Chinese world, just how eager people are to submit to an authority figure – to *any* authority figure, even one whose job it is to lead people through karaoke and tell them the name of the area they are passing through. Of course, in this case, it was completely harmless, but such submission, historically speaking, has been disastrous – and yet it continues; the pattern is never seen. Individualism is sometimes tolerated, but it is seldom encouraged. Whenever I saw people trading in their self-determination for a leader-headed collective (and Chinese people will appoint a leader for something as simple as a picnic – honestly), I always thought of the Monty Python film *Life of Brian*, where Brian admonishes the crowd assembled outside his door for mistaking him for the Messiah.

Brian: "Look. You've got it all wrong. You don't need to follow me. You don't need to follow anybody. You've got to think for yourselves. You're all individuals."

Crowd: "Yes, we're all individuals!"

Brian: "You're all different!"

Crowd: "Yes, we're all different!"

In a few hours we arrived at Tiger Leaping Gorge, and I must admit that it didn't disappoint. Located in the upper reaches of the Yangtze, the gorge is one of the world's largest, measuring in at 16 kilometres and with as many as 3,900 metres separating its torpedoing currents from its high-ceilinged peaks. The Yangtze originates in the nearby Tibetan Plateau, hence its forcefulness at this point. The waterway continues to twist its way through nine provinces, becoming appreciably weaker in its middle and lower portions until it trails off with a weary sigh into the East China Sea. Observing it surge through the narrow gorge, however, was enchanting. It looked completely unreal, with the man-made objects in the chasm below appearing laughably undersized. Scanning upward and then lengthwise, craggy summits could be seen angling out in all directions. It was if mountains were sprouting mountains. It was all quite humbling, but it mightn't remain so for very long.

Even though the gorge constitutes a UNSESCO World Heritage Site, the central government has drawn up plans to dam it and has even begun some of the initial blasting. Construction of the dams themselves, to be spread out over 564 kilometres, was begun in 2008. Of course, such a massive undertaking will include the usual hiccups: the displacement of 100,000 people (principally the Naxi), the flooding of massive tracts of farmland, the elimination of countless heritage sites and plant specimens, along with the distinct possibility of triggering landslides and earthquakes, just to name a few things. To say that China has a fondness for dam construction would be to engage in oversimplification; it has 85,000 of them. Interestingly, one of the companies spearheading this scheme is led by Li Xiaopeng, son of former president Li Peng, the man chiefly responsible for the Three-Gorges-Dam project as well as the massacre that occurred near Tiananmen Square. Mr. Peng's role in the latter earned him the handle 'The Butcher of Beijing.'

We left the gorge and continued on, making our way through some more riveting scenery and stopping at various spots of "cultural interest," which is to say a jade market and a bazaar selling ground deer antlers, dried duck gizzard, and other Chinese remedies and aphrodisiacs. I had known the bus would stop briefly in the gorge, but I hadn't been informed of the additional diversions. Just before we reached the hotel, the guide announced that we were 3,200 metres above sea level and would most likely feel the effects of altitude sickness. To counter this we would need to take an occasional puff from an oxygen canister, an item he just happened to have an entire duffel bag of. I have never seen Chinese people's wallets open so fast. Subsequently, we were instructed to open our windows a crack before we went to bed that night.

"What should you do before going to bed!?" asked the guide.

"Open our windows!" responded 39 voices in unison.

"Right! And don't forget *not* to bathe or take a shower! Otherwise you will certainly faint! Understand!?"

"Understood!" responded 39 voices in unison.

I had to get away from them.

The guide, his assistant, the woman from Shanghai, her family, the boy who called me a foreigner, and several others were genuinely dismayed and more than a little distraught upon hearing that I wouldn't be joining them for dinner, or for a night of traditional Tibetan dancing and barbequing yak meat, or for the rice gruel and pickled-cabbage breakfast the following morning. I was asked to sign a waiver stating that I was leaving the tour voluntarily and that I was a satisfied customer, a document the guide produced from his oxygen-canister-filled duffle bag. I happily complied.

The town was called Zhongdian and our hotel was located in the middle of the main thoroughfare. Zhongdian, it should be noted, has only one main thoroughfare. The hotel was new. In fact, it was so new that it wasn't quite finished. Neither was my room. A third of the light switches didn't work, the doors to the television cabinet were lying on the floor, and the bathroom counter featured an assortment of hinges, screws, and tools. After getting cleaned up, I went out for a walk. The two receptionists couldn't tell me the name of the street we were on. The reason for this, one explained, was that the hotel was "too new." It had been built only six months ago.

Upon exiting, I came upon a canine form: a ribcage atop four uncertain legs choking pitiably on a branch. Out on the main road, all was silent. There wasn't a car in sight. Zhongdian was a Tibetan town and its Tibetan name was Gyeltang, sometimes spelled Gyalthang. At one end there lay another quaint albeit decidedly new-looking Old Town, while at the other there could be found a monastery. In between there existed the main road along with a dusty collection of lesser streets. Everything was dusty and shabby and everyone stared. People came out of their houses to stare. There were open-fronted pool halls with teenagers smoking and drinking old-fashioned bottles of Coca-Cola. Restaurants featured tables that were partitioned into private booths. In a place where everyone knew everyone else, this made perfect sense. In a convenience store, the clerk's eyes seemed to double in size when she saw me enter. She got off her stool and anxiously followed me around as I searched for bottled water and peanuts. Back outside, an elderly couple sitting in front of their home watched me as I approached. They watched me as I passed, and they watched me until I became a dot a dozen blocks away. Zhongdian made me think of the Neil Young album, *Everybody Knows This Is Nowhere*.

I have seen plenty of skies in my day, but none like the one I saw that evening, and that is not an exaggeration. Ballooning mushrooms skewered a thick blanket of puffy whites while motionless formations of pearl hung overhead, streaked and tinged in shades of peach, ginger, and scarlet. It was as though I were scrutinizing an enormous oil painting.

Back at the hotel, I relaxed and watched TV. The phone rang four times. "*Ni yao bu yao anmo!?*" barked a gruff-sounding female voice. Did I want a massage or not? A laminated list of services had been placed on the pillow. From least expensive to most expensive, it read: foot massage, half-body massage, full-body massage, Thai massage, special massage. I took a long, hot shower and slept very soundly – and warmly – with the window completely closed.

The next morning, I caught a cab to the monastery known as the

Ganden Sumtseling Gompa. Brown and white with a golden roof, it was perched on a hill above a collection of simple grey houses with dark windows. It was a dimly lit, musty affair characterized by vibrant murals, thangkas, mandalas, angling shafts of particle-heavy sunlight, burning yak butter, burgundy-clad monks grumbling invocations, and a gargantuan golden Buddha. I had a good long look around, after which I exited an anterior door in order to get some fresh air.

As I was taking in the surrounding view, I noticed a man raise his camera as though he meant to take my picture. When I turned to face him, he lowered it nervously. Then he snapped a shot of a ditch and another of a pile of firewood before turning around and striding off. Later, I spotted him photographing other Western tourists as they made their way up the building's front steps. His tourist outfit was just a little too perfect, causing him to resemble an overgrown Boy Scout. And then there was the giveaway of giveaways: he was alone.

At the foot of the stairs lay a gritty parking lot packed with hawkers. In addition to the usual offerings of Mao Zedong statuettes and Deng Xiaoping plates, vendors were selling prayer flags, tiger pelts, and yak skulls. There was also a ceramic plate I hadn't seen before; it featured a picture of the Nationalist Party politician from Taiwan, Lien Chan.

I jumped on an idling public jalopy filled with extravagantly clad Tibetans and we rumbled back into town. Along the way, we passed a hill that had been manicured to read 'WELCOME TO SHANGRILA.' That was the name Zhongdian had officially adopted as a tourism ploy, or so I garnered from a brochure I had picked up.

Auspicious LandShangila

The origin of Shangrila: In 1933, a British plan crashed in an unknown place with several survivors. They found an unimaginable, mystique and fairy land with snow-clad mountains, thousands up thousands of years' glaciers, deep valleys, primitive forests, fertile grassland, clear and pure lakes inhabited by a tranquil and peace-loving people. People here believed in various religions but they were all living in harmony without any conflict, let alone crimes. Tibetan Buddhism became the most influential religion in this area. When Tibetan Buddhism was at its peak nearly every household had a monkey or nun. James Hilton, a British writer, published a novel according to the survivor's intriguing experiences. Only until 1995, people found that there are great similarities among the scenes, cultures and cultures in the novel and in Zhongdian County, so in 2002, The State Council of China ratified that the name of Zhongdian County was change to Shangrila.

I spent the remainder of the day contentedly wandering about the sawdust-scented Old Town, where I escaped a brief downpour, did some reading, and chatted with a few of the locals. No one seemed to be from Zhongdian. They had all moved here to work.

I spoke to a man named Mr. Li from Heilongjiang province, in China's northeast, who told me that he missed snow and the rumbling sound of snow ploughs. I chatted to a bubbly waitress from Chengdu named Dora Dong, who wore a jean skirt and a cotton top that said 'Milk Balls – Everybody Likes You.' The café in which she worked was attached to a guest house. She suggested I stay the night there.

"I've already got accommodation," I informed her.

"Your hotel can't be as good as this one," she pitched.

"Probably not," I said, and then went on to tell her about the two receptionists and how they didn't know the name of the road the hotel was on.

"Oh, that's because they've lived here for too long," she said.

"Sorry?"

"Well, it's like me. I've lived in Chengdu my whole life, so I don't know where anything is anymore."

I arranged for a travel package to Tibet at a place called the Tibet Café. Foreigners wishing to enter the so-called autonomous region were required to purchase a special (and especially pricy) permit in addition to joining a travel group, although in reality such a group could comprise a single person. No physical permit was ever issued nor was one asked for upon arrival.

After an imitation Western meal (the French fries were cut from yams; the only thing identifying ketchup as ketchup was its colour), I caught a cab back to the hotel. The driver was the same one I had gotten that morning to the monastery. Zhongdian (or Gyeltang, or Gyalthang, or Shangri-La) was a very small place.

Hotels in China almost always ask for a deposit. The unfinished one located on Zhongdian's anonymous main street asked for 100 *yuan*, or 12 dollars. They refused to return it because I had taken a map from the room. When I had checked in, they suggested that I do so, so as to avoid getting lost. When I reminded them of this, they insisted that they had made it clear that if I used the map, I would have to pay for it. Of course, they never said any such thing, and of course we got into a bit of a row, one that I ended up winning. "Perhaps I should knock on everyone's door and ask if they're aware the maps are worth a hundred *yuan*," I said calmly. "I imagine you can get the same one at a convenience store for twenty." A receptionist retrieved my money from a drawer and threw it at me.

It is often said that in China you must never get angry at anyone or cause them to lose face, but if you are being given the short end of the stick, that is precisely what you must do – provided, of course, that there is no way for the situation to come back and haunt you. There is nothing more childish, and to that end, more telling, about Chinese culture than the concept of face; it is merely a licence for people to behave however they please. Mind you, I didn't feel singled out when people tried to con me. I knew that Chinese people had been conning each other since time out of mind.

I returned to the Tibet Café in the morning and was introduced to the rest of my travel group: an elderly woman from Japan dressed like a Christmas tree. Nearing her seventies, she wore dreadlocks ornamented with red and green beads and had green fingernails, green pants, and a red blazer. She immediately handed our driver a tip after which she handed me a vial of foul-smelling brown liquid that she called "high mountain medicine." She had a daughter who lived in Los Angeles, she said. She liked America, but she didn't like George Bush, and she couldn't stand hot dogs. And which state was I from anyway? On the way to the airport, she did calisthenics and frequently addressed me in Japanese. In the waiting area, she asked me if I knew what a prayer wheel was.

"Sure," I said.

"Do you know what is the prayer wheel do?" she then asked.

"It sends prayers up to heaven?"

"Yes! Right! It sing the prayer of to the heaven! You look! I am the prayer wheel!" she exclaimed, and with that she stood up and began spinning around and around with arms outstretched, repeating the lines, "Sun so *big*. Sun so *big*," in poorly pronounced English. Nearly everyone in the room noticed this and began to stare at us. I made a face and a feeble gesture: a denial of association. Until I gave her the slip in Lhasa, we were practically conjoined at the hip. Owing to the language barrier, she couldn't quite comprehend that we were a tour group in name only.

CHAPTER NINE

From the shiny-new Gongkar Airport I hopped on a bus and embarked on the 95-kilometre journey through the Kyichu Valley toward Lhasa. The vistas were heart-stirring. A parade of tawny mountains studded with stubborn tussocks of grass was bolstering a sky of luxurious turquoise. What few clouds there were looked as though they were suspended from threads.

Passing by military installations and oncoming convoys of army trucks, we eventually entered the city and within no time were driving past the Potala Palace. It was the strangest thing; one minute we were stopped at a traffic light in the grey Chinese section of town, and the next we were rolling by one of the most splendid architectural achievements ever conceived. I made my way to the lively though odorous Tibetan quarter (Lhasa is divided into very distinct sections) and got a room at an establishment called The Yak run by a friendly Dutchman.

The first order of business was to get a ticket to the Potala Palace. Hailing a taxi, I headed to the main gate. The driver was a Chinese fellow who disclosed that he had first come to Tibet with the PLA back in the fifties. He had fallen in love with the place and requested to stay. His wife had joined him and the two had never regretted their decision. He seemed like an affable sort, and I desperately wanted to ask him about things he had seen or done; to find out his opinion of Tibet's absorption, but decided against it. I didn't want to arouse any suspicion. In Tibet especially, one had to be careful.

The man told me that getting a ticket for the Potala was becoming increasingly problematic. "They sell the tickets in blocks to tour guides who pay a bribe to have first crack at them," he said. "And scalpers snatch up most of what's left. If you're not in a tour group, it can take days to get inside."

He wasn't kidding. At the building's western gate, I discovered a long, immobile queue wrapped around the perimeter of a grubby courtyard. I fell in with three friendly Americans named Lynn, Toni, and Krishna and we spent the next five hours holding the line for each other and going off for toilet breaks, water runs, and rests in the shade. The clouds I had seen earlier had been tugged out of sight, and of course the sun's rays were intensified at this altitude.

To fill the time, I chatted with the Chinese tourists and asked them what had brought them to Tibet. "To understand a little of their culture," they all replied beamingly. They all said the exact same thing, in the exact same tone. I also overheard them saying this to each other, but in a manner that betrayed that they viewed the Tibetans as little more than a novelty.

During my breaks, I walked around the palace, dodging hordes of vendors and pilgrims as I went. I craned my neck repeatedly to take in the edifice's attractive veneer and atypical symmetry. I thought it was beautiful.

Begun in the year 631, the Potala Palace consists of two main sections named after the tint of their outer walls. The White Palace, completed in 1682, houses a seminary, a printing shop, and living quarters for monks and the Dalai Lama. The Red Palace, finished in 1693, is dedicated to religious study and prayer. It contains an assembly hall, a superfluity of shrines and mandalas, and the remains of eight Dalai Lamas, which have been entombed in a series of golden, jewel-laden stupas.

The Red Palace and the White Palace are built into an enormous whitewashed base, and this is built into the steep and stony Red Hill, the geomantic centre of the Lhasa Valley. At 13 stories, the Potala rises to 400 metres in height and boasts approximately 1,000 rooms. Of course, in photos, the front of the structure is always what is shown. The footpath behind it is a litter-strewn, makeshift market dominated by puddles and vendors with carts and megaphones screeching out announcements. "Buy three pairs of socks, get a fourth pair free!" The front of the palace featured large-character banners thanking the Communist Party for its undying support.

At five o'clock, the ticket booth finally opened and the line inched forward. At seven o'clock, an announcement was made that all tickets had been sold and that we ought to come back the next day. The large contingent of mostly Chinese tourists emitted a collective sigh and shuffled off. The man behind me smiled at me and said, "In China, it's always like this! What can you do?"

I presented myself to the ticket counter and began to complain – in Mandarin. Much to my surprise, it worked. A Tibetan man instructed me to take my American friends, and a Spanish couple we had picked up along the way, to the main gate at eight sharp the next morning and inform the staff there that we had an appointment with him. He wrote down his name on a card and passed it to me. And so, that's what we did. Without looking up, a woman behind a desk asked, "Ticket?" When I said 'no,' she asked, "Appointment?"

Exploring the Potala Palace is thrilling. It is also disorientating not to mention exhausting. There is simply too much for the senses to accommodate. Along with hundreds of other tourists and pilgrims, you are shepherded through a warren of ill-lit chambers, stuffy corridors, and dusty stairwells where you eyeball one intricate display of religious art after another. There are literally hundreds – sometimes thousands – of carpets, thangkas, mandalas, statues, scrolls, Buddhist tomes, murals, and paintings. There are also articles of copper, brass, jade, porcelain, and ivory as well as galaxies of gold and gemstones. It is all very impressive, and it is all very overwhelming. Incidentally, the Chinese name for Tibet is Xizang, which means "Western Treasure House."

With their hair in plaits and their sheepskin, ankle-length, sash-bound robes (*chubas*, they are called), the Tibetan pilgrims murmured mantras and stuffed altars with cash and ceremonial scarves while adding dollops of yak butter to candles by spooning it out of sacks they clutched in their dark hands. Monks could be seen sitting on the floor chanting or carting around large pots of smouldering juniper incense. Uninterested Chinese soldiers paced about with hands clasped behind their backs. I gazed out of a top-floor window only to find the view of the mountains beyond disrupted by a monument rising up from People's Square, a cement plaza situated across from the palace on Beijing Middle Road. The monument was meant to commemorate the peaceful liberation of Tibet. It looked like an oversized tombstone.

The highlight of the tour was a brief inspection of the Dalai Lama's plush living quarters, occupied nowadays by impatient sentries who whisk you along with a grimace and an annoyed flailing of the arm if you happen to dawdle. The Potala Palace once served as the Dalai Lama's winter residence in addition to the seat of the Tibetan government. Currently, it is a state museum and a UNESCO World Heritage Site. If you are lucky enough to enter through its main gate, as I was, you will see that it also houses a sizeable and well-staffed police station. The Fourteenth Dalai Lama resides in Dharamsala, India, where he heads the Tibetan government-in-exile, having fled his homeland in 1959.

Early the following morning, I headed to the Barkhor, a

neighbourhood-turned-pilgrimage-circuit situated in the heart of the Tibetan quarter. The circuit runs clockwise around the Jokhang Temple, Tibet's most venerated site. Joining a multitude of tourists, pilgrims, and plain-clothed police officers, I embarked on a brisk circumambulation. Flanked by whitewashed walls and row upon row of dim windows, the way was lined with tables piled high with souvenirs and the ubiquitous yak butter. A walk around the Barkhor is nothing if not interesting. It is an echoing affair characterized by disparate sounds (clapping, chanting, singing, neighing), puzzling smells, and smears and daubs of almost hallucinogenic colour. At the entrance to the Jokhang, more than 50 muttering believers were vigorously prostrating themselves on the dusty pavement. After observing them, I paid and then pushed my way inside.

Constructed in 639 CE in order to house the dowry of a Nepali princess married to the legendary King Songstän Gampo (who, by the way, is always described as legendary), the Jokhang evidently hadn't seen the likes of a broom or mop since. It contained Tibet's most revered relics and a gazillion germs at the least. It was a garish, sooty affair filled with smirking, gilded statues and penny-dreadful, eye-bulging gods. The few inches that existed between visitors and objects were occupied by smoke and the incalculably rancid tang of yak butter. Inspecting the Jokhang is certainly entrancing, but not what I would call pleasurable. Sharp-elbowed pilgrims are there to worship, not to be held up by loitering tourists. And the pilgrims smell *awful*, something difficult to ignore when sandwiched among them. Tibetans, you see, are not in the habit of bathing.

For Westerners, Tibet is an archetype nestled in the recesses of consciousness. It is that rough and remote land placated by creamy zeniths and sapphire skies. It's the Rooftop of the World, the Land of Snows, the heart of Buddhism, the *real* Shangri-La. It's perennially idealized and has become sleekly sanitized. It's the Dalai Lama's smile radiating from *The Art of Happiness*; an endorsement from Steven Seagal or Richard Gere; a T-shirt; a bumper sticker: *Free Tibet*. To a large extent, and much like China itself, its harsh realities have been replaced by myth. Nietzsche might have explained why: 'We possess myth lest we perish from the truth.'[1]

As Chinese writer (and outcast) Ma Jian notes in his exquisitely crafted *Stick Out Your Tongue*, "The need to believe in an earthly paradise, a hidden utopia where men live in peace and harmony, seems to run deep in those who are discontented with the modern world. Westerners idealize Tibetans as gentle, godly people untainted by base

---

1   In fact, Nietzsche said that we possess art lest we perish from the truth.

desires and greed. But in my experience, Tibetans can be… corrupt and brutal…." In his book, Ma Jian admits that he too idealized Tibet, until he travelled there in 1985 while fleeing the police and the "soulless society that China had become." Ma Jian's writing in *Stick Out Your Tongue* is fluid and beautiful and in stark contrast to the dark topics he explores and documents: the crippling effects of poverty, backwardness, superstition, sorcery, quackery, barbarism, mental illness, and incest.

In the first of five vignettes, Ma Jian chronicles a sky burial. The deceased is a young woman, and through her former lover, a forlorn PLA soldier from Sichuan, the author learns her story. As a young girl, she was sold to another family for nine sheep hides. The father of her adoptive family sexually molested her. Later, she married two brothers (simultaneously) before having an affair with the lonely soldier. Then she got pregnant and died during labour. The child was not delivered. Ma Jian, a complete stranger, and foreigner for that matter, was permitted to take part in the subsequent ceremony.

After the presiding lama determined that the woman's spirit had wafted up to heaven, "The younger brother hacked off a chunk of thigh and sliced it into pieces. Her right leg was soon reduced to bone. With her belly squashed to the ground, sticky fluid began to trickle from between her thighs." "The vultures surrounded us and fought over the scraps of flesh. A pack of crows landed behind them." "I picked up the axe, grabbed a severed hand, ran the blade down the palm and threw a thumb to the vultures. The younger brother smiled, took the hand from me and placed it on a rock, then pounded the remaining four fingers flat and threw them to the birds." "The crows had now joined the vultures… and were picking at the roast barley that had been mashed up with scraps of brain."

This scene, although graphic, is no more disturbing than those that follow, and the theme of incest crops up three times, in three unrelated incidents.[2]

The Martin Scorsese film *Kundun* opens with the line: "Tibetans have practised non-violence for over a thousand years." Not only would such a statement seem to deny human nature, but it also denies Tibetan history.

Starting from the early seventh century, Tibet was a land of warriors and the legendary Songstän Gampo was their warrior king.

---

2   *Stick Out Your Tongue* was labelled "vulgar and obscene" by the Communist Party, which lambasted its author for having 'defamed the image of China's Tibetan compatriots' and for failing to depict "the great strides the Tibetan people have made in building a united, prosperous and civilized Socialist Tibet."

Under his tutelage, Tibetan males received comprehensive military instruction. They rode horses, wore chain mail, wielded swords and lances, and were renowned for their archery skills. Indeed, the Tibetans were prototypes for the Mongolians and over the subsequent decades they conquered vast tracts of land, including Nepal and swathes of Burma and India. Tibet's expansion also made for battles and skirmishes with the Chinese, which the Tibetans usually won.

In 755 CE, Songstän Gampo's great-great-great-grandon, Trisong Detsen, took over the Tibetan throne, and it was under his rule that Buddhism became Tibet's official religion. However, Trisong Detsen was both a Buddhist and militarist, and his military pressed into both western and northern China after which it pushed far into its interior. At present-day Xian, the Tibetans temporarily dethroned the Chinese emperor. Eventually, there were peace talks, and these led to the formation of an agreed-upon Sino-Tibetan border in 821 CE. Satisfied, the Tibetans withdrew from the Middle Kingdom, but kept control of the western Central Asian trade routes, thus ending China's domination there. The actions of the "barbarian" Tibetans illustrated to the continent that the mighty Chinese were in reality weak and vulnerable.

Tibetan history is filled with violence. In fact, it has only been in the past few decades that Tibetans have ceased practising mutilation as a legal punishment. Applying pressure to the guilty party's cranium until their eyeballs popped out is said to have been one such penalty.

As Ma Jian reports in his book, Tibetans also practise polygamy and polyandry. In fact, the word 'polyandry' was coined by the first British explorer to reach Tibet in the year 1774. Paradoxically perhaps, and in spite of Buddhism's claim to be a religion of tolerance, the Dalai Lama has publicly condemned homosexuality as well as acts of oral, anal, and manual sex.

Another inconsistency has to do with the government-in-exile's territorial claims. The Fourteenth Dalai Lama and his administration have stated that they are the rightful rulers of all land occupied by Tibetans. However, since the majority of Tibetans reside outside of Tibet (chiefly in the contiguous and rather spacious provinces of Qinghai, Gansu, Sichuan, and Yunnan) that claim covers an area roughly twice the size of Tibet itself.

Here's something else to consider: the Jokhang was once called Piccadilly Circus and the Potala was dubbed Windsor Castle, and this, of course, has to do with the British invasion of Tibet in 1903. When British forces reached the Potala, they found that the Thirteenth Dalai Lama had already decamped – to Mongolia. Even with a bad start (the

British gunned down some 3,000 defenders), the Tibetans were soon being wooed by soccer, polo, bangers and mash, and various other facets of British culture. Although Great Britain courted Tibet, there would be no wedding bells. In fact, after demanding a large indemnity from the Chinese government, which had held a tenuous grip on Tibet *only* since 1720 (not since the dawn of time, as the Chinese government currently claims), the British signed an agreement acknowledging China's suzerainty of the region. This done, the British packed up their wickets and cricket bats and headed for home.

But Britain wasn't the only Western power to lead Tibet down the proverbial garden path. After "liberation," the CIA trained a *chuba*-wearing guerrilla force that attacked and harassed the PLA for years. All the while, the insurgents believed that Uncle Sam would one day reward them by helping to recover their homeland. It wasn't until Nixon's *rapprochement* with Beijing that they realized they'd been duped, once again.

And although it's often overlooked, the Fourteenth Dalai Lama *did* flee the invading Chinese (in 1950) – but then he returned and accepted the Seventeen Point Agreement for the Peaceful Liberation of Tibet. He believed – although he was very young and naive at the time – that reform was exactly what Tibetans needed, and that the Chinese Communists were the ones to deliver it. According to the Dalai Lama himself, he had both "admiration and respect" for Mao when he first met him, although he defected nine years *after* "liberation" (in 1959) in part because he believed the Chinese were plotting to have him assassinated.

In 2008, the Fourteenth Dalai Lama effectively abandoned his government's claim on Tibet, saying that he now accepted Chinese sovereignty. "Tibet is a backward country, economically (and) materially," said the spiritual leader. "Therefore, for our own interest as far as material development is concerned, we want to remain within the People's Republic of China."

And here, perhaps, is the biggest incongruity of all: when commenting on atrocities committed by the Chinese in Tibet, the number of deaths cited is invariably a neat 1.2 million, 1.07 million of which are said to be male. But in 1950, the year of the Chinese invasion, there were only 1.25 million Tibetan males in existence. As Patrick French, former pro-Tibet activist, Tibetophile, and author of the profoundly engaging book, *Tibet, Tibet*, discovered for himself in a file room in the government-in-exile's headquarters, 1.2 million is a number that was pulled straight out of the air. The truth is that it isn't known how many Tibetans have died at the hands of the Chinese. It may be 50,000 or it may be 500,000. But, of course, even one is one too many.

The Chinese insist that their involvement in Tibet is a mission of mercy; that they are simply rescuing the Tibetans from their own ignorance. To some observers, this has become a kind of justification: what the Chinese have done may be wrong, but they genuinely believe it to be right. However, listening to whatever it is or isn't the Chinese believe is not where the cause of their actions can be found. To do that, as always, one must look to the past.

For the Chinese, Tibet also represents an archetype. It is a gorgeous land, to be certain, but it is also a vulnerable one filled with hordes of long-haired, hot-headed, dagger-wearing savages. The Chinese have traditionally painted Mongolia and Taiwan with a similar brush. Such borderlands were to be Sinicized and made safe the first instance it became possible. Taiwan got away. Mongolia remained a Soviet suzerainty in exchange for aid and advice. Tibet, however, which had long since traded in its martial tradition for peace and religion, was ripe for the picking. The Cold War was on and larger players were distracted. Although there were other factors involved – the Chinese were anxious about the post-war French presence in Indochina as well as the ambitions of a young and charismatic Dalai Lama – the primary motive for Tibet's subjugation was revenge. The Chinese have a long and merciless memory.

By briefly toppling China's emperor at Xian and refusing to play the role of vassal state, Tibet shamed the Middle Kingdom, and, in doing so, sealed its fate in the late eighth century. Once Tibet was secured, the Chinese carried out a program of cultural genocide, striking at the heart of traditional life: Buddhism. Before 1950, Tibet boasted over 2,500 monasteries. Presently, there are around 70 and they are closely monitored by the police. But then, everything in Tibet is closely monitored by the police, and what a lot of police there are. There are regular police, traffic police, the Barkhor police, the People's Armed Police, the People's Liberation Army, the Public Security Bureau, and the notorious State Security Bureau. There are also loads of informants, mostly Tibetans who have been compromised. The Fourteenth Dalai Lama is considered a non-person in Tibet and his image is banned. Monks are required to denounce him and Tibetans must receive patriotic education and sign conduct agreements.

The authorities' chief concern is that of revolts as they tend to make headlines. There have been several of these, and they have all been ruthlessly suppressed. I suppose I could go on about Tibetans being incarcerated, "re-educated," electrocuted, burned, sexually humiliated, executed, or beaten to within an inch of their lives with sand-filled hoses, but it strikes me that there is little point. Independent campaigns have made for zero change in Tibet. Neither have UN resolutions.

As Ma Jian points out in the epilogue of *Stick Out Your Tongue*, the majority of Chinese people "know nothing of the destruction the Chinese have (wrought) in Tibet." Rather, they have "swallowed the Communist Party's nationalist propaganda concerning China's 'liberation' of the country, and would fiercely oppose any moves to break up the 'integrity of the Motherland.'"

Incidentally, it's not just the so-called mainland Chinese who are almost totally in the dark in regard to Tibet's history and assimilation. After the Communist Party crackdown in Tibet during the run-up to the Beijing Olympics, I asked some of my adult students in Taiwan (over 50 of them, in fact; in three different classes) if they had read anything about the event in the news, as we were studying a chapter about news, where we got it from, and so on. As I discovered, not one of them was aware that Tibet had once been a country, never mind a country that China had invaded shortly after kicking out Chiang Kai-shek and his feckless Nationalist clique. Not one; and this in a nation that is often said to have the freest press in Asia. When I asked how they thought this ethnically, culturally, and linguistically distinct territory ended up within China's borders, I was answered with blinks. When I asked why Tibet's absorption was something someone from Taiwan might want to know about, no one offered a reasonable response. It was suggested, however, by more than one student, that China must have occupied Tibet in order to help it.

I made my way to the Muslim quarter, where I saw children with white prayer caps streaming out of a mosque. I reckoned this was the restored version of the building that once had been converted into a cinema for watching propaganda films. I knew, from having read *Tibet, Tibet*, that this district had been divested of all its historical records, documents, and copies of the Qur'an whereupon a bonfire was made – by *Tibetan* Red Guards.

I found the area's coarse, narrow streets to be fascinating and spent quite some time sauntering around them, gawking into shops and observing the goings-on of everyday life. Surely, this was one of the best parts of travelling: observing people doing what they do in an altogether unfamiliar setting.

In one street, I saw a government poster saying, in Chinese,

'Lhasa's Tomorrow – To Become Beautiful is Good!' It showed the city filled with futuristic skyscrapers. There was an elevated highway and what looked to be a bullet train. The Potala lurked in the distance, only a fraction higher than the highest glass-skinned tower. Oddly, other hallmarks of Chinese civilization – shopping plazas, American fried chicken joints, karaokes, whore houses – didn't merit a spot in this vision of the future.

I had lunch at a café in the Barkhor, opting for something called a Tibetan tortilla over a yak burger. I also ordered a cup of yak butter tea, remembering that it was the only thing Heinrich Harrer couldn't stomach during his *Seven Years in Tibet*. I took a wee sip, put the cup down, and called for the bill.

I took a taxi to a monastery located outside the city, halfway up one of the many beige versants. There were no tourists here and I spent a pleasant couple of hours wandering about a labyrinth of white buildings under a sky so blue and close, it was as though it had been folded around the edges of the Earth. Only occasionally did I spot a burgundy-robed monk as most of them were pottering about inside to avoid the searing heat. None seemed interested in talking to me, though most offered genuine hellos. I had gotten so accustomed to the strident, mocking, Chinese hello, and the subsequent string of tittering giggles, that the Tibetan version seemed wholly out of place.

I had to wait a long time to get a taxi back. I sat on a rock and studied the valley and all its folded hills. The driver was a grinning Chinese woman who picked up three monks after she picked me up. Two of them got in the front seat, with the second one failing to fully close the door.

"The door isn't shut," the woman said.

"He doesn't understand Chinese," said the man in the middle.

"Well, translate then," she suggested.

The man turned and grumbled something in Tibetan to his colleague who uttered an, "Oh," before rolling down the window.

The woman was possibly *the* worst driver I have ever seen; sincerely confused as to the difference between braking and accelerating. Winding our way down the mountain, we very nearly went off the road – twice. I put my seat belt on and made little whimpering noises as the three monks stared stoically straight ahead. When our driver got to the highway, she just about smashed into the back of a police car waiting at a stop sign. On the highway, she drove for a full five seconds on the wrong side of the road as she fumbled to light a cigarette. Pulling into my hotel's parking lot, she caused the security guard to do his best impression of a crab. If the Tibetans noticed any of this, they gave no indication.

That evening at The Yak, I socialized in the bar with my American friends. The beer, the backpackers, and the sixties' music lent the place a decidedly bohemian air. After a few drinks, we took in the view of the Potala Palace from the rooftop. Heat lightning caused it to reveal itself in flashes of brilliant white light. Back in the bar, Bob Dylan's 'Chimes of Freedom' played.

Even though a cloud's white curtain in a far-off corner flashed
An' the hypnotic splattered mist was slowly lifting
Electric light still struck like arrows, fired for the ones
Condemned to drift or else be kept from drifting

CHAPTER TEN

The scene at the Gongkar Airport was one of sheer mayhem. Everybody shoved and jumped the queue and the officials couldn't be bothered to acknowledge it. The situation on the plane wasn't much better. The flight was full of voluble Chinese tourists and befuddled Tibetans, few of whom seemed capable of locating their seat. An olive-clad soldier commanded me to relinquish my own seat so that he might sit with his cohort. This, understandably, annoyed me.

"Move to another seat!" he barked in Mandarin.

"I don't understand Chinese," I replied in Chinese.

"Changee sheet," he attempted in English.

"I don't understand English," I replied in English, and went back to reading my book. He gave me a puzzled look before he began to whine and grab at my arm. He didn't stop until a flight attendant directed him to his actual seat. Once there, he turned around continually to cast me hateful looks. Whining and pouting, by the way, are perfectly acceptable methods of expressing sentiment in Chinese society. They're seldom, if ever, discouraged, and are even regarded as cute.

Take-off was delayed by nearly two hours as we had to wait for clearance. In Lhasa. On a Monday morning. During this holdup, there were no other landings or departures. Once in the air, we were treated to cotton-framed glimpses of rugged, snowy mountaintops and meandering waterways. The soldier next to me was flipping through a magazine when he burst into a bout of unmanageable laughter. When I turned toward him, he said in Mandarin, "Look! This is hilarious!" It was a picture of a monkey in a business suit sitting in an office and using a computer. "It looks just like a human!" he cried, shaking his head in disbelief. He laughed so hard that he started to cry. He then passed the magazine around for all his colleagues to inspect and guffaw at. Only moments before we touched down, and with everyone finally silent and behaving themselves, a middle-aged fellow stood up, retrieved his suitcase from the overhead compartment, and headed for the exit. When the flight attendants started to scream at him, he looked genuinely surprised.

We landed in Chengdu, the capital of Sichuan, a province known far and wide for its fiery contribution to Chinese cuisine. The Sichuanese are a pretty fiery lot themselves. Throughout history, their province has repeatedly been at odds with the capital and has witnessed a staggering amount of warlordism, violence, and upheaval – even by Chinese standards. In modern history, Sichuan has seen the deaths of millions as a result of one conflict or another. Until the Communists took control, it was a tremendously untamed and backward domain, rife with opium smoking, disease, and illiteracy.

Customarily described as being just larger than France, Sichuan, which means "Four Rivers," is also one of China's most populous provinces, with more than 87 million residents. Claiming nearly 10.6 million of those, the provincial capital represents China's fifth largest city.

I caught a bus downtown and was soon moving along a dismal highway flanked by legions of dreadful little factories and broken billboards. Eventually, these were replaced by car dealerships and the trademark grey apartment blocks. My seat had had a puddle of urine on it, but the female ticket attendant had wiped it up and found a magazine for me to sit on. Seated behind me was a European couple and within no time the man was arguing with the attendant because the bus wasn't going where he had been told it was. "You lied to me!" he shouted. "You Chinese people…. You're all the same! You're all a bunch of fucking liars!"

After we alighted, he and his wife began petitioning me with their grievances. They had experienced nothing but dishonesty since the moment they arrived in China, they said. That was three weeks ago. Didn't the Chinese realize what a bad impression they were making? Were they so pathetic that they would lie over a 20-*yuan* bus ticket? Wasn't this country supposed to be modernizing and opening up? Where was the evidence of that? The couple didn't like being lied to, they said. Then they said this again. I nodded sympathetically and told them truthfully that I wasn't interested in hearing about it. A cab to their destination would have cost them 15 *yuan*, or 2 dollars.

I stayed in an attractive, traditional-style guest house complete with lanterns, a garden, and a fish pond. For lunch, I ordered a pizza that contained no sauce and came delivered in a cellophane bag. There were also cellophane gloves with which to eat it. This was preferable to eating in the hotel's restaurant, which smelled of mould and cigarette smoke. After getting cleaned up, I set out for a stroll around town.

Chengdu was recently rated China's fourth most liveable city by *China*

Daily. This is fitting as Chengdu means "Perfect Metropolis." Standing in the city centre, I noted that it was indeed a place of near perfection. Wherever I looked, my eye was met with stately glass towers and wide boulevards flowing with orderly traffic. Sidewalks were similarly broad and featured smiling pedestrians who padded past trimmed bushes and tidy rows of trees; they were mostly families holding hands. The sky was blue, the air clean, and there wasn't a scrap of rubbish anywhere. Or at least that's how it was portrayed on all the government billboards. The real picture, however, was in complete disagreement.

Pretty much the entire city centre was under construction. Side streets were walled by grim apartment blocks and the footpaths overflowed with debris and cigarette butts. Main arteries coursed with fume-spewing buses and torrents of impatient cars. On this day, it also featured the *worst* pollution I had ever seen. A suspended mass of exhaust roasted slowly in the July sun and every road and every alley was choked with the same foul asthma.

One of China's three so-called blast furnaces, Chengdu was comprehensively Dickensian and marked by a shirtless, phlegm-ejecting class of people who pointed, gawked, and offered disingenuous hellos. It was a working-class town that manufactured everything from silk to aluminum. It was also the first city in the world to have issued and utilized paper money, a phenomenon that began around 960 CE. In the mid-1980s, Paul Theroux remarked that Chengdu was "oversized and charmless," and that "though some of its markets and shop-houses remained, too many of them had been torn down to make room for workers' barracks and tower blocks." He also commented on the spitting, describing how restaurants were fitted with spittoons.

Things to do in Chengdu included visiting the Mao Zedong statue (dire), sipping tea at a traditional tea house in People's Park (interesting), inspecting the Taoist Green Ram Temple (worth an hour), and sampling spicy hot pot (daunting). Even in the extreme summer heat, the Sichuanese slurp this capsicum-enriched stew partly in order to sweat as they believe that that will help them cool down. I'm not a big fan of spicy hot pot, although I do like other peppery Sichuan specialties, namely *gongbao jiding* (kung pao chicken) and *mapo doufu* (mapo tofu), so I found a well-known restaurant specializing in both and ordered a sizzling and satisfying plate of each. The beer was warm, as usual.

Early the next morning, I got on a minibus filled with foreign tourists that shuttled us through the city's dismal fringes: block after block of slums and battered buildings, only a handful of which possessed window panes. Wherever there wasn't decaying brick or concrete, rubble-molested weeds stood a metre high.

We were going to the Giant Panda Breeding Research Base. When we arrived, our guide got out and approached a guard stationed at the gate. Within seconds, they were arguing. They opened at eight-thirty, said the guard. It was only eight now. We would have to wait. Our guide wanted to know what that had to do with running a business. The faster the "foreign friends" were processed, the faster he could transport the next batch. He had a family to support. A rule was a rule, replied the guard, and the two went back and forth in slurry Sichuanese before our guide returned to the bus and informed us we would have to wait. He did this by scribbling '8:30' on a piece of cardboard and holding it up for all to see. Neither he nor the driver spoke a word of English. I ended up acting as translator.

Currently, there are 50 reserves in China for the protection of the giant panda, which is an endangered species in addition to being China's national symbol. The animal is now classified as a bear, but for years scientists wondered if it weren't a variety of raccoon or a separate genus altogether. Unlike other bears, pandas don't hibernate, nor do they vocalize by roaring. Instead, they bleat. And although they are capable of consuming meat, they are first and foremost herbivores.

Estimates of the number of pandas in existence vary considerably. However, the World Wide Fund for Nature (whose logo is the panda) believes that there are 980 living on reserves and another 1,600 in the wild. The vast majority of the creatures are strewn throughout the mountains of northern and northwestern Sichuan, where they face a staggering array of problems ranging from habitat loss to an extremely low birthrate. In addition to being rather solitary, the bears possess a famously low libido. In captivity, they are actually shown the equivalent of pornographic movies, which has yielded some success.

In 2006, seven reserves were granted UNESCO World Heritage Site status, implying that China's hand would be forced in taking panda protection much more seriously. Human encroachment and poaching are, and always have been, other major concerns, although the government has recently taken a tougher stance on poachers. However, 2006 was the same year officials began auctioning licences to foreigners wishing to hunt wild animals in China, *including* endangered species. A spokesman for China's animal protection department justified the action by proclaiming, "Hunting is not slaughter," before adding that proceeds from the hunting would be put toward wildlife protection.

Naively perhaps, I had been expecting to see a contingent of the adorable bears lounging about on lawns and munching bamboo, but it wasn't like that. Instead, we were led through what was supposed to be a nursery, but mirrored a prison. Behind bars and within damp, concrete cells there sat a handful of inert, dejected-looking cubs, one of which was staring at the wall in a manner that gave the distinct impression it was contemplating suicide. This scene was wholly at odds with the host of cutesy signs and messages posted everywhere. One of these warned us not to "speak aloud" or feed the bears as they would "prefer to eat healthy food prepared by their mum." Another informed us that one of the cubs had been "adopted" by Microsoft and named Microsoft. Microsoft (the company) had chosen this name over Intel Panda 1, Power Point Panda, and Bill. "Wildlife is not food," another message read.

The red panda, which resembles a rust-coloured raccoon, appeared to be fairing much better in an environment of actual trees and grass. A sign here said, "Walking in my territory after the delicious meal."

Inside a stupendously insipid museum, we were treated to an English-language film on the giant panda's breeding habits, which was really the only decipherable information provided on the entire excursion. The male, accented narrator's voice explained: "The mother cleans the yearling by licking it. She even eats its feces. This intense mothering is something that I can really relate to..."

Seeing pandas had been my chief reason for visiting Chengdu. Goodness knows I hadn't been expecting much, but I still came away feeling deeply – nay, profoundly – disappointed. We finished the tour early, and then drove around in circles downtown. When I asked why we were doing this, the guide said that if he got back too soon, his boss would reprimand him. This made the 8:00 a.m. shouting match all the more peculiar.

In the afternoon, I walked around the city again and visited People's Park, where I sat and drank tea for hours on a rickety chair at a chipped table under the fluttery awning of a clutch of bamboo trees. I can't tell you how hot it was. Shirtless, white-haired men sat about chatting and fanning themselves as they smoked and gulped tiny cups of piping-hot green tea. The park possessed a man-made lake and canals that people paddled on. It was crowded, but not unpleasant. An old man walked over to me and poked me in the arm.

"You want ears clean?" he asked in English. "It feels very comfortable." He then showed me a long, rusty acupuncture needle. Its tip had been fitted with a brownish cotton swab. He banged a tuning fork against it and pressed it against my arm. The needle quivered and the swab danced against my skin. "You See?" he said. "It feels very comfortable."

In the evening, the park filled up with people, which was odd because there were virtually no lights. Groups of elderly women danced to traditional music, men wailed into microphones hooked up to generator-powered karaoke units, and children blew bubbles and licked ice-cream cones.

As I was leaving, I noticed a pair of men trailing me. One was jotting something into a notepad and the other was speaking into a walkie-talkie. After I had made enough turns to be sure I wasn't being paranoid, I stopped and waited for them to catch up. Seeing this, they stopped, too. I got out my camera and snapped their picture. Then, I started walking toward them. Much to my surprise, they turned around and headed in the opposite direction. I followed them out of the park, where they got into a cab that sped away. I also caught a cab, but went in the opposite direction. I figured that my reading and note-taking had attracted someone's attention.

That night in my hotel, I watched some TV. Admittedly, I had been watching TV almost every evening and had come to the conclusion that Chinese television consisted almost entirely of Chinese news, Chinese sports, Chinese soap operas, kung fu films, movies about the Communists thumping the Nationalists, movies about the Communists thumping the Japanese, and shows depicting kids in costumes and makeup singing, dancing, and bounding about brightly lit stages. CCTV had the ability to make even the most mindless of Western programming appear cerebral. Tonight, there was a movie about a supply-filled Japanese train in Manchuria bound for some remote base. Before it could reach its destination, however, it was commandeered by a handful of Communist guerrillas who had disguised themselves as Japanese soldiers. They even spoke Japanese. When the signal was given, they slaughtered every last Nip onboard, customarily screaming, "Die, you Japanese dog!" before shooting them in the face. Their plan went off without a hitch. In the penultimate scene, the heroes were awarded medals of honour. The film closed with everyone standing around singing patriotic songs. It made me think of what happened at the Guilin Train Station.

A second-grade reader in China includes a tale of a young female cowherd who "led the Japanese devils into an ambush" by the Communist Eighth Route Army. In the end, the girl sacrifices her life out of patriotic obligation.

CHAPTER ELEVEN

The next morning, I caught a jittery, odiferous bus to the city of Chongqing. Something was wrong with the front axle, so the driver pulled over and endeavoured to fix it – with a broom handle. Although the highway cut through a swath of fecund countryside, the pollution was so bad that trees 50 metres away were out of focus. Once more, I was probably the only person onboard to notice this. All the other passengers were grinning inanely at the television set, which was showing *The Gods Must Be Crazy*, slapstick about Bushmen from Botswana who have no knowledge of the outside world. The Chinese, by the way, prefer their comedy to be visual and slightly cruel, *schadenfreude* comprising a muscular cultural undercurrent. Charlie Chaplin is still enormously popular in China and banks play Mr. Bean videos in an apparent attempt to keep their waiting clientele calm.

Three hundred and forty kilometres later, and we came upon the burg: a blur of skyscrapers domed in a frightening miasma. We were greeted by skeleton-like, half-finished buildings cemented to violated, trash-strewn streets. The skyline was skewered with cranes and I saw a bridge with missing spans hovering above a corridor of rubble. The pollution was so thick that it mimicked smoke. The traffic was intense.

The bus stopped in front of the train station and I battled my way through a tangle of touts and beggars in the hopes of finding a cab. Along a dingy sidewalk, shirtless men smoked, spat, and shouted at one another as they shuffled about with bamboo poles slung over their shoulders. Part of the rank-and-file of a 100,000-member militia known as the *bangbang jun*, or "stick-stick army" ("stick-stick" being a reference to the bamboo poles), these men were porters and a part of the city's landscape. Hucksters and vendors glanced past them intently. There were women selling peaches, men offering shoe shines, and children peddling newspapers. Like in Guilin and Chengdu, people pointed and gawked in that patented, bovine, slack-jawed manner, and every few seconds a '*HOIRRRRRK!*' could be heard, followed by the sound of spittle being dispatched to the pavement.

After an extremely long wait, a minivan pulled up and the driver – a thin man with sunglasses – said, in English, "How do you do?" and opened the door to let me in. This was an unofficial taxi driven by a Mr. Huang. Mr. Huang informed me that he wished to practise his English conversation skills.

"Fuyuan Hotel," I said.

"Fuyuan Hotel," he echoed, pulling away. "But I feel there is not the better hotel. I know the better hotel. Fuyuan Hotel is too old, too dirty." I told him my guidebook listed it as being quite new and very clean, but he just passed me a card for another hotel and insisted I go there until I threatened to get out. Mr. Huang went on to suggest that I pay a visit to his cousin's tea shop. I told him more than once that that wouldn't be necessary. There was a sullen pause after which he asked me which country I was from. After I told him, he asked, "Is Canada independence country?"

"Yes." I said.

"So, it's not same to USA?"

"No, it's not."

"USA is the policeman of the world," he declared, betraying that this phrase had been memorized. I asked him if there was always so much pollution here.

"What's mean 'pollution?'" he wanted to know.

"*Wuran*," I said in Mandarin.

"Oh. I feel Chongqing pollution is not so much," he responded. Even buildings a block away were unclear.

During the war with the Japanese, Chongqing had earned the unenviable distinction of having become the single-most bombed city of all time. Ernest Hemingway described it as a "gray, bomb-spattered, fire-gutted, grim stone island." As we drove, I wondered aloud if there hadn't been another, much more recent conflict.

"Pardon?" my driver asked.

"A *war*," I repeated. "It looks like there's been a war here." Suddenly, Mr. Huang jerked the wheel, pulled over, and came to a stop. Swivelling around, he lowered his sunglasses and looked at me absorbedly. "What's mean 'war?'" he asked.

When we finally got to the hotel, I saw that the train station was diagonally across the street.

In the hotel restaurant, the staff decided to ignore me, so I left to get a taxi downtown. None would stop, so I ended up jumping on a bus that looked to be headed in that direction. The driver admonished me for not having the correct change. Three elderly male passengers appraised me in disgust and readjusted the grips on their canes.

I wanted to go to a travel agency located at 165 Zhongshan (Sun Yat-sen) Road. No one had the slightest idea where it was; not the cabbies I asked, not the half dozen or so people I questioned on the street, not even the two women who worked in the office two doors down from the place. *They* weren't certain of the name of the street they worked on. I left them arguing about what it was called. I ended up finding the place by accident. Afterward, I tried to get a taxi to Minzu Road (the city's main street), but two taxi drivers claimed they'd never heard of it. After squinting at my map, one asked me, "Chongqing?"

I walked.

Chongqing is not a city for walking. It is a rocky, hilly affair and one of the only municipalities in China where you won't find people riding bicycles, hence the army of porters. Mainly, the porters gather together on the docks and the downtown area where they eke out an existence lugging goods up and down the city's lengthy and precipitous stone steps.

The narrow city centre could have passed for Hong Kong. I looked down this corridor of glass buildings and then that one to note that it was almost agreeable provided you viewed it from just the right angle. As you moved away from the core, however, each street appeared shabbier and more chaotic than the last. And everywhere you cast your eye, you were met with a magazine cover. Silver luxury sedans rolled past collections of bronzed stick-stick soldiers. Peasants gaped at manikins in Italian suits. Pale young men with puffy hair and purse-like handbags sipped lattes as they sashayed past noodle shops filled with sweaty, hunched-over, brown-skinned labourers.

One of China's four provincial level municipalities, along with Beijing, Shanghai, and Tianjin, Chongqing is home to some 31.5 million people and is roughly the size of Austria. In terms of population, it is the world's largest city. It is also the world's fastest-growing city with roughly half a million people arriving every year. It is an inland port (and was a treaty port) situated at the confluence of the Jialing and Yangtze rivers. Like its counterpart, Chengdu, it is a major manufacturing hub, rich in natural resources such as coal and strontium. Additionally, it is the chief transportation centre for goods moving from the country's southwest to its east. It is the communist country's biggest boomtown and authorities hope it will spark economic growth in the west. Comparisons may be odious, but a rough parallel may be drawn between Chongqing and Chicago; perhaps Old Chicago.

I bought a ticket for a cable car and was soon looking down on a

decaying collection of oyster-tinted houses marked by weed-choked
courtyards and shattered roofs. I saw people hanging laundry and staring
blankly out their pane-less windows. I was pulled up and over the flat
brown Yangtze, on which an assortment of white boats moved this way
and that while many more suckled the long concrete piers. Chongqing
resembled a miniature Manhattan, complete with a replica of the Empire
State Building. Just above the enveloping murk, a fiery disc was dropping
and causing the remainder of the sky to cascade in brilliant bands of
orange and yellow. I turned around to inspect the far side of the river: a
bedraggled assortment of buildings and debris.

During the war with Japan, Chongqing, or Chungking as it was then
spelled, served as the Nationalist provisional capital, an idea Chiang Kai-
shek claimed he got while pursuing the long marchers. With China having
had much of its northeast occupied (since 1931), things took a turn for
the worse in 1937 when the Japanese seized Shanghai before moving
on to the capital, Nanjing. Chiang believed that all he needed to do was
hunker down in Sichuan (of which Chongqing was then a part) as well
as Yunnan and Guizhou where he could defeat the Japanese in a war of
attrition.

During the war, Harvard professor John King Fairbank likened
Chongqing to "a junk heap of old boxes piled together…. There is no
color," he wrote. "Nothing grows out of the rock, the stone is all gray
and slightly mossed; people, houses, pathways all blend into gray, with the
gray river swirling between." Others noted how the city's drab dwellings
"hung from the cliffs like birds' nests" and they commented on the
vagabonds who constantly rummaged through the hillocks of refuse that
were affixed to the slopes. Enormous rats scurried hither and thither and
human waste coursed through open sewers. It was collected by porters
who transported it to the Yangtze where it was stirred by naked labourers
before being shipped off on the imaginatively named honey barges
as fertilizer. The river itself saw an estimated 500 hundred tonnes of
excrement dumped into it every day, yet it represented Chongqing's chief
water supply. Disease was endemic and so was starvation. The Yangtze
bobbed with corpses and each morning bodies had to be cleared from the
city's streets.

Yet, despite all of the death and misery, those who could afford to
lived it up. Cinemas and ice-cream parlours did a brisk business whereas
the foreign community had French wine and American whiskey flown in
to be consumed at an exclusive club. Indeed, the capital of "Free China"
was brimming with foreigners, not to mention "down river people," and
many others. Its ranks swelled from 300,000 to 1 million, and for the

first time it possessed a sense of colour. In addition to the diplomats and their staffs, there were prayer-capped Muslims, Xinjiang merchants, Shanghai film stars, and Tibetan monks. There was a novelist from India, a ballet dancer from Trinidad, a Living Buddha from Mongolia, and a doctor from Bulgaria. From America, there were dentists, academics, aid workers, reporters, and so on. Celebrity appearances were not unknown. In addition to Earnest Hemingway, Henry Luce was on hand (the cofounder of *Time* magazine and the man behind *Fortune*, *Life*, and *Sports Illustrated*), and Indian Congress leader Jawaharlal Nehru once made a visit. Chongqing became the home of Chinese from nearly every province and citizens from nearly every nation. The surly tempered locals despised them all.

Once across, I found a man with a motorbike who agreed to give me a lift. We drove past cinder-block neighbourhoods where road workers were breaking up old streets with sledgehammers and iron spikes. I spotted a mêlée outside a karaoke and noted an oil truck whose gas cap had been replaced by a punctured, deflated basketball. Straddling the yellow line, we moved past an incredible traffic jam: an endless chain of honking, immobile cars that wound its way into the hills. Continuing on, I saw what had caused this: a traffic controller was sitting on a lawn chair with his stop/yield sign resting between his knees. He was smoking and snarling into his cell phone with his back to the traffic. Things became greener and we came to a shaded parking lot with a short flight of steps. Nationalist sentries, with their German-style helmets, Mauser pistols, and khaki uniforms, had once stood guard here. In the 1930s, Nazi Germany supplied elite units of Chiang Kai-shek's army with weapons and training. Chiang Kai-shek's adopted son, Chiang Wei-kuo, became a second lieutenant in Adolf Hitler's army, where he commanded a Panzer unit and participated in the 1938 annexation of Austria.

This was Chiang Kai-shek's former residence; his cottage, really. His wartime headquarters had been located in a squat villa in the city. Chiang and his wife, Soong Mei-ling, were shuttled across the river by motor boat when in need of a break. She used to have marmalade made from citrus fruits in the garden. He used to relax next to a gramophone. Out of the public eye, both could smoke imported cigarettes. During the war, they had urged the nation not to do so as part of something called the New Life Movement.

Chiang Kai-shek and Soong Mei-ling had married in Shanghai in what the *Shanghai Times* called "the outstanding Chinese wedding ceremony of recent years." Thirteen hundred guests turned out, including just about all of that city's foreign diplomats, not to mention the commanders of the American and British navies. The American-educated Soong was a member of China's leading westernized Christian family. Her father, a Methodist minister, had made his fortune printing Chinese editions of the Bible. By marrying Soong Mei-ling and converting to Christianity, Chiang Kai-shek enhanced his standing among foreigners. Moreover, because Soong was the sister of Sun Yat-sen's widow (the aforementioned Soong Ching-ling), it appeared to the Chinese that Chiang was the saint's successor. The hotel in which the two were married was made to resemble the interior of a church and the ceremony involved a great deal of bowing before Dr. Sun's portrait.

I walked up past a set of shaded, well-preserved western-style homes, where I peered into windows and admired the greenery. I looked toward the direction of the city and saw a toxic cloud above the dense foliage. I peered back at my driver. He was smoking and examining his feet. Then, satisfied with my snooping, I rode back to the cable car station, where a sign said, 'THE ROPEWAY OF YANGTZE RIVER.'

"How much did you make from the foreigner?" bellowed a woman from the window of a glorified hut, after I had climbed off the bike.

"I didn't do too badly!" the man shouted back.

I ate dinner at a Western restaurant called Pizza Almalfi. I was the only diner there, though, and the staff took turns walking around and pretending to clean already-gleaming tables so that they might have a bit of a stare. The manager began to pace around in circles. He would walk by, gawp expressionlessly, continue on, and then walk by again. He did this a dozen times. I was on the verge of asking if he wanted to take my picture when *he* asked me.

"What for?" I wanted to know.

"For memory's sake," he replied.

"No thanks," I answered. I knew that the memory would be preserved forever at the restaurant's entryway as proof of how good their food was.

After an hour on the street, I still hadn't found a taxi to take me back to the hotel. Drivers would scrunch up their faces and say things like, "The train station? Where's that?" One told me he didn't know where my hotel was because it was "too small." I ended up hiring another motorcycle driver, who, miraculously, knew the locations of both the train station and the hotel.

Back in my room, I got the customary late-night telephone call. "Not interested," I said, and hung up. Moments later, there was a knock on the door and I opened it to find a thickset woman with nasty, fang-like teeth and huge hands. "Yes?" I asked. She tried to slip by me, but I blocked her.

"Look, do you want a blowjob or what!?" she thundered. No sooner had she done so than a family of three walked by. The phone rang four more times. It only stopped after I did my best impression of a woman.

The following morning, I was jolted awake by the clamour outside. I pulled up a chair and drew back the curtains. Now, it was my turn to stare. A drunk was rolling on the sidewalk in a puddle of his own urine while another man was explaining something to an unimpressed contingent of police officers. I witnessed yet another scuffle, and bodies and vehicles zipped about like subatomic particles. The pollution mirrored that of the day before and I thought, 'Welcome to the Third World.' I also thought of all the recent China books I'd seen with titles that included the words 'rising' and 'superpower.' I wondered if the people who'd written them had ever been inland. I doubted they'd ever been here, to China's largest city. In the thirties, British writer Pierre Stephen Robert Payne wrote of Chongqing: "There is no sign of the greatness of China here." Nearly seven decades on, it wasn't difficult to come to the same conclusion.

It took an hour and all of the usual hassle to find transport to where I wanted to go: the Stilwell Museum. After being treated to the scenic route and overcharged, I was let out near a park on the southern bank of the Jialing River. I made my way down a driveway where I was met by a bust of General Joseph Stilwell. At its foot was a stone tablet etched with an appreciative and spirited message to the people of Chungking from the president of the United States, Franklin D. Roosevelt.

The museum (Stilwell's former residence) had on display a good deal of photos and personal effects. It was squeaky-clean and tastefully done. Moreover, captions were rendered in flawless English; a rarity. But then, the museum's very existence was novel as it presented the United States in an unequivocally positive light. To this day, the Chinese government openly and frequently refers to that country as "the enemy."[1]

Joseph Stilwell was a straight-talking, no-nonsense, four-star American general known for the genuine concern he exhibited toward his men and the equally authentic disdain he displayed toward officiousness and ceremony. Much to his approval, he was referred to by the soubriquet Vinegar Joe for the harsh criticism he could dispense for substandard performance. Just as he was about to head the Allied command of the invasion of French North Africa, Stilwell was handpicked by Roosevelt to act as commander of the China-Burma-India Theatre. He was to be stationed in Chongqing, where he would also be responsible for all US

---

1   In the late 1990s, China's vice-commandant of the Academy of Military Sciences said, "(As for the United States), for a relatively long time it will be necessary that we quietly nurse our sense of vengeance. We must conceal our capabilities and bide our time."

Lend-Lease aid. On top of that, he was to serve as Chief of Staff to Generalissimo Chiang Kai-shek, an unprecedented move. Stilwell was deemed the right man for the job in part because he had been stationed in China previously and – with his aptitude for languages – could speak and read Mandarin. In retrospect, Joseph Stilwell almost certainly *was* the right man for the job. He was a figure of great integrity. He was honest, he was direct, and he was hell-bent on getting things done. And that is why he was doomed to failure.

Chiang Kai-shek was never very keen on taking the fight to the Japanese, a fact which can be evidenced in part by the drastic retreat he made into his country's interior, a move which left something like 40 percent of the population at the mercy of a merciless enemy. Chiang's principal aim was to conserve his forces while putting on a good show, a long-standing Chinese military tradition. In Chinese traditional warfare, firecrackers played a key role as did hexes, gongs, stink-bombs, and various other evil smells. In the early twentieth century, when warlords got their hands on modern weaponry, seldom was it used for anything but effect. The objective, as author and historian Sterling Seagrave has noted, was to first frighten one's opponent by making a lot of noise and then to strike a political settlement.

After Pearl Harbour, Chiang knew that all he had to do was to survive and make sure that no one became powerful enough to challenge him. In the meantime, it would be necessary to stockpile equipment and minimize casualties in order to resume fighting the Communists after the United States had dealt with Japan. His principal military strategy was something he termed "magnetic warfare," which involved luring the enemy in, causing it to overextend itself, and then hitting it with a counterattack. This did work, but only occasionally. The Nationalists may have harassed the Japanese, but significant victories were few and far between. In fact, in more than eight years of fighting, Chiang's army routed the enemy a grand total of once.[2] And, like the government itself, the Chinese Army was shot through with inefficiency and corruption.

One of the main problems was the manner in which orders were given. The generalissimo would issue commands to far-flung armies to advance or retreat based on reports from the front that were often

---

2   This occurred at a place called Taierzhuang, and the conflict is sometimes referred to as China's Stalingrad. Even though the Japanese were badly defeated here, the Chinese still incurred more casualties. Nevertheless, the Chinese illustrated what they could do if they focused, but alas, they could only focus for a moment. The Japanese regrouped and took the area. Instead of attacking the dazed Imperial Army from the air, Chiang ordered his planes to fly over Japan and drop leaflets urging citizens to cease supporting their military in its attempt to conquer China, an act which had zero impact on Japanese morale or opinion.

woefully and fatally inaccurate. His orders, in turn, were forwarded by generals who were equally in the dark as to the enemy's true position and strength as they too were normally unwilling to get anywhere near the front line to verify such reports. Nor were they much interested in observing whether their commands were executed or not. Additionally, officers often refused to use or even deploy heavy equipment – even in critical situations.

Overwhelmingly, Chiang's commanders were incompetent, and this was because they had been chosen for their loyalty and obedience, not their capability. Chiang himself had little faith in them. "I have to lie awake at night, thinking what fool things they may do," he once said. "Then I write and tell them not to do these things. But they are so dumb, they will do a lot of foolishness unless you anticipate them. This is the secret of handling them – you must imagine everything that they can do that would be wrong, and warn them against it. That is why I have to write so many letters." As for the few generals who *were* capable, Chiang often gave them assignments with the aim of reducing their political power.

There were also immense problems with intelligence and logistics. Medical services and supplies were sorely lacking, and this had much to do with the fact that provisions were being sold on the black market and to the Japanese directly.

The Chinese soldiers themselves were poorly trained and ill equipped. Many had never received or completed basic training and many more had been press-ganged, as has been mentioned. Morale was never high, and discipline and the enforcement thereof was a major issue; so too was profiteering, desertion, and even starvation.

Chiang Kai-shek's troops were simply no match for the regimented and pitiless Japanese Army, an army with which the Chinese had conducted training exercises prior to the First Sino-Japanese War (1894-95). The Japanese were stunned by what they saw, and concluded that any fighting force that used its weapons for hanging laundry was not to be taken seriously.

After assessing the situation, Stilwell called for drastic measures. He wanted a well-trained, well-equipped, efficient army that wasn't afraid of meeting the enemy head on. He believed that the Chinese soldier was as good as any provided he received the proper training and support. But Chiang Kai-shek had other ideas. As Chiang biographer Jonathan Fenby has noted, China's leader "saw military units as chess pieces to be manipulated for his benefit. The generalissimo was a distant commander on a white horse."

It has been suggested by Jonathan Fenby, Sterling Seagrave, and other historians that Chiang was hopelessly out of touch with reality. As part of his and his wife's New Life Movement, Chiang published a list of 86 instructions to the people. Citizens were to be economical and exhibit good moral behaviour. They were to be punctual, stop spitting, dress neatly, and kill flies and rats to combat disease. Women's gowns were to be ankle-length and they were to cease curling their hair. Any female working for the government had to follow a strict dress code; there would be no more "lascivious and fantastic fashions," as Chiang put it. Even coats without buttons were prohibited. Film makers were to produce material that was 70 percent educational and 30 percent entertaining. To spread the message, slogans were drawn up and parades were held. In Chongqing, a couple of pigs spotted eating sugar cane in a park were shot because they were deemed to be offensive to public decency.

With the enemy swiftly gaining ground and the nation coming apart at the seams, Chiang Kai-shek, the fastidious, white-gloved martinet, issued a similar set of behavioural instructions to his officers and officials: "No smoking, no drinking; Sleep early, rise early; Thrifty life; Absolutely no gambling; Absolute obedience to superiors; All uniforms to be made of cotton; No office stationery to be used for private correspondence; No badges of office to be worn in places of amusement; No public banquets unless absolutely necessary." Immediately after making this announcement, a series of Japanese advances left some 200,000 Chinese troops dead. Chongqing was on the verge of being bombed to smithereens, yet Chiang was more concerned about people's pants being pressed and whether their coats had buttons or not.

Chiang Kai-shek was born on October 31, 1887 in the three-street village of Xikou, south of Ningbo in the coastal province of Zhejiang. His family owned the Yutai Salt Store, and because salt was a government monopoly, the Chiang family enjoyed a certain degree of standing. As a child, Chiang showed a fondness for bossiness and melodrama. He loved ordering his peers about and putting himself at the centre of attention. At the same time, he exhibited a strong partiality to being alone. He went on long exploratory walks and became known for his lengthy spells of quietude inevitably shattered by his violent fits and outbursts. Supposedly, when he spiralled into a bad mood, even his neighbours became anxious.

By the age of 8, the boy's father and grandfather were dead, and Chiang's mother was left alone to raise him. There had been little love between Chiang and his father, but Chiang's mother was the centre of his world. She was, according to Chiang, "more a disciplinarian than any strict teacher" as well as "the personification of Confucian virtues." By all accounts, Chiang Kai-shek's mother was austere, and she devoted herself wholly to him, hoping he'd make a name for himself.

At the age of 14, Chiang entered into an arranged marriage; his bride was five years his senior. The age gap was highlighted by Chiang's leaving the wedding banquet in order to go play with a couple of his friends. After a few years, he reportedly took to beating his wife. He admitted later that he could not so much as bear hearing her footsteps or seeing her shadow.

After traditional schooling in Ningbo, Chiang Kai-shek decided on a military career. He was influenced by *The Revolutionary Handbook*, which proposed the elimination of the Qing and the adoption of an American-style government. Realizing that proper military training could never be achieved in China, the young man snipped off his cue and set sail for Japan, where he attended the Shimbu Gakko military academy. After graduating, he joined the Japanese Imperial Army, which he served in between the years 1909 and 1911, or until he heard of the collapse of the empire, at which point he returned home.

As a Japanese soldier, Chiang Kai-shek did not make much of an impression on his superiors. However, he did make one on a compatriot named Chen Qimei, a man who introduced Chiang to a Tokyo-based anti-Qing society that had been established by none other than Sun Yat-sen. Back in China, Chiang became a member of the Nationalist Party, but was sent packing when Yuan Shikai embarked on his purge. Chiang Kai-shek hid in both Japan and Shanghai before heading to Guangzhou after Yuan Shikai's death in 1916.

Like Mao, Chiang came to see himself as China's great patriarch, saviour, and teacher. His world view was informed by Confucianism, which had been instilled in him by his severe teachers and mother. Confucianism does not lend itself to co-operation and the hierarchy it calls for must be continually maintained. Obedience is all. Benevolence is a sure sign of weakness. Anyone caught criticizing the Chongqing government was executed or given life in jail. Chiang treated his officers like children. They treated their soldiers like children. The soldiers treated the populace like children, something that would be remembered when the Chinese Civil War resumed in earnest.

Chiang Kai-shek was all but incapable of entrusting responsibility to subordinates. At one point, he held a total of 82 posts ranging from the president of the government to the president of the Boy Scouts. This resulted in affairs being handled without his knowledge and an administration working at cross purposes.

Not surprisingly, when the generalissimo's new foreign chief of staff arrived on the scene, he was greeted coolly. With his top-down world view, Chiang saw Stilwell as a threat to his authority; a temporary inconvenience that needed to be tolerated so American aid could continue to fill government coffers. When all was said and done, that aid would total approximately $3 billion, a whopping-huge sum in those days. The American general and the Chinese generalissimo became embroiled in dispute more or less immediately, and Stilwell watched in awe as his proposals were ignored and his commands countermanded. He had had a decent idea of what he would be up against, mind you. As he told a reporter from *Time* magazine shortly after receiving his assignment: "The trouble with China is simple. We are allied to an ignorant, illiterate, superstitious, peasant son of a bitch." Stilwell was soon referring to Chiang as 'Peanut' because of the odd shape of his head. Later, he would refer to him as 'The Rattlesnake.'

Indeed, Chiang Kai-shek's temper tantrums were now legendary. As a gang-associated thug during his debauched, post-Japan Shanghai days, Chiang once got into a violent quarrel with a man who posed a threat to Chen Qimei, who had become Chiang's mentor. The argument came to a halt when Chiang whipped out a pistol and shot the man dead. In point of fact, Chiang Kai-shek's criminal record in Shanghai's British-administered International Settlement would eventually include murder, extortion, several counts of armed robbery, and a batch of lesser crimes. Although indicted on all charges, the future president of "Free China" and the supreme commander of the Allied forces in the China-Burma-India Theatre managed to elude both trial and jail.

The very deep and very real connections to the underworld that Chiang cultivated in Shanghai (namely in regard to the Green Gang) would remain with him throughout his entire life. Before the situation with the Japanese came to a head, Chiang had made China's chief drug czar and criminal kingpin, Du Yuesheng, a major-general, and put his assistant in charge of the Opium Suppression Bureau. In 1931, Du Yuesheng himself became the head of the Opium Suppression Bureau. Under the guise of confiscating and eradicating the drug, the Chiang regime came to monopolize its trade. One of the key reasons the Nationalists were so intent on eliminating the Communists (who also sold opium) during the war with the Japanese was so the sale of the narcotic would not be disrupted. On Chiang's fiftieth birthday, Du Yuesheng, whose nickname was Al Capone of the Orient, presented the leader with an airplane christened *Opium Suppression of Shanghai*.

Chiang Kai-shek's regime can be seen, not as some sort of aberration, but rather as a natural extension or reflection of Chinese culture and society. The Chinese had but a single task: to fight the enemy, but they lacked the co-ordination and focus to do so. Every time the wind changed, so did their strategy, and those making the decisions were too busy proselytizing, "conserving their energy," or lining their pockets to possess any genuine concern about the fate of the nation. Furthermore, Stilwell's appointment and America's continuing support for Chiang are emblematic of the unsophisticated approach that Westerners have taken at times when dealing with China. Americans saw the smart-looking generalissimo and his refined, Americanized wife as the embodiment of hope for a backward and impoverished country. The Chinese could, it was believed, aspire toward modernity, democracy, Christianity, and the American way; all they needed was a little bit of help.

For their part, the Chiangs put on a good show, with him hosting banquets to which foreigners were invited and her undertaking a massive speaking tour in the United States, which included an appearance before Congress. The couple made the cover of *Time* under the banner 'Man and Wife of the Year.' Many were convinced they were the genuine article. Roosevelt, especially, chose to see things in this light and never ceased treating Chiang as a major player and his client state as a crucial ally, even when reports began streaming in from Stilwell and others to the effect that all was not as it seemed. One advisor described the Nationalist philosophy as "a combination of Confucianism and European authoritarianism modelled on Italian and German fascism, with a dash of the YMCA type of Christianity." A good many, however, went on believing what they wanted to.

The spell wasn't broken until the Truman years. The new president summed up the Nationalist clique as "grafters and crooks" (hence, echoing what Stilwell had been trying to say all along) and refused to send any more aid. Chiang Kai-shek's excessive demands came to be seen for what they were: financial blackmail. In Washington, the leader of Free China was given a new nickname: Cash My Check.

I left the Stilwell residence and walked across the street to the Flying Tigers Museum. The Flying Tigers was the stage name, as it were, of the American Volunteer Group, a fighter group of about 90 aircraft (known for the trademark fangs and eyes painted on their noses), which operated within the Chinese Air Force. Although it never achieved the success hoped for, it was made up of talented pilots and was a thorn in the side of the Japanese. Unlike the Stilwell Museum, entry to the Flying Tigers Museum was free. A woman behind the counter suggested I buy a painting of what looked to be Tibetan art. She explained by saying the museum received no funding from the government and had to rely on cash from artwork and souvenirs.

"Right," I said. "And your government still won't thank the United States for its role in the war. They supported the wrong side."

"Oh, our government understands why America supported the Nationalists," she countered. "They were the officially recognized government at the time. The Communist Party was still illegal."

"Yes, but they still haven't thanked them," I pressed, but she thought I meant that the Communists still hadn't thanked the Nationalists.

"Well, our government and the Nationalist Party have had some problems in the past, but things are much better now."

By "problems," I assumed she was referring to the Chinese Civil War, which lasted from 1927 to 1950 and saw the deaths of roughly 1 million soldiers and perhaps 10 million civilians. Technically, the conflict has never ended. I asked her what she meant by things being better.

"Don't you know? We've offered to send Taiwan two panda bears," she said smilingly. "And Lien Chan is about to make his second visit here." Lien Chan had just recently stepped down from the position of chairman of the Nationalist Party. He was the man whose image I had seen on the decorative plate in Zhongdian. "Even now," the woman went on, "we have the Nationalist Party in China."

This puzzled me. "Don't you have just one party?" I asked.

"No," she said laughingly. "We have many. We have the Nationalist Party, the Democratic Party, and many others."

"Can you vote for any of them?"

"They're all legal," she replied.

"Yes, but can you *vote* for any of them?"

"No," she said after a pause. She was still smiling.

I left and walked down a road. I spied a station with the name Sky Train on it and felt relieved to think that I wouldn't have to wait for an hour for a taxi. My relief was short lived.

Inside the brand-new, empty station I presented myself to a man and woman standing inside the ticket booth. They exchanged nervous glances as I drew near.

"I want to go downtown," I said in Mandarin.

"Which station?" the woman stammered.

"It doesn't matter, as long as it's somewhere downtown."

"Well, there are several stations downtown," said the man.

"All right, do you have a map?" I asked. The woman handed me a notepad and pen.

"No, no. A *map*," I repeated.

"Just write down where it is you want to go," she instructed.

"I don't know where I want to go and I cannot write in Chinese. That's why I want a map – a route map. Haven't you got one?"

"No," said the man.

'Right,' I thought. 'And why would you?' I glanced around at the immaculate interior noting only restrooms and a row of potted plants. The place looked like it had been finished yesterday.

"Oh, wait," beamed the woman. "There's a map upstairs on the platform."

But of course there was. You bought a random ticket downstairs and then made your way through the turnstile and up to the platform in the off chance that it might actually take you to where you wanted to go. Realizing that I could have stood there all day waiting for them to make or even attempt to think of a suggestion (they hadn't been programmed to do that), I asked them to sell me the most expensive ticket there was. As it happened, the Sky Train itself, or monorail, as it also called itself, was state-of-the-art and a pleasure to ride. But then, it should have been. It was built by Hitachi.

After lunch at a restaurant that offered 'crispy spring pigeon,' 'grilled kidney,' 'pig bowels,' 'pepper and salt duck beak,' and 'sliced vegetarian' (a meat dish?), I strolled around Chongqing's grotty streets once more before heading back to my hotel to wait for the car that was to pick me up and deliver me to the travel agency on Zhongshan (Sun Yat-sen) Road. From there, I would be driven by minivan to the pier. At the travel agency, the man who had sold me my ticket solemnly informed me there was a problem.

"You see, when I took the US dollars you paid me in to the bank yesterday, well, they told me that it wasn't enough. They said you made a mistake."

"Oh?"

"Yes. The exchange rate is seven point one nine RMB to the US dollar, not seven point nine one, so that's a difference of twenty-four dollars."

"So, I guess you owe me twenty-four dollars," I deadpanned.

"No, you owe me twenty-four dollars," the man replied.

"But the exchange rate *is* seven point nine one," I said. "You told me so yourself. The banks are closed now, so we can't ask them…. I know. Maybe we can ask the police. Perhaps they can tell us what the exchange rate is. Is it okay if I use your telephone to do that?"

He didn't miss a beat. "Oh, wait," he said, punching some numbers into his calculator. "*Wo suan cuo le.*" "I miscalculated. You only owe me one dollar."

I sat there staring at him.

"Okay, forget it," he said, waving his hand. "How about I arrange a hotel for you in Yichang? You'll be getting off the boat at around ten o'clock at night and won't feel like searching around for a place to stay, so I'll arrange for someone to pick you up and drive you to our three-star hotel. It's only a hundred and sixty-eight *yuan*, very reasonable. You can pay me now and I'll write you a receipt."

"I don't think so," I said.

"Why not?"

"Well, it's just that, as a foreign tourist, I wouldn't feel comfortable giving a travel agent from Chongqing money for a hotel that's in another province. No offence, but my impression of people from Chongqing hasn't been very favourable. To be frank, people here seem to be a little on the dishonest side. In fact, I've been ripped off more than once."

I usually speak in a quiet voice, but I amplified the message so as to draw attention from the crowd of people seated behind me. I was, of course, attempting to cause the man to lose face. I figured he deserved it. My little ploy worked; something of a hush came over the room. The clerk shifted toward his colleague and said, "Hey, Mr. Chen. Did you hear that? This foreign friend here says he's been ripped off – right here in Chongqing!"

"Really? Here in Chongqing? No, I don't believe it!"

"Yeah, I know. I'm surprised, too," he said, and the two men emitted mechanical chuckles. Turning toward me again, the man said, "I'll tell you what. If you don't want to pay now, you don't have to."

I fixed him with a look and left wordlessly.

The boat that would take me down the Yangtze was disembarking at 8:00 p.m. At 7:00 p.m., I was shown to my first-class cabin: a simple affair with two beds, an imitation hardwood floor, and an unambiguously third-class bathroom.

In the lobby, a man behind a desk urged me to make my way to the upper deck, so I did. There, I met a man whose job it was to block the door. He was smoking and counting money. The smoke was curling up and into his eyes, causing him to squint. When he spoke, his cigarette danced between his lips.

"Do you have a pass?" he asked brusquely. He touched a laminated card that hung around his neck on a string. "You can't come up on deck without a pass. It's fifty-five *yuan*."

"You must be kidding," I said. "I have a first-class ticket."

He smiled and replied, "That only entitles you to stay in your room or below deck. If you want to go to the lower or upper deck, the snack bar, the karaoke, or the lounge, you need a pass." Just then, a woman came back inside muttering how she couldn't believe she had to pay sixty-five RMB just to stretch her legs.

"Is it fifty-five or sixty-five?" I wanted to know.

"It's fifty-five," he said.

I handed him the money and the cigarette danced again. He wanted ten more.

"What for!?" I demanded.

"It's a deposit," he explained. "You'll get it back when you return the pass."

After grudgingly giving him the remainder, I asked, "Is that all? Any more fees? Are you going to charge me for breathing, or perhaps for taking a photograph?"

"No," he replied.

"*Bu laoshi,*" I said, moving past him. "Dishonest."

"Who's dishonest?" he wanted to know.

"You are," I said, but this only yielded a dismissive grunt.

On the bus in Chengdu, I had found the exasperated, expletive-hurtling European a bit much. Travel, after all, is supposed to toughen you up. The lie he and his companion had been told had probably set them back a mere two dollars and ten minutes, and the tongue-lashing he had given the innocent attendant was uncalled for. But after only two days in China's largest city and fifteen minutes on a boat about to leave it, I was perilously close to the point of imitating him.

CHAPTER TWELVE

The boat was christened *Changjiang Guanguang* or Yangtze River Tours and its name was written in both languages. The word 'Tours' had been spelled 'Toursy,' which somehow seemed fitting. The vessel was white with blue trim and, uniquely, had the fuselage of a blue and white airplane attached to its top. Its members-only upper deck contained a few dozen dirt-caked plastic lawn chairs, so I sat on one and read. The railings were in the process of being converted into clotheslines. By the time we got underway, a traveller on a passing ship would have seen 40 people seated within a ring of socks and underwear.

The immense hills that guide the river grew dim, becoming featureless masses which rose up at intervals to lick the thinning strip of hazy blue which hovered just above. Overhead, the sky drained itself of colour. It turned wine dark and offered a pair of glistening stars for consideration. Before long, we were moving atop an onyx slate dotted with visual echoes of extinguished suns. Lengthy stretches of shadowy nothingness were punctuated by towns and villages that appeared in the distance as bracelets and pendants. Our searchlight remained fixed on the southern bank, illuminating man-made bits and pieces (a window pane, a guardrail) within a circle of murky green. When the horn sounded, 80 hands shot up to cover as many ears.

When I returned to my room, I could hear a rustling noise inside. I unlocked the door, expecting to find someone rummaging through my belongings, but instead found a blond-haired man in a white tank top lying on my bed.

"Don't be alarmed," he stammered, noting my expression. "They paired me up with you because the roommate I got didn't want to turn the air conditioner on. Can you imagine? In this heat? Why would he buy a first-class ticket in the first place?" He stood up and offered his hand. "Sorry to frighten you. My name's Trevor."

Like me, Trevor had been told his ticket would entitle him to a cabin of his own. We brought this to the attention of the staff, but to no avail. I wasn't happy with the arrangement and neither was he. As far as roommates went, however, I could have done much worse.

Trevor was from Seattle and was the manager of a bookstore. He was travelling around the world. He was cheerful and polite and he imparted his itinerary to me in precise detail. Indeed, he was big on detail and everything about him implied preciseness and efficiency: the impeccably polished boots, the elaborate digital watch, the two pairs of designer socks – the inner white pair pulled an exact inch above the outer grey pair. He was intelligent and good-natured, if a bit neurotic. I got the impression that if I asked him for, say, a thimble or a map of Alaska, he would have had no trouble producing either from one of his well-packed bags.

I gave the early-morning tourist outing a miss, but was woken by Trevor's tour guide. "The time change again," she said. "Now we go at nine-twenty. I know before I say nine, but there have some change. I know you buy the all-inclusive ticket, but that isn't included transportation. You must to pay more twenty *yuan*." Two hours later, Trevor returned grumbling and shaking his head. "That was the biggest fiasco you can ever imagine," he declared. "Why did I even bother?"

In the early afternoon, I went up to the deck to have a look at the river. Even though we were moving again, there was no breeze. The brown enamelled waterway arced gently into the distance where it was pinched by a pair of lush hills. It rippled at its edges, as though an elongated pane of tinted glass had been scratched repeatedly by a diamond. Among these scratches were scissored silhouettes of men in conical hats standing atop uncertain rafts. Sagging coal barges puttered past, and occasionally an obnoxious hydrofoil would growl by leaving bluish brushstrokes of exhaust suspended in the air. The hills were flecked with concrete houses and markers indicating where the water level would be after the completion of the Three Gorges Dam. We passed pagodas, tombs, and factories as hawks soared high overhead. I imagined I saw Mao Zedong floating along with his big belly sticking out of the water and a boatload of panicky cadres following after him.

In the late afternoon, we docked at Wanzhou, a city in the process of retreating to higher ground. As the sun fell behind it, the slanting town and its doorstep of rusty-bottomed boats faded under a brilliant crown of sunlight.

Trevor and I had agreed to meet for dinner. At 6:00 p.m., we made our way to the restaurant only to find that it was empty. All the tables had been laid out with food.

"Do we seat ourselves?" I asked a man behind the cash register. Like the doorman, he was counting money, and didn't even bother to look up.

"You can't order anything now," he replied.

"Why not?"

"We're entertaining guests."

"Yes, I know. *We're* the guests."

"No, no. Guests that just came today. You can come back when they've finished."

"When will that be?"

"I'm not certain."

"Are the guests tourists who are visiting Wanzhou?" I asked. I knew that many of the river towns had become major tourist attractions. I pictured brochures saying things like 'See Wanzhou Today, Before We Sink It.'

"I'm not certain," the man answered again.

"You don't seem to be certain of very much," I said.

His mask dissolved and a faint smile came over his face, as though he had just farted in his sleep. "Do you or your friend need a massage? I can arrange for a woman to be sent to your room."

The following day, we approached the first and shortest of the Three Gorges: Qutang Gorge. Once a rushing corridor of turbulent water, this glazed section of the river passed leisurely between a colossal sand-coloured cliff and a mountain that was exploding with peaks and fraught with crevices. It was all very dramatic and impossible to fit into my view finder. A Song Dynasty poet, Su Dongpo, wrote of the gorges:

Above the river, heavy on the heart, thousandfold hills:
layers of green floating in the sky like mist.
Mountains? clouds? too far away to tell
till clouds part, mist scatters, on mountains that remain.
Then I see, in gorge cliffs, black-green clefts
where a hundred waterfalls leap from the sky,
threading woods, tangling rocks, lost and seen again,
falling to valley mouths to feed swift streams.

On the lower deck, a dozen megaphone-wielding tour guides standing amidst a hundred camera-clicking tourists made literary and historical references of a similar nature. "The Tang Dynasty poet Li Bai said Qutang Gorge was like a thousand seas poured into a single cup!" one yelled proudly. "Five thousand years of history!" shouted another. When it was announced that the most arrestive scenery was behind us, the deck cleared in under a minute.

Trevor and I headed to the lobby. We were going to transfer to a smaller boat that would take us on a six-hour jaunt up the diminutive Daning tributary in order to see the Mini Three Gorges. Regardless of a sign urging everyone to 'Meet and Discuss with Care,' the lobby wasn't exactly a picture of order, and Trevor wasn't dealing with it very well. He was standing only inches from the wall when a man tried to squeeze past him. He refused to budge, however, resulting in the man being pancaked. "And just where do you think *you're* going?" Trevor asked the back of his head. Moments later, Trevor was trying to whip the mob into shape. "People *please*!" he yelled, waving his arms. "Single File! *Single File*! Here, line up behind this woman," he instructed and touched an elderly lady gingerly on the shoulder only for her to recoil, raise her arms defensively, and cautiously back away from the barbarian. People clucked disapproval and shook their heads.

The Mini Three Gorges were wonderful. The sheer size of the slopes and cliffs made passenger boats like ours look like little toys. However, of the six hours we spent exploring the gorges, five were blighted by repetitive and continuous announcements ("We're boat number thirty-four! Thirty-four! Don't forget: we're boat number thirty-four! You'll have an hour when we dock! One hour! You'll only have one hour once we dock! Then you must return to boat number thirty-four! One more time: that's thirty-four!"), more eardrum-rattling horn blasts (made for no apparent reason and in the narrowest part of the gorge no less), and by passengers who smoked, spat on the floor, and tried to squeeze past you when there was no room or reason to do so. People on other boats pointed and laughed when they spotted foreign faces and this really upset Trevor. "What's *wrong* with these people?" he asked. At one point, he buried his face in his hands and said, "Maybe I should just catch a flight to Sydney."

That evening, back on the ship, Trevor and I bought a couple of warm bottles of beer and headed to the deck. Within the circle of now-parched laundry, we were joined by all the other foreign passengers: a woman from Norway, a couple from Denmark, a trio from Spain, and two chemical engineering students from Germany who were in China doing their practical training.

"We are here to oversee the construction of a water treatment plant designed to pull heavy metals out of the river water," one of them explained.

"And how's that going?" I asked.

"Good. The plant is up and running and we taught the local engineers how to operate it."

"It's been an amazing experience for us," his colleague added. "We never could have done something like this in Germany, but here a German student is much more knowledgeable than a Chinese engineer. But we estimate that one or two months after we leave, the plant will become inoperable."

"Why's that?"

"Because no one here has the slightest idea what they are doing. All they want to do is cut corners. And this is really amazing because they dump *everything* into the river. You wouldn't believe some of the dioxins and chemicals we found. It's unimaginable. If you swam in this water for fifteen minutes, I guarantee you'd get cancer."

The next morning we were awoken by a stampede of people headed to the deck to snap pictures of Wu Gorge. I watched it from my cabin while in a supine position. Xiling Gorge appeared a while later, and it too was captivating, but like the entire affair, it would have been immeasurably better had it been witnessed from some other context.

To state the obvious, a cruise down the Yangtze should have been pleasurable, but that was the one thing it wasn't. It was passengers meandering about in their pyjamas and littering in the corridors. It was pushing and shoving in the lobby. It was manic tour guides constantly knocking on doors. It was being denied access to the restaurant at dinner time and charged extra for going outside. It was an entire deck draped with bras and panties. It was having your eardrums nearly blown out by the horn – repeatedly – even when anchored. It was never being provided with accurate information and receiving daily schedules that changed and then changed again. It was the rancid, smoke-filled lounge and its non-stop mahjong game and 24-hour karaoke. It was a floating microcosm of Chinese society and I desperately wanted out. So did Trevor. In the middle of the night, he went next door to confront the people who had woken us up by pounding on the wall. "What in heaven's name are you doing!?" he demanded of a middle-aged couple, more shocked than angry. "Don't you know people are trying to sleep!? Why would you beat on a wall!? *Why*!? Why are you people so rude!?"

In the afternoon, we set out to see the Three Gorges Dam. After taking a tram up an embankment, we transferred to a bus. At the station, a sign in English read, 'Please Safeguard Yourself from Fire, Theft, Robbery and Dishonest Trick.' Our first stop was an aquarium characterized by static creatures in tanks of unclean water. Like the panda breeding centre, pictures provided the contrast: happy dolphins in bright blue pools leapt and smiled for the camera. Attached to the museum, improbably, was a supermarket and our troupe was led through it. Trevor and I left them and headed for the exit. "If you see something you like," chirped the leader through her megaphone as they passed through the dairy section, "please don't hesitate to buy it."

That an aquarium had been constructed near the dam was no coincidence. It was the government's way of making it look as though it cared. It is believed that the construction of the dam has already aided in the extinction of the Chinese River Dolphin and it is certain to have an adverse impact on the Yangtze sturgeon as well as the critically endangered Siberian Crane. But then, it is believed the dam will have an adverse effect on a great deal.

The government has said that construction of the $30-billion, 22,500-megawatt, hydro-electric power station is necessary and that its benefits will be manifold. They've argued that it will make China less reliant on oil (China is the second largest consumer of that product) and coal (by more than 30 million tonnes per year). There will also be the advantages of flood control and drought relief, they say. Furthermore, the higher water levels, along with the dam's lock system, could make for a fivefold increase in shipping. Navigation, once extremely tricky, should become much easier and much safer. And then, of course, China simply needs the extra power. Its modernization efforts have put a serious strain on power grids and there are still widespread blackouts. Of course, the dam is also a symbol: it shows the world just how far China has come and it shows Chinese citizens that its government is focused on a future where the economy will be paramount.

Critics have argued that the dam was poorly planned, having been built atop a geological fault and with a weight that could induce seismic activity. They have also noted that the 660-kilometre-long reservoir created by the barricade has already become extremely polluted – as they predicted it would. Raw sewage and pollutants are likely to contaminate water supplies, no small matter when you consider that more than 350 million people, or one out of every twenty on Earth, live in the Yangtze's watershed. There are already 300 million people in China who do not have access to safe drinking water and there are 750 million who lack proper sanitation.

Another major concern has to do with siltation. The Yangtze carries a thousand times more silt than the muddy Mississippi and it is projected that 500 million tonnes of the stuff will settle in the reservoir every year. Not only are the riverbanks downstream (not to mention the city of Shanghai) dependent on the stuff, but its accumulation upstream could lead to catastrophe. As China-writer Peter Hessler has pointed out: 10,000-tonne freighters might have a tough time attempting to navigate a

660-kilometre-long bog. But infinitely more disquieting is what that build-up of sediment might spell for the dam.

In 1975, sedimentation contributed to the failure of the Ru River's Banqiao Dam. Thought to be indestructible, it crumbled after a typhoon. The upshot was the formation of a 10- to 14-kilometre-long wave, which moved through the countryside at a speed of 14 metres per second while inflicting ineffable devastation. Sixty-one additional dams failed in the disaster, which took the lives of roughly 166,000 people and affected 11 million more. The government did what it could to cover up the debacle; the Banqiao Dam also had critics, and they too were ignored.

With the Three Gorges Dam, 13 cities, 140 towns, and 1,352 villages will be inundated, as will 1,300 archaeological sites. The project will see the displacement of 2.3 million people, and it has recently come to light that compensation promised by Beijing is being siphoned off by local officials. In order to maximize the dam's efficiency and to combat siltation, a series of additional dams is in the works.

Interestingly, the Three Gorges Dam was originally conceived by none other than Sun Yat-sen. Chiang Kai-shek supported the idea and commissioned an American engineer to perform a survey. The generalissimo had hoped to start construction after the war. This task fell to Mao Zedong, the dam's most enthusiastic proponent. When his engineers objected to the project, he had them jailed. Public debate over the Three Gorges Dam has been banned since 1987.

Half disappeared in mist and not yet operational, the dam failed to impress. It appeared as a great, notched slab of grey ornamented by evenly spaced red cranes. The surrounding bushes were wired with speakers explaining why it was beneficial lest tourists be tempted to think of why it wasn't.

That night, as we sat anchored upriver from the structure, great tangles of light and colour burst above it. Fireworks. I watched them silently with Trevor and the group of Europeans. A shiny-white luxury cruiser docked alongside us and we had no trouble seeing into its well-appointed rooms. On the lower deck, tuxedoed waiters whisked steaming plates of food and bottles of wine to diners seated at candle-lit and fan-cooled tables. A live band embarked on a light jazz number. We stared silently for some time, and I imagined everyone was thinking the same thing. 'Oh, well. I'll be off this fucking junk heap tomorrow.'

During the night, we passed through the lock system. It was very loud, with lots of echoing creaks, crunches, and shudders. I peeked out the window every now and again only to find myself looking at a metal wall and rows of yellow lights. At dawn, I went to the lower deck and took one last look at the river. If I were a painter, I could have made its far bank by running my thumb sideways along the top edge of the water, smearing in the hills, breaking here and there for clumps of colourless buildings. I followed the long smudge of shoreline with my eye until it and the bronzed river it abutted vanished into a ghostly mist.

I tried to return my deck pass to two members of the staff, but neither would accept it and both claimed not to know to whom I should give it. On the gangway, I casually dropped the pass into the muddy water. On the pier, I turned around and chucked the key at the boat's hull. It made a delightfully satisfying clanking sound before falling and making an equally gratifying splash.

CHAPTER THIRTEEN

It was a bright morning, yet the waiting area at Yichang's bus station was so dark that I could hardly make out the print on the pages I was reading. Its wooden walls and pews brought to mind a small-town church. Members of the congregation dozed with their arms crossed and their feet propped up on their luggage. Those awake were gazing at me: a bearded Westerner doing something you never see people in China doing: reading. Or perhaps they were gazing past me at the object of veneration that hung on the wall: a prodigious oil painting of the Three Gorges Dam.

In the summertime, rice is the leading crop in Hunan, and for the next eight hours I passed by one fogbound rice field after another in the fertile province's northern alluvial plain. Vast tracts of nodding stalks were dotted with bleak concrete houses, which gathered every so often to form villages that doubtlessly hadn't changed in half a century. The highway was just a crumpled old country track barely wide enough for two vehicles. Besides a handful of bulky homes, there were few signs of prosperity or modernity. I never saw a single piece of farm equipment.

It was these rural areas, of course, which were helping to fuel China's great boom. During the past two decades, more than a fourth of the country's 800 million rural inhabitants had packed up and headed to the city to work on production lines and so on. Although tempting to get excited about a country that is suddenly, and quite literally, on the move, it is important to remember that such migration is technically illegal. In China, there is a system of household registration known as the *hukou*, which essentially confines residents to their place of birth and to their work unit. Moving requires a permit, and the process involved in moving from the country to the city can take years. Even city dwellers wishing to study in another city require a temporary residence card. If a man from Hunan were to move to Shanghai to look for a job, he would be hard pressed to find one that was legitimate, and more than likely, his existence would be harsh: a reduced wage, poor living conditions, and the

possibility of being rounded up, beaten up, and then sent home. If the
man had a child, the child would attend a migrant's school if it attended
school at all. Access to national health care or government services would
be denied.

Yet, in spite of this, and all of the very real discrimination that such
people are accorded, many find it worth the risk; preferable to life on
the farm where wages are one sixth of those in the city and taxes are
three times higher. By its own calculation, China has the largest disparity
between urban rich and rural poor in the entire world. Some provinces
have considered abolishing the *hukou*, but worry about an unchecked
flood of migration to urban areas, which was mainly why the system was
devised in the first place. Household registration in China dates back to
the Xia Dynasty, 2100–1600 BCE. Status is hereditary.

The girl next to me was young and pretty. Her seat was broken, so
that when we made a right turn it would shift and move her toward me.
Left turns would move her away. We made a right turn and then drove
straight for some time. She had fallen asleep and her head was now
resting on my shoulder. Other passengers noticed this and began to
whisper (inasmuch as Chinese people *can* whisper) and stare. A few felt
morally bound to swivel around at intervals to make sure the foreigner
wasn't copping a feel. I could have explained, but what was the point?
They wanted to think the worst, so I let them.

In the afternoon, we came upon Changsha's periphery: a sprawl of
mustard-tiled apartment blocks streaked with rust stains that ran from
air conditioner frames and the bolts that fastened cages around windows.
Across the street from the terminus was a KFC, so I headed there to grab
a bite. Three female employees were outside doing a synchronized dance
to the song 'Funky Town' in order to drum up business. Three old men
sat on a bench and ogled them lasciviously.

I took a cab across the Xiang River and entered Changsha proper.
Hunan's capital had wide boulevards, tall buildings, and McDonalds. At
the hotel I stayed at, a male receptionist jotted down the particulars of my
passport. As he did this, his female colleague peered over his shoulder and
asked him where Canada was. "*Bu zhidao*," he said. "I don't know." But
regardless of not being very geographically astute, the staff was at least
honest. At the first place I had gone to, they tried to charge me an extra $50
for "insurance" after promising me there would be no deposit or additional
fees. Insurance, they reasoned, was neither a deposit nor a fee.

Customarily, Chinese cities are enhanced by nightfall, but that wasn't
the case with Changsha. Away from the socialist thoroughfares and
shopping plazas, it was a matter of decay and desperation. There seemed

to be brothels on every street and the sidewalks were so thick with
trash that in places you had to kick your way through it. In front of a
convenience store called Whacko Market, three girls of perhaps 13 asked
me for money. They claimed they were hungry.

"You don't look hungry," I told them. From their attire and the bags
they were carrying, I guessed they'd spent the day at the mall.

"Well, can you at least buy us some beer then?" one asked. The
strange thing was that she did this in flawless English.

Ever since Chongqing, I had become something of a bad traveller.
I freely admit it. I was abrupt with people and awfully distrustful. I
shook my head so often I feared it might come off. I glared. I scowled.
I did what many Western people do when lied to or harassed: I became
confrontational. I suppose the extreme heat didn't help; the temperature
had been in the mid-to-high thirties every day and the humidity was
agonizing, but I felt I should have coped better. I had figured a jaunt
around China would be relatively easy; that my language skills and
knowledge would make me more or less impervious to the types of
troubles that most outsiders encountered. But I had figured wrong.

I felt like blurring the edges with a drink, but couldn't find any of
the watering holes recommended in my guidebook. I settled for a mango
juice in a restaurant run by the friendliest people I had met so far; they
were from Taiwan.

They didn't like living in China, they said, but it was easy to make
money. They hoped to save enough to move to Vancouver, where
they had relatives. They asked me questions about life in Canada and
complimented my middling Chinese. They were kindness itself. The
mango juice came garnished with parsley and looked and tasted exactly
like penicillin. When they asked me if it was good or not, I grinned and
told them it was great.

The following morning, I caught a bus an hour out of town to a place
called the Lei Feng Memorial Museum. I bought a ticket and strolled up
a stone walkway flanked by thin strips of grass. Planted in the grass were
low signs with messages written in both English and Chinese. As usual,
the English made between little and no sense.

One flower one grass all life, one first life always concern feeling

Protect the environment, but treat oneself kindly

The small grass of mattress mattress is very quiet, the roadside
pedestrian does not bother

Lift a finger for beautification of the environment, one goodness of fine long hair see spirit

Inside, I was greeted by the bronzed upper body of Comrade Lei Feng. He was smiling. As I was about to discover from the cornucopia of posters and photos bearing his likeness, Comrade Lei Feng was always smiling.

According to the story, Lei Feng, a native of Hunan, became an orphan when his peasant father was murdered by the Japanese and his mother committed suicide after being harassed by her landlord's son. Young Lei Feng was then taken in and raised by the Communist Party, where he joined its youth corps and grew up to be a model citizen. He spent his days doing good deeds: he read to children, he helped old ladies cross the street, he volunteered to do heavy labour, and he gave demonstrations in gymnastics. At the age of 20, he joined the People's Liberation Army, where he wasted no time in becoming a squad leader. He donated his measly salary to flood victims, served officers tea, and massaged his fellow soldiers' feet. He even darned and washed their socks, and he did so in the manner in which he did everything: with an ear-to-ear grin etched onto his mug.

It seems that the only occasion Comrade Lei Feng didn't smile was the time he posed for a Che-Guevara-like portrait in which his eyes are narrowed and focused and he is brandishing a machine gun. To be certain, Lei Feng's cheery selflessness had its limits; it would not be extended to class enemies, for example. In his diary, he wrote that his sole purpose in life was to act as "a screw in the machine of the revolution." Young people, he opined, ought to submit unquestionably to both the Party and its leader.

Unluckily, Lei Feng died when he was just 22. He was helping to direct a truck that was backing up when it struck a pole that came crashing down on his head. A year later, in 1963, the government embarked on a nationwide campaign dubbed 'Learn from Comrade Lei Feng,' which saw his diary reproduced and disseminated for study. (Excerpts of the journal are still required reading in elementary schools, which are also obliged to display his portrait.) The campaign saw the production of movies, comics, and a plethora of posters. The phrase 'living Lei Feng,' used to describe a person who goes out of their way to assist others, earned a spot in the national lexicon.

After Mao's death, the movement lost momentum, but it was revitalized following the Tiananmen Square protests in an effort to remind the masses of the importance of obedience. China's firefighters have been encouraged to follow the hero's example as have jailed members of Falun Gong, who have been required to study his diary as part of their "re-education."

In 2003, the soldier-turned-paragon was dusted off once more, this time to illustrate that his spirit was still relevant in a world of 'socialism with Chinese characteristics.' Lei Feng was marketed as a homeowner, the possessor of a bank account, and was used to promote pharmaceuticals. He got his own webpage that features an educational online game where players perform philanthropic acts in the hopes of winning a virtual copy of the *Collected Works of Mao Zedong*. One company went so far as to sell Lei Feng condoms, although these were swiftly banned.

Comrade Lei Feng is a page straight out of George Orwell's *Nineteen Eighty-Four*. Precisely, page 49. "There were occasions when Big Brother devoted his Order for the Day to commemorating some humble, rank-and-file Party member whose life and death he held up as an example worthy to be followed. Today he (the protagonist, Winston Smith) should commemorate Comrade Ogilvy. It was true that there was no such person as Comrade Ogilvy, but a few lines of print and a couple of faked photographs would soon bring him into existence."

I had read that many Chinese people considered Lei Feng to be a joke, but the museum claimed to have had 11.5 million guests and although there were only two other families visiting when I was there, it was obvious they didn't think it was funny at all. Viewing the ceramic jars that Lei Feng's mother had used to preserve vegetables was clearly going to be a highlight of the summer vacation. True, they became morose when they got to the photo of Lei Feng's corpse, but their exuberance was restored upon learning that he had been the "first excellent tractor driver" at a farm he worked on in Hunan. At the tour's end, they beamed with delight as their guide snapped their picture and one of the mothers stood at attention and began to sing a song dedicated to the Good Samaritan. Its lyrics and notes had been affixed to the wall.

I left and spent an hour wandering around aimlessly. Past a battered stretch of shabby houses and roadside shrubs (with nearly as many bits of litter as leaves), I came upon a neighbourhood of newly built, Western-style homes. They were white and had lawns and wrought iron fences. They hadn't been completed, however, and lacked window panes and doors. I assumed that the project had been abandoned. A roadside banner read, in English, 'WELCOME TO ENGLAND.' Another showed a neat row of town houses surrounded by perfect trees. I glanced around at the empty, fenced-in shells, the hillocks of trash, and the forsaken construction material while noting the odd silence. The wind had picked up, and ashen rags of cloud were now spinning across a gunmetal-tinged sky. I walked back to the bus station.

Back in Changsha, I paid a visit to the Former Office of the Hunan Communist Party Committee. It was situated within a large courtyard dominated by a statue of Mao 'made of an aluminum magnesium alloy with a total height of 12.26 metres and a foundation support of 5.16 metres.' It also contained Mao's former residence and another museum.

In one of the museum's drab stairwells, a portrait of a young Mao hung on the wall. He was standing on a mountaintop wearing a black robe and staring determinably at something out of view. I followed his gaze with my own and saw what he was looking at: brown ladies' underwear hanging inside the caged window of the adjacent building. Again, you would never have known it was a place of historical significance. There was trash everywhere and dozens of shirtless vendors lying like junkies next to their wares.

I took a taxi to the Hunan No. 1 Teacher's Training School where young Zedong studied and later taught. It was an attractive, well-preserved building with some nice greenery. I nosed around the corridors and poked about the reading room where Mao once pored over newspapers while trying to figure out how the world worked.

The next day, I caught a cramped minibus to Shaoshan, Mao's birth place. I sat next to an elderly woman who had brought nine Santa-Claus sacks of foodstuffs with her. It was a frenzied, two and a half hour drive marked by repetitive scenery: tumbledown houses, farms, fields, factories, smokestacks, tumbledown houses.... I witnessed several pedestrians saunter across the road without the slightest regard for traffic. Surely, they had a death wish. Our driver rear-ended another vehicle, and, though it had been his fault, got out to admonish the other driver. In Chinese society, an elaborate system is in place to ensure that wrongdoers are never in the wrong. It involves lying, denial, shifting the blame, recrimination, and intimidation.

Shaoshan itself was pretty. It was white, decent-looking houses hugging verdant hills. Drooping willows and contorted pines stood watch over ponds of giant lilies and jumbo lily pads.

Mao's home, a coral-coloured bungalow capped in slanting black tiles, had been neatly restored. His parents' bedroom was guarded by a pair of soldiers whose job it was to remind people not to take photos. A sign behind them explained that this was the room where Mao was born. His mother was described as a compassionate Buddhist and his father a '... hardworking, thrifty, smart and crackajack man.' Mao's father may have been hard-working, but his relationship with his son was often strained. Like Chiang Kai-shek, Mao Zedong adored his mother and considered her to be a saint, but such feelings were never extended to his domineering father.

Mao Zedong started to work on his father's farm at the age of 6. At the age of 8, he was enrolled in the village school, where he was to be educated in the Confucian classics, the idea being that he should acquire literacy and math skills enough to successfully run the farm. Literacy led to a fascination with historical novels, which the boy read and reread until his story-telling abilities rivalled those of the village elders. At 14, he was married off to girl in a neighbouring clan and they lived together on the farm for three years, until she died. According to historian Jonathan Spence, it was either this event that altered Mao's trajectory or a book that his cousin sent him entitled *Words of Warning to an Affluent Age*. If China no longer wished to be subjugated by Western powers, the volume argued, it would have to westernize. Otherwise, it was doomed. Mao said later that it was this message that awoke both his political sensibilities and his intellectual curiosity.

With his father's consent, Mao registered at a school in a nearby township that emphasized both the Chinese classics and Western education. Thereafter, he continued his studies in Changsha, a city big enough to detect the nation's political tremors. The year was 1911 and the empire was on the brink of disintegration; many in Changsha were intent on helping it on its way. Mao became caught up in the fervour. He participated in demonstrations, he clipped off his cue, and he became a supporter of the exiled Sun Yat-sen. After the accidental mutiny in Wuhan, Mao joined the Republican Army (where he only saw guard duty), but quit after six months to go back to school, assuming the revolution was over.

As China descended into chaos, Mao spent his days in a library intently studying its history. He became deeply intrigued by the Qin Dynasty, which unified the country in 221 BCE under the First Emperor (Qin Shi Huangdi), a powerful but brutal ruler fond of laws, grand projects (the Great Wall, the Terracotta Army), and eradicating Confucianism. One of the Qin Dynasty's leading statesmen was a fellow by the name of Lord Shang, a man who helped turn the hesitant Qin state into a dominant and highly centralized entity. He did this by promulgating a series of laws, which became codified in a volume called *The Book of Lord Shang*, and which were later denounced by academics for their severity and for allegedly reducing the citizenry to subservience and sycophancy. Lord Shang's laws (sometimes referred to as the Law, capitalized) called for the elimination of the aristocracy. Land was to be transferred to soldiers based on military success and citizens were to be grouped into units where agriculture was encouraged and commerce discouraged. To ensure that everyone did as they were told, people were forced to monitor one another. Failing to report a transgression would result in being boiled alive or cut in half. Anybody found profiteering or not pulling their weight was made a government slave. Mao Zedong endorsed these measures wholeheartedly.

In 1918, a 24-year-old Mao graduated and moved to Beijing, where he got a job as a clerical worker in the Peking University library. Here, against the backdrop of a sham government and a nation ruled by warlords, he found himself at the periphery of a movement that sought drastic change. At its centre was the head of the library, Li Dazhao, an intellectual who subscribed to Marxism. His writings, published in the progressive journal *New Youth*, were widely read and well respected. Mao began to emulate Li, which resulted in his own articles being published in journals in Changsha.

In 1920, under the supervision of the Soviet Union, Li Dazhao and a fellow named Chen Duxiu established the Chinese Communist Party in Shanghai. The First Congress was held the following year, and Mao Zedong was invited as one of two representatives from Hunan's capital, although it isn't known precisely why. The meeting was fraught with tension and its 15 attendees (membership totalled just 53) narrowly escaped being captured by the police. Mao was ordered to return to Changsha in order to begin recruitment, a task he threw himself into.

At the Second Congress, it was decided that the fledgling and borderline insolvent party had no choice but to form an alliance with the Nationalists in what came to be called the United Front. As a member of the Nationalist Party, Mao rose through the ranks. In Guangzhou, where the Nationalists first set up their base of operations, he worked as a liaison between the two factions before being transferred to the propaganda department.

The United Front may have been tenuous, but it functioned, and support for it was growing. The nation was seething over a series of events involving foreign malevolence and governmental complicity, and the up-and-coming coalition hoped to channel that anger into action. Under the command of Chiang Kai-shek, a hybrid military force trained at Huangpu embarked on what came to be known as the Northern Expedition: a series of northward thrusts meant to "unify the nation," although in reality this entailed striking deals with warlords or buying off their armies. Nevertheless, the campaign was a violent success and the Nationalists saw their territory extended to Nanjing, some 1,500 kilometres away. The speed and viciousness of the expedition made both warlords and foreign interests anxious.

The following year, Chiang set his sights on his old stomping ground: Shanghai. The plan was to smash the city's 499 labour unions and then arrange for "loans" from businesses and banks. The Nationalists required funding and Shanghai's 821,282 union members represented potential converts to communism. In joining the Nationalists, the Communists had hoped to compromise its members, but Chiang was one step ahead of them; there would be no dictatorship of the proletariat under his watch. When a hundred-thousand-strong group of Shanghai protesters marched against a Nationalist-troop presence, they were fired upon. Sixty-six died and five times as many were wounded. Arrests and executions over the next few weeks would take the lives of up to ten thousand more.

The city's bankers and industrialists had bankrolled the takeover by allotting Chiang Kai-shek $3 million (in 1920s money) and agreeing to support a Nationalist government in Nanjing. Labour had begun to organize, and they wanted it put back in its place. They believed that helping Chiang Kai-shek would put him in their eternal debt, but they were sorely mistaken.

In effect, Chiang held the entire city for ransom. First, the business community was called on to extend astronomical amounts of "credit" to the new government. Then it was asked to purchase "bonds." Most readily complied; those who didn't often had a change of heart when their daughter was kidnapped or their own coffin was delivered to their door by the Nationalist Party collection agency: the Green Gang.

Meanwhile, in Beijing, a warlord seized the Soviet Embassy, which just happened to be sheltering Li Dazhao and his 17-year-old daughter, who were both slowly strangled to death. Chiang Kai-shek telegrammed Moscow, whose help he had enlisted at Huangpu, to express his "outrage" and "regret" over these incidents. It was all a terrible "misunderstanding," he said. What a pity.

The crackdown spread to other areas, including Hunan. Mao fled there and hid in the mountains with a large rabble of peasant soldiers. Eventually, he headed to the neighbouring province of Jiangxi, near the Fujian border, where he established the Jiangxi Soviet and expanded his Red Army. From 1930 to 1934, this ragtag force was repeatedly attacked by the Nationalists before finally being encircled. Miraculously, or so it is always described, the encirclement was broken, thus marking the start of the legendary Long March.

Although now heralded as a grand achievement (I had seen two

Long March movies during my late-night TV watching), the exodus was in fact a less-than-glorious event and much more complicated than the version commonly relayed. To begin with, there wasn't really one long march, but rather three long marches: successive retreats made by a trio of Communist armies. The concept of a single trudging column of 86,000 men (and 35 women) weighed down with equipment while being tracked by Nationalist regiments and gunned down by the tens of thousands at the Xiang River crossing by Chiang Kai-shek's air force has been taken from the ash heap of Communist propaganda. There were more desertions than deaths, and, to put it mildly, the soldiers weren't always impeccably disciplined. The 1st Red Army (the army that initially fled the Jiangxi Soviet; the one Mao belonged to) press-ganged young men in addition to robbing and even killing civilians. But then, this isn't surprising when you consider that there were soldiers so ignorant that they didn't know what a light bulb was, believing it would go out at dawn, just like the moon disappeared. The Communists did have to pierce and skirt Nationalist blockades, but never mentioned are the blockades by and attacks from hostile tribes, warlords, and Chinese Muslims.

Even though the Long March has been simplified and mythologized, it was still a resounding success. After travelling as far west as Tibet, the Communists swung north making it as far as Yanan, in the arid and impoverished province of Shaanxi, where there was already a Communist base. Out of practicality, the long marchers made their homes in caves, after which they got rested and reorganized. Of the original 86,000, only 7,000 to 8,000 had endured. They had covered a distance of roughly 9,600 kilometres in approximately 370 days.

Before the Long March, Mao's importance had been in decline. He had been sidelined because of bloody purges he'd carried out – purges which undermined local support; purges which left him out of the march's planning. However, his leadership during the march lent him considerable prestige, and once the faction was out of the woods, as it were, he began to close in on the position of Party leader. But this was by no means assured. Quarrelling, which had been present ever since the party's inception, and which had erupted during the march, erupted again and there was no shortage of individuals vying for top spot. Mao realized that in order to rise above them, he would have to utilize the Confucian paradigm, which is to say: he would have to become a teacher. So, with the aid of an expert, he began boning up on Marxist theory.

Just as Chiang Kai-shek's ascent was fuelled by a contingent of fiercely loyal supporters, so too was Mao's. As he sat in his cave acquainting himself with dialectical materialism, a group of followers

compiled and published a series of his writings. Posters were drawn up
too, and Mao was soon being touted as the new Confucius. Propaganda,
remember, was something Mao understood well, having learned it from
the Nationalists.

No sooner had Mao begun to gather a following than he started to
behave like a tyrant. He flew into rages. He took to lecturing people. And,
like his nemesis in Chongqing, his view was the only view. He was so
intimidating that few had the nerve to challenge him. At the same time,
he began to betray his peasant roots. While speaking one day, he searched
his groin for lice. In the midst of an interview, he took off his pants to
cool himself down.

During the war with the Japanese, Mao and his long marchers stayed
safe in their caves. Besides the brief Hundred Regiments Campaign of
1940, where Communists in central-northern China battled the Japanese
Army head on, the Reds did little more than pester the Japanese. Even
with their good intentions, they were too peripheral, undermanned, and ill
equipped to be anywhere near effective.

Under the protection of American dignitaries, Mao was flown to
Chongqing to meet with Chiang, but little came of the summit. Although
the United Front was rekindled, both sides promptly began double
dealing one another. When the Communist New Fourth Army attacked
and defeated a Nationalist army in the lower Yangtze, Chiang became
concerned. Communist presence in that area wasn't provided for under
the new pact and he asked that the force withdraw north, going so
far as to guarantee them safe passage. When they began to head east,
presumably to their old lair in Jiangxi, they were ambushed and as many
as 10,000 were killed. The majority of those captured were poisoned,
tortured, shot, or buried alive. The Japanese, as Chiang Kai-shek was fond
of saying, may have been a disease of the skin, but the Communists were
a disease of the heart.

In 1945, the Japanese guns fell silent, a shock to both the Communists
and the Nationalists as neither had had any knowledge of America's
intention to use the atomic bomb. They hadn't been privy to the
conference at Yalta, either, where Roosevelt, Churchill, and Stalin decided
that the Soviet Red Army ought to oversee the Japanese surrender in
Manchuria.

The Chinese Communists poured into the area, where they were
greeted by the Soviets and armed to the teeth with Japanese weaponry.
Nationalist troops were airlifted to the region by the Americans and large-
scale battles ensued, with Chiang's troops quickly gaining the upper hand.
By the summer of 1948, however, not only had the People's Liberation

Army recovered all of their lost territory, it was on the verge of taking all of Manchuria, thereby putting itself within easy striking range of all Nationalist-held cities north of the Yangtze.

Although Mao would take credit for the victory, it was Chiang who helped make it possible. Once the war with the Japanese was over, the dictator returned to his bad old ways. To be sure, he had never abandoned them. Chiang's post-war campaign was described by one American diplomat as, "one of the biggest carpetbagging operations in history."

When billions of dollars in aid began streaming into China from international relief agencies after the Japanese surrender, the Nationalists simply seized it. Auctions were held, and what wasn't moved in this manner was traded on the black market. Even blood plasma donated by the American Red Cross was diverted to drug stores and sold at sky-high prices. The Nationalists then embarked on a mission to penalize "collaborators." Virtually anyone who had survived the war with their property or wealth intact was accused of colluding with the enemy whereupon they were jailed and relieved of all possessions. People who lived in cities other than Chongqing were considered unpatriotic; writers and intellectuals were executed; students and professionals were required to take courses in Nationalist ideology. During this time, Chiang was committing 80 percent of the federal budget to military spending, i.e. operations against the Communists. With such a pitiable dearth of funds, the economy, already in a bad way, slumped even further.

The solution to the country's economic woes was found in the printing press, and before long the Chinese dollar was worth less than the paper it was printed on, as evidenced when a paper mill in Guangdong purchased hundreds of cases of the stuff to use it as raw material. Shops would readjust their prices several times a day, or even close early knowing that the next day their commodities could be sold for considerably more.

Rather than adopt measures to increase legitimate revenue or curb spending, Chiang's party unveiled a new currency, which was to be pegged to the US dollar. Under penalty of death, all citizens were required to forfeit any and all capital, including gold and silver, in exchange for the new bills. In cities like Shanghai, trucks were sent into affluent neighbourhoods and people were terrorized into compliance. Those found hoarding were publicly executed. The upshot was that virtually the entire middle class exchanged their life savings, out of either hope or fear, for a monetary unit that would prove to be as valueless as its forerunner within a single month.

Back on the front lines, support began to swing to the left, with one

Nationalist general after another defecting, often taking his entire division with him. Beijing was captured in January, 1949, and within six months virtually all of China was under Communist control. The Nationalists decamped to Taiwan.

On the crisp, clear morning of October 1, 1949, Mao Zedong appeared at a podium overlooking Tiananmen Square where he announced the inception of the People's Republic of China. Speaking in his soft, Hunan accent, he declared, "The Chinese people have stood up!" The banner-waving crowd went wild. "Long live the People's Republic of China!" they shouted. "Long live the Chinese Communist Party!" Every person present had been handpicked and instructed on what to say and do.

Mao and the other leaders took up residence in the regal, walled neighbourhood of Zhongnanhai, within the grounds of the old Forbidden City. A swimming pool was built for the chairman and he was reunited with his children. He lived with his fourth wife, Jiang Qing.

After nearly four decades of occupation and warfare, China lay in ruins. Yet, a program of national reconstruction wasn't embarked on until the end of the Korean War – nearly four years later. The conflict on the adjoining peninsula became Mao's chief obsession, and he ordered a million "volunteers" into North Korea to 'strengthen China's borders and protect its Communist ally.' "If we don't send troops," he said, "the reactionaries at home and abroad would be swollen with arrogance when the enemy troops press to the Yalu River border." Mao also believed that a mammoth 'Aid Korea, Resist America' campaign was just what China needed as it would serve to unite the country politically, thereby helping it to heal emotionally.

On the eve of China's intervention in Korea, an attaché to Kim Il-sung named Yu Song-chol was dispatched to Beijing to confer with China's leader and request assistance. Yu Song-chol wound up defecting to South Korea where he reported that after he had delivered his pitch to Mao, Mao "began by informing (him) that the Politburo had already decided to send volunteer forces to Korea." Mao then explained his military strategy to the Korean, and others in attendance, by using himself as a visual aid. He asked that his audience imagine that one of his legs was the American Army and the other the South Korean Army. The South Korean Army would be encircled and then decimated, Mao explained, hence rendering the American Army powerless. According to Mr. Yu, Mao then "raised one leg of his bulky body and hopped around on one foot" to bring the message home.

About the only "reconstruction" that China did undertake during the years of the Korean War involved land reform, which is to say the brutal seizure and redistribution of property. In reality, this was little more than the settling of old scores, a long-standing Chinese tradition. Mao later admitted that, between 1950 and 1952, 700,000 "bullies and evil gentry" were justly put to death. When a newspaper in Hong Kong put the number at 20 million, the chairman exploded, "How could we possibly kill twenty million!?"

It had been Mao's charisma and accessibility that had helped make him so popular. He had appeared unpretentious and sincere; the very antithesis of Chiang, a man who disdained the people. But after settling into Zhongnanhai, Mao became cloistered and left much of the administrative work to his subordinates. He spent his time chain smoking and lounging about in his bathrobe. He read copiously, delving ever deeper into China's imperial past. He kept erratic hours and was attended to by servants who dressed him, groomed him, and wiped him down with moist towels. Mao never bathed and he refused to brush his teeth, preferring instead to rinse them with green tea. The military leader, Peng Dehuai, once remarked, "The chairman's teeth look like they are coated with green paint." When Mao's dentist implored him to brush, Mao replied, "A tiger never brushes his teeth. Why are a tiger's teeth so sharp?"

Mao's tone was often liturgical, not to mention rife with factual errors, logical fallacies, and clichés. He believed that China's three greatest contributions to civilization were *Dream of the Red Chamber*, mahjong, and Chinese medicine, yet he didn't believe in Chinese medicine. He was also extremely vulgar. He made frequent analogies to farm animals and seems to have been obsessed with the words 'shit,' 'fuck,' and 'motherfucker.' He developed serious and lasting addictions to barbiturates and sleeping pills. In his biography of Mao Zedong, historian Jonathan Spence wonders aloud whether the Chinese leader wasn't "simple-minded."

Despite having banned dancing, the chairman held weekly dances to which young girls were always invited. Like every emperor, he believed that sex with virgins and young women would add to his years.[1] Mao retained his concubines for as long as they held his interest. Sometimes they were kept around for years; he would simply forbid them from leaving or marrying. Most, however, were honoured to serve him. They were even honoured when he infected them with disease. Mao was also

---

1   China's Yellow Emperor (2696-2598 BCE) is alleged to have become immortal after having made love to a thousand young virgins. The Yellow Emperor is regarded as the father of the Han race, that is: the man from whom all Chinese are descended.

apparently bisexual. A masseur once ran out on him after refusing his advances.

Eventually, Mao's policies and style of leadership came under fire from within the Party. His now-famous response was to let 'a hundred flowers bloom and a hundred schools of thought contend.' Party members and intellectuals were encouraged to come forth and let their criticisms be heard. After they had done so, Mao initiated a campaign of counter criticism, a movement which came to be called the anti-rightist campaign. The task of identifying rightists was assigned to work units, which were given a quota of five percent. This netted a half a million people, who were sent to labour camps to be reformed. Reform was simple: prisoners worked until their bodies broke. When that happened, it proved they *were* rightists. They were then forced to confess and betray others, whereupon they were murdered.[2]

In any event, it finally dawned on Mao that his policies were wanting, especially in the realm of land reform. Even with the seizures and the establishment of some 700,000 communes, private ownership was still the norm. This was in opposition to the chairman's vision of a truly pure form of socialism, a wish that slowly ripened into The Great Leap Forward.

Seen by Mao as a continuation of the Hundred Flowers Movement, The Great Leap Forward was meant to spawn a socialist utopia that would see the creation of 20,000 super-collectives. On these, people would wear the same clothes, receive the same state allowance, and eat free meals. By utilizing more effective farming methods, they would produce an overabundance of food, hence ending hunger. The excess would go to poor countries. The Chinese people wouldn't need machines to help them. Instead, they would engage in good old-fashioned physical labour, and, in doing so, would become healthy and happy to the extent where they would never have to see a doctor again. When Mao outlined this arcadian proposal at a Party meeting, there wasn't a single objection.

In addition to agriculture, the nation was to focus on steel production. The plan was to better the British in that area within 15 years. To accomplish this, and to circumvent the costs involved in constructing steel plants, the masses were ordered to make their own steel in their courtyards and fields using "mini-steel mills," or what the masses called "backyard furnaces." Suddenly, people everywhere took to the task of

---

2   The premise behind the Hundred Flowers Movement was hardly new. Emperor Qianlong once asked his subjects to donate books for a government-subsidized compilation project, after which he hunted down and executed those authors whose writing he found offensive.

producing steel – mainly through the use of household implements. Knives were melted into ingots, which were collected by the government and made into new knives. Because of excessive quotas, 60 million peasants were forced to leave their fields to attend their furnaces. Ultimately, people became so desperate for material to melt down that they began tearing apart their homes. With no cooking utensils, there was no option but to eat in rowdy, tension-filled public mess halls.

With the Great Leap Forward in full swing, Mao toured the country in his private train. He was overjoyed by the mass mobilization and wanted to see it close up. Wherever he went, he saw smiling, colourfully dressed peasants working fields that, according to reports, were yielding thousands of times what they had just a year before. He saw the new farming techniques being implemented. He saw hard-working local officials. He saw mini-steel mills stretching away to the horizon. He saw an extravagant show staged by the entire nation and directed by the Party secretaries in order to please an audience of one. Indeed, the furnaces did stretch away to the horizon, but only along Mao's route. The rice in the fields that he saw had been planted so close together that electric fans were set up to keep it from rotting.

In the fall of 1958, agricultural production reached an all-time high. By mid-December, the country was on the verge of famine. Rather than being dismissed, the preposterous statistics were documented and the peasants taxed accordingly. In order to pay, they had to hand over every last bit of grain they had. Ironically, most of it was then exported to the Soviet Union in order to cover the national debt. Many of the fields were simply never harvested as there were no tools to harvest them with. The exact number of those who died as a result isn't known, but the majority of academics and researchers put it at 30 million.

As for the steel ingots, nothing of significance was ever done with them. It was often enough to simply have them collected and weighed. When Mao visited a proper steel plant and discovered that the ingots were useless, he refused to halt their production as he didn't want to dampen people's spirits. The economy, which had only just begun to recover, was shattered, yet Mao's popularity soared. Just catching a glimpse of the leader was the highlight of many people's lives. Those fortunate enough to shake his hand wouldn't wash it for weeks. When news got around that someone had shaken his hand, friends and family would journey from far and wide to shake hands with them. But the madness was only beginning.

Mao refused to take blame for the Great Leap Forward. Instead, he called it fundamentally good.[3] Initially, he browbeat its detractors, but in the end, under mounting pressure, he agreed to a shift in policy. The peasants would be permitted to live and farm as they saw fit. Thereafter, Mao became increasingly detached from politics, preferring instead to ride around the country in his train. He liked to swim (i.e. float down rivers) and to stay in lavish guest houses, where he worked on adding to his longevity. Meanwhile, a movement began within the Party to have him retired and made a figurehead. The crevice that had existed in the Party for nearly a decade widened into a chasm.

On the one side were the moderates: people like Liu Shaoqi (chairman of the PRC from 1959 to 1968; Mao had stepped down, although he was still chairman of the Party), Peng Dehuai (the straight-talking military commander who had no time for political intrigue), and the capable Deng Xiaoping. On the opposite side were people like Lin Biao (another military leader) and Jiang Qing, who were convinced that the Party was riddled with so-called bad elements (revisionists, counter-revolutionaries, capitalist-roaders, rightists, Nationalist spies, etc.) and that they needed to be destroyed. Mao, who was fixated with the notion of continuous revolution, agreed. He felt that the nation's dampened socialist zeal could be reignited through the elimination of its class enemies. What China needed was another political crusade. But this crusade would be different from the others. It would be a "great upheaval," and Mao estimated that a thousand people would be dead when it was over. "Great chaos," he said, "will lead to great order. The cycle appears every seven or eight years. The demons and monsters will come out by themselves. Their class character dictates it." Mao saw the Great Proletarian Cultural Revolution as the third part in his trilogy of grand campaigns.

Initially, the "investigations" were conducted behind closed doors. They tended to involve torture and usually resulted in written confessions. Depending on your label, you might be sent to the countryside to shovel shit for the next eight years, or you might have your skull split open with an axe. It all depended on how the wind was blowing that day. Having said that, the interrogations took on a whole new dimension with the advent of the Red Guards, the militant student faction that sprang up after Mao urged the nation's pupils to attack their teachers. "To rebel is justified," declared the chairman. "Bombard the headquarters." Lin Biao and Jiang Qing added that the students ought to "wage civil war"

---

3   In fact, he called it 70 percent good and 30 percent bad, which is, of course, ironic given that that is precisely how the Party has appraised his own rule. Certainly, this is a formula. When Mao Zedong had Deng Xiaoping rehabilitated, he described his record as 70 percent good and 30 percent bad.

and "overthrow everything." Throughout China, the Red Guards began by sacking their local party headquarters. They were given free train rides to the countryside to do so. They were also given free transport to Beijing, where they were received by Mao at Tiananmen Square in the imperial tradition.

We now know that 2 million cadres alone were interrogated. Many committed suicide whereas many others most certainly wished they had. Liu Shaoqi was labelled a traitor and a scab and was publicly "struggled against" until he was psychologically shattered. He was then tossed in jail where he died in agony. When his 70-year-old body was retrieved, it was covered with vomit and diarrhea and there was a foot of hair on his head. Peng Dehuai, who had quietly tried to tell Mao that the Great Leap Forward was not working, was tortured and beaten until his organs were crushed and his spine splintered. Supposedly, he pounded the torture table so hard with his fists that the walls of his cell shook. Remarkably, he survived this ordeal, but died some eight years later of cancer. Deng Xiaoping survived, though his son was thrown from a window at Peking University and paralyzed from the waist down. Except for Mao, no one was immune from the charges, which could be as trifling as "having known foreigners." In *Nineteen Eighty-Four* (published in 1949), George Orwell writes, "The story really began in the middle sixties, the period of the great purges in which the original leaders of the Revolution were wiped out once and for all. By 1970 none of them was left, except Big Brother himself."

There were also massacres, like the one organized by the Public Security Bureau in Daxing County outside of Beijing. A writer by the name of Yu Luowen described the incident, which took place between August 27 and September 1, 1966. "Beating a person to death was a common scene. On Shatan Street, a group of male Red Guards tortured an old woman with (chains and belts) until she could not move anymore, and still a female Red Guard jumped on her body and stomped on her stomach. The old woman died on the scene…. Near Chongwenmeng, when the Red Guards searched the home of a landlord's wife (a lonely widow), they forced each neighbour to bring a pot of boiling water to the scene and they poured (it) down the old woman's collar until her body was cooked. Several days later, the old lady was found dead in (her) room, her body covered with maggots…. There were many different ways of killing, including beating to death with batons, cutting with sickles and strangling to death with ropes…. The way to kill babies was the most brutal: the killer stepped on one leg of a baby and pulled the other leg, tearing (it) in half."

The Cultural Revolution also bore witness to cannibalism, as documented in writer and political activist Zheng Yi's *Scarlet Memorial: Tales of Cannibalism in Modern China*. Within the book's covers, Zheng Yi describes how the movement, which appears to have started in Guangxi, developed in three stages. The translation is somewhat rudimentary.

"The first was the beginning stage when the terror was covert and gloomy. County annals documented a typical scene: at midnight, the killers tip-toed to find their victim and cut him open to remove his heart and liver. Because they were inexperienced and scared, they took his lung by mistake, then they had to go back again. Once they had cooked the heart and liver, some people brought liquor from home, some brought seasoning, and then all the killers ate the human organs in silence by the light of the oven fire.

"The second stage was the peak, when the terror became open and public. During this stage, veteran killers had gained experience in how to remove hearts and livers while the victim was still alive, and they taught others, refining their techniques to perfection. For example, when cutting open a living person, the killers only needed to cut a cross on the victim's belly, step on his body (if the victim was tied to a tree, the killers would bump the lower abdomen with the knee) and the heart and other organs would just fall out. The head killer was entitled to the heart, liver and genitals while others would take what was left. These grand, yet dreadful scenes were adorned with flying flags and slogans.

"The third stage was crazed. Cannibalism became a massive widespread movement. In Wuxian County, like wild dogs eating corpses during an endemic, people were madly eating other people. Often, victims were first 'publicly criticized,' which was always followed by killing, and then cannibalism. As soon as a victim fell to the ground, dead or alive, people took out the knives they had prepared and surrounded the victim, cutting any body part they could get hold of. At this stage, ordinary citizens were all involved in the cannibalism. The hurricane of 'class struggle' blew away any sense of sin and human nature from people's minds. Cannibalism spread like an epidemic and people enjoyed cannibalistic feasts. Any part of the human body was edible, including the heart, flesh, liver, kidneys, elbows, feet, and tendons. Human bodies were cooked in many different ways including boiling, steaming, stir-frying, baking, frying and barbecuing.... People drank liquor… and played games while eating human bodies. During the peak of this movement, even the cafeteria of the highest government organization, Wuxian County Revolutionary Committee, offered human dishes."[4]

---

4   China's best-loved literary classics contain abundant examples of carnage and cannibalism. In *Outlaws of the Marsh*, a character takes revenge on an enemy by tearing out his heart and liver. Later, he and his supporters dine on another victim – eating his flesh and drinking his blood. In *Romance of the Three Kingdoms*, a man kills his wife in order serve meat to the character Liu Bei, an act for which he is later rewarded.

At its height, Mao's Cultural Revolution was unadulterated insanity: an entire populace at each other's throats. Everything one said or did could have dire consequences. So much as nodding to a neighbour might yield a knock on the door in the middle of the night. Factories, offices, schools, and even hospitals were divided and then subdivided politically. The Red Guards began battling each other while Party leaders faced off in power struggles. Students criticized teachers and ridiculed their parents. People snitched on one another and China became a nation living under mob rule. As society fell to pieces, Mao's personality cult reached its zenith. Everyone had to wear a Mao button, carry his little red book, and recite his quotations – and his quotations were displayed everywhere. So was his portrait. It was mandatory in all homes, buses, trains, and even on bicycles. Millions began their day by praying to it and every intersection was wired with loudspeakers to broadcast his ideas. When the chairman gave some workers a few mangoes one day, they boiled them into a magical elixir and drank it in a mass ceremony. When an earthquake struck Yunnan, killing 15,000, the army was sent in; not to distribute food and medicine, but rather copies of *The Thoughts of Chairman Mao*.

In his early days as a Communist and Nationalist Party organizer, Mao had shown himself to be sharp-minded and meticulous. He compiled extremely detailed and helpful reports and was a shrewd negotiator. But there was no sign of that now. Apart from a few disparate statements in regard to what he was trying to accomplish ('to learn from the masses,' 'to eradicate old elements'), Mao, as historian Jonathan Spence has noted, "never wrote a single comprehensive analysis of what he intended to achieve by the Cultural Revolution, or of how he expected it to proceed." Yet, he believed until his dying day that it was never completed and hoped that young people would take it up after he had passed on.

Inevitably, the deeply disturbed Lin Biao and the psychopathic Jiang Qing had a falling out. Lin Biao devised a plot to assassinate the chairman and take over. When his scheme was discovered, he commandeered a plane that left for the Soviet Union, but crashed in Mongolia. Immediately thereafter, Mao became depressed and his health slipped and never recovered. When he was visited by Richard Nixon and Henry Kissinger just a short while later, he could hardly talk and needed help getting around. As it happened, Mao had Lou Gehrig's disease.

As the political turmoil he had unleashed continued to swirl all around him, Mao Zedong spent much of the last four years of his life bed-ridden and in a very bad way. His doctors, who worked tirelessly to help him, were accused of fabricating the diagnosis and much else. Certainly there was no such illness. And even if there were, how could someone as strong as the chairman get it? And who did they think they were fooling with all their fancy tubes and equipment? Administering poison was what they were likely doing. If their medicine was so helpful, why didn't they take it themselves?

After Mao succumbed, his personal physician, Li Zhishui, a man who served the chairman faithfully for 22 years and spoke to him nearly every day he was in power, was purged and sent to the countryside to do heavy labour. He was 57 years old. In his amazing 736-page memoir, *The Private Life of Chairman Mao*, he characterizes Mao as having been "devoid of human feeling, incapable of love, friendship, or warmth."

It is interesting that the jury is still out on Mao (all over China, you can find Western tourists buying Mao memorabilia). At the Second Plenum of the Eighth Party Congress on May 8, 1958, the Helmsman derided the First Emperor, asking, "How great was he really? He buried (or 'buried alive') only 460 Confucian scholars. We have buried 46,000.... You democrats scold us for being like the First Emperor. You are wrong. We are a hundred times worse than him. To the charge of being like the First Emperor – of being a dictator – we plead guilty. But we need to add to your accusations. They are not enough!"

Mao Zedong's reign was a weird mix of Qin Dynasty principles, pseudo-Marxist-Leninist theory, and that classic and ever-present Chinese theme: revenge. He wanted to show everyone who had ever slighted him – from the Changsha schoolmates who had laughed at his bumpkin ways to the intellectuals in Beijing who were too busy to talk to him – what he was capable of. Most of all, he wanted to punish the Chinese people for their backwardness and blind obedience. To do this, he used their Confucian values against them. "Rebel," decreed the emperor, and his subjects duly complied.

To many, Mao's rule, and the Cultural Revolution in particular, was an anomaly; as if China began to suffer from an acute psychosis that had never been present in imperial times and has since been cured by the forces of the free market. Nothing could be further from the truth. Mao's reign (just like Chiang's reign) simply highlighted cultural behaviour which has been in existence for millennia.

If we look at a random year in China – say, 1887 – we can see some of the events which were recorded. In Shanghai, a criminal was forced to stand in a cage without food or drink until he died. In Guangdong province, a crusade to eliminate "evil characters" resulted in 906 summary executions. In Guangzhou, the God of Plague was sighted and described as "a semihuman monster with huge feet." In Beijing, a Manchu prince fell ill and his doctor prescribed a course of river otter livers. At a murder trial on the Yangtze, a magistrate summoned the ghosts of the dead.

The madness is still there. To see it, just stand at any intersection and observe. Care to witness a struggle session? Attend a company meeting. Think that self-criticisms are a thing of the past? They are a regular part of education in China, beginning from elementary school. In Taiwan, students caught cheating must write signed confessions. School principals and directors employ student informants who report on both their classmates and their teachers. Snitches exist in companies, too. Lhasa is rife with them; you could be betrayed by a family member at any given moment. In the run up to Taiwanese presidential elections, workplaces become so politically divided that colleagues stop speaking to one another. So much as hugging your friend in public could have all kinds of ramifications, and perceived slights and offhand remarks could (and almost certainly will) come back to haunt you *years* down the road. Sloganeering is widely practised as is the labeling of "bad elements." In 2008, the Chinese government called the Dalai Lama "a devil with a human face and the heart of a beast." Previously, it branded him a "jackal," a "reactionary feudal serf-owner," a supporter of "rape, murder and child cannibalism," a "tool of Western anti-China forces," and much else. Chris Patten, the former governor of Hong Kong, was called a "serpent," a "strutting prostitute," and a "tango dancer."

The Great Leap Forward was no one-off either. Customarily, employees in Chinese companies are given impossible workloads resulting in copious mistakes and an almost systematic lack of quality. But because mistakes can be used as evidence, they are not reported. Objections or even constructive proposals are infrequent, too, as they can be interpreted as undermining one's superior. There is even a modern-day analogy for the metal ingots. In 2000, Taiwan's government launched a massive campaign dubbed "the Trash Revolution." Suddenly, there were recycling bins and notices in every business, school, and apartment block in the country. Six months later, it was discovered that the processing plants weren't recycling anything.

And this is what habitually gets glossed over in the China analysis: Chinese culture remains locked in a self-replicating state of chaos, myopia, inefficiency, intolerance, violence, and irrationality. It is, in a word, backward. Sun Yat-sen knew it. So did Mao Zedong, and Mao Zedong's thought process was described by his doctor as having been "prescientific." Mao, like many Chinese, believed that eating the ash from josh sticks might be beneficial to one's health. China may be embracing Western trends and technology, but so what? It's been doing that for more than a century. Culturally, and psychologically, it remains anchored to the distant past. It is highly ironic then, that it has suddenly become linked to, or touted as being, the future.

I took a rickshaw down the road to an avuncular Mao statue looming above a row of feathery pines. Sixty plus people were clustered in front of it, posing for a group picture. Some were grinning and giving the peace sign. Above the door of the Shaoshan Train Station, there hung the same portrait of the Great Leader that can be found at Tiananmen Square. There was another one of him announcing the inception of the People's Republic in the waiting area. I boarded the last train to Changsha, which chewed through the green, heat-hazed countryside in the receding daylight.

The next morning, I flew to Shenzhen, China's most prosperous city in addition to being one of its most soulless. An endless mass of recently built apartment blocks, office towers, and factory outlets, my guidebook described Shenzhen as being a "shopping mall for Hong Kong residents" with "formidable hordes of whores." In the 1980s, Shenzhen was one vast construction site with parallel roads leading into empty fields. Peasants would stream here dressed in their best clothes in search of work. That stopped when the government decreed that Chinese nationals could only enter Shenzhen with a special permit.

On this dreary day, going from Shenzhen to Hong Kong was like watching a grainy, black-and-white film turn to Technicolor. After clearing customs in a typically grungy and gaudy cement building, I walked across a glass-enclosed overpass spanning the Shenzhen River and saw that the menacing barbed-wire fence was on the Hong Kong side and angled out at the top toward China.

In Ma Jian's Red Dust, a memoir from the 1980s in which the Beijing native has a run-in with authorities and spends the next three years wandering around the country, he mentions, while in Shenzhen, that a tributary of the Pearl River was often mistaken for the Shenzhen River. He writes, "… visitors from the north always assume the opposite bank is Hong Kong. In the dead of night they swim to the other side, crawl up the beach, and have just enough time to shout 'I'm free at last!' before the police pounce and put them in handcuffs."

Hong Kong's metro was clean and fast and its passengers were quiet. It got more crowded with each stop and it was impossible not to notice how much more healthy and happy everyone looked. They smiled, they laughed, they read. Absent were the mask-like expressions, the aimless shuffles, the vacant gazes, the thousand-yard stares, and the mocking hellos. There were no placards ordering you to be civil, and no one smoked, pushed, spat, argued, or gawked. It was, in a word, normal.

I stayed in a guest house on Hong Kong Island run by a man named Tommy Hou. After spotting the 'Occupation' box on my completed guest form, he told me, with great enthusiasm and in that obsequious way Chinese people tend to take for normal, that he had great interest in the English language and hoped to master it one day. Later, I heard him tell a man from Malawi that he'd always wanted to visit that country, and just which part of South America was it in anyway?

The smog the following day was astonishing. I picked up a newspaper to find that the day before the city had seen some of the worst pollution on record. One district had witnessed hail as well as 1,550 lightning strikes in two hours.

I caught the subway to Lantau Island and flew back to Taiwan. Walking toward Immigration at Taipei's Chiang Kai-shek International Airport, I noticed a security detail walking next to me. I glanced over to see who they were protecting. It was Lien Chan, the stiff, sour-faced former Nationalist Party chairman (and present Chairman Emeritus of the Nationalist Party) who lost in both the 2000 and 2004 Taiwan presidential elections.[5] We had been on the same flight and were now walking side by side. This was his second visit to China since cross-strait visits were legalized in the 1980s, although he was born there.

In 2005, and in spite of not holding any post in the Taiwan government, Lien Chan met with Chinese president Hu Jintao in the most significant Communist-Nationalist exchange since Mao Zedong met with Chiang Kai-shek. Supporters from the Nationalist Party and its rival, the Democratic Progressive Party (DPP), drove to Taipei's airport to give Lien Chan a "send off," which took the form of a mêlée despite a 3,500-member police presence. On the news, I saw a wild-eyed man wearing a headband and brandishing a machete as well as an elderly fellow being kicked and stomped as he lay on the floor. People threw rocks and eggs and lit off firecrackers. Most of this occurred *inside* the airport. In China, Lien Chan attended a welcoming ceremony where schoolchildren chanted, "Grandfather Lien, you've come back. You've finally come back."

To the casual observer, Lien Chan's visits to China might seem like treason, but the truth is collusion is something of Nationalist Party tradition. During the war with Japan, the lines of communication between Chongqing and Tokyo were never down and the two sides even held secret meetings in Hong Kong. In point of fact, Chiang Kai-shek wanted the US to know about them (which it did) so as to guarantee financial

---

5   During the 2000 campaign, Lien Chan accused a rival candidate of positioning his family graves so as to interfere with his *fengshui*. Naturally, Lien Chan was forced to reposition his own graves.

support. Foreigners in Chongqing were staggered to see locals driving brand-new Japanese cars in between Japanese air raids.

During the taxi ride home, my garrulous driver asked me what I had thought of China.

"It's quite different from Taiwan," I remarked.

"*Dui a!*" he replied. "You got that right! It's *totally* different. Taiwanese are friendly. Chinese are con-artists. I should know. I lived in Guangzhou for nine years. The things I saw, you wouldn't believe. They see you coming and they think, 'I wonder how much money I can get out of this guy.' They're always scheming and conniving, and they hate Taiwanese people, you know – almost as much as they hate you foreigners. A lot of Taiwanese businessmen get kidnapped there. I'm telling you, those people would sell their friend for a single *yuan*. It's because of communism," he theorized. "Being controlled all the time has made their hearts black. You probably noticed that. It's easy to see." After a pause, he added, "Good food, though, and beautiful women. Did you try a massage?"

PART TWO

FROM A PLACE FOR DRYING FISHING NETS TO THE GATE OF THE GRAND MANSION

Chapter Fourteen

Back in the other China, I taught an uneventful semester of high school and enrolled in more Mandarin classes. Admittedly, the frustration I had experienced toward the end of my summer journey gave rise to feelings of trepidation in regard to returning to China, but such thoughts were rapidly supplanted by a desire to escape my daily routine. By the time the Chinese-New-Year break rolled around, I had conjured a healthy degree of eagerness to explore China's Dongbei, or Northeast. I would start my winter journey in Haerbin, the capital of Heilongjiang ["Black Dragon River"], a province that borders Russia to the north and the east. But first, I needed to buy some winter clothes, which I did at a store on Taipei's Zhongshan (Sun Yat-sen) Road. I purchased a wool hat, wool socks, a scarf, a hooded sweater, a good pair of gloves, and a sturdy set of boots. I already had a winter coat. There is something very strange about shopping for winter clothing in a subtropical climate. There is something even stranger about a Canadian being apprehensive about winter weather.

"The first condition of right thought," wrote T.S. Elliot, "is right sensation – the first condition of understanding a foreign country is to smell it…" The plane from Hong Kong to Haerbin smelled of heating oil. The flight attendants didn't greet the passengers, the seats were worn and stained, and people jostled and squabbled with each other in the aisle. I thought, 'Yup. Here we go.'

As it was, the flight was also cooking-hot. The old man seated next to me took off his shoes and socks and promptly fell asleep. I sweated and read through the list of prohibited items on the customs form. According to the first of 10 points, I wasn't to enter China with any of the following:

> Printed matter, films, photos, gramophone records, cinematographic films, loaded recording tapes/video-tapes, CDs (video & audio), storage media foromputers (sic), (and) articles which are detrimental to the political, economic, cultural and moral interests of China.

In *Nineteen Eighty-Four*, part of Winston Smith's job description
is to continually alter the state's "…newspapers… books, periodicals,
pamphlets, posters, leaflets, films, sound-tracks, cartoons, photographs…
(and) every kind of literature or documentation which might conceivably
hold any political or ideological significance."

When a flight attendant roused the old man next to me to say we
would be arriving soon, he sputtered and asked, "Arriving? Arriving
where?"

At the airport in Haerbin, a sign announced that it was 1:47 a.m. and
16 degrees below zero. I flipped open my guidebook to recheck the name
of the hotel I wanted to go to, and within seconds I was surrounded by
three ruddy-faced soldiers wearing olive overcoats and matching *shapkas*,
the Russian-style fur hats. They were just curious.

"How's it goin' fellas?" I asked in English.

"What language is that?" one asked another.

"It must be Russian," the other replied.

As I headed for the orange taxi lights on the other side of the glass
doors, I could see them in the reflection standing and staring after me.

A rotund ginger moon with a portion missing followed us along
a frigid corridor of insufficient lighting, leafless bushes, and dormant
apartment blocks. It was a very long drive.

I had booked a room at the Heavenly Pearl Hotel and was pleased to
note that it was fairly clean and relatively well appointed. I went to sleep
at three-thirty in the morning. At six in the morning, the phone rang. It
was a woman asking when my friends would be arriving and how many
of them to expect. I awoke for good sometime before noon.

Drawing back the curtain, I found I had a sweeping view of London,
1837. Smokestacks disgorging colossal columns of smoke retreated
into an aura of smog, as did outlines of low smudgy brick buildings. A
cacophony of horns ricocheted off walls, and at the intersection below I
counted three near accidents in a single minute.

I went outside and walked around in a mild state of awe. The
buildings were monotonous and utilitarian and everything – even the
snow – was layered in soot. Old men sold peanuts and sunflower seeds
from large metal pots, and steam billowed from dumpling stands.
Everyone was bundled up with little wisps of breath-steam wafting from
their fur-lined hoods. The hawkers rubbed their hands and stomped
their feet in an attempt to stay warm. I passed a man with long matted
hair sitting on concrete steps and talking to his shoes. I turned around
to see another halting traffic at an intersection with his horse-drawn
wagon; he was squinting against the wind, transporting a load of battered

cabbages. The flaps of his *shapka* angled out like wings. There was so much grime on the sidewalks that they had become treacherous and black. Improbably, many were plastered with stickers advertising *anmo* – massage. 'Want to Relax? Call this Number.'

I caught a taxi to a branch of the Bank of China that reminded me of an old rural Canadian ice-hockey arena. The cabbie was friendly and wanted to talk. I had to tune my ear to the dialect.

"Canada? Oh, it's my dream to immigrate to Canada. Well, actually," he clarified after a pause, "that's not entirely true. It's my dream to immigrate to any Western country."

"Why's that?" I asked.

"Why's that? Are you kidding me? Do you even have to ask that question? Look at this place. Look around. Look at all the people! China has too many people! It's a total mess!"

We passed by a Carrefour; the French department store had been built into an old Soviet-style wedding-cake building. Above the store's logo there hung the red and gold starred national emblem. "That used to be an exhibition hall," my driver stated disapprovingly. "Now, it's a department store from France. People think it's a big deal to go in there and push a cart around and fill it up with stuff – red wine and other foreign products. Cheese! I've never tasted anything so disgusting in my entire life. But it gives them face to buy those things. In China, we're trading in culture for capitalism."

We drove past a few large and decaying Jewish houses, with their dark, diminishing walls and their steep, retreating rooftops. If it had been overcast or twilight, the homes would have appeared medieval and slightly sinister, but the sunlight and blue skies exposed them as simply old and decrepit.

Starting from the late nineteenth century, Russian Jews, escaping the pogroms of their homeland, fled to and settled in Haerbin, bringing their culture and entrepreneurial acumen along with them. They ran a hospital, a theatre, bakeries, cafés, banks, publishing companies, newspapers, hotels, coal mines, and various other enterprises and industries, and were almost solely responsible for turning a few scribbles of dwellings along the Songhua River into a bold dot on the map. 'Haerbin' is derived from a Manchu word meaning "a place for drying fishing nets."

It is always claimed that the Jews were greatly respected by the Chinese and never harassed, but I didn't believe it. It seemed impossible to me that any group of outsiders could have lived in Haerbin or anywhere else in China for nearly five decades in perpetual peace, harmony, and security. It would have been more believable if it were said that there had been only a few incidents of friction, but it was always maintained that there were none. I knew that this was part of the pattern of disinformation that the Chinese are so fond of: "*All* Chinese people are law-abiding and patriotic," "*Everyone* supports this policy," "China has *never* invaded a foreign territory," etc., etc.

However, I didn't doubt that many everyday Chinese people liked or at least respected the Jews. I had read one account of a man who considered one Jewish family to have been his friends, and he became upset when he lost touch with them. To some Chinese, the Jews must have seemed a hazy reflection of themselves. To the more observant, the Semitic predilections toward industriousness, shrewdness, clannishness, and familial piety would have struck a chord. Perhaps even a few were able to identify with their persecution complex.

Although a handful of Haerbin's Jews lived out the rest of their lives here (the last one died in 1985), their general departure coincided with the Japanese arrival. Many fled to Shanghai only to be rounded up and put into ghettos along with other Jewish refugees. There, they were reduced to poverty and harassed by the guards of a Japanese officer who referred to himself as "King of the Jews." Altogether, there were 16,000 of them. Non-Jews were treated little better, mind you, and the Japanese, even with their racism and barbarism, ignored Nazi requests to exterminate them.

Any Haerbin Jews who didn't flee Hirohito's army faced nine months of oppressive post-war Soviet rule. An untold number was sent to the Gulag in Siberia, presumably for having fled persecution in the first place. After the torch was passed to the Chinese Communists, it appears that things became even worse. As historian Paul Johnson writes, in his *A History of the Jews*, "… it cannot be denied that the cataclysmic events of the twentieth century virtually destroyed dozens of Jewish communities, many of them ancient. The post-war Communist regime in China, for instance, imposed its own final solution on China's Jewish population, much of it a refugee exodus from Soviet Russia and Hitler's Europe, but including descendants of Jews who had been in China from the eighth century onwards. All fled or were driven out, Hong Kong alone, with about 1,000 Jews, and Singapore with 400, constituting lonely outposts in the Far East."

In 1958, Haerbin's Jewish cemetery (Guidebook: "… 583 tombstones engraved in Russian and Yiddish….") was actually "transferred" by the Communists from its location downtown to a spot outside the city. In Chinese culture (as with others), the ultimate sign of disrespect involves tampering with or desecrating the graves of one's ancestors. Yet, the oft-repeated message these days was that the Jewish people never had any problems in China and were always treated kindly and with a great deal of hospitality. As a rule of thumb in the Chinese universe, the more something is said, the more you can assume it to be untrue.

Recently, the local government had been spending millions on the restoration of buildings and synagogues along with the construction of a Jewish Museum in order to drum up tourism. This wasn't such a bad idea. Haerbin's old European architecture, its Ice Festival, and its relatively reduced amount of urban industrialization were really the only things it had going for it. 'Come see Haerbin's rich heritage!' 'The Chinese have always respected the Jewish people!'

I made my way to Central Street, which was lined with tawdry Chinese shops and fine Russian buildings. It was a clear, windy day and so cold that every 10 minutes or so I had to dart into a store to get warm. Most stores sold Russian dolls, headscarves, *shapkas*, pictures of Lenin, impossibly heavy watches, bottles of vodka, rubles, model tanks made from bullet casings, and lighters in the shape of double-barrel shotguns.

I also sought refuge in a bookstore, where I perused some chemical-scented volumes that had been deemed safe by the Party. Books in China are of such abysmal quality that to even call them books could be considered begging the question. That said, both Western and Chinese classics are available for as low as one dollar. I bought a few and stuffed them in my bag. Near a rack of locally produced English textbooks, a CD player was booming out a listening activity:

Woman: Eez these your handabaga?
Man: No, eet eezn't.
Woman: Eez these your waelleta?
Man: Yes, eet eez. Shank cue ferry much.

I walked to Stalin Park, located on the southern bank of the Songhua River, a waterway that had been the site of a major chemical spill a little over a year earlier. In the neighbouring province of Jilin, a petrochemical plant had exploded causing an 80-kilometre-long toxic slick to pass along the Songhua and through the middle of Haerbin, a city dependent on the river for its water supply. Upon learning of the disaster, city officials announced a water stoppage for reasons concerning maintenance. This led to widespread fear and conjecture. Was there an impending earthquake? Had terrorists filled the waterway with poison? People began panic-buying and camping outdoors. Eventually, the government came clean, but only after all the denial, disinformation, and poor decision-making it has become known for. Oddly, when I asked people about the spill, no one claimed to have any knowledge of it. But then, industrial tragedies, largely the result of neglect and corruption, have become commonplace in China's Northeast.

Planted by the Russians and Japanese, Manchuria's iron tree came to fruition under Mao after he visited a foreign-built steel mill in Shenyang and quietly realized that industry and agriculture were mutually exclusive. By the 1980s, the region accounted for 16 percent of China's industrial production, but had since become a colossal liability. The three provinces that comprise the Northeast, Heilongjiang, Jilin, and Liaoning had morphed into a checkerboard of aging and inefficient state-run factories manufacturing blanket-like air pollution, contaminated landscapes, urban poverty, squalid workers' barracks, derelict dorms, vacant warehouses, an unhealthy labour force (whose workers were lucky to make three dollars a day), and an unemployment rate of around 15 percent. Say the name of any city in the region to a Chinese person and it will be associated with an industry; Changchun – car manufacturing, Benxi – steel, Mudanjiang – rubber, Tumen – paper, Daqing – oil and gas, Tonghua – steel and coal, Qitaihe – coal, Jiamusi – coal, Fuxin – coal, and so on. Indeed, China produces and consumes more coal than any other country, and a staggering 80 percent of its electricity demands are met by coal-fired power plants. China is also the largest maker and consumer of steel, accounting for just under a third of the world's total.

Currently, the central government was attempting to revitalize the area through funding and privatization efforts, but widespread graft was seeing to it that growth was slow. A pervasive lack of business ethics had also scared away many foreign direct investors. Land deeds had been transferred without the relevant foreign partner's knowledge, new plants had gone up only for managers to siphon off funds and establish identical plants across town – and that was if the managers stuck around. There were several cases where they simply emptied the accounts and headed for the hills. Bank managers who allowed for the total-sum withdrawals headed for the hills with them. Foreign investors had discovered that attempting to remove corrupt managers often led to strikes and riots. Investigations on behalf of the country's anticorruption bureau were possible, but necessitated bribes.[1]

Stalin Park had all the trappings one might expect of a recreation area named after one of history's greatest mass murderers. There were few people, its concession stands were closed, and its grey trees were wired with speakers blaring dance music into the frigid wind.

---

1   China's culture of dishonesty in business (and beyond) has been excellently documented by Tim Clissold in his informative and entertaining book, *Mr. China*.

I'm a Barbie girl, in the Barbie world,
Life in plastic, it's fantastic,

I headed to Dali District, a zone marked by onion cupolas, tall arched windows, wrought-iron verandas, and determined spires. I stopped to admire the Church of St. Sophia, an imposing edifice composed of brick and topped with turrets and a forest green dome. Scores of pigeons rested on its many perches. On the ground, parents helped small, wobbly legged children to feed them. Above the building's lofty golden crosses, an ivory moon peered through a thin blue sky.

The interior – which featured some gorgeous paintings, including a *Last Supper* that had been done on a concave canvas and hung on the curved wall of the enormous dome – had been converted into a Chinese-themed museum. Photos from the early twentieth century showed ramshackle Chinese houses and squinting peasants selling ducks from coarse roadside stalls. A large sign explained their presence.

'We pay so much attention to historical pictures, because merely as fixed images of historic twinkling periods, they contain a wealth of messages and implications which will render the visitor in deep thoughts.'

A girl at the entranceway's souvenir shop asked me if I wanted to buy a change purse featuring an image of a large-breasted nymph wearing a taut T-shirt. Most of the souvenirs were adorned with cutesy characters or were just bits of plastic junk. A sound system played Whitney Houston's 'I Wanna Dance with Somebody (Who Loves Me)' too loudly. Undoubtedly, someone had realized that the Orthodox cathedral outshone anything the local people had ever constructed. After all, once you leave downtown, Haerbin is mainly a matter of cereal-box housing and grim industry. As a face-saving measure, the church had been Sinicized.

That evening, I partook in the Ice Festival, which is to say I strolled around Zhaolin Park and inspected a host of very big and very nice ice sculptures. I liked it very much, even though I had to constantly evade free-lance tour guides and people peddling DVDs of the very carvings I was looking at. If ever something didn't require an explanation, I reflected, it was a 12-metre-tall ice bunny.

In a nearby underpass, I spotted a poster warning pickpockets that their days were numbered. Two Chinese police officers bookended a man in handcuffs. The purse he had snatched was on a table in the foreground. The criminal, whose identity was partly obscured by a black line over the eyes, was not Chinese. He looked to be Uighur or perhaps Caucasian.

I felt like drinking, but settled for some CCTV (China Central Television) instead. The most interesting thing I could find was something called 'The Welfare Lottery.' I watched as two stone-faced, olive-clad soldiers plucked numbered-balls from a whirring machine and was asleep within minutes.

At seven the next morning, the phone rang. "Hello," a woman said. "Is this Mr. Chen?"

"No."

"Oh, so what's your name then?"

After breakfast in the hotel restaurant (fried rice, pickled cabbage, peanuts, and *mantou*, or steamed buns), I exited the building to find a taxi waiting there. The driver was a woman in her mid-forties. I told her I wanted to book a cab for the day. We agreed on a price and she took the highway across the river. She told me her name was Miss Xie, at which point she began hammering me with all the customary questions. They seldom vary.

"Oh, Canada!" she exclaimed. "I want to move there."

"Really? Why?"

"Because it's a good country," she answered.

"All right, but why is it a good country?" She didn't have an answer. "Let's put it this way," I said. "When you think of Canada, what do you think of?" At first she pretended not to understand me. Finally, she admitted that she couldn't think of anything. She only knew she wanted to move there.

I got tired of telling people I was Canadian, so I began to get inventive. I told them I was from the United States, Iceland, England, Ireland, Scotland, Wales, Norway, Sweden, Finland, France, Germany, the Netherlands, Italy, Greece, Australia, and New Zealand. If the person seemed genuinely interested or if we were going to spend any amount of time together, I told them the truth. But when I didn't, I almost always asked my interlocutor what they associated with my homeland and almost always they dithered. For Germany I once got Hitler and for Canada I twice got a physician turned missionary (who was also a devout communist) named Norman Bethune,[2] but that was all. When people asked me where I learned Chinese, I would often say that it was compulsory in my country

---

2   Norman Bethune is still something of a household name in China, mainly owing to an essay Mao penned called *In Memory of Norman Bethune*, which was required reading in elementary school during the Cultural Revolution. It is only recently that he has become widely known in his own country, but what Canadians don't know is how much Dr. Bethune despised capitalistic societies. He was, in fact, a fascinating figure.

("Everyone in Scotland is required to learn Mandarin now."), and never once did anybody express dismay.

"So, how long have you been driving a taxi?" I asked.

"Eight years."

"Ever get into an accident?" She was all over the road.

"No, and I don't think driving is dangerous."

All around us, cars were zigzagging and blasting their horns. I tried to put on the seat belt, but Miss Xie wouldn't have it. "You don't need to wear that," she said. "That's for driving fast. Now, we're driving slowly."

I asked her some more questions, including if she were married or not. She hesitated and stammered that she wasn't. I could tell she was lying. At the next red light, she asked if I were married. After I said 'no,' she examined my profile for a second too long.

The landscape became bleak. Fractured roads lined with black gnarled trees divided brown fields and grey bushes ornamented with pink and white trash. I knew that in orchards (especially in arid regions), the Chinese sometimes wrapped plants in plastic bags to create moisture, but there were no orchards here. There were factories, warehouses, scrap yards, garbage dumps, train tracks, suspension towers, and cottage-cheese-coloured apartment blocks with tiny windows; designed that way presumably so people couldn't jump out of them. The window panes had turned silver, at charitable variance with the leaden sky. There was no one – not a soul – outdoors. It was all incredibly glum.

Finally, we arrived where I had wanted to go: the Germ Warfare Base. A notice in the foyer announced that the Japanese had built the base in order to dominate Asia and "rule the rooster in the world." But, truly, this base – now a museum – was no laughing matter.

It was here where the Japanese developed and tested the effects of disease-carrying microbes, such as anthrax, cholera, bubonic plague, dysentery, and typhoid. The germs were tossed into water supplies, injected into food, and even dropped on cities like Shanghai and Ningbo by way of infected fleas, although this method had little effect. Conservative estimates put the germ-warfare death toll at just under 4 million. In total, it is believed that the Japanese killed some 19 million Chinese during their occupation. Of those killed by deadly microbes, it is thought that 4,000, including British, Russian, and American prisoners of war, were used as laboratory rats at this centre, known as Unit 731. None survived.

The museum was housed in a single structure, but the original compound consisted of 150 buildings and employed thousands of people. The Japanese told the locals that they were building a lumber mill and jokingly referred to their subjects as logs. The exhibits included haunting pictures and video-taped interviews with Japanese doctors that made my eyes water. "We used to perform live vivisections," one physician said. "We did about a thousand of them and never gave the patient anesthetic. We just cut them open and let them bleed. Their blood would run like tap water. Sometimes, subjects would wake up in the middle of the procedure. Once, a woman woke up and asked for her children."

Incredibly, the post-war trials conducted by both the Americans and the Russians were, by and large, mockeries of justice. Although some criminals were hung, others received light sentences. Others still were granted immunity in exchange for information.

As I was walking around, I noticed a herd of young *shapka*-wearing soldiers being led down a hallway by their commanding officer. As he passed by, he cast me a venomous glance. Most of his soldier boys, who looked absurd in their giant coats and caps, only grinned. I watched as they were indoctrinated inside one of the rooms. As the officer barked an explanation, one of his men laid on an enormous fart, which sent titters throughout the squad. The commander rolled up a thick stack of papers and smacked the offending soldier across the face. "Idiot!" he screamed, and the giggles and tee-hees ceased.

At the exit, there was a counter selling junky Russian souvenirs and toy helicopters. I tried to take a picture, but the two female cashiers wouldn't let me. "This is a history museum!" one yelled angrily. The other nodded and pointed toward the door. I walked around to the front of the building to see another truckload of soldiers arriving in order to be processed. My driver spotted me across the icy parking lot and drove over to pick me up.

"What is this place?" she demanded.

I tried to explain it to her, but had some trouble.

"World War Two?" she asked. "What's that?"

"Like the war with Japan," I said.

"Well, I know about the war with Japan, but I don't know about any world war."

We drove in silence for an hour to the Siberian Tiger Park, where we were greeted by a giant plastic tiger and a tourist shop where grinning vacationers were posing for photos by kneeling next to a stuffed tiger. The image was then manipulated by software to make it look as though it were a real tiger, something for the living room wall.

The park's stated aim was to eventually reintroduce the tigers back into the wild, yet tourists were encouraged to feed them. A menu had been posted on the ticket office in both Chinese and English.

'Price for Live Animals – domestic chicken 40 *yuan*, domestic duck 100 *yuan*, beef 10 *yuan*, pheasant 100 *yuan*, sheep 600 *yuan*, cattle 500 *yuan*.'

The birds were fed to the giant cats via special chutes that were built into minibuses that had caged-up windows. Larger meals, such as sheep, were delivered by a small blue dump truck that deposited the startled creature into the midst of several hungry predators. However, because no one on the bus I got on had splashed out for food, and because we were followed by no such truck, the park's inhabitants weren't at all interested in seeing us. The conditions in the park were appalling, but in terms of barbarity it paled in comparison to a zoo outside of Beijing, where live goats are hurled into a lions' den as families cheer and clap.

As I saw it, the Chinese affinity for animal cruelty stemmed from a denial, at least on some level, of their own animal nature.[3] Animals, even domestic ones, are often mysterious to the Chinese. What does it mean when a dog wags its tail, puts its ears back, and cautiously sniffs at your shoe? Who could say? In Taiwan, I had witnessed more than a few dog owners pick their beloved pets up by their paws and necks, and I had even seen people trying to reason with their animals. As for cruelty, there is no scarcity. I once watched a male bank teller kneel down and blow cigarette smoke into a street dog's face while two of his female colleagues looked on and laughed. On a television show, I saw a man at a farm walking around stomping pigs in the snouts with the heel of his boot. Each strike was matched by a *boi-oi-oing* sound effect. The studio audience was practically rolling in the aisles.

On the way back to Haerbin, it started to snow. After another spell of silence, Miss Xie asked me if I had received any phone calls at my hotel.

"Someone called this morning," I told her.

"Do you know why?"

"Massage?"

"That's right," she said. "*Special* massage. Was there a card on the night table?"

"Yes." There always was.

"Did you call the number?"

"No."

"Why not?"

"I don't know."

---

3   In 1931, the province of Hunan banned Lewis Carol's *Alice's Adventures in Wonderland* because animals were anthropomorphized, or endowed with human characteristics.

"But it's normal," she said. "Especially for you. You're a man. Don't you know that China has become *hen kaifang*?" she asked. "Very open."

She said this in a tone that was at once giddy, naughty, and energized, and I thought how sad it was that she equated rampant prostitution with sexual liberation.

It was apparent that Miss Xie had been doing some serious thinking while I was visiting the museum and tiger compound. "Why aren't you married?" she wanted to know. "What kind of women do you like?", "Am I your type?", "How long is a flight to Canada?", "How much for a ticket?", "Is it easy to get work there?", "When are you going to leave Haerbin?", "Would you like to have dinner before you go?" She gave me her card and asked me to call her. She smiled, revealing a mouth of black gums and brown teeth. I gave her a tip and said goodbye.

By eight o'clock that evening, Haerbin was in the midst of a snowstorm. It had been quite some time since I had seen one of those. I caught a taxi to the railway station to get the train that would take me to Dalian. In the waiting area, I was standing about a metre from the wall and reading when a man decided he was going use the space behind me to put down his bags. There was plenty of room, but he made up his mind to walk straight into me. This set me off.

"Why don't you watch where you're going!?" I shouted. Actually, I can't write what I shouted.

"Farger you!" the man yelled back, spinning around and raising a fist. A crowd of people stopped talking and glanced over and I recalled the book *River Town* by Peter Hessler, where he and his compatriot were joking around with a group of Sichuanese that suddenly turned on them. I ignored the man and the crowd and went back to reading my book. I heard him say, "*Shi laowai*," before he trod off. *Shi laowai* is a racial slur. It literally means "shitty foreigner."

I once watched a television program in Taiwan where a panel of Mandarin-speaking foreigners was asked what the most annoying thing about living there was. The majority said, 'The way people walk,' which totally mystified the host and the audience and required a great deal of nervous explanation. A guidebook I had read in Taiwan described the way local people walked as akin to a "falling-leaf pattern." What they forgot to mention is that leaves don't aim for you. Not only will people walk straight at you if they want to get by (even in an open area with no one else around), but they come to abrupt halts on flights of stairs, congregate at the tops and bottoms of stairs (not to mention entrances, exits, and elevator doors), and will occasionally – and this is not invention – stop in their tracks and begin to walk backwards. If you are passing through an open door while keeping to the right, there's a very good chance you'll be met by someone trying to push through the five centimetres of space between your right elbow and the door frame; never mind that it would only take a second to either let you go or step around to pass you on your left. In Mandarin, 'Go ahead,' or 'After you,' is *Ni xian zou*. It's seldom said. High school civics textbooks feature lessons on how to walk, how to form queues, how to use a public toilet, and so on and so forth. Public notices and service announcements do the same. Hardly anyone pays the slightest bit of attention.

My compartment was relatively clean, but oven-hot. I grabbed a warm beer from the trolley and watched out the window as Haerbin's flurry-streaked, snow-mantled buildings became squatter and sparser, yielding in the end to a line of vague outlines, fuzzy phosphorescent blots, and fat particles of angling snow.

Chapter Fifteen

We arrived at Dalian at six and I headed to the station's KFC to get some scones and a cup of tea. There was no snow here, and I watched as the rising sun panelled the city in its golden glow. Despite the early hour, the place was filled with people. A woman at the next table asked me in English if she could join me. She seemed interested in my guidebook.

"I can look?" she pidginized.

"Sure," I answered, and she picked it up and squinted.

She told me that her name was Miss Zhou and that she was a Chinese teacher at a Korean high school in the coastal city of Weihai in Shandong province. She had taken an overnight ferry to Dalian to visit her mother. She asked me where I had learned my Mandarin, so I told her. She then asked me if I were interested in Chinese literature and I said, "Somewhat," before explaining that I was more interested in Chinese history and culture.

"Well, I don't understand," she said. "If that's the case, why are you only travelling in China? Why don't you live here? Why would you choose to live in Taiwan?"

At first, I was surprised she said this. It was as though she were admitting that Taiwan wasn't part of China, but then I realized that it wasn't a political statement. She simply meant that it wasn't the "real China." It was just some trifling, uncultured appendage.

"Oh, I don't know," I began, but of course I did. "I live in Taipei, and Taipei is more... suitable for foreigners."

"What do you mean by that?" she asked, insulted.

"It's more... open," I said quietly. "More free."

She bristled, and I could tell what she was thinking: 'Those bastards. How did *they* manage to get away?' It was also evident, after I showed her the route I was taking (she had asked), that she envied me for being able to travel abroad. On her salary, that probably wasn't possible – even if the government granted her permission to leave the country. In Taiwan, even taxi drivers often volunteered that they'd visited two or three countries (usually Japan, Australia, and the United States), but in China I had learned not to ask people if they'd been overseas. In *The Private Life of Chairman Mao*, Li Zhishui writes, "Under the Nationalists, no matter how bad things got, it was always possible to run away. Under the Communists, there was nowhere to go."

"What's it like teaching Korean kids?" I asked.

"It isn't so bad," she replied. "They are very respectful, although sometimes their parents have unreasonable expectations. And I don't understand why they have so much money."

"What do you mean?"

"I mean Korean people. How is it that they have so much money? Chinese people don't have that much money, and Koreans only copied our culture and language..."

"But things are getting better in China, aren't they?"

"For some people," she said, bitterly.

I slept until noon and awoke to find that my watch had stopped. I found a nearby restaurant serving Taiwanese beef noodles and then set out to find the bus station. Using the petite map in my guidebook, I walked to where it should have been, but couldn't find it. I asked a woman at a newsstand and she said, "It's that way." Against my own better judgment, I asked for a clarification, and soon half the street was standing around me eavesdropping.

"I know where it is," said one old man. "It's that way."

"No, it isn't," a woman differed, and a debate began. One fellow led me by the arm away from the deliberating crowd only to – and I am not toying with hyperbole – point me to a row of potted trees. Yet another man led me down an alley to a parked van, and a woman guided me to the front door of the post office. Honest. I gave up and caught a taxi. It drove around the block and dropped me off 20 metres from the spot I had flagged it down. About 45 minutes later, a young woman walked me straight down the street to the station's ticket office. The grandmotherly woman behind the counter was the picture of kindness: she welcomed me to China, reminded me not to be late, and suggested I prepare a snack for the long journey.

A port city, Dalian was not a terribly cultural place, but it exuded a quietude and mild dignity that I found reasonably refreshing. Typically, there was more than a healthy dollop of pollution and construction and it was obviously ringed with industry, but it really was, as my guidebook said it was, "both bustling and relaxed, as if the entire population is on holiday – or shopping." It was a municipality of slopes and angled streets and probably the only city in China apart from Beijing that featured a focal point, the circular Zhongshan (Sun Yat-sen) Square. Cities in China were designed without town squares in order to deter crowds from gathering.

I caught a cab to the undulating Labour Park (the driver knew where it was), and strolled around for a bit. A miniature ski hill had been packed with artificial snow and some kids were receiving lessons, which was nice to see. The park, best-known for its jumbo-sized red and white soccer ball, was heavy with somnolent conifers and burgundy lanterns. My guidebook recommended taking the chairlift "up to the TV tower for an excellent view of the city," so I followed the cables to a ticket booth that was built into the first floor of small house.

"Closed?" I asked the man inside. He was smoking and tinkering with a radio.

"We're only open in the summer," he said.

"How can I get up to the tower?"

"Climb the hill."

I looked at the hill. "Can I take a cab there?"

"I don't know."

"Well, there must be a road that goes up there. Is there one on the far side?"

"I don't know," he said again, and went back to fiddling with his radio.

Next to a frozen lake, I spied a group of old men milling about a clutch of trees. I walked over to see what they were up to. They were inspecting pieces of paper, which had been thumb-tacked to the bark. "What are you doing?" I asked, and a man growled something I couldn't understand. In the northern accent, words often culminate in a heavy 'r' sound, instilling the language with a coarse, growling quality. It's as if the tip of everyone's tongue has been Superglued to the roof of their mouth. "You want to find a job?" I clarified.

"Nor," he said in English. "Rweer rwantr tor farndr ar girrr. Here, you rook."

I have (even more) trouble reading simplified characters, and reading handwriting is almost impossible for me. Finally, I found a message that had been typed and could make out every word, which caused the group of seniors to clap. 'Are you out there?' it asked. 'Do you love me? Would you marry me? Are you my ideal match? If so, please contact me at this number.'

"You talk like a southerner," one man commented.

"You should call," another suggested. I told him I would and pretended my glove was a phone, which brought the house down. "On second thought," I said. "I think I'll order a pizza. What's the address of this tree?" One fellow laughed so hard, I was worried we might have to call for an ambulance. They were an easy audience.

Back in the city, I found a repair shop and dropped off my watch. Surely, the two men working there were twins. They both wore slick comb-overs, large gold-rimmed glasses, yellowing lab coats camouflaged in grease, and shoes that matched their hair. They were very polite and said to come back in half an hour. I browsed around a department store (many people were ordering prefabricated bathrooms imported from Europe) and then returned to the shop. One of the technicians polished my timepiece with the bristles of a blackened toothbrush after which he wiped it with an oily rag and handed it to me.

I spent the rest of the day strolling around and popping into cafés to warm up and drink tea. It was frigid outside. At one such place, I was leaving when a well-dressed woman in her fifties blocked me and handed me a pamphlet.

"What's this for?" I asked.

"Massage," she replied.

A man carrying a tray of food yelled at her, "*Taitai*! Would you come on and sit down!?" *Taitai* means 'wife.'

I made my way to Zhongshan (Sun Yat-sen) Square and inspected the marble interior and antiquated décor of the Dalian Hotel, as seen in the movie *The Last Emperor*. I checked my e-mail in its business centre and tried to log on to the BBC and CNN, but neither could be accessed. Innocently, I asked the receptionist why this was and she told me she'd never heard of the BBC or CNN.

A giant TV screen had been attached to the hotel's roof so that people could gather and watch soccer matches. Just down the way was Friendship Square, a smaller traffic circle with a giant disco ball in its centre that continuously morphed into new colours. Buses with digitalized signs swooshed by this psychedelic mirror ball as skyscrapers with marching computer-generated characters loomed in the background. The air felt as though it were filled with iron filings and it was much too cold to be outside.

I ate at a Korean restaurant and then walked back to my hotel. On the front steps of another restaurant, a man had come outside to have a violent coughing fit. I paused and watched as he hacked and convulsed, hunching over with hands on knees. When he had finally finished, he straightened up and lit another cigarette.

The Chinese government is the largest producer of cigarettes in the world and China has the world's largest number of smoking-related deaths. Nearly three quarters of Chinese men smoke, and a comprehensive survey conducted by both Western and Chinese scientists found that two thirds of Chinese people believe smoking is all but harmless. Sixty percent believe it doesn't cause lung cancer while ninety-six percent think it bears no relation to heart disease. I learned this from an article I read from the BBC.

That night on CCTV, a panel of Chinese scientists was explaining how the Americans had never landed on the moon. Not only were the lunar missions faked, they said, but the Apollo program itself was largely a matter of science fiction. The shadows were all wrong. Where were the craters? And just look at that ridiculous flag – not moving even with solar winds. Their tone was both mocking and disdainful, as if even having to explain why this was the biggest fraud of all time insulted their very intelligence. It was announced that part two of the program would air the following evening and I made a mental note to remember to watch it. I reckoned I might be able to learn where Elvis had been hiding and why Princess Diana was murdered by Britain's secret service.

The next morning, I caught a cab to the bus station. I had taken a picture of it and the buildings all around it to show the cab driver – which I ended up having to do. I had a ticket to Dandong, a city northeast of Dalian and some 315 kilometres away. Before I boarded, I peered through a couple of low-quality newspapers and oily comic books at a newsstand and bought some *mantou*, or steamed buns, for the ride.

For the first hour, the woman behind me shrieked into her cell phone. Then she took out some sort of miniature portable karaoke device along with a songbook. I turned around and watched as she programmed the machine with a number, flipped to the corresponding page, and began to sing. No one asked her to stop. "Here," Orwell writes in *Nineteen Eighty-Four*, "were produced rubbishy newspapers containing almost nothing except sport, crime and astrology, sensational five-cent novelettes… and sentimental songs which were composed entirely by mechanical means…."

Under a broad clear sky we passed a procession of tawny furrowed fields, frozen creeks, skeletal-trees splotched with birds' nests, striding columns of transmission towers, and tiny white abodes flanked by greenhouses and collapsing storage sheds. As we drew upon Dandong, I saw high concrete buildings and low brick hovels with patchwork roofs and courtyards of lumber and laundry. On the sidewalks, wool-capped people with puffy coats and high cheekbones exchanged notes for sorry-looking vegetables resting on filthy quilts.

Dandong proper was surrounded by bunches of cardboard-cutout apartment blocks situated below snowy bluffs and naked trees. The downtown area was an eye-assaulting mishmash of splintered concrete, graffiti, and trash. Men huddled around flaming barrels and garbage pickers could be seen in the lanes, their carts piled high with scrap. There were whole rows of work-shed-like restaurants and tiled, dark-windowed drinking establishments. A sign on one said, 'Three Rivers Dog Meat Restaurant.' Next to this was the, 'Northeast Drinking House.' My first instinct was to jog to the railway station and catch the first train leaving.

By Chinese standards, Dandong is practically a village. It has a population of 643,000 and a downtown area that can be traversed in five minutes. My cabbie didn't know where the hotel was, the receptionist didn't know the name of the street the hotel was on, nor could she tell me where the local branch of the state-run China Travel Service was located. When I asked her if she could find out, she gave me a look that said, 'Oh, for pity's sake. Can't you see I'm trying to do some knitting here?'

"And which way is the river?" I wanted to know.

"What river?" she asked, but I was ready for this one.

"Do you mean to say there's more than one river in this town?"

"No," she muttered.

"Right. So obviously, I'm talking about the Yalu River, the one that runs between your country and another country and empties into the Yellow Sea. It can't be more than one kilometre from here. I'm guessing it's that way. Am I right?"

"I don't know," she answered, and started to pout.

"Well, thanks anyway," I said, and stepped into an afternoon so cold that my eyes hurt.

It brings me no joy to report this, but this is the way it is: it can seem that every single time you ask for information or the availability of some product or service in China you are supplied with an automatic negative response: 'No,' 'I don't know,' 'I'm not sure,' 'We don't have that,' 'We can't do that,' 'You can't do that,' 'It can't be helped,' 'It's out of our hands,' 'That's impossible,' 'You can't get there from here.' Because information is typically dispensed by higher-ups, everyday people have been habituated to neither seek nor disseminate it. The upshot, then, is that you are left to play *Twenty Questions* in order to find out where the nearest toilet is. Furthermore, the manner in which you are informed some basic commodity (bottled water) or service (internet access) is unobtainable is utterly astonishing: as if proprietors wouldn't dream of belittling themselves by offering it. You want a hand job? No problem. What's your room number? A fax machine? Here? In our state-licensed hotel? Just what, pray, do you take us for?

I caught a cab to the Museum to Commemorate US Aggression, perched on a hill overlooking the city. An airy, cavernous affair, the structure was a socialist leftover from Mao's 'Aid Korea, Resist America' campaign. It was even more preposterous than I had presumed.

Within its high-ceilinged lobby, there stood a towering statue of Mao conferring with Peng Dehuai (the general who had his organs crushed and spine snapped at Mao's behest), as well as two wall-sized messages denouncing the American Imperialists and their running dogs. Here is the short version:

'Despite warnings from both China and the global community, the Americans invaded North Korea with the aim of conquering China and then the entire world. At the point where the Americans "drew the flames of war toward the Yalu River," 2.9 million Chinese volunteers had little choice but to intervene in the interest of peace. The Americans were forced back to where they had started from, whereupon the amiable leaders of the Soviet Union persuaded them to accept a cease-fire.'

Of supplementary interest was an exhibit dedicated to Zhang Taofeng, "a famous sharpshooter who killed and injured 214 enemies with 442 bullets in 23 days" (without the aid of a scope no less), and another offering evidence of American war crimes, that is: the tattooing of Chinese prisoners with traditional Chinese characters. There was also an exhibit on germ warfare. Although it's widely agreed that germ warfare has not been used since WWII (although it has definitely been researched), China and North Korea claim that the United States conducted a widespread campaign in which they bombed the Communists repeatedly with infected snakes, crickets, and centipedes. Arguably, the oddest of the exhibits was a pedestal with a bronze rifle lying across its top and a bronze coat draped over part of the rifle. On top of the coat there sat a bronze scarf and a *shapka*. A placard read, in Chinese, Russian, Korean, and English, 'To the Most Loveable Person.' I took out my camera and snapped a photo.

"Do you understand?" asked a female staffer.

"Not really," I said.

"I didn't think so," she replied. "It's very deep. You foreigners wouldn't get it."

At the Germ Warfare Base, I had been treated pretty coolly by the staff. I had stopped in a stairwell to deal with a piece of dirt in my eye and had been ordered – vocally and repeatedly – not to loiter. But here, it wasn't just the staff that glowered at me; it was the guests. After all, I looked identical to the thugs from Wales and New Zealand who had been caught trying to sneak into their country's backdoor. People did a double-take when they saw me and it was impossible not to notice their mouths curving into frowns. When I entered one room, a man grabbed his son by the arm and hurriedly departed in an air of unconcealed disgust.

I got an opportunity to speak to one of the 1 million (not 2.9 million) volunteers the following summer in a suburb of Taipei. My co-worker's father-in-law, a cheerful native of Sichuan named Mr. Lin, agreed to tell me about his time spent fighting the Americans and their running dogs. At his house, I was greeted by a huge smile, a mountain of sliced pineapple, and all the Coca-Cola I could handle.

"I joined the army to get food," Mr. Lin began with a grin. "Food and clothes. We were so poor, you know, and always hungry. Then one day we were told we were being shipped off to the Northeast to fight the Americans. We didn't know why. We just did as we were told. We were marched across the Yalu into Korea, and soon we were under enemy fire. It was scary as hell! Half of us didn't even have rifles. Only the vanguard did, and we just picked up theirs after they fell. It was horrible – dead bodies everywhere, arms, legs, hands, heads…. My god! And the Americans, they had tanks and cannons and airplanes! Airplanes! My god! I'd never even seen an airplane in my whole life. There were shells exploding all around us – *boom*, *boom*, *boom*, *boom*, *boom*. It was really impressive!"

Rather than use tanks, the Chinese strategy had been to use overwhelming numbers of ground forces, the same strategy they later employed in Vietnam. Many of the men were hardened civil-war veterans. A US colonel by the name of Logan marvelled: "They could go on for days with a bag of rice, an army coat, ammo and a rifle." Nonetheless, it has been estimated that the Chinese lost hundreds of thousands of troops, if not a million. I asked Mr. Lin how he'd gotten captured.

"Well, I was with my company on the top of a mountain – Korea's full of mountains – and the Americans simply surrounded it. We didn't know any English, so we just marched down the slope with our hands up and said, "Hello!" He did an imitation and gave me a big smile.

"What was captivity like?"

"Oh, I remember the first night, we were so scared. The Americans were giving everyone these black cubes and we thought it was poison. Of course, it was chocolate. They ate some first to show us it was okay. To be honest, I never ate so well in all my life. We all thought the food was great. But then, after a year, we were transferred to Jeju Island, where we were guarded by the South Koreans. They hated us. We slept in tents with no bottoms. We slept on the ground! In the winter, too! And we were so deprived of food and drink that we would sometimes eat grass and drink from puddles." He smiled as he said this.

After the war was suspended, the Americans gave the captured Chinese a choice: they could go to either of the two Chinas.

"They built an office with a front door and two back doors," Mr. Lin explained. "If you chose the Republic of China, you went out one door, and if you chose the People's Republic of China, you went out the other. If your friend went out the other door, you never saw him again. I chose Taiwan over China because I knew who Chiang Kai-shek was. I didn't know Mao. To prove we would be loyal to Chiang, we all got tattooed with… well, here, let me show you."

He took off his T-shirt to reveal some faded tattoos, among them: *Zhonghua Minguo Wan Sui* (Long Live the Republic of China) and *San Min Zhu Yi* (the Three Principles of the People). They were all over his chest and arms. They looked like the tattoos the Americans had used to "brand" Chinese prisoners of war.

When the ex-Communist soldiers arrived in Taiwan, they tended to congregate in the same shabby communities. Mr. Lin's neighbourhood was full of old PLA soldiers. Initially, the locals despised them for their peculiar accents and "humble" origins, but the soldiers ended up assimilating by doing what Taiwanese people seem to have been born to do: work. Mr. Lin had spent his life collecting recyclable trash. He had done well for himself and owned three properties. He had owned a fourth one, but sold it so he could give his friend a loan. The friend had long since disappeared, but Mr. Lin wasn't all that concerned. Neither he nor his local wife had any education to speak of. She proudly informed me that she had never had any formal study. All of Mr. Lin's fingernails were black, and dirt was ground into his skin. He told me this was the first time he had ever spoken about that period in his life. No one had ever asked him about it before. When our interview was over, he grinned at me again and said, "More pineapple?"

Chiang Kai-shek had wanted to send troops to Korea, but at the time, the Americans were keeping him on a short leash. However, even though an ROC military victory was impossible, Chiang managed to score a political one. The reason Mr. Lin had been allowed to defect to Taiwan had to do with Beijing ditching its demand for Chinese prisoners of war to be repatriated. This was done in order to pave the way for the armistice, which Mao very much wanted. In order to encourage Chinese captives to make the right decision, Taipei sent them welcome letters and 14,000 gifts along with tutors to help them answer interview questions correctly. The upshot was that 14,000 out of 20,000 PLA soldiers (many of whom were either Sichuan peasants, like Mr. Lin, or former KMT soldiers) decamped to Taiwan on January, 23, 1953. To celebrate, the Nationalist government on Taiwan declared January 23 World Freedom Day.

Just as I was wondering how I was going to get back into town, a moss-uniformed woman approached me and said, "Your driver is waiting for you."

"My driver?" I asked. "I don't have a driver."

"Well, there's a taxi waiting for you outside and the guy driving it says he's your driver."

I opened a door and saw the snow-cordoned parking lot. It contained S-shaped wisps of white powder and a single crimson cab. In the driver's seat, a square-faced man with a crew cut was waving at me. I saw a rectangle of happy teeth. I walked over, got in the front seat, and told him the name of my hotel. He began driving and said, "How would you like to go to North Korea instead?"

"Just the hotel, please."

"Come on," he said. "We can cross *into* North Korea. Isn't that exciting? That's why you came here, isn't it? You wanted to see it. What are you going to do?" He hit me playfully on the arm. "Go to Yalu River Park and snap a few photos? You can't take a river tour because the river's frozen, but... *but*... you can go *into* North Korea. I will take you there."

This was Mr. Deng, a highly animated native of Dandong who spoke in a *bang-bang-rat-a-tat-tat* staccato. He would swat me on the arm with an outsized mitt before he wanted to tell me something, he frequently repeated himself, and he lit each cigarette off the butt of the last. His car was awash in peanut shells and empty cigarette packages. I agreed to let him take me for a drive. At first, I thought he might rob me, but the more he talked, the more I trusted him. He seemed knowledgeable and was clearly a character. He explained how, contrary to popular belief, the middle of the Yalu River did not constitute the Sino-Korea border. Rather, it did for a stretch, but once you drove out of town, the two countries were connected by land.

"Is that because the river has changed course?" I ventured.

"No, it's because no one in Dandong ever leaves Dandong to find out," he said. "People don't even know what street they work on. It's true. I've got friends who don't know what street they work on. Go ahead and ask the maids at your hotel what street it's located on. I bet they can't tell you."

My trust level shot way up. Mr. Deng lit up another smoke.

"I used to be a tour guide," he explained. "I took people on tours to Pyongyang, but I can make more driving a cab, and tourists are such idiots – like sheep."

"What's Pyongyang like?" I asked.

"Everything is fake. Even the pedestrians are fake. It's nutty."

We followed the river until it veered south. Under an inflated orange sun, I saw what he was talking about: a brand-new galvanized fence appeared and ran along the edge of the road.

"You see?" said Mr. Deng. "*That's* the border."

On the other side there was an endless field of high, corn-coloured grass. Occasionally, we caught a glimpse of barracks or the dark outline of a pair of North Korean soldiers.

"They're always patrolling," Mr. Deng explained. "In the summer, they dig and dig, and in the winter, they patrol and patrol. You wouldn't believe how many foxholes are over there. They need them because, in the summer, that grass is gone. You know why?" He swatted me again. "Because they eat it. They are *so* thin. You look at their faces and you think, 'My god, they're not even human.' Hey, grab that bag behind my seat, would you? Got it? Okay, now open it."

Inside were several stacks of 100-*won* bills. North Korean *won*. I read the *hangul* or Korean script at the top of a note. "The Central Bank of the Democratic People's Republic of Korea."

"You can read Korean?" Mr. Deng asked. "What are you, a spy?"

"No, no. I'm not a spy," I said. "I lived in South Korea for a couple of years."

"Oh, well that's what they pay me with," he explained. "I get them food and cigarettes and they pay me in *won*. Look!"

Some people had parked their minivan and were at the fence passing items to a pair of gaunt soldiers.

"They're South Koreans," Mr. Deng said. When I asked how he knew they weren't Chinese, he replied, "Just look at their clothes!"

We pulled over and got out and Mr. Deng scanned the grass. "Listen," he said. In the distance I could hear, just faintly, "*Pengyou, pengyou. Xiangyan. Dolla.*" "Friend, friend. Cigarettes. Dollars." Two black lines were cutting through the grass. They looked like pencil tips. Mr. Deng shouted the Chinese word for 'friend' and they shouted it back. We watched as the two lines blipped through the stalks. They were making their way toward the fence. "Come on," Mr. Deng said, after a minute. "I don't have anything to give them and it wouldn't be good if they saw me with you. Let's get out of here."

We drove on toward the setting sun. The sky, which had been a dusty yellowish grey, had since blossomed into a rosy pink causing the landscape to glow and give up crucial details. We passed some road workers and huts and old people bent under enormous bales of hay. Then, we rolled past a series of battered fishing boats and Mr. Deng explained that he wanted to visit his associate.

"You see how the boats have two flags?" he asked. "That's because we rent them out to the Koreans. In fact, we do a lot of trade with them." When I asked him what kind of trade, he replied, "All kinds."

We pulled into the driveway of a good-sized house that practically had its own dry dock in the backyard. Beyond the dozen or so fishing vessels lay an iced-over rivulet and beyond that sat the motionless ochre grass of North Korea. Mr. Deng's friend lived quite literally on the border. Several men were huddled about smoking. When they saw me, their jaws dropped slightly. Mr. Deng knocked on the door and a man dressed in black answered and motioned for us to follow him upstairs. His office was arctic and Spartan, although there was a large watercolour painting of a cherry blossom tree.

As Mr. Deng and his acquaintance talked shop, I flipped through a Hong Kong girlie magazine. My ears perked up when I heard Mr. Deng say, "… he was caught smuggling heroin and they shot him…" but the man in black didn't seem very concerned. Then he asked who I was. Mr. Deng explained.

"So you do business with North Koreans?" I said to him after a bit of small talk. Mr. Li was his name.

"Yeah, I rent them boats that they use for fishing. They also use them for transport. They bring me copper, nickel, silver – stuff like that – and I pay them with American dollars. Then, I turn around and sell at a nice profit. That's all they have over there, whatever they can get out of the ground."

"And you deal with them often?" I asked.

"Sure, two of them were here just an hour ago, two soldiers. They come all the time. They just appear out of the grass like ghosts. We also sell them food and cigarettes. And these," he added, holding up some more magazines. "So what business are you in?" he asked, leaning forward.

"I'm an English teacher," I said.

There was a pause after which he leaned back, chortled, and slapped his knee. Mr. Deng choked on his cigarette and the two of them looked at each other and laughed.

"No, really," Mr. Li said, becoming serious. "What do you do?"

Mr. Deng and Mr. Li told me that if I wanted to cross the line, I'd have to leave my wallet behind and "prepare a bit of cash" in case I got caught.

"They might pop out of the grass with their guns," Mr. Li explained. "But, don't worry. They won't shoot. We don't even think they give those kids bullets. Their only interest is money or goods. Just say, 'Dollars, dollars,' and show them the cash. They'll take it and run away."

I wound my scarf around my face, and started walking. I turned around to see Mr. Deng, Mr. Li, and the group of men watching after me, wafts of smoke rising above their wool hats. I toddled over the ice, marched up the small embankment, and strode over some matted-down grass. I was in North Korea. I scanned the horizon, but only saw sky and straw. Still. I wondered how many Western people had stolen into the Hermit Kingdom this way and concluded it couldn't have been many. It put me in an impossibly good mood.

On the drive back to Dandong, I stared toward Korea as Mr. Deng smoked and talked. A luminous full moon had been stitched into an indigo sky. It caused the Yalu to shimmer and stars to vie for attention. The once vivid expanse of golden grass was now the shade of milk tea. I spotted an enormous grey mound on the distant horizon and asked Mr. Deng if it were natural.

"No," he said. "That's a mine. That's all the dirt and rock they dug out of the ground. I told you, they are always digging, digging. The Koreans," he went on, "are such a problem. They won't listen to us and they won't listen to the Americans. They fired a missile over Japan and Kim Jong-il is even worse than his father Kim Il-sung. If a country can't feed itself, what kind of a country is that?"

Mr. Deng wanted to know how to say 'friend' in Korean, so I told him. He then wanted to know if I wanted to visit some Korean defectors working in a textiles factory the following morning (Dandong is full of textiles factories), but I told him I had other plans.

"They are my friends," he said. "I have friends from all over: Japan, America, South Africa.... People know me. People trust me. I'm not trying to cheat you."

I told him I knew that and that I thought he was honest. He seemed content with that; that and with the wad of cash I handed him.

I had dinner in one of the many restaurants lining Binjiang Road, the boulevard parallel to the river. The Korean side was a collection of smokestacks and mean little buildings. The Chinese side was a parade of brash, neon-predominant Korean eateries. I took a sip from my Yalu River Beer and thought, 'Not bad.' Then I noticed the label. 'Made with Pure Yalu River Water.'

Chapter Sixteen

The next morning, I walked through decrepitude and Manchurian winds to get to the bank. I half expected to see a film crew with a foreign correspondent holding a microphone saying, "As you can see behind me Peter, there has been some intense fighting here in the past few days…" Dandong's side streets were a virtual war zone. There were dilapidated huts, abandoned businesses, walls marked with spray paint, and hundreds of stickers advertising for massage. There was shattered glass, boarded-up windows, and the charred remains of sidewalk bonfires, customarily with the singed remnants of liquor bottles lying among the ash. Women peered out of brothels (at nine in the morning) and one tried to wave me into her apartment from her fire escape. I assumed she was a housewife.

The local branch of the Bank of China contained a dozen people offering unofficial exchange rates. "Yolo? Dolla?" they asked ("Euro? Dollars?"). As they paced back and forth hounding the queues, the security guards and tellers pretended not to notice.

At the bus station, I climbed aboard a minibus crammed with nattering, shoving, smoking peasants and crates of chickens. To ward off the bird smell, I wound my scarf around my nose and mouth. The seats had been upholstered with imitation leopard skin, there were footprints on the ceiling, and the radio was blasting a terrible, static-filled song by Bon Jovi. "A Russian!" one woman exclaimed and everyone agreed that I did indeed look like a Russian.

Out in the countryside, I got off the bus, bought a ticket, and walked down a long desolate road past a few simple farm houses with thatched roofs and granaries stacked with corn. This was Tiger Mountain Great Wall, the easternmost section of the legendary barrier, or so it was claimed. My guidebook said, "Unlike other sections of the wall, this one still sees comparatively few tourists." It was true. I only saw two (a pair of South Koreans) the entire day, and what a day it was: freezing but beautiful, with hardly a cloud in the sky.

The wall was the colour of charcoal, solidly built with brick and white lines of grout. It had parapets and was punctuated by regal towers. It snaked its way up Tiger Mountain, a jagged, snow-dusted protuberance of grey stone and dead leaves. The views from the mountain were magnetizing: the village below, the gleaming river, the copper-hued fields, and the distant range of white-brown Korean mountains. I climbed until I reached the summit, which offered a tower and respite from the whipping wind. After a rest, I walked down the other side, carefully gripping the rail in a vertiginous descent. At the foot of the mountain, there lay a snow-covered building made of the same slabs of stone as the wall. The path led to its roof, on which I made a circle of tracks in the virgin snow before descending the attached flight of stairs. Thick smoke was spewing from a pipe sticking out from one of the windows. This was the museum to which my ticket included a visit.

I walked around to its doorway and read the Chinese sign: 'The Ten Thousand *Li* Wall's Easternmost Starting Point.' In English, it said, 'It is the startin of easter the Great Wall.' Next to the door lay two sacks of coal. Without any more snow to silence my footsteps, a chained dog around the back began to bark insanely.

I opened the door, but it was dark, smoky, and silent inside. I crept through the blackness until I saw the outline of another door and pushed it open. It was the room with the pipe. In the haze, two young women were sipping tea next to a stove and staring at a fish tank. I got to within two metres of them before they noticed.

"*Ai ya!*" one yelled, jumping to her feet. "*Xiale wo yitiao!*" "You scared me to death!"

"Sorry," I said. "But why are you sitting in the smoke?"

"What do you mean?"

"What do I mean? It's bad for your health."

They laughed. "We'll sit further away from the stove next time," one said, and she smiled. Her teeth were the same colour as the fuel they were burning.

The other went to throw a switch and there was a shudder and a cicada-like buzz and then all the lights went on. The museum was cool and dusty, but otherwise mildly interesting. Supposedly, I was looking at Ming Dynasty weapons and armour, but who could say? A large map showed the wall meandering from Dandong's Tiger Mountain all the way across the country to Jiayuguan in Gansu province, but I knew that the notion of a single, stegosaurus-backed, tower-predominant stone wall gracefully rising and falling across two thirds of the Middle Kingdom was pure myth. For starters, there is no "wall," and there never has been.

Rather, there existed an entire series of *walls* (and gaps) built at different times, by different rulers, of different styles and materials, and for different reasons. The fragments cannot be linked together. Consequently, any statistics concerning "the wall" are meaningless. The section I had traversed on this day was probably younger than I was.

The original had been little more than a procession of pounded earth guarded by an occasional fort. More than five centuries ago, it was upgraded by the Ming into parallel rows of stakes that were filled with dirt (indeed, many of the walls were made of dirt), but it was never deemed important enough to be constructed of stone, as the walls north of Beijing were. The Tiger Mountain Great Wall was secluded and lovely, but it was also completely fake. The easternmost starting point of the Ming wall is called Old Dragon's Head and is situated hundreds of kilometres away in Shanhaiguan, where it rests its chin in the sea.

Not only were China's walls disparate and disconnected, but they were seldom successful in helping to repel invasions from nomadic hordes, which may have had something to do with the fact that they were never actually meant to do that. Rather, to reiterate, they were built for a whole host of reasons, chief among them a wish to restrict the movement of the Han so that they could be organized and taxed. The first wall was begun by the despotic First Emperor in order to impose his will and/or the will of the state. As soon as he got the people organized, he set about turning them into slaves. After his death, the trend continued. As historian John Man notes in his absorbing *The Great Wall*, "… ambitious leaders built walls as potentates built palaces, keeping their people cowed by displays of power and fearful of alien threats."

John Man goes on to note that the Chinese traded and interacted with the northern "barbarians" for centuries, but that these nomadic tribes were never all that barbarous, comparatively speaking. In fact, their cultures rivalled that of the Chinese in both refinement and sophistication. However, during times of war, the northerners did invade – at will. The walls were seldom effective at even slowing them down, let alone keeping them out. John Man also reminds us that those who were supposedly being kept out actually ruled China during the Yuan and Qing dynasties as the Mongols and the Manchus. In fact, they did so for 356 out of the last 728 years.

Although tempting to view the barrier(s) as an architectural wonder indicating consistency, supremacy, and a glorious past, they were, in reality, a muddled failure; a colossal waste of life and limb, successful only in maintaining prejudice and the subjugation of a populace. Until the installation of the People's Republic, the Chinese themselves saw the walls as symbols of either the tyrannical First Emperor or the discredited

Ming Dynasty, and they failed to fathom why foreign missionaries and envoys requested to see "it." John Man describes "the wall" as having been "ignored, reviled, abandoned, eroded, torn apart for building materials, and cut through to make roads." Within China, it was Mao who singularized the walls and raised "it" to its current status of national symbol. Communist troops had resisted the Japanese at some of its most remarkable stretches, such as Badaling and Shanhaiguan. Hence, it fit as an emblem of opposition, of keeping the shitty foreigner out.

It is from Europeans that non-Chinese derive the idea of a singular and great wall. Prior to the twentieth century, published accounts of the divide constituted little else than ornate passages of Victorian prose. A sketch of a section near Beijing (even though it was inaccurate and later embellished) closed the deal when it became widely circulated on the Continent. Consequently, the mythical image became seared into Western consciousness.

Incidentally, you cannot see any of the walls from space. They cannot even be seen from low orbit. That notion was championed in 1932 by Robert Ripley, creator of the cartoon *Believe it or Not!* Furthermore, although Richard Nixon did say, "I think that you would have to conclude that this is a great wall," reporters failed to complete the sentiment: "and it had to be built by a great people."

When I purchased my ticket, the clerk explained that a path next to the museum wound around the side of the mountain to the starting point. I had assumed that this would be a relative breeze, but I was mistaken. I spent quite a bit of time clambering up and down overhanging rock formations, searching for toe-holds, and wondering if anyone would find me if I happened to survive the 20-metre plummet to the ice below. The most harrowing part was a lengthy wooden suspension bridge that rocked wildly the instant I set foot on it. The chances of it giving way while I crossed it were slight, I knew, but that was all I could think about.

Back on the main road, I began to hitchhike. I waited for nearly two hours, although I didn't really mind. It was nice not to be moving even if it was cold. A donkey cart went by and then stopped. Its driver got off and set up a little stand to hawk skewered candied-fruit. Vehicles pulled over to buy some, but they were going in the opposite direction. Finally, a taxi picked me up, although he too was going in the opposite direction. He told me he'd turn around once he deposited the passenger in the front seat. The man had gone into town to buy a part for his car.

"Hey, he speaks Chinese," the passenger said. "Where do you think he's from?"

"I don't know," replied the driver. "Russia?"

"Yeah, probably Russia," said the passenger. "He looks Russian."

I told them I was from Canada.

"Did you hear that?" said the passenger. "He says he's Canadian. How old do you think he is?"

"I don't know," said the driver. "Thirty-five?"

"Yeah," the passenger said. "Probably thirty-five."

I told them I was indeed thirty-five.

"Did you hear that?" said the passenger. "He says he *is* thirty-five. What do you think he's doing here?"

After dropping the man off at his house and getting turned around, the cabbie laid into me with questions. But they were much more probing and thoughtful than the usual ones. He wanted to know how many countries I had been to and which ones. After I told him, he went off.

"Ten? You've been to ten countries? I'm older than you and haven't been anywhere. Do you want to know why I haven't been anywhere? Because I'm not allowed, and even if I were, I couldn't afford it. Not only that, but how would I communicate with anyone? If you asked me a question in English right now, I wouldn't have any idea what you were saying. Thanks to our government, we have no education. None. Unless you count patriotic education. What nonsense. Even people in India speak English, isn't that right?"

I mumbled that that was right.

"India! We're worse off than India! But then, I imagine we're worse off than a lot of countries. And look at those hills! No trees!"

It was true. All of the hills looked to have been draped in suede. From the tower on the top of Tiger Mountain I had only seen one tiny patch of pines on the Chinese side.

"They don't even cut down the trees in North Korea," the driver went on. "And do we plant new ones? Of course not. The future doesn't matter. All that matters is right now; money! Do people cut down all the trees in your country?"

"Well, they cut down quite a few, but then they usually replant them."

"That's what I'm talking about. And I bet that in your country, you don't have to worry about products and foodstuffs filled with toxins. Am I right?"

"For the most part," I said.

"Food in China is packed with shit – shit that will make you sick and kill you. I have a daughter, you know. I'm worried about what she eats. But what am I supposed to do? Complain? Yeah, right. The government would say, 'Well, that's very interesting, sir. Why don't we take a walk and talk about it? Please, tell us whatever it is that's on your mind.' And then they'd shoot me in the back of the neck. *Bang*! And that would be the end of that."

Orwell writes, "For a moment (Winston) was seized by a kind of hysteria. He began writing (in his diary) in a hurried untidy scrawl: *theyll shoot me i dont care theyll shoot me in the back of the neck i dont care down with big brother they always shoot you in the back of the neck I don't care down with big brother -------*"

CHAPTER SEVENTEEN

"*HOIRRRRRK!*" That was the first sound I heard in Beijing – the instant my toe touched the platform. "*HOIRRRRRK! PAA-CHU!*"

The night before, I had taken the overnight train from Dandong. I had walked past the battered Mao statue, had entered the dimly lit, grubby station, and had tried to buy chocolate in a convenience store, only to be proudly informed that they didn't sell it. I had woken early and sat on one of the fold-down seats in the corridor squinting into the sun and watching a post-apocalyptic slideshow of raped earth, dark hovels, pig pens, yard fires, piles of rubbish, and twisted, sooty trees. 'Certainly,' I kept thinking, 'people don't actually *live* in those buildings.'

I left Beijing's carnival-like main station and crossed the street to hail a cab. A man in front of me, who had judged correctly that a car had come much too close to him, walloped the offending vehicle with his suitcase. The car stopped. The driver got out. Angry words were exchanged and the two began to grapple and growl. A crowd gathered, a snarl of traffic honked accusatorily, and I recalled the last time I was here.

I was going into a restaurant when two families began to manhandle each other on the sidewalk. A full-scale battle eventuated. They rolled around on the ground, slapping, and spitting on each other. They carried the struggle into and out of a clothing store. They uncoupled and tried to catch their breath. Hands on knees, someone said, "Okay, that's it. It's over. Go home," and someone from the other clan said, "Okay, okay. You're right. It's finished. *Fuck your mother!*" and they clashed again, hands at throats. People came out of the alleys to watch and soon there were 70 or 80 people standing around. Finally, the two cliques disentangled and ran away. When I stepped into the restaurant, a girl was kneeling on the floor and watering a large plant. Its holder had holes around the bottom; the water had gone straight through and was in the process of inundating the floor. The girl had had a serene expression on her face, but the instant she saw me, she grimaced.

Beijing residents, or *Beijing ren*, are not the world's softest, most cuddly people. China, after all, represents the cultural centre of the universe, and Beijing represents the cultural centre of China. The capital's inhabitants are notoriously conceited, strident, aggressive, and obtuse. They seem to be in constant possession of a horseradish temper and appear to like nothing more than a good argument. They absolutely must have the last word, and they smoke and spit like there is no tomorrow. 'The emperor once lived here, don't you know? And who the hell do you think *you* are, anyway?'

But regardless of its bitter bearers of civilization, not to mention its sombreness, and intense police presence, I like Beijing. It has great restaurants, it's almost impossible to get lost, and it's authentic and full of history and culture. Much of that has been destroyed, mind you (Mao blocked a proposal for beautifying the city, saying he'd rather see it lined from end to end with smokestacks), but much remains. Wandering around Beijing in the dead of winter, one might wonder why the Chinese chose this harsh, windswept plain to establish their capital, but it wasn't the Chinese who did so. It was Kublai Khan in the year 1264.

I checked into a hotel in an alley off the central shopping boulevard of Wangfujing. It was flanked by restaurants and bordellos and came with a lumpy carpet, cardboard-like walls, and a view of brick and barbed wire. I emerged to find a man ladling shit from the sewer into a bucket, which he swung onto the back of his rickshaw to be delivered as fertilizer. I saw city workers putting down lines on the sidewalk with some thunderous, smoke-spewing contraption that shot out a foot of flame, and later I spotted a horse-drawn cart go by. An eight-lane, car-choked thoroughfare of glass towers and five-star hotels was only a ten-minute walk away. Beijing is a city where you can round a corner and enter a whole other world.

I spent a contented afternoon visiting the world of the *hutong,* or old neighbourhoods, near the man-made Shisha lakes, which once served as the finishing point for a series of canals built by the Mongolians. Within the constricted lanes of grey-walled single-storey courtyard houses, life was going on much as it had for the last hundred years, or so I imagined. If it had been warmer, I would have seen people outside knitting, playing chess, and drinking tea, but it was chilly and the greyish arteries were practically devoid of human activity. Except for the odd painted plank advertising laundry service, or an occasional empty tea house, the web of dwellings, lanterns, bicycles, rickshaws, and clutter was delightfully non-commercial. I could have walked around here for days.

The *hutong* are habitually described as "lacking in amenities," a polite way of saying they have no running water. Instead, most lanes possess a public toilet, which you can smell before you can see, although these don't have running water either. Roughly a fifth of *Beijing ren* reside in these neighbourhoods.

Alas, it is old ideas, not old buildings, that endure in the Chinese universe and structures spray-painted with the character *chai* had an appointment with the wrecking ball. "Demolish." But the Chinese were no Philistines. They would strive to ensure that the cultural legacy of the historical *hutong* lived on in construction site banners and placards throughout the city.

On one of the lakes, some men had chopped a rectangular hole in the ice and were swimming. One of them would steady himself, dive in, front crawl for 20 metres, touch the ice, swim back, be helped out, and then stand around shaking while encouraging the next fellow.

I retired to a tea house overlooking an arched bridge and a row of icicle-tipped trees as the sun turned the lake's surface to the hue of an unripened peach. The tea house played songs by Blondie and Abba, except they weren't really sung by Blondie or Abba. I headed back to the Drum Tower Subway Station where I found a bronze statue of a boy attempting to climb a wall. His pants were split open revealing the crack of his ass and a pair of dangling testicles. A sign in the station said, 'Please Wait for the Train in a Civilized Manner.'

The following day, I did some serious sightseeing starting with Tiananmen Square. I must say that it felt peculiar to be visiting the site of a massacre, or would have had a massacre actually occurred here. The sad fact is: the "Tiananmen Square Massacre" is a non-event; something the Western press got horribly wrong.

In the early hours of June 4, 1989, a massacre did occur in Beijing, but it happened a few kilometres west of the square – mainly on Changan Street [or "The Street of Eternal Peace"] and mainly involving workers and onlookers, not students. Workers had been targeting and lynching soldiers, burning and beating them to death. The army retaliated and the Chinese government admits that there were some 300 resultant fatalities; Western estimations make for a number somewhat higher. A few hours earlier, on the evening of June 3, the government carried out its crackdown on the student protestors at Tiananmen Square, but those still present when the army moved in were permitted to leave unscathed. In fact, there is no evidence to suggest that anyone died in Tiananmen Square that night, although people were most certainly killed when they tried to prevent the PLA from getting near the square, and at other times during the days to come. That there were no students mowed down in Tiananmen Square itself has been reported by both *The New York Times* and *The Washington Post*, but it has not been enough to rein in a myth hatched by false eyewitnesses and perpetuated by indolent reporters.

But if Western people don't know the truth about Tiananmen Square, neither do the Chinese. Many Chinese know that something called the June Fourth Incident occurred here, though they have little clue as to its true nature or conclusion. They have never seen the photo of the tank man, and this is because the government has worked tirelessly to expunge references to the incident.

Later, I caught up with the Canadian journalist and author of *Red China Blues*, Jan Wong, and asked her about what she had seen on June 4, 1989 from the balcony of her Beijing Hotel room. Mrs. Wong informed me that she had a clear view of two lines of soldiers standing guard just outside the square. A group of approximately fifty people assembled some distance away and began screaming at them: "Blood debts will be repaid with blood!" The group didn't approach, she said, and the soldiers took no action – until ordered to by their officers.

"The soldiers were in double formation," she explained, "one row kneeling in front of the other. They'd raise their rifles and the people would run away, but instead of running into a side street, they would run straight down Changan Street. The soldiers shot people in the back as they ran. This went on all day. The group would assemble again, start cursing at the soldiers, and the soldiers would fire on them when their officer gave the order."

"And how many times did that happen?" I asked, delicately. After all these years, I sensed that she still found it a bit difficult to discuss.

"About four of five."

"And how many people would you say were shot and killed during each of those four or five rounds?"

"Two or three," she said. "I just don't know why they didn't run into a lane. They didn't have to run straight down the boulevard. I think it was because they believed that the soldiers wouldn't do this, or couldn't believe they *were* doing this. They had been *so* brainwashed into believing the People's Liberation Army was their army."

"And you say this went on all day?"

"Until about four in the afternoon. Then it started to rain and the group left. I just thought it was so strange. They weren't afraid to die, but they didn't want to get wet."

But Beijing has always been a place of brutal suppression. The Forbidden City was so named (in English; it's called the Imperial Palace in Chinese) because just approaching its outer walls could result in the loss of one's head.

In Ma Jian's *Red Dust*, the author recollects attending one of Beijing's executions in the 1980s. "Public executions take place throughout China in the run-up to National Day," he writes. "I have grown up reading these death notices and have attended several executions. I once watched an army truck stop, a young man called Lu Zhongjian come out, handcuffed, and two soldiers escort him away. When he started to scream, they slung a metal wire over his mouth and tugged it back, slicing through his face. Then they kicked him to the ground and shot three bullets into his head. His legs flailed and his shoe flew into the air." Later, the writer comments on what a spectacle the events were. "When the police drive criminals to the execution ground, the streets fill with gawping crowds. Women are always treated the worst. In a Beijing suburb I saw a woman being dragged through the streets by a wire hooked between her vagina and anus, while the male prisoners were just hooked at the shoulder blades. When a woman steps before the firing squad, people point and whisper, 'Look, it's a woman.'"

Tiananmen Square was filled with hucksters ("Would you like to buy some precious Chinese art?"), tourists, kite-flyers, families, and plain-clothed police officers dressed as sightseers and country bumpkins. Their disguises were excellent: one glove missing, faces smeared with dirt; you would never know they were cops. The square's periphery was dotted with white police vans with the words 'Public Security' written in blue on their sides. I wondered if any of them were the so-called death vans, the mobile execution units that administer lethal injections.

I visited the Chairman Mao Mausoleum, arguably the only place in China where you will find an orderly and quiet queue. Indeed, the reverential hush exhibited by the Chinese as they shuffled past Mao's crystal crypt was extraordinary; if only they knew they were most likely paying homage to a wax dummy.

After Mao died, at 12:10 a.m., September 9, 1976, an emergency meeting was called by the Politburo to decide on what to do with his body. Despite a signed wish to be cremated, it was determined that he should be permanently preserved, as Lenin and Stalin had been. The problem, however, was that no one had the faintest idea how to do this. Asking the Soviets was out of the question, and the only thing a task force sent to Hanoi learned was that the technique was poorly understood – Ho Chi Minh's nose had rotted away and his beard had fallen off.

By default, the chore of figuring out the procedure fell to the man who had assumed he would be charged with Mao's murder: Dr. Li Zhishui. When he protested, it was reasonably suggested that the Institute of Arts and Crafts construct a wax model of the chairman, just in case. Meanwhile, two officials were dispatched to Madame Tussauds in London to report on the quality of dummies there. They concluded that the Chinese replica was superior. So did Dr. Li, who described it as "remarkably lifelike" and "uncannily like Mao Zedong."

This was a stroke of luck, as the twenty-two litres of formaldehyde injected into an artery in Mao's leg ("some six more than the formula called for") caused the Helmsman to bloat "… as round as a ball" with his neck widening to the breadth of his head, his ears sticking out at right angles, and formaldehyde seeping from his pores like sweat. While trying to massage his face and neck back to normal proportions, a piece of his cheek came off. Luckily, within a day, Mao's face looked fundamentally as it had, and his new bulk was concealed by the national flag.

In 1977, when the mausoleum was completed, both Maos, so to speak (along with jars containing his vital organs – proof that there had been no foul play), were moved to an underground vault. Every day, one of them is raised by an elevator to be viewed by foreigners and the faithful. Dr. Li wrote that the existence of the effigy was known to only a few. He doubted that even Jiang Qing was aware of it.

I passed on the Mao watches, commemorative plates, and tanks made out of bullet casings being hawked on the back steps, and walked to the Great Hall of the People, which a free-lance tour guide offered to steer me through, describing it as "China's parliament." (The Great Hall of the People is where the National People's Congress deliberates.) I didn't need a tour guide, however, and went there alone.

My visit to the cinder-block building was emblematic of sightseeing in China. You approach the front door only to be informed that the ticket office is located 200 metres away. Once there, you hand your money to a sour-faced individual who wordlessly tosses your coupon and change at you. After that, you proceed to the entrance only to be curtly informed by a scruffy-looking guard that you were supposed to check your belongings in at the ticket office. Back at the ticket office, at a counter located next to the one where you purchased your ticket, and staffed by the same people, you forfeit your bag in return for four decayed lumps of wood of various lengths and widths with flecks of green and yellow paint on them. As you stare dumbly at these, your bag is opened and its contents are revealed and itemized ("One booka! One sunglassa!"). After that, you go to the next counter and exchange your rotten wood for a tag. You show this and your ticket to the guard, who glares at you, mutters something under his breath, and spits a gob of phlegm a metre from your feet the instant you turn to leave. In the end, you realize you've done all this to inspect a building that is both austere and inelegant not to mention largely inaccessible.

Each of China's provinces (in addition to Taiwan) was represented here by a room that had been unimaginatively adorned with indigenous artifacts, such as rocks, paintings, and bronze vessels. Only a handful of them were open and they were dull in the extreme. I knew from my reading that Mao had set up temporary residence in Room 118, where he entertained the female attendants of the Fujian and Jiangxi rooms during the halcyon days of the Cultural Revolution, when it became impossible for him to hold weekly dances.

Next, it was on to the Forbidden City, which didn't seem nearly as interesting as it did the last time I was here. In part, this had to do with its being renovated, although I was even more disappointed to note that the audio tour featuring the voice of Roger Moore was no longer available. That was a shame as it had been both informative and entertaining, and surely that was the reason it was no longer available.

The Forbidden City housed 24 emperors of the Ming and Qing dynasties, but the new audio tour seemed to consist of little else than statistics regarding its construction materials and dimensions. I was about to switch it off when the female, accented voice urged me to examine a pair of gold vats, explaining that they had been "… filled with water and used to extinguish fires. I hope you notice the scrape marks reminding us of the bitter history. The unscrupulous Eight-Power Allied Forces robbed and plundered the Imperial Palace, not even leaving the gold on the urns…." I knew from my previous visit that the Summer Palace and the Military Museum contained placards bearing similar reminders.

I tried to visit the Museum of Chinese History and the Museum of the Revolution (lumped together in the same somnolent building), but they were closed for "revisions" and were heavily guarded. The history museum, I knew, dealt mainly with the nineteenth century and was heavy on such captions as "foreign aggression" and "colonial oppressors," or so a book I own said. Apparently, it featured an exhibit labelled 'Weapons used by the British against the Tibetan people,' which I very much wanted to see. The Museum of the Revolution was almost always closed (during the Cultural Revolution, it shut down for 12 years) as it was constantly required to reinvent the past so as to remain consistent with the present.

I also wanted to visit something called the Beijing Underground City, a complex of tunnels built beneath the streets of Beijing as a shelter from a nuclear attack from the Soviet Union. I showed three taxi drivers the name in Chinese, but they claimed not to know where it was.

I gave up and bought a huge piece of walnut fruitcake from a lone and gracious Muslim who had converted the back of his bicycle into a display for his product. It was really quite good and I ate it happily, trying not to think about where or how it had been made.

In the subway, I joined a crush of commuters and pushed my way onto a train. With an elbow in my ribs, another in my back, and a man with rotten teeth and feral hair smiling in my face, I realized that living in Taipei had made me commuter-train-spoiled. The metro I took to and from work every day was spotless and filled with people who regularly showered and were no strangers to hair brushes and hygienic products.

At Dongdan Subway Station, I got out and hailed a cab. After we had driven a couple of blocks, the driver confessed that he had no idea where the Temple of Heaven was. I would have thought he was lying, except he hadn't made any detours and looked genuinely perplexed. I showed him the name in Chinese, showed him a map, and even a photo from my guidebook, but he just flatlined and scratched his head. He had heard of it, he said, but didn't know where it was. Was he from Beijing? Of course he was. I reasoned that if he didn't know where the meeting point between Heaven and Earth existed, it wasn't worth the effort. I got out and walked back to my hotel.

The following day, I padded about the streets of Beijing, exploring this district and that without any real plan or focus. In a CD shop, I found a film or mini-series about the germ warfare centre, Unit 731. On its cover, in addition to the phrase 'Unit 731,' there were pictures of attractive, bound-and-gagged, half-naked women kneeling in front of Japanese soldiers and their national flag. In a bookstore, I bought a pair of weighty (and copied) linguistics textbooks for a mere $16 along with an inexpensive copy of the *Analects of Confucius*. I recalled my visit to this bookstore on my previous trip when I observed an American man pacing about and muttering to himself. As I pretended to read *Romance of the Three Kingdoms*, I watched as he picked up a book on Tibet, squatted, and scanned its preface. "You lie!" he yelled at the page. "Everything you say is a god-damned lie!" After he left, I picked up the book and read the same page. It began by claiming that in spite of what Western people may have been led to believe, Tibet has always been an inalienable part of the Chinese motherland.

I ate dinner at an ancient-looking restaurant with thick wooden doors. It also possessed staring patrons and Jackson Pollockesque stained walls, one which contained a giant photo of Mao Zedong. The owner hovered over my table and smilingly told me that her immigration application to Canada had been denied. I had told her I was Canadian. She had asked. She wanted to know if I had any *guanxi* with my government. 'Sure,' I thought, 'I'll ring up the Canadian High Commission first thing in the morning.' I suggested she try Australia.

"That one was denied, too," she said. "Next, I'm going to try New Zealand."

"What about Britain?"

"Well, maybe. But I think there are a lot of hooligans there, soccer hooligans. It's very dangerous."

"America?"

She made a face and said, "Too many black people."

So far, I had seen one television program about hooliganism in England and had heard one radio program about it. Of all the things they could have focused on regarding British culture and society. The message was obvious, and there was a message with everything. Rarely were you supplied with information just for the sake of it. As for black people, as long as none were around, Chinese people had no qualms about disparaging them.

Once, in Taiwan, I had a student whose major was agricultural science and whose dream it was to go to Africa and educate people on how to break the cycle of subsistence farming. At her college, there were several African students studying on scholarships, and she made no secret about how much she liked them and how handsome she thought the men were. Her classmates (all adults) openly ridiculed her, and she confided to me that her father was on the verge of disowning her. But she was a one-off. I had heard innumerable students denigrate blacks and any race deemed darker than themselves. In Taiwan, skin-whitening cream is wildly popular, so I imagined it would be in China, too, once people got money enough to waste on such quackery. Racism isn't exclusively a Chinese trait by any means, but the Chinese can be terribly racist. By making such a statement, the restaurant owner had betrayed what it is most bigots believe: that everyone else is just as prejudiced as they are.

I strolled through the *hutong* near my hotel where I enjoyed teleporting myself back in time and inspecting the courtyard houses and their gargantuan, soot-coated lanterns and imposing wooden doors. Whenever I approached a *gong ce*, or public toilet, I wound my scarf tightly over my mouth and nose and held my breath.

China's public toilets (which you usually have to pay for) are literally nauseating. Words like 'putrid' or 'foul' fail to convey the stench you are met with when you walk into one of them. They are little more than sheltered troughs.

Interestingly, the Chinese claim to have invented the toilet some 2,000 years ago in the province of Henan. They claim to have invented toilet paper a few decades later. But then, the Chinese claim to have invented quite a number of things, including beer, the fork, the kite, soccer, playing cards, the menu, the oar, the rudder, the ploughshare, the wheelbarrow, the toothbrush, and even the urn. Whenever it's determined that the Chinese discovered something (as with the toilet), it has a way of being reported by the Xinhua News Agency, the official press agency of the Chinese Communist Party, as though it were fact. Orwell writes "… Winston remembered, in the late 'fifties, it was only the helicopter that the Party claimed to have invented; a dozen years later… it was already claiming the aeroplane; one generation more, and it would be claiming the steam engine."

Young women behind glass doors giggled and waved as I passed by and two came out to call me in. I waved and smiled back and kept walking. The flesh is weak, as they say. But not that weak.

Traditionally, prostitutes in China have been seen as occupying the lowest rung of the Confucian ladder. In *Nineteen Eighty-Four*, Winston reflects that "it was easy enough, provided that you could avoid being caught in the act. The poorer quarters swarmed with women who were ready to sell themselves. Some could even be purchased for a bottle of gin…. Tacitly the Party was even inclined to encourage prostitution, as an outlet for instincts which could not be altogether suppressed. Mere debauchery did not matter so much, so long as it was furtive and joyless, and only involved the women of a submerged and despised class."

Wherever lanes intersected with boulevards, vendors in wool caps, mittens, and puffy coats sold candied fruit or yams from carts. Many shops featured the single Chinese character *chuan*, or 'kebab,' a vertical line skewering two rectangles. Other peddlers sold sketches and trinkets from blankets fitted with drawstrings; one sign of the police and all they need do was tug the strings and duck into a blurry alley.

I ambled down Wangfujing and was solicited for sex once every 50 metres or so. "Massage? Drinking beer? Sing song? Sexy girl?"

I stopped to admire St. Joseph's Cathedral, which looked quite striking at night: the moon hovering just above its matching, floodlit facade. A placard read, 'The cathedral is a mixture of classic Western architecture and traditional Chinese detailing.' This "detailing" could be found in a pair of door-frame epigrams. I heard two Englishmen scoff that it probably owed its local influence to having been built on the site of a duck shop. In point of fact, it was built on the site of a Jesuit missionary's residence.

I was going into a McDonald's to buy a cup of tea when a woman in a beige jacket and a matching beret began talking to me in fairly good English. She told me she was a school teacher and hoped I could take a moment to help her improve her language skills. "Maybe we can have a cup of tea," she said.

"I was just going in here to get one."

"I know a better place," she replied, and pointed to a building just across the street.

The tea house was on the fourth floor. When we entered, the woman, whose name was Miss Liang, said something to the waitress about a "special menu," assuming that I didn't understand. We were led to a Japanese-style room with a raised floor, a low table, cushions, pine walls, and a sliding pine door with opaque vanilla windows. Miss Liang scanned the list of items on the menu and then passed it to me, pointing to a kind of tea I'd never heard of before: *Gongfu cha*. In English, it said, 'Kung Fu Health Tea – 575 *yuan*.' That was about $73. I looked at the other teas. You couldn't get away with a pot for less than $25. I hadn't seen pots of tea anywhere else for more than $3.50, and even that was steep in China. Usually, they were a buck.

"It's very good for health," Miss Liang said.

I said, "I'll tell you what. If you just want to practise English, why don't we go back to McDonald's?"

She protested, but I stood up to leave. Just before we got to McDonald's, she pretended to get a call on her cell phone. She spoke to no one for a second or two before imparting that she had to go. Her friend needed her help. "Bye," I said, but she walked away without saying a word.

The next morning, I paid a visit to the nicely presented Lu Xun Museum, which I found at the end of a short lane lined with low-end restaurants and massage parlours. A woman sitting on her front steps couldn't tell me where the place was, never mind that Lu Xun (1881–1936) is a household name in China, generally considered the nation's finest modern-era writer, social critic, and intellectual. And, partly because he wrote in the vernacular and not in classical form, his works are wholly accessible and have been widely consumed by the masses.

As a young man, Lu Xun was deeply affected by his father's sickness and death along with the fact that traditional medicine failed to help him. In 1902, he set off for Japan to study Western medicine, but returned four years later in the belief that what China needed most was a cure for the illness afflicting its collective soul, something he aimed to treat through the mediums of the essay and the short story. He came to this decision after one of his professors gave a slideshow presentation that included images of an alleged Chinese spy about to be beheaded. Surrounding the condemned man stood a group of Chinese nationals who looked on in detached amusement. Lu Xun wrote that their facial expressions revealed "all too clearly that spiritually they were calloused and numb," and that they "had come to enjoy the spectacle."

In his first major work, *A Madman's Diary*, the author struck at Confucianism and feudal values believing that they had spawned a society of paranoiacs who believed their only choice in life was to cannibalize or be cannibalized. In his most popular story, *The True Story of Ah-Q*, Lu Xun tells the tale of an ignorant and hostile peasant who stumbles from one disaster to another while convincing himself that each of his catastrophes is in fact a conquest. The character, Ah-Q, embodies all that is wrong with Chinese society. He "used to be better off." He has "a very high opinion of himself and (looks) down on all the inhabitants of (his village of) Weizhuang." He views anything different as "ridiculous" and employs "cunning devices to get even with his enemies."

Whenever Ah-Q has a brush with another villager, he customarily gets his cue pulled until he admits that he's a beast. During one such altercation, he admits that he's an insect and walks away from the scene thinking that he's the 'number one self-belittler.' Cleverly, he removes the phrase 'self-belittler' thereby becoming 'number one.' Ah-Q asks, "Was not the highest successful candidate in the official examination also number one?"

Ah-Q's standing is temporarily lifted when he is beaten by Mr. Zhao, a man of stature. Mr. Zhao, who is younger than Ah-Q, quips that beating the old codger is like a son beating his father, and although the villagers are quite certain the two are not related, they lend Ah-Q a degree of prestige in the off chance they are. Eventually, everyone goes back to treating Ah-Q like a worm, so he decides to join a revolution, but is caught and quickly executed. When it comes time to sign the confession, he stammers that he doesn't know how to write. His captors suggest that he draw a circle instead, but because he is nervous and has never held a writing brush before, he ends up drawing what looks like a melon seed. Ah-Q soothes himself by thinking, 'Only idiots can make perfect circles.' After facing the firing squad the story closes with the following paragraph: "As for any discussion of the event, no question was raised in Weizhuang. Naturally all agreed that Ah-Q had been a bad man, the proof being that he had been shot; for if he had not been bad, how could he have been shot? But the consensus of opinion in town was unfavourable. Most people were dissatisfied, because shooting was not such a fine spectacle as a decapitation; and what a ridiculous culprit he had been too, to pass through so many streets without singing a single line from an opera. They had followed him for nothing."

A staunch leftist, Lu Xun was glorified after the Communist takeover, with Mao himself professing to be a lifelong admirer. Lu Xun never joined the Communist Party, however, and his ideas concerning socialism were the very antithesis of what would come to pass. He was, at heart, a humanist, and it is probably for that reason that his works were banned by the Nationalist Party in Taiwan until 1988. Lu Xun once compared warlord-dominated Nationalist China to syphilis: congenitally rotten and with "dark and confusing elements" in its blood vessels; a phenomenon requiring absolute purification.

Taking up Lu Xun's cause was another writer by the name of Bo Yang (1920–2008). A member of the Nationalist Party, Bo Yang fled to Taiwan in 1949 and was jailed there the following year for six months for having listened to Communist Party radio broadcasts. In the late 1960s, he was jailed again; this time for nine years and for satirizing Chiang Kai-shek's dictatorial rule in a comic strip. When his sentence expired, authorities refused to release him and only did so under pressure from Amnesty International, an organization whose Taiwan chapter the author later came to head. After his release, Bo Yang began working on a book called *The Ugly Chinaman and the Crisis of Chinese Culture*, which ended up selling hundreds of thousands of copies throughout East Asia; it was widely disseminated in China. He chose the title in order to "shock (his) compatriots into self-understanding."

Within the volume's covers, the author savages Chinese culture and society. He describes Chinese people as petty, mean, sloppy, filthy, muddleheaded, arrogant, narrow minded, loutish, irrational, apathetic, cruel, slavish, childish, maudlin, racist, judgmental, belligerent, neurotic, pusillanimous, crude, backward, brainless, cunning, duplicitous, argumentative, paranoid, and sadistic. He asserts that the Chinese are afraid of the truth, incapable of introspection or admitting error, and "addicted to bragging, lying (considered a virtue), equivocating and slander." They are "devoid of humanity and morality," "light years behind the Japanese and Koreans," unable to say 'sorry,' 'excuse me,' or 'thank you,' oblivious to the benefits of democracy, civility, generosity, co-operation, and the rule of law, "unaware of the backwardness of their own culture," stuck in the rut of feudal thinking, perpetually "stew(ing) in the juices of emotional provincialism," and – most damning of all, perhaps – "the same everywhere."

Far from being a rant or some tawdry slanderous tract, Bo Yang's thesis is concretized by a profusion of examples and elements customarily absent in Chinese argumentation: logic and objectivity. Bo Yang says that while Chinese people put on their best face for foreigners, they treat each other "with the gentility appropriate to a blitzkrieg." This is because they still suffer from what he calls the Ah-Q mentality. "Narrow-mindedness and intolerance," he writes, "result in an unbalanced personality constantly wavering between two extremes: chronic inferiority on the one hand, and overbearing arrogance on the other. A Chinese with an inferiority complex is a slave; a Chinese with a superiority complex is a tyrant. As individuals, Chinese lack self-respect. In the inferiority mode, they feel like a heap of dog shit, so the closer they get to influential people, the wider their smiles. In the arrogant mode, everyone else is a heap of dog shit. These radical swings in self-esteem make Chinese people imbalanced creatures with psychotic tendencies."

In another paragraph, he writes, "America is full of psychiatrists, but you will have a hard time finding one in China. The reason for this is, when you see a (shrink), you're supposed to tell the truth. Chinese people *never* tell the truth. If they've got a pain in their buttocks, they tell the doctor they've got an earache. If a woman doesn't like a particular man, she'll tell the psychiatrist the man doesn't like her. How can the doctor do a proper job if his patients always tell lies?"

Like Lu Xun, Bo Yang heaps the blame on all of these shortcomings on 5,000 years of traditional culture, which he compares to a virus (transmitted from one generation to the next), a soy paste vat (a large pot in which the sludgy sauce continues to accumulate and congeal), and a river filled with five millennia of historical detritus. Chinese history is not glorious at all, he argues, but rather thousands of years of uninterrupted warfare, carnage, violence, oppression, mayhem, and misery. When the author speaks of Chinese civilization, he puts that word in quotation marks. Chinese people have evolved only to the level of troglodytes, he conjectures. "On paper, China is a highly civilized country. In the flesh, however, Chinese people are barbarians."

Crucially, he points out that the Chinese notion of a harmonious society revolves around the quote-unquote harmonious relationship between inferiors and their superiors. Beyond that, harmony does not exist. Like most Chinese virtues, it is something that can only be found in books. Bo Yang goes on to argue that China has contributed virtually nothing to civilization. He characterizes the Cultural Revolution as entirely natural; the Tiananmen Square Incident as "back to normal."

Bo Yang urges Chinese people to stop living their lives for the sake of their ancestors and to embark upon independent thought. To achieve this, he says, they must abandon Confucianism (which he blames for turning the people into "dimwits"), break the fetters of traditional education (which he labels "anti-education"), and unreservedly embrace

Western civilization.

However, he casts serious doubt as to whether westernization can ever be attained in anything more than a superficial capacity. He notes that China believes it *is* westernizing when it stockpiles weapons and builds movie theatres. Bo Yang says, "As for the more fundamental aspects of (Western) culture, such as education, art, manners, social intercourse, and world view, not only is there no room for these things (in Chinese culture), one glance is enough to make the Ugly Chinaman itch uncomfortably all over." False pride, he asserts, prevents learning anything new. Besides, 'learning' to Chinese people is something strictly conceptual; they lack the fortitude and foresight to put theory into practice. Moreover, they believe they don't need to learn foreign ways. They know in their hearts that their civilization is not only superior to all others, but that it is indestructible. The Chinese hold that "China as a nation will never perish." The reason cited, says the writer, is its "ability to absorb and Sinicize other nations."

The Ugly Chinaman and the Crisis of Chinese Culture opens with a dialogue between a doctor and patient. The doctor regretfully informs the patient that he has tertiary tuberculosis. The patient contests the diagnosis to the point where he accuses the doctor of faking the test results and harming the motherland. The patient barks, "It's people like you who are to blame for China's problems. You make foreigners look down on Chinese people because you give them the idea that we're all suffering from TB. Traitors like you suck the blood of the Chinese people and kiss the arses of the barbarian devils. God will strike you dead! Imperial court guards! (*coughs*) Take him away!"

Nearly as interesting as Bo Yang's pronouncements are the 61 pages of challenges (more than a third of the book) that follow them. In this section, one academic after another contests the author's diagnosis, customarily by employing recrimination, elliptical reasoning, and jingoism. One such rebuttal, entitled, 'We Must Sweep Our Faults Under the Rug and Parade Our Virtues in Order Not to Demean Ourselves: Some Criticism and Suggestions for Bo Yang,' makes the case that the task of modernization belongs not to the West (which is now studying Chinese culture), or the Japanese (who merely copied Chinese culture), but instead to – traditional Chinese culture. By criticizing Chinese civilization, people only become the unworthy descendants of those who created it.

Taken together, the ideas for reform espoused by Sun Yat-sen, Lu Xun, and Bo Yang provide the prospectus that China must adhere to if it ever hopes to become a *truly* great nation. The changes which are occurring presently are totally unrelated.

After I left the Lu Xun Museum (which I thoroughly enjoyed), I headed back down the lane and saw a group of people arguing in front of a restaurant. A small mob of darkly clad onlookers had already gathered.

"The owner tried to cheat me!" a man was screaming repeatedly.

The owner, a woman, was screaming back. "You get out of here or I'll call the police!" She was trying to have a go at the customer, but was being held back by two men.

I spent most of my last day in Beijing at a bank. While sitting in a taxi during an impossible traffic jam, I had noticed an advertisement on the back of the passenger seat for a Roger Waters concert to be held in Shanghai the following week. Instantly, I turned into a teenager. I got the promoter's details from the internet and took them to a bank only to discover that they couldn't transfer funds to an "English" account. Not only could no one read it, but their computers couldn't process it. Two hours later, I returned with the Chinese details and watched two episodes of Mr. Bean. Once I got to the counter, it took another full hour to have the money remitted to the bank in Shanghai. I had to fill in five identical forms, which were stamped three times each and put into a folder that was casually tossed onto a jumble of other folders on a dusty desk in the corner. If even so much as a single character were misprinted, the staff informed me proudly, the transaction would not go through. Three employees were assigned to my case: one to operate the keyboard, one to control the mouse, and one to give instructions. By the time I finished, it was 10 minutes before closing time and the waiting area was still filled with people being placated by the television screen.

That evening, I met my American friend, Steven, for dinner. We had met on my previous visit to Beijing when we took the same course together. He lived in Beijing with his Chinese wife and had done so for many years. During our chat, I told him that I had forgotten how unfriendly and difficult *Beijing ren* could be.

"Well, the thing is," he said, topping up my glass with warm beer, "they're just peasants, but they don't know they're peasants. As for being unfriendly, yeah, they are, and it's getting worse. In the past couple of years, there's been inflation, but wages haven't gone up. People are angry. You can feel it. Oh, well," he concluded with a resigned shrug, "they're still friendlier than the French."

Chapter Eighteen

"A world away from China's drab industrial towns," my *China: Eyewitness Travel Guides* guidebook explains, "the breezy seaside city of Qingdao is a colourful port on the Shandong Peninsula. Known to foreign nationals as Tsingtao, where its namesake beer is brewed, pretty Qingdao's charms derive from its German textures, namely its cobbled streets, red roof tiles, distinctive stonework, and tree-lined avenues. Its German legacy dates from 1897, when the city came under German jurisdiction, but was returned to Chinese control in 1922. Modern-day Qingdao is a clean, entrepreneurial, and forward-thinking city, a kind of miniature Shanghai with high ambitions."

Other descriptions I had read of Qingdao were of similar stock. The coastal city was China's answer to Brighton or Nice; a place to get away from the megacities like Beijing and Shanghai and be reinvigorated by the ocean air. You could stroll along the beach and dream about retirement. You could go for a dip. You could dine on seafood and stare at the water, imagining what lay beyond. I thought Qingdao was dreadful. It wasn't a world away from China's drab industrial towns. On the contrary, it *was* a drab industrial town. There was nothing whatsoever to set it apart from the dirt and dreariness of any other Chinese metropolis save for its littoral nature and a few slender strips of sand that separated it from the indistinct Yellow Sea. As for its being miniature, it was home to 7.6 million people. My notes for Qingdao begin, 'First impression: slums, dirt, poverty. Qingdao – a desperate affair.'

The city was fringed by a cosmic assortment of rotting apartment blocks, hazy grey streets, pipe yards, construction pits, factories featuring stout brick smokestacks, and clotheslines strung from people's homes to telephone poles and tilted street signs. To avoid the clotheslines, pedestrians had to duck underneath them every few metres. On a single drive, I saw scores of beggars and a group of elderly people cooking over a bonfire on the sidewalk. The German architecture (which looked remarkable in the software-modified tourist posters) had either been neglected or converted into restaurants that were covered with large tattered banners and sign-boards. The houses looked as though they were inhabited by squatters. Mind you, this was the old section of town. Later, I passed through a much nicer district, one built on Korean *won* and industriousness. That said, in my three days in Qingdao, I never once saw anything I would have labelled pretty.

Forty minutes after I checked into a draughty hotel, I got a phone call from the receptionist saying that they needed to close. This was followed by a request to leave. I was given a full refund at the counter. My new hotel was located next to an elephantine construction pit. The old German railway station, minus its clock tower and tiny frontage, had been razed to build a new one in time for the Olympics. Qingdao was set to host the sailing competition.

It was morning and people were eating breakfast in garage-like *zao dian* (breakfast shops), consuming rice gruel, fried crullers, *mantou*, and soy milk. I made my way to a Lutheran church for no other reason than its having been listed in my guidebook as the city's third most appealing sight, after St. Michael's Catholic Church and a fish market. The old Protestant house of worship was minimalist and empty. The Catholic church, situated across the way from an establishment called WHAT RESTRAUNT, had but a single worshiper: a middle-aged woman preserved in cosmetics and blond hair-dye. She wore huge gold glasses and a cross around her neck, which she fingered during supplication.

The Roman Catholic Church is prohibited in China. People who consider themselves "Catholic" must practise at state-approved churches that reject the primacy of the Roman Pontiff and require their members to break communion with the Holy See. Many circumvent such restrictions by practising surreptitiously. Since the Communist takeover, missionaries have not been permitted in China, unless they obtain employment of a non-religious nature. Given China's experiences with imported religions, there are good reasons for this.

By the end of the nineteenth century, the 2,800 missionaries in China were doing a roaring trade. There were more than 700,000 Catholic converts and roughly 85,000 Protestant ones. So eager were the 850-plus priests and nuns to undermine local superstition that they would accept anyone into the fold. In densely populated, poverty-stricken Shandong, this meant the conversion of peasants who would agree to renounce ancestor worship and false idols in exchange for food, employment, and preferential treatment in matters of law and land claims; protection that was leveraged through foreign pressure, which is to say: intimidation.

Naturally, this didn't sit well with the remainder of the populace, who labelled the converts Rice Christians. Any two-bit thug could escape justice and gain immunity by claiming to have seen the light and by getting baptized, and Shandong was a province rife with two-bit thugs. In the last years of the nineteenth century, the region suffered from a chain of natural disasters, creating an economic crisis. Consequently, men turned to crime in order to survive, and it wasn't long before Shandong became a breeding ground for bandits, opium smugglers, charlatans, vagrants, opportunists, rival militias, and vigilante mobs. The unemployment of soldiers, who were discredited after the First Sino-Japanese War because of their ineffectiveness, and Grand Canal bargemen, who were made redundant by foreign-built steamships and locomotives, only added to the misery – and to the resentment. The people's woes were ascribed to the foreign devils. Not only had the "red-haired barbarians" worsened unemployment, but they had disrupted the great balance. Their church spires interfered with the *fengshui* and their railway and telegraph lines irritated the spirit world by cutting through ancient burial grounds.

In several provinces, including Shandong, there arose a wave of anti-Christian sentiment fuelled by the mass distribution of leaflets. The missionaries were accused of drugging and sodomizing their converts, castrating the men, and using the children's eyes as medicine, and it was also rumoured that their orphanages were in reality dining halls where fetuses and infants were cooked up and served as meals. The upshot of this campaign (and it never came to light who sponsored it) was that Christians and their outposts were attacked in every one of China's provinces. There were riots in Sichuan and a massacre occurred in Fujian. Officials in Beijing were forced to punish participants as they feared Western reprisal. An edict was announced stating that any further harassment of Christians, no matter whether foreign or native, would not be tolerated.

Figuratively, officials in Shandong had their hands tied, and were forced to watch as the number of "Rice Christians" continued to climb. Whole packs of criminals took up the Bible, realizing that the imperial edict meant imperial protection. Once having gained patronage, many of these converts embarked on crime sprees. Others used their security to provoke and harass rival factions.

Alarmed by the situation, the governor of Shandong, a capable and patriotic man, tacitly approved the persecution of Christians. There followed the deaths of two German missionaries, just the pretext Germany had been looking for as it desperately wanted a naval base in Shandong as well as mineral and railway rights. Beijing capitulated to all of Germany's demands. The Shandong governor was replaced and the Germans were granted a 99-year lease on Qingdao and the nearby Jiaozhou Bay.

This greatly upset a sect called the Iron Hats, whose plan was to eradicate the foreigners and restore China to its former glory. Clairvoyants were consulted and a time was set for an assault: July, 1900. Meanwhile, the natural disasters continued: the Yellow River surpassed its banks and a million people were made homeless. This was followed by a plague of locusts and a drought that caused two years of famine. Clearly, the gods were annoyed.

Against this backdrop there suddenly emerged a new breed of anti-Christian clique; a military faction that didn't require rigourous physical training or the tedious acquisition of martial arts. They called themselves the Society of Righteous and Harmonious Fists, and they stressed the magical elements of martial arts. Foreigners dubbed the movement Spirit Boxing.

All a Spirit Boxer need do was throw himself into a shamanistic trance aided by charms and incantations and by allowing himself to be possessed by his favourite superhero – taken from Chinese fiction or street plays. Achieving this hypnotic state could be learned in less than a week; perhaps an afternoon. During training, one apprentice was blown to bits by a cannonball whereas others failed to repel live rounds, but this only demonstrated that one must never be negligent in performing preparatory rituals. The prospect of becoming immortal *and* expelling foreigners proved too attractive to resist for many and the group's ranks swelled with drifters, criminals, farmers, charlatans, and the out-of-work.

The Spirit Boxers set their sights on Chinese Christians and soon a series of clashes ensued and a handful of foreigners lay dead. Naturally, the legations in the capital protested to the imperial court, which issued a set of Delphic statements that seemed to condone the actions. The foreigners were stunned, although they wouldn't have been had they known what was afoot in the Qing government.

China's imperial court was split down the middle. On the one side, there were the moderates, those who realized that conflict with the foreign powers could only result in disaster. They also realized, especially after the Boxers sacked the nearby city of Zhouzhou, where they harassed local officials and members of the gentry, that this new and popular peasant-sect would likely turn on the throne if threatened.

On the other side, there were the extremists, most of whom were affiliated with the Iron Hats. They saw the Boxers as useful: an anti-foreigner rabble unassociated with the government. The extremists, led by a man named Prince Duan, did what they could to keep the moderate Dowager Empress Cixi misinformed. When this ceased to work, they kept her as a virtual hostage, issuing edicts on her behalf.

As tensions flared in cities and areas outside of Beijing, members of the foreign legations became anxious. They called for weapons and reinforcements (which they got), and a fleet of naval vessels anchored itself in the waters off of Tianjin. The Boxers entered Beijing, although they were kept well away from the legations, which were sited just outside the Forbidden City. Eunuchs donned the Spirit Boxer uniform: a red headband and matching sash. People hired Boxers as private guards and burned incense to prove there were no Christians about. Those who owned foreign items, such as clocks and matches, hid them. But even with the show of support, the armed superstitionists flew into spastic fits and embarked on a three-day rampage.

Just south of the capital, the grandstand of the foreign-built Beijing Racecourse was burned to cinders, and members of the legations went by horseback to survey the damage. Not surprisingly, they discovered a group of Boxers. An Englishman named Bristow took out his pistol and shot one of them dead.

This detail was never passed on to the foreign press. In fact, a great deal was never passed on to the foreign press, and the stuff that was transmitted was routinely embroidered if not wholly fabricated. The intention was (and had been for some time) to mask foreign malevolence in China by characterizing the Chinese as a treacherous, hedonistic lot headed by a sexually deviant sorceress who dispatched of her enemies by feeding them poisonous cakes. In point of fact, Cixi was a simple, indecisive woman, often out of her intellectual element in matters of politics and intrigue. At home, she was the victim of a plot. Overseas, she was the victim of fraud, perpetrated by resident correspondent to the *Times*,[1] George Morrison, along with author Edmund Backhouse, the same men who would falsify accounts of the siege of the legations and the foreign occupation.

After the German minister beat, abducted, and then murdered a boy dressed as a Boxer, the moderates began to lose their footing. This caused riots in the area adjacent to the legations, although the legations themselves were never threatened. Nonetheless, the rioters, which did include Boxers, were fired upon the next day by the legations. A throng of angry Chinese tried to retaliate by storming the consular district, but they were thwarted by imperial soldiers. Cixi issued a lethal warning to

1   Now *The Times*, or what is sometimes referred to as the 'London Times' or 'The Times of London.'

anyone found even threatening foreigners and ordered that Boxer altars in the capital be dismantled. Still, the members of the legations continued to target Chinese, killing perhaps 100 of them.

Things went from bad to worse when George Morrison and others began marauding about in small cavalries rescuing Chinese Christians and shooting those who got in their way. With the situation nearing boiling point, Prince Duan hatched his plan. He presented Dowager Empress Cixi with a forged ultimatum, one he passed off as having come from the Allied commanders. It contained a list of excessive demands, ones the court could never submit to. Coincidentally, at the same time Prince Duan was goading the throne, the anchored admirals issued a genuine ultimatum, one tantamount to a declaration of war.

Positioned off the mouth of the Beihe River, the foreigners noticed that the four Chinese forts defending that waterway (two to the north and two to the south) were receiving reinforcements and readying torpedo tubes. Incredibly, it was decided to send the commander of the forts a demand for surrender. Just over an hour before the deadline, the Allied ships weighed anchor and advanced toward the coast. They were fired upon, of course. A six-hour battle ensued, with the Allies gaining the upper hand when their rounds landed in powder magazines in forts on both riverbanks. The Chinese were staggered by the explosions. Japanese, British, German, Russian, and French troops rushed ashore and secured the area. Brutally.

The following day, the Chinese attacked foreign settlements in Tianjin. Two days after that, Dowager Empress Cixi issued an edict to the effect that China and the Allied powers were now embroiled in a *de facto* state of war. She did not unilaterally declare war. That was a choreographed lie; the foreign admirals had issued their ultimatum without the knowledge or consent of their home governments.

There eventuated the legendary Siege of Peking, a 55-day episode of sheer terror for the foreigners holed up inside the legations. For nearly two months, the Christians and diplomats were surrounded by packs of wild-eyed, Oriental berserkers: possessed Boxers who fired at them incessantly. Certainly, if these savages were allowed to pass through the barricades, the women would be defiled and the men tortured. Every last one of them would be murdered. Or so it was believed. But it never happened that way.

The Boxers had been a tool of the extremists, but even the extremists could see what a menace they were. With a state of war now declared, the Spirit Boxers' services were no longer required. They were hastily disassembled and absorbed into the imperial guard, various militias,

and the police. The diehards were sent far out of the city to form the
first line of defence against the Allied Army. Those who refused to co-
operate were tracked down and executed. Thus, the legations were not
surrounded by Boxers, as the foreigners believed and reported, but rather
by an assortment of imperial regiments, each under the command of a
different general.

The most significant force was led by a General Ronglu, a moderate
who had been instructed by Dowager Empress Cixi to protect the
legations at all costs. His was a considerable predicament: while ensuring
that the legations were made safe, he also had to ensure that it appeared
as though he were blasting them to pieces. His solution was to use
firecrackers – hundreds of thousands of them. There was real firing,
mind you, but the majority of this occurred within the first two weeks
of the siege and most of the casualties were either marines shot at point-
blank range as they defended the barricades or Chinese Christians who
had been herded into the courtyard of an appropriated private residence.
Others died from ricochets as they casually strolled around. General
Ronglu's men did their best to fire at empty buildings or over rooftops.
However, the besieged never understood this (although a few of them
figured it out afterward) and chalked it up to a Chinese inability to take
proper aim. When the foreigners fired on the Chinese (and they shot
hundreds, including many they knew to be civilians), the Chinese were
naturally inclined to fire back. However, much of the siege passed in a
state of cease-fire. This the foreigners understood at the time, but when
the ordeal was over they refused to admit it. Instead, they claimed they
were ceaselessly attacked and heaped all the blame on Dowager Empress
Cixi and General Ronglu, the very people who tried to protect them.

Although it must have been harrowing to imagine what would have
happened had the combatants surrounding the legations gained entry,
in reality, and as long as one took cover during the sporadic clashes, the
siege arguably wasn't such an ordeal. There was no shortage of food, for
the Westerners at least – the Chinese Christians nearly starved to death.
Europeans and Americans spent their time consoled by champagne
and considerable stockpiles of liquor. During the protracted cease-fires,
the Germans drank schnapps and played the piano. The British played
cricket. What the foreigners fought more than anything was tedium.
Luckily for them, things were about to get very exciting.

Having seized the coastal forts, the Allies, 20,000-strong and
spearheaded by the Japanese, regrouped and advanced on the capital.
They met little resistance. As they closed in on the city, burning and
looting as they went, there occurred one final (and genuine) assault on

the legations. It was quelled, and by the time foreign forces arrived, they found that nearly all of the Chinese soldiers had fled. After gathering their wits, the foreigners – both the members of the legations and the rescuers – set about plundering the city, stealing whatever wasn't nailed down.

Figures such as George Morrison and Edmund Backhouse scoured Qing palaces, while common soldiers pillaged temples and ransacked shops and storage depots. The various nationalities divided the city into zones of control whereupon they had a field day. The Forbidden City, the Temple of Heaven, the Summer Palace, and a bevy of private residences were gutted. The Forbidden City was then occupied by the commander in chief of the Allies (and would remain occupied by the Allies for more than a year), the Temple of Heaven was turned into British military headquarters, and the Summer Palace was sacked and then set alight. Missionaries didn't do too badly either, moving into the mansions of the aristocracy. Auctions were held and precious works of art left China by the boatload, making their way to museums and private collections around the globe.

Cixi and her court fled to Xian, where they were forced to sign the Boxer Protocol, by which they were compelled to erect monuments to the dead foreigners, outlaw imperial examinations in cities where the massacre of foreigners had taken place, outlaw the importation of weapons for two years, put to death any leading Boxer supporters, and pay an indemnity: nearly twice what the state earned in a year.

Of course, at this point, the foreigners were free to carry out their own punitive measures, or sit back and watch as others did it for them. The fatso general, Yuan Shikai (the walrus-mustached warlord who later sent Sun Yat-sen on his fool's errand of heading the national railway), killed more than 40,000 "Boxers" in order to curry favour with the Americans and British and to strike fear into the hearts of the Chinese. The foreigners themselves committed all sorts of atrocities. Women threw themselves down wells to escape being raped and scores of frightened Chinese committed suicide. The invaders went well beyond scraping the gold off vats.

I know most of this from having read Sterling Seagrave. When it comes to Chinese history, there are several scholarly authors, but there is no one more adept at bringing the subject to life. *The Soong Dynasty* and *Dragon Lady*, two riveting accounts of China during the late nineteenth and early twentieth century, are handbooks for any China hand.

Near a slope in Qingdao, where the Germans used to play golf, I came across a government notice board filled with execution announcements: pictures of handcuffed individuals flanked by guards in sunglasses. One claimed the guilty party was a smuggler. A separate photo displayed the contraband: a treasure chest filled with gold coins. It looked like a clip art image that you'd find in Microsoft Office. Two girls in their early twenties were looking at the notices and laughing. I began with some small talk before asking their opinions of the death penalty.

"Sure it's a good thing," one replied. The other nodded.

"But how do you know they're really guilty?" I asked. I knew from having read *The Christian Science Monitor* that Chinese courts had a conviction rate of between 95 and 98 percent.

"Because the court found them guilty," the other answered incredulously, and I thought of the line from *The True Story of Ah-Q*: "Naturally all agreed that Ah-Q had been a bad man, the proof being that he had been shot; for if he had not been bad, how could he have been shot?"

"What if the court made a mistake?" I asked, and gauged from their expressions that I should never have brought the subject up.

The men in the photos probably were guilty, but there was always the chance they weren't. They could have fallen afoul of some powerful official (who didn't get his cut, say), or the proceedings might have been a show trial (substituting, for example, a petty criminal for a big-time smuggler) to frighten would-be smugglers or prove to the fickle masses that the government was clamping down on crime. In such a system, how could one ever hope to determine what the truth was?

At a nearby police station, there were more notice boards, but these contained posters of cutesy cartoon characters driving cars. One car was flying over a line of others while pedestrians looked on in cutesy disapproval. 'Drive in a Civilized Manner,' they read.

I spent the following afternoon climbing a sizeable hill that offered a sweeping view of the entire city: compressed apartment blocks for as far as the eye could see. Many of them were the same sort of grey, featureless cuboids that you see everywhere in northern China (in the south, it is always tiles and bars) only they had been outfitted with Bavarian-style roofs. The effect was absurd, like pigs sporting berets.

That evening, I ate dinner at an excellent Japanese restaurant. I ordered a pork cutlet on rice, a side dish of pickled cabbage, and a 7-UP.

"And would you like that hot or cold?' the waitress asked.

"Would I like what hot or cold?"

"The 7-UP."

"You have hot 7-UP?"

She thought for a second and then said, "No."

In Haerbin, I had ordered a pot of green tea only to be told that a pot was much larger than a cup. When I said I knew that, the waitress said, "Oh, I don't think you do," and galloped off to fetch an example of each so I could compare. At a McDonald's in Beijing, I had been asked if I wanted my orange juice hot or cold. No kidding.

As I ate, a girl of about 20 was sitting next to me and studying English. When she went to the bathroom, I grabbed her textbook and scanned it. "Especially when the economic advancement of developing countries plays a pivotal role in the international currency and financial systems, the present financial order led by so-called developed western countries can no longer adapt to change," one sentence read. I turned the page and saw a line I was already familiar with: "America is the policeman of the world."

The book was a series of unrelated sentences accompanied by translations. No context was provided. It seldom is. I flipped to the back and scanned through a list of vocabulary: 'cryonics,' 'resuscitation,' 'oceanographer.' I could tell by the way the girl studied (mechanically mumbling the words) that if I asked her, in English, what time she had woken up that morning, or what her favourite colour was, she wouldn't have been able to answer. It wasn't her fault, mind you. This was a university textbook and I knew that Chinese professors of English customarily hid their own inability to use, understand, or teach the language behind a veil of impractical lexical items and pedagogically meritless reading lessons based on stilted passages of academic prose. By and large, English in China is a subject to be studied, not learned.

By travelling to Qingdao, I had fooled myself into thinking I would be spared China's perennial weirdness and petty annoyances, but it was the most bizarre place I had visited yet. Locals seemed to be either slightly daft or emotionally unhinged. Service in restaurants and hotels ranged between non-existent and abysmal. Initially, I chalked it up to being the low season, but then I reflected that this was the *real* Qingdao, not the Why-not-have-a-gander-at-our-splendid-European-architecture?-tourist-season Qingdao that drew *Beijing ren* and Shanghainese in the warmer months.

I walked into a travel agency only to be told that they didn't book tickets – for anything. Not only that, but they couldn't tell me who did. Usually, it was possible to buy just about any type of ticket from just about any hotel. But not in Qingdao. I caught a cab to the train station to buy a ticket (the driver was an absolute madman, and only luck prevented us from being creamed by a cement mixer), after which I changed money at a bank, where I had the pleasure of being screamed at by a female teller for filling in a form with blue ink instead of black. The woman only stopped shrieking after I lied and told her I was an Olympic representative. A sign behind her announced that hers was a 'Civilized Work Unit.'

Fortuitously, the following day was much better. I went on a tour of the Tsingtao Brewery. When I arrived, the workers were in the midst of an early, end-of-year celebration. Below a rooftop row of giant beer cans half hidden in billowing steam, they were singing and firing off party poppers. There were about 150 of them and they all had on red bandanas, green jackets, and blue pants. Bits of coloured paper fluttered everywhere and those that landed on the grass were immediately swept up by old men using straw brooms. On one lawn, there was a statue of a muscular, loin-clothed Dionysus carrying a keg of beer under one arm while hoisting a froth-capped stein with the other. A sign explained.

'Dionysus (is) the god of wine and the god in charge of brewage and bacchanal. The god of wine is coming facing the sunglow, treading the spray, and raising the glass full of sincere Tsingtao Beer liquor.'

Despite the garbled signage (company motto: 'We Aim to Satisfy Your'), dull exhibits (purchase orders), and less-than-scientific technical explanations ('The purpose of yeast propagation is to produce more yeast....'), the tour wasn't bad. In fact, it was pretty good. The second best part was the complimentary four shooter glasses of beer we were given halfway through the inspection. The best part was the complimentary litre of beer we were given at the end – in a mock Bavarian beer hall with Chinese characteristics. The ale was so refreshing, in fact, that I went to a bar district nearby and spent the rest of the day getting blissfully pickled. This made Qingdao, and all of China for that matter, seem like an infinitely more agreeable place.

CHAPTER NINETEEN

The following afternoon, I collected my baggage and my hangover and caught a train to Shanghai, boarding just six minutes before it left. We clacked through a lengthy stretch of industrial wasteland, which thinned to intermittent cement farm houses, russet plots of land, and garbage-filled ponds. The air pollution, even here in the middle of the countryside, was tremendous. China is now the most polluted country in the world, laying claim to 16 of the 20 most despoiled cities on Earth. By its own estimation, 10 percent of its farmland has been seriously contaminated. Certainly, I was passing through some of that farmland now.

I went to the dining car for a little hair of the dog. There was hardly anyone there, but I was asked to leave after an hour. A waitress informed me I couldn't occupy a place unless I ordered something.

"I already ordered a beer," I told her.

"You have to order food."

"Give me a dish of *gongbao jiding* and some rice," I said.

"You have to order food for two people," she replied, but I refused to budge. She served me, but returned every thirty minutes to order me to leave. But suddenly, I lost my ability to understand Chinese. "This is China," she scolded, realizing what I was doing. "You cannot do whatever you please. This is not a Western country." I continued to ignore her. "You foreigners," she hissed. "Too proud, you are. You're all too proud."

As it happened, I was proudly reading the *Analects of Confucius*, which was fitting as Shandong (formerly the state of Lu) was the Sage's birthplace. The tome's preface began, "Chinese traditional culture is a treasure among the cultures of the world, and *Analects of Confucius* is the brightest pearl in its depository." Subsequently, Confucius' ideas were described as "brilliant," "profound," and "widespread throughout the world." They were responsible for the economic success of Japan, they formed the social fabric of Vietnam and Korea, they had been translated into every major language, etc., etc.

In the *Analects*, Confucius essentially argues that morality, ritual, and obedience will generate order and civility. Additionally, people ought to strive to attain wisdom and cultivation. They should, in a word, become virtuous. Confucius' chief concern is that of ethics, and to that end he has much in common with Socrates. To be sure, there is considerable overlap between the two, one definitely worth examining, if only briefly.

Confucius and Socrates lived around the same time (their life spans overlapped), and, or so it is thought, to roughly the same age: 72 and 70 respectively. Both made their livings from teaching and neither had much use for wealth or possessions. Little is known about the men themselves. Glimpses of their lives, along with their ideas, are known to us through the writings of their adherents, namely Mencius and Plato. Although it can be said that they were both obsessed with the concept of righteous living, their philosophies on how to attain such a state are rather different, which is to say: antipodean. Whereas Confucius implies that virtuousness can only be attained by following the teachings that he prescribes (or transmits, as he claims to be only passing on the wisdom of antiquity), Socrates holds that virtue is something that can only be realized through reflection and examination, that is: questioning; what has come to be known as Socratic questioning or the Socratic method – the same method I am applying to China and its culture.

Before one can possess a virtue, so says Socrates, one must first understand it, and in order to understand it, one must subject it to scrutiny; a great deal of scrutiny. It is all fine and well to encourage people to act, say, benevolently, but what *is* benevolence? According to Socrates, it is not simply what someone tells you it is, rather you must work out its meaning and essence for yourself. By extension, all opinions, exhortations, traditions, beliefs, ideologies, laws, and so on, must be analyzed and distilled by the individual so as to arrive at some fundamental truth or knowledge. Granted, such truth or knowledge may fall short of genuine or pure wisdom, but it is the best available option.

Once a virtue is understood, it ought to be practised primarily in order to benefit oneself, or one's soul. By extension, society will be benefitted, but the emphasis of Socrates' philosophy is placed on the individual. Indeed, not only did the Socratic method give rise to the scientific method, but it helped create a movement of individualism. Conversely, Confucianism spawned a civilization that stresses conformism and collectivism. In the *Analects*, excessive reflection and questioning are explicitly discouraged. One acquires knowledge not by testing a hypothesis or by thinking on it, but by finding a teacher familiar with the ways of the ancients and then imitating him. Whereas Socrates' ideas do not constitute a dogma (he never claimed to *know* anything, and considered himself to be a mere guide or "midwife" to discovery), the tenets of Confucius make no allowance for rival doctrines. "Confucius says, 'The plague of heterodox theories can be eliminated by fierce attack.'"

Socrates believed that the *status quo* ought to be continually questioned and challenged. That would make for a better and more just society. Furthermore, citizens are morally bound to scrutinize those in authority. Confucius believed that the *status quo* must never be questioned or challenged. It may only be altered by those in authority. Consequently, change in a Confucian society occurs incrementally, if it occurs at all. Presently, China and its culture and society are being touted as dynamic, but that is the very thing they aren't.

As I read the *Analects*, a book called *Notes on Reading the Analects* was flying off of China's bookshelves. Supposedly, it sold 3 million copies in just four months. It has since gone on to sell at least 3 million more. The Chinese government, ostensibly in an attempt to bolster its soft power (the attractiveness of a nation's culture, policies, and political ideals), recently announced a massive project of retranslating virtually the entire corpus of Chinese literature, first into English and then into other languages. Called the "Library of Chinese Classics," the *Analects of Confucius* was listed as top priority, followed by *The Art of War,* and *Dream of the Red Chamber.* This large-scale task has gone hand in hand with the establishment of Confucius Institutes around the world. As touched upon, Confucius Institutes are non-profit, public establishments meant to advance the Chinese language and culture.

I had tried to read the *Analects* when I first arrived in Asia, but quickly gave it up, which is probably just as well as it's doubtful that I would have understood it then. I found it fascinating now, however. The volume, with all its thinness, vagueness, oversimplification, dictums posing as wisdom, and if-A-then-B reasoning constituted the blue print for two millennia of civilization. Parenthetically, the corresponding Chinese translations included something the English did not: dozens of exclamation marks, as if the lessons were being shouted. I knew from years of marking writing assignments that Chinese people used these liberally. The instinct is to yell, even while writing.

I sat in the dining car for four hours and counted five arguments among the staff and passengers. At one point, a police officer looked to be on the verge of throttling one of his underlings, but stopped short when someone reminded him there was a "foreign friend" in his midst.

People would shuffle in, get out their cigarettes, order beer or

100-mililitre bottles of pungent Red Star *baijiu*, and moodily assess one another after they'd gotten a bit of a glow on. Twice, I heard someone say, "What do you think *you're* looking at?" Before long, the car was filled with smoke and dull, wounded expressions. Above the windows, there was a series of pictures: Party leaders smilingly shaking hands with foreign Olympic committee members. I picked up a magazine someone had left on a nearby seat and flipped it open. Coincidentally, I found myself examining a glossy photo of a handcuffed and crestfallen fellow sitting in a dining car. Two policemen sat across from him, filling in a report. It was an article about public security. Other photos showed rows of riot police dressed in Darth Vader costumes. Presumably, these were meant to instil in the reader a certain peace of mind.

At noon the following day, I exited the Shanghai railway station and found myself swimming in a sea of stone-faced people. My notebook reads, "… masses of people – unbelievable, men dressed like Old Chicago gangsters, women wearing inflammable outfits – one match; Poof! Incredible pollution! – I immediately start to cough."

At four o'clock in the afternoon, I set out for a stroll. My hotel was in a neighbourhood dominated by scruffy streets walled by rambling brick buildings, every one of which had laundry hanging from protruding bamboo poles. Clusters of electrical wire coursed from one knotted, pole-top mass to the next, and suspicious-looking men loitered about alleyways, smoking and fingering their cell phones. The alleys contained old grey homes, more hanging laundry, and leathery duck carcasses. Like the undergarments, these dangled from metal bars and bamboo poles that were 10 or even 20 metres above the ground.

I made my way to the Bund, which by now was dark and bitterly windy. Atop the Huangpu River, there floated a junk strung with hundreds of yellow lights. From the opposite direction, a barge drifted past: a floating, jumbo-sized television set. It showed various nature scenes: a butterfly dancing atop a flower, a time-lapse sequence of a burgeoning mushroom, and so on. Across the cold, hazy river stood the gaudy Oriental Pearl Tower and the flashy skyscrapers of Pudong, an electric circus of primary colours. What struck me the most was how quiet it all was. There were nearly 17 million people in Shanghai, yet it was as though someone had switched off the volume.

I surveyed the colonial buildings behind me, concluded I would come back during the daytime, and walked up Nanjing East Road, with its blinding neon and repeating Pepsi signs. Young boys with dyed hair, tattoos, and pamphlets huddled on the sidelines. They would accost foreigners and hound them until told to get lost. They were ill tempered and dangerous-looking. I heard one guy swear at couple in their fifties. I walked on until I got to People's Square, and it was here where I discovered Shanghai's terrible secret: it was next to impossible to hail a cab. At least at night. Or so it seemed to me.

The next morning, I did the walk again. The Bund was one of those places you couldn't take in just once. It was a crisp, cold day and I crossed the Huangpu via the Bund Sightseeing Tunnel. I stepped onto a rail-guided car that tracked though a channel of psychedelic lights, lasers, inflatable puppet-like creatures with flailing arms, and digital images of lava and tropical fish. The pod-like vehicle was fitted with a sound system that played spacey music and offered terse commentary in English and Chinese. "Sea Cadence," the voice droned, and then, "Meteor Shower."

Just before leaving the terminal, I spotted a sign saying, 'Chinese Sex Exhibition – 20 *Yuan*,' so I stopped abruptly and bought a ticket. It was advertised as being the first exhibition of its kind in more than 5,000 years, which just might have been true.

It was interesting enough. There were vases adorned with penises and there were dowry paintings: instructive scrolls given to daughters on their wedding day. The most unusual exhibit was entitled, in English, 'This Part of the Body Could Not be Locked.' It was a wooden carving of a tubby bald man bound in chains. The only part that remained unchained was his member, which was longer than he was tall and nearly as wide.

I left and walked to the 88-storey Jin Mao Tower where I was cannoned to the viewing deck by the futuristic elevator. On all sides, buildings stretched away until they vanished into the smog. The deck's windows included the following signs.

Siberia – 4,750 km	Ulan Bator – 2,200 km
Beijing – 1,080 km	Tianjin – 960 km
Lu Xun Park – 6 km	Chongming – 38 km

No places outside East Asia were listed.

In mining for evidence of China's "great rise," Shanghai is customarily held up as the most lustrous example; home to a new breed of Chinese: an erudite and motivated class of *nouveau riche* that has embraced materialism, wealth, and Western tendencies with a reckless and magnificently capitalistic abandon. Without question, Shanghai is a city of relative modernity and opportunity; however, it is important to remember that it has been so ever since the mid-nineteenth century.

As author Stella Dong reminds us in her book, *Shanghai: The Rise and Fall of a Decadent City*, the present-day manifestation of this grand metropolis owes its existence to an illicit union between the East and the West, one founded on the opium trade. By the time the Treaty of Nanjing was signed, 10 percent of China's population was addicted to opium, and Shanghai, sited in the dead centre of China's coastline and only 22 kilometres from the mouth of the Yangtze River, was judged to be the ideal spot from which to peddle the "foreign mud" inland. Shanghai swiftly unseated Guangzhou in becoming China's foremost port. All the major foreign trading firms moved their headquarters here and the area of marshlands and mudflats west of the Huangpu River was carved up into foreign settlements.

To the south, there was the French Concession, which greatly outsized and outflanked the nugget-shaped Chinese City, whose population had spilled over to the wastelands of Pudong, where I was now. North of the French Concession was the much larger International Settlement, a district initially comprised of mainly Britons and Americans. North of this was the impossibly crammed Chinese district of Zhabei.

As the foreigners, or Shanghailanders, as they called themselves, employed coolies to build the foundations of their houses and buildings atop piles driven deep into the loamy soil, the semblance of a city emerged: churches, warehouses, courtyard homes, and roads built along the curves of creeks and cow paths.

There was a real-estate boom followed by the rise of the cotton industry, which took advantage of the American Civil War to supply that product to Europe. Trade flourished, and by the 1850s the greasy jetties at the southern end of the Bund scurried with coolies, long-robed merchants, and cigar-smoking brokers who were whisked about in sedan chairs as they scanned the newest rates shipped in from London and New York. As saloons, hotel bars, and private dining rooms shot up to accommodate the surge in income, a steady stream of speculators and schemers poured into the city, as did sailors, smugglers, thieves, prostitutes, and intrepid tourists. Shanghai, the "Whore of Asia," refused no one and asked for no papers or passports.

Because the vast majority of the émigrés were uncommitted men, the city came to embrace a level of decadence that might have caused ancient Rome to blush. On the backs of such ignoble industries as the "poison trade" (opium), the "flower-selling trade" (prostitution), and the "pig trade" (the slave trade, whereby labourers were forced onto ships – or shanghaied – and sent to all corners of the world), gambling houses, opium dens, brothels, and cabarets grew like weeds. The 'City Upon the Sea' turned into the 'City of Sin.' Undeniably, it became the most ravenous, brazen, licentious, corrupt, and depraved conurbation in the entire world. By far, it had the highest incidence of prostitution anywhere, and by 1859 it was believed that nearly half of all British soldiers in the city suffered from a sexually transmitted disease. A physician from France considered syphilis to be practically an epidemic. By the 1880s, missionaries were referring to the city as "the Sodom and Gomorrah of the Far East," and after thousands of destitute White Russians arrived on the docks, the burg's flesh trade became so notorious that it was investigated by the League of Nations. Shanghai was a place where morality was simply immaterial.

The enormous white piles driven deep into the Bund by teams of coolies who chanted, 'Ah ho! Ah ho!' from dawn to dusk signified the beginning of Shanghai's "million-dollar skyline," or "magnificent mile," a curved stretch of European lavishness bookended by the British Consulate and the Shanghai Club. This embankment would come to include the Astor House Hotel, the Cathy Hotel, the Hong Kong Bank, the Shanghai Bank, the Chartered Bank of India, the Customs House, the *North China Daily News* building, and such influential firms as Jardine, Matheson and David Sassoon and Company.

World War I saw yet another economic spike, and this time it wasn't just the foreigners and compradors (go-betweens) who got rich. Local investment gushed into the city and a generation of Chinese tycoons was born. Mostly Cantonese, these moguls moved into villas in the foreign settlements, where they hired throngs of house boys, coolies, gardeners, cooks, and amahs (or nannies). Children, many of which were born to concubines, were sent to Western schools while their parents went about mimicking the habits of the Shanghailanders. Shanghai's original *nouveau rich* were without question the most progressive Chinese to be found anywhere, but they were also the most materialistic. As author Pearl S. Buck recorded, "The streets (of Shanghai) are crowded with hungry, sullen, half-starved people and among them roll the sedans and limousines of the wealthy Chinese, spending fabulous sums on pleasure, food and clothes, wholly senseless to others."

To be certain, the very evident gap that existed between the privileged and the poor was something often commented on by outsiders. While tai-pans and Chinese magnates feasted and caroused, and their wives splurged in Nanjing East Road's well-stocked department stores before breaking for tiffin, conditions in the Chinese quarters were horrendous. Along the edges of industrial areas there arose shanty towns and boarding houses where migrant workers slept, quite literally, on top of one another; and those were the ones who could afford to live

248   WHY CHINA WILL NEVER RULE THE WORLD

on land. Many were forced to exist on sampans, thousands of which
floated atop the fetid Suzhou Creek. The town's factories were filled
with women and children who were required to work 12-hour shifts
and often with materials that had been banned in Europe or America.
Mothers often took their babies to work. Whereas women wove silk and
children worked in match plants, boys toiled in oil mills, tanneries, and
shipyards. Most men eked out an existence as coolies or rickshaw drivers.
As you would expect, conditions in all industries were abhorrent; disease
and malnutrition were endemic and wages frequently fell below the cost
of living. The upshot was that nearly 150,000 people, or half the city's
workforce, were eternally in debt. Pawnbrokers and moneylenders made
fistfuls of cash.

Meanwhile, the more stylish of the Shanghailanders were trading
in their antiquated villas for the grandeur of apartment buildings, ones
fitted with air conditioning, high-speed lifts, restaurants that served
Western food, room service, ground-floor nightclubs, parking garages,
and stunning views. The socioeconomic rift that existed in Shanghai was
perhaps best described by American journalist Vincent Sheean when
he wrote, "The confrontation of European power and the swarming,
fluid, antlike life of poverty-stricken Chinese is more obvious here than
anywhere else in China."

Thanks to Chiang Kai-shek, neither the labour movement nor the
massive anti-foreigner protests of the 1920s managed to hinder the
city's growth, and with the ushering in of the 1930s, Shanghai reached
its economic peak. Its port was the world's fifth busiest, and foreign
investment, estimated then to be in the $3-billion-dollar range, exceeded
that of any city outside the Western world. There was another real-estate
boom and parcels of land near the Bund sold for more than they did
on Fifth Avenue or the *Avenue des Champs-Élysées*. Still, it was clear to
everyone that the good old days were gone.

Practically since its inception, the 'City of Mudflats' had been a place
of routine, if not casual, violence. But in the thirties, partly owing to a
ban on opium trafficking, the number of triads and criminals operating
in the metropolis caused Al Capone's Chicago to appear as a picture of
parochialism. In short, Shanghai became an extremely dangerous place to
live. Crime was eventually halted, mind you, but not in a way anyone had
foreseen.

Naturally, after the Japanese Army took control of the city on
December 8, 1941 (the same time they attacked Pearl Harbour), they
seized everything in it, including the International Settlement, after which
Britain and America signed treaties with Chongqing concluding their

licences in China. The Vichy regime had already surrendered the French
Concession, and so, 101 years after the Treaty of Nanjing, Shanghai
ceased to be a treaty port.

After the war ended, and after the Nationalists' great carpetbagging
campaign, the city was occupied yet again – by a peasant army that
marched into town gawking awkwardly at all the hotels and homeless
people, not knowing what to think. Their leader knew what to think,
though. In the years to come, Mao would make certain that Shanghai was
stripped of both its dignity and its decadence.

I had read several news magazine articles on present-day Shanghai
and they tended to hype its worldly wise, well-heeled, wine-sipping
denizens as a phenomenon that was entirely new.

I walked around Pudong craning my neck at its corporate cathedrals
before jumping in a cab that drove under the Huangpu toward the former
French Concession. I paid a visit to the heavily guarded former residence
of Sun Yat-sen, which I found to be immaculately preserved and quite
interesting. In addition to a speech which played on a gramophone, there
were various gifts from supporters and sympathizers. One such item was
a book called *Construction of Railway Curves* by G. Watanabe. Certainly, this
was to set Dr. Sun straight on just why railway lines couldn't be straight.
After Sun Yat-sen showed his master plan to the Australian advisor and
journalist, William Henry Donald, Donald reported, "I saw evidence of a
most convincing nature that Sun is not only mad as a hatter, but that he is
madder."

The building was charming and featured a hearth and a lovely
lawn-covered courtyard, as did many of the area's houses. When they
were built, these "English manors" possessed large, airy rooms filled
with marble-inlaid mahogany furniture, European couches, and wing-
backed chairs. In addition to the lawns, there were often stables, tennis
courts, swimming pools, and even indoor gymnasiums. Segments of the
former French Concession looked much as they did a century ago: regal
mansions moderately obscured by trees and *fleur-de-lis*-topped wrought
iron fences.

I spent the rest of the day strolling around the area and found it to
be such a pleasant contrast to the brashness of Nanjing East Road that
I returned the next day and strolled around some more. Still, I didn't
exactly enjoy Shanghai, which surprised me enormously. I kept expecting
to find examples of the sort of sophistication that one finds in Hong
Kong or Singapore, but never did. The 'New York City of China,' I found
Shanghai's residents to be pushy and callous. But then, they are famous
for that.

I stayed in the city for five days and got into four arguments with the staff at my hotel, and I am not big on arguments. I had called a travel agency to book an air ticket, which was supposed to be delivered to the front desk between eight and nine one evening, but never came. I called the company several times the next day, but couldn't get through. The following morning, they called me, but by then I had already booked a train ticket. When I told them I no longer wanted their ticket, they became annoyed. While exiting the hotel afterward, a receptionist called me over to explain that the agent had called them and that they had decided a penalty of 10 percent would be deducted from my room deposit. The hotel and the agent were in no way affiliated. A great quarrel ensued, one which ended when I threatened to call the police. That evening, I picked up my laundry at the front desk. Only after I left Shanghai did I discover that all of the items had been stapled and sewn together.

But it wasn't just how *I* was treated; I found the way people treated each other on the street, and especially in the subway, to be inexcusable. And, with the exceptions of Hanoi and Saigon, the traffic situation was the worst I had ever seen in any city. Indeed, motorists seemed to take great delight in roaring past women and children caught in the middle of crosswalks. If Shanghai had a motto, it would have been, "Get outta my way! There's money to be made!" But, perhaps I shouldn't have been so surprised. Once, I met an American who lived and worked in Shanghai. Not only did he dismiss the Shanghainese as "rude," he claimed that following 9/11, many of them celebrated.

On my last night in Shanghai, I went to see the Roger Waters concert. As he and his band performed Pink Floyd's *The Dark Side of the Moon*, complete with futuristic special effects, grey-clad police officers shuffled back and forth in front of the stage while staring at the floor. What they must have thought when hundreds of middle-aged foreign businessmen wildly applauded the appearance of a large, flying pig, I can only speculate.

One year earlier, The Rolling Stones had played the same venue. As with Roger Waters, it was their first concert in China, although they had been slated to play there in 2003, an event that was cancelled due to SARS. In 2003, part of the agreement was that the Stones wouldn't perform the songs 'Beast of Burden,' 'Brown Sugar,' 'Let's Spend the Night Together,' or 'Honky Tonk Women' because of their suggestive lyrics. In 2006, a new song, 'Rough Justice,' was added to the no-no list.

Roger Waters has a song about the Tiananmen Square Incident called 'Watching TV,' a duet sung with Don Henley, although he didn't perform it. It wasn't part of the tour's set list. I heard one person calling for it as an encore.

Before the show, I had gone to a nearby McDonald's to wait and drink tea. I sat with a local fellow who had come to do the same thing. He was an accountant whose English name was Sam. We got to talking about music, something we both enjoyed, but no longer had much time for. We had remarkably similar tastes and ended up chatting for more than an hour just about music.

"I like Roger Waters's music, but I like his lyrics more," Sam said. "It's like poetry. He's anti-politics and anti-war, and his words are like, I think the word is sarcasm? Like irony. But behind it is fear and love. His words are very powerful, very meaningful."

This had been a recurring theme on my journey so far: just when I was nearing the end of my tether, I somehow managed to run into someone who was friendly, polite, or hospitable. I was reminded, too, that there were probably heaps of friendly Shanghainese; they were just too busy for me to see it. Sam and I walked to the concert together where he met and introduced me to his girlfriend. He and I then shook hands and said goodbye.

The next day, I ate lunch at a sushi restaurant located on the third floor of a department store. From my table, I watched as a couple bickered next to a railing in the middle of the complex. The woman tried to climb over it and jump, but the man tackled her and wrestled her to the floor. She screamed. He yelled. A large crowd gathered. People left the restaurant to go see what all the fuss was about. I left and battled my way through swarms of unsmiling people in Shanghai's beat-up railway station.

Chapter Twenty

The train to Nanjing (or Nanking, as it is still sometimes spelled) was startlingly clean and I spent three and a half hours sipping tea and glaring out the window at a pageant of factories and factory towns. There was the usual 'Please! A Civilized Train!' reminder flashing across an electronic sign, and the usual hassle of finding anyone who knew where the street my hotel was on was located once I arrived. At the hotel's in-house foreign-exchange counter, I had a ridiculous experience with a dim, no-can-do clerk after which I walked outside into the drizzle grumbling to myself. I dined in some rudimentary back-alley restaurant as the other patrons whispered and stared. If the door opens to a Chinese restaurant's kitchen, you should never look in. I did, and noted that the kitchen in this place was the colour of charcoal.

When I returned to the hotel, there were five staff members arguing with seventeen guests in the lobby. They were all men. The guests, each of which wore black trousers and dark jackets, had clearly been drinking and it was as if they were all talking at once. I went to the business centre, which offered a front row seat to this scene. I checked my e-mail and watched for an hour, or until the cops showed up and the throng of disgruntled customers was cleared from the premises. I retired to my room to watch CCTV news. "*Zhongguo dao le!*" the newsreader began proudly. "China has arrived!" As evidence, images of Americans shopping at Wal-Mart were paraded across the screen.

The next morning, I went for a walk around town. Nanjing was, and I hesitate to say this, nice. In fact, it was by far the nicest city I saw in China. To be sure, it had some grotty alleys and more than a few caged-up windows, but comparatively speaking, it was a marked improvement. There were proper roads, proper street signs, and, in most places at least, proper sidewalks.

I hailed a cab and told the driver that I wanted to go to the Memorial Hall of the Nanjing Massacre, but he informed me it was closed.

"Why's that?" I asked.

"Guess," he said.

"Because they don't want foreigners who are coming for the Olympics to visit it?"

"Nope," he replied. "They're expanding it."

I settled for the Taiping Heavenly Kingdom History Museum instead. I knew something was up when I saw the 33 bronze placards at the gallery's entranceway. These assured me that the museum's staff represented not only a civilized work unit, but a model one; one that had been honoured with the Priority Landscape Architecture prize, the Key Unit of Fire Safety Award, and a host of other accolades extolling its contributions to patriotic education, the national culture, and so on and so forth. As this bevy of bronze squares foretold, the museum was a propaganda piece meant to validate Communist rule by linking it to the Taiping movement.

The Taiping Rebellion was depicted as a grass roots movement that strove to advance society by overthrowing the Qing, eradicating feudalism, and combating the "aggressions of the Western powers." Its leaders rose up boldly, fought heroically, *ad nauseam*. On display, there were silk-gown uniforms embroidered with dragons along with garden spades affixed to crude bamboo poles. The Taiping soldiers wore not helmets, but flimsy crowns, and instead of bugles they employed conches. These items, along with a host of hand-drawn military formations, were intended to impress upon you that the movement represented "a classic chapter of Chinese military history."

And that was it, really. The museum was smallish and there wasn't a critical word to be found anywhere. Like the Boxer Rebellion, the Taiping Rebellion, along with its leader Hong Xiuquan, had received the official stamp of approval. They were, in a word, 'Good.'

In 1814, Hong Xiuquan was born to Hakka parents in the province of Guangdong. Having failed the examination that would have qualified him as a scholar, and therefore a civil servant, he travelled to Guangzhou to study. There, he came in contact with a Protestant missionary who handed him a translated passage from the Bible, one which he only glanced at and filed away. After failing his test for the third time, the frustrated Hong had a dream in which a blond-haired, bearded man conferred upon him a sword, and a younger man explained how to wield it in order to slay evil spirits. After his fourth examination failure, Hong Xiuquan retrieved and read the Biblical passage whereupon he concluded that the two men he had seen in his dream could only have been God and Jesus Christ. Logically, he must have been the second son of God, Jesus' younger brother.

Believing that he had been charged with the divine mission of expunging the demonic Qing and erecting a "Christian" state, Hong Xiuquan, unlike China's myriad other demagogues, began to spread his message publicly. After reading the Bible in its entirety, he began baptizing converts, preaching asceticism, and destroying Confucian and ancestral shrines. Naturally, this drew negative attention and he and his supporters were expelled to the countryside.

From the remote and mountainous region of Guangxi, the prophet began subjecting his flock to rigourous military training. In 1850, after a Qing force sent to destroy the sect was routed, Hong's group of silk-gown-wearing, pike-wielding, long-haired Christian soldiers (they had unbraided their cues) set out on an ultimately triumphant northwesterly campaign that put them in Nanjing – some 1,400 kilometres away – a little over two years later. In order to enlist new recruits, the crusaders utilized propaganda literature that combined Christian themes with anti-Qing rhetoric. They also championed equality of the sexes, and, most importantly, land reform. Their numbers grew exponentially, as did their funds.

The city of Nanjing was simply overwhelmed by the invaders, and, supposedly, every single one of its 40,000 Qing supporters was killed. Any of the "demons" who weren't sent back to hell in battle, including women and children, were burned, stabbed, or drowned. Thereupon, the Christian sovereign entered the city atop a golden palanquin borne by 16 men. He occupied the former Ming Dynasty palace and commenced ruling his Taiping Heavenly Kingdom under the title of Heavenly King, something he did for the next 11 years.

The pillars of Hong Xiuquan's new state, at least in theory, were Old Testament Christian morality, regimentation, social equality, and collectivization. In addition to bans on opium, alcohol, dancing, and prostitution, there existed strict segregation of the sexes. Funds were held in a common treasury and a land law was introduced whereby tracts of soil were to be distributed to Taiping families based on their number. Men and women received plots of equal size and excess produce was delivered to common granaries. There was military service and a state examination system based on translations of the Bible and Hong's own teachings.

Despite such utopianism, Hong's scheme ultimately failed – resplendently so. Not only were his initiatives infinitely more potent on paper (the Taipings actually put an enormous strain on land, ruining vast tracts of once fecund territory), but his administration, based on collective rule, soon became rife with infighting and power struggles. Hong Xiuquan had a falling out with two of his staunchest and most able supporters, one who believed that he was the Holy Ghost, and therefore more powerful than Hong, and another who tried to establish his own kingdom in Sichuan, only to be caught and slowly dismembered by Qing troops. Hong himself withdrew to his pleasure dome, where he surrounded himself with concubines. He spent much of his time underlining passages in the Bible that he perceived to be references to himself. The Taipings, many of whom were Hakka or former members of ethnic hill tribes, were also despised by locals who believed they were just as alien as the Qing and nearly as weird as the foreign devils.

Ultimately, it was the foreign devils that brought the kingdom to an end. Reacting to a Taiping advance on Shanghai, the British and French, worried about the threat to their business interests (including the opium trade) and the prospect of dealing with a different administration, allied themselves with Qing forces and crushed Beijing's rival capital. It is believed that between 10 million and 20 million people died during the rise and fall of the Taiping Rebellion. Incidentally, the name Taiping means "Great Peace."

From the museum, I made my way east through the reconstructed city gate toward Purple Mountain. The road cut through a patch of pretty forest, something rarely seen so close to a city in China.

After purchasing an ambitiously priced ticket, I walked past a throng of gimcrack souvenir shops featuring what looked to be government-issued signs. In English, they read, 'Rong hua cigarette wine edible drink,' 'Purple sand pot monopolized shop,' 'Genuine pearl jade article monopoly,' and 'Pixiu fabulous wild beast luck; mascot monopoly.' I walked along a corridor walled by pines (symbols of longevity), ascended 392 steps, and reached a square hall with a life-sized marble statue of Sun Yat-sen sitting under an elaborate ceiling designed after the Nationalist flag. There were signs ordering me to salute and be quiet. At least I was quiet. From this room, I entered a domed chamber that held Sun Yat-sen's marble sarcophagus. It lay on the floor, a level below a circular observation area, with another statue of his body resting atop his crypt's lid. People gazed downward in silent veneration. Nearly everyone bowed or saluted. This was a place of pilgrimage.

I went outside to amble around. I tried, unsuccessfully, to ignore the Communist Party signs (in listing Sun's goals, not one mentioned the word 'democracy') before casting my eye to the west. The views were striking. Trees extended forever under a dull haze. Shadowy hills rose and fell and I could just make out the gleam of the Yangtze off in the distance. In ancient China, people believed that the Yangtze River and the Purple Mountain offered geomantic protection from evil influence, "like a coiling dragon and a crouching tiger." Nanjing, with only its southern portion discernable now, was where the tenets of Chinese painting and calligraphy were set and where the four-tone system of the language was established.

I wanted to take a cab back to the city, but as I approached a group of drivers they started to mock me. "Yeah, yeah, okay, okay," they repeated, slapping their thighs and howling. I caught a bus and within minutes we passed by a bicycle that had been pulverized by something much larger. A lone black glove lay among the twisted wreckage.

After the bus swung onto Taiping South Road, a minivan from the opposite lane crossed the centre line and did a U-turn. It just missed crashing into us. Its driver failed to get straightened out and careened into a stone guardrail, ripping his fender off and destroying about 10 metres of rail in the process. As we passed him, I looked back to note that he was laughing hysterically.

That night, I went to a pub filled with expatriates. I ended up talking to a man from Boston with red hair and an Irish name. He asked me about my travels and then told me about a few of his. "Don't go to Inner Mongolia," he warned. "I travelled there last summer with a buddy of mine and we got chased down the street by a bunch of Han Chinese carrying planks and bricks. There's so much tension in this country," he said. "It's like a tinderbox."

He went on to tell me that he firmly believed that China was preparing for war. "Oh, you can just feel it," he said. "They hate us. They hate everyone. I tutor a guy who's a fairly-high-ranking military officer, and he told me that after the Olympics, the army is going to pull off something big. I think they are, too. The signs are everywhere. This is a country mobilizing toward combat."

Back at my hotel, I watched an English-language talk show on CCTV 9 about Chinese negotiations with North Korea that absolutely simmered with anti-American rhetoric. Nearly six decades after the fact, the Chinese were doing their utmost to finish something (they claimed) the Americans had started. It was a great day for Chinese diplomacy and an auspicious occasion on the cusp of the Chinese New Year.

The next morning, I walked to the Presidential Palace. In front of its entranceway, there were beggars and some old men sitting on a bench. When one of them saw me, he jumped up and shouted, "*Huan, tu, sili!*" ("One, two, three!") while waving his arms madly. His cohorts cackled and yelled, "Yes, yes, no, no!" I ignored them and bought a ticket to the historical spot.

This was the site of the Ming Dynasty palace, Hong Xiuquan's residence, the place where Sun Yat-sen had been sworn in as provisional president, the spot where the Nationalists had made their headquarters for 10 years, and where the Japanese had made theirs after the Nationalists retreated to Chongqing. The site's theme had been carefully selected by the present administration. The first hall I entered was filled with photos of Japanese soldiers shooting people in the head. I watched as all the children and parents shuffled by them, the former saucer-eyed and the latter scowling. They were so focused that they didn't even notice me taking pictures of them. Given what happened in the city, however, it was little wonder. Nanjing, of course, was the site of one of the worst atrocities in modern history.

In 1937, Chiang Kai-shek *finally* decided to take the fight to the Japanese in the city of Shanghai. Despite some incredible blunders[1] his ground forces got stuck in and made life very difficult for the invaders, at least for a while. In the end, Chiang's forces were badly defeated, but not before 40,000 Japanese soldiers lay dead. The Japanese had expected to take all of China in three months, but they got pinned down in Shanghai for nearly that long. This would set the stage for what happened next.

Having already softened up the Nationalist capital of Nanjing with bombing runs, the Japanese pressed forward, razing other cities and villages and engaging in killing sprees as they went. Chiang Kai-shek pledged that Nanjing would never fall, but as the enemy came ever closer, he made plans to evacuate, which he did a mere five days before the city was taken.

Responsibility for the city's defence was delegated to Tang Shengzhi, a former warlord who had never displayed much loyalty to Chiang Kai-shek. Indeed, their relationship was so strained that Chiang had had Tang banished from China twice, once to Japan and once to Hong Kong. Tang Shengzhi only accepted the assignment under the advice of his Buddhist spiritual advisor.

Once in command, Tang Shengzhi gave a press conference where he vowed to defend Nanjing or die trying, although in the end he did neither. Hundreds of thousands of people had already fled, and the 600,000 to 700,000 who remained were defended by 90,000 ill-equipped and poorly trained soldiers, many of whom couldn't understand each others' dialects,

---

1   Not only were the Japanese expecting an air attack on their warships, as they had intercepted and decoded a secret telegram, but Nationalist pilots grew nervous when the ships' guns turned on them. One pilot prematurely released two bombs, one which landed in front of the Cathy Hotel, and another which went through the roof of the adjacent Palace Hotel. Ambulances were late on the scene as two more Nationalist bombs were dropped on an intersection serving as a sort of refugee soup kitchen. Those four bombs caused the deaths of 1,740 people and wounded 1,431 more.

and many more of whom had only recently been conscripted at gunpoint. To make matters worse, Chiang Kai-shek had run off with the entire air force and nearly all of the communications equipment.

When Japan dropped leaflets on the city ordering it to surrender, Tang Shengzhi balked and commanded his troops to "defend every inch of the front line." Meanwhile, Tang sought a cease-fire, but Chiang vetoed it. Then, incredibly, after three days of bloody fighting, and just as the Japanese were on the threshold of engulfing the city, Chiang Kai-shek ordered Tang Shengzhi and his men to withdraw across the Yangtze.

To say that Chang Kai-shek's belated order to ditch the capital at the last second caused disorder would be an understatement of the highest magnitude. For starters, once having received the command, many officers fled immediately, without relaying the message to their troops. Consequently, many in the field mistook a mass retreat for a mass desertion and hundreds were gunned down as traitors. As anyone wishing to leave the city for the river had to do so via the northwest gate, the withdrawal turned into a stampede. Tanks rolled over soldiers, and soldiers and police wrestled civilians for their clothes. Zhongshan (Sun Yat-sen) North Road, the artery leading to the passageway, became clogged with abandoned weapons and vehicles. Hundreds of thousands of evacuees, along with trucks, cars, and horse-drawn wagons forced their way through the 21-metre-wide gate tunnel, although scores never made it. Owing to all the discarded grenades and bullets, a fire broke out and quickly spread. Hundreds of soldiers burned to death or were trampled in the tunnel by frightened horses. Along the river, as officers squabbled about which equipment to destroy and which boats to take, tanks were strapped to rows of vessels that were tied together only to capsize and sink. When boats became scarce, the situation became dire. In the end, some 10,000 troops fought to gain access to three ships. Those who managed to claw their way onboard fired warning shots so that others would give up their efforts. Those who clung to hulls were chopped at with axes until they gave up or fell. The last of those fortunate enough to depart that night would have seen a city in flames and hundreds of their compatriots clutching buckets, logs, and doors in a vain attempt to cross the icy river.[2]

When the Japanese entered the city the following morning, December

---

2   In 1933, a novel called *Cat Country* was published by a writer named Lao She. About a space traveller who arrives on another planet to find a nation of cats being attacked by a diminutive but resilient race, the story represented a thinly veiled attack on China's inability to put aside its social and political differences and repel a common enemy. In the end, the cat people tear each other apart as their occupiers look on.

13, 1937, they were met by cheering crowds. But they weren't cheering for long. As historian Jonathan Spence has noted, there ensued a campaign of terror and death that has few parallels. Civilians were clubbed and hacked to death in the streets. Men were rounded up, jailed, starved, and then marched to various points in and around the city to be executed. Many were used as bayonet practice. Many more were beheaded. Live burials constituted another method of extermination. There occurred killing contests, one of which was widely publicized in the Japanese press, and there was widespread and systematic rape, almost always followed by murder. The victims were as young as 8 and as old as 80. Buddhist nuns and pregnant women were gang-raped to death. Women were bound to beds, chairs, and poles as permanent fixtures of rape. Others spent the rest of the occupation working in military brothels; the Japanese referred to the women as "public toilets." Men were also sexually molested in addition to being made to commit acts of incest and necrophilia. The Japanese set up a lab like the germ warfare centre outside of Haerbin. They lit children on fire. They engaged in cannibalism. They sold the Chinese opium and heroin to turn a quick buck and turn the Chinese into junkies. According to a host of eyewitness accounts and photographs, they did much of this while laughing and smiling. Estimates on the number of people murdered vary, but a very reasonable figure is 300,000.

If the six- to eight-week orgy of violence and murder can be said to have had a bright spot, it was in the erecting of the Nanjing Safety Zone, which came to accommodate 200,000 to 300,000 people, or roughly half of the remaining populace.[3] This zone was established by some two dozen foreigners who lived and worked in the Chinese capital. They did whatever they could to protect people from being molested and murdered. They wrestled Chinese men away from execution sites, tore Japanese soldiers off of women, and put themselves between the Chinese people and the Japanese guns. They also documented the genocide and got stories to the international press.

Among the heroes – and these were heroes in the truest sense of the word – were two Americans: Dr. Robert Wilson, the only surgeon in the entire city trying to help civilians (he performed operations on people around the clock for weeks), and a woman named Minnie Vautrin, the dean of studies at a women's college who turned her school's campus into a sanctuary for women, children, and wounded soldiers.

Most extraordinary among the protectors was John Rabe, a Nazi who chaired the safety zone committee and opened the doors of his home

---

3   In fact, the Rape of Nanjing lasted for months, but it was most intense during the first six to eight weeks. Occupation of the city lasted until war's end.

to refugees. Rabe was so incensed by the occupiers that he roved about the city with his swastika-adorned armband waving it in their faces while ordering them to stop their raping, looting, and murdering. After filming some of the horror, he sent the reels along with a missive to Adolf Hitler himself imploring the leader to take action.

Like the others, Rabe wasn't always successful. As the occupation wore on, the Japanese showed the safety zone organizers less and less respect. The foreigners were often threatened and occasionally roughed up. All of them expected to be shot in the back at any moment, and all too often they were simply powerless. However, they tirelessly pressed on, doing whatever they could to save lives, and it has been calculated that they may have saved as many as 250,000 of them. Rabe has been called the Oskar Schindler of China, and rightly so. When he returned to Germany, he was arrested by the Gestapo and forbidden from speaking on Nanjing. After the war, he lived in extreme poverty although he did receive money from the new mayor of Nanjing. Most organizers of the Nanjing Safety Zone were never the same afterward. It probably didn't help that the Communists either expelled any that were still living in Nanjing at the time of the takeover, or kept them under virtual house arrest. After Minnie Vautrin returned to the United States, she committed suicide.

The Chinese survivors didn't fair very well either. They certainly didn't receive any preferential treatment. In conducting research for her book, *The Rape of Nanking*, author Iris Chang (who herself committed suicide in 2004) visited the city in the 1990s in the hopes of interviewing some of them. She writes, "What I found shocked and depressed me. Most lived in dark, squalid apartments cluttered with the debris of poverty and heavy with mildew and humidity. I learned that during the massacre some had received physical injuries so severe they had been prevented from making a decent living for decades. Most lived in poverty so crushing that even a minimal amount of financial compensation from Japan could have greatly improved the conditions of their lives."

But the Chinese Communist Party never asked Japan for reparations. Neither did the Nationalist Party. Both were too busy jockeying with each other for recognition and support from Japan in the post-war era to worry about such trivialities. In *The Ugly Chinaman and the Crisis of Chinese Culture*, Bo Yang says, "Chinese people are very clever. No ethnic group in the world, not even the Jews, is as shrewd as the Chinese. So shrewd are they, in fact, that once they've been sold off for the kill, they continue haggling over the price of their own flesh all the way to the slaughterhouse. If they can earn five extra bucks before the knife passes through their necks, they will die in ecstasy, knowing they had not lived in vain."

After the Communists took charge, they filled newspapers with articles blaming the Nanjing Massacre on the United States, a country which supposedly aided the Japanese in their carnage. The Xinhua News Agency reported that the American government protected its "companies, churches, schools and residences with the blood and bones of the Chinese people." The safety zone committee was depicted as a gang of marauding imperialists that had worked in "faithful collusion" with the Japanese Army.

Of course, there ought to have been a museum dedicated to the committee, but there wasn't so much as a plaque. That wasn't part of the plan. Besides, the organizers of the Nanjing Safety Zone were merely in the business of saving lives, whereas righteous factions like the Boxers and the Taipings were in the business of taking them.

Next to the Presidential Palace, in the Ming-style garden, I heard someone say, "Hey, didn't I see you yesterday at the Sun Yat-sen Mausoleum?" It was a Canadian man named Dave. He was visiting Nanjing with his wife, a native of that city, and his father, a retired professor. He and his wife were very friendly, and I strolled around with them for a bit and chatted. The father wanted to know how far away Taipei was from Nanjing.

"Taipei is in Taiwan," his son explained.

"Oh, Taiwan," he said. "Taiwan is part of China."

"Well, not according to many of the people living there," I replied.

"Taiwan is part of China," he repeated. "That's where that rotten Chiang Kai-shek got to after the civil war."

Ergo, Taiwan was a part of China.

After surveying some nearby tile-and-cage buildings, the ex-professor professed, "It looks to me like the Chinese are building their society on the basis of science and technology; science and technology." He said everything twice, the second time with more assurance. The first time was merely a warm-up.

I attempted to challenge him on his Taiwan theory, but after years of lecturing, he appeared to be incapable of discussion or debate. The theme of his discourse was China and its great rise. I made sure I took notes. "The Chinese are playing a game of catch-up; a game of catch up," he declared sagaciously. "But they can do it; they can do it."

It was a variation on an argument that I had heard many times before. China is destined for greatness. Why? Because I said so, and there will be no questions as to why it won't. Subscribing to the idea of China's greatness and its inevitable supremacy wasn't unlike subscribing to a religion. Proponents needn't provide evidence; it was just something they knew. Others were required to either believe or be quiet. Sceptics were heretical, incapable of seeing the light.

I took a taxi to the university district and got to talking with the driver. It was odd, but talking to taxi drivers was one of the only times I felt as though I could ask whatever questions I wanted and really communicate with people. Alone, and in private, Chinese people are infinitely more candid than they are even with their friends, and for a traveller like me, catching a cab made for a rare moment of closeness. I knew too that the Chinese sometimes felt safer sharing their thoughts with foreigners as there was almost zero chance of their words coming back to haunt them.

The driver, Mr. Zhang, asked me if I'd been to Sun Yat-sen's mausoleum yet, before adding that he went there at least once a year to pay his respects. I told him I had, and asked him whether he thought his life would have been different had the Nationalists not been kicked out of the country. "Sure it would have," he said. "For one thing, I probably wouldn't have spent my entire life driving a cab. I might have actually made something of myself. I might have some money saved in my bank account. *All* Chinese people might have some money saved in their bank accounts, not just a few. Our government," he went on, shaking his head, "is extremely stupid. Many people in Nanjing think that, but not young people. Young people will believe anything."

Sun Yat-sen's ideas and those of the Communist Party were, of course, worlds apart, but he was the one person the Party could never criticize or vilify. Sun Yat-sen was untouchable. But he wasn't beyond censorship, as the signs at his mausoleum attested.

I spent an hour strolling around Nanjing University's campus examining women's underwear, but only because it was hanging in nearly every barred-up balcony I passed. In an adjacent student ghetto filled with cheap restaurants and coffee shops, I talked to a fellow from Uganda who was in Nanjing doing a business degree. He said he enjoyed studying in Mandarin even though writing reports was "a killer."

"I like living in China," he declared in a thick accent. "It's not so bad. Good food. Beautiful women. And I should be able to get a good job when I go back home. The Chinese are investing a lot of money in Africa." By the looks of things, Africa was investing a lot of students in China.

In a record store (everything was pirated), I ran into a young French couple and a young German who were living and studying Mandarin there. They were all cheerful and spoke fluent English.

"Why study Chinese?" I asked them.

"Why not?" the French fellow answered smilingly.

"Do you think China is a rising superpower?" I asked.

"Just look around!" he said, as though I were a bit daft.

"Are you only interested in the language, or aspects of culture, too?"

"Everything," said his girlfriend. "Culture, history…"

"What's an aspect of Chinese culture that the West ought to copy?" I asked. They were still smiling, but they were stumped. "What's something Chinese civilization has to teach Western civilization?" I rephrased, but they just looked at each other and nervously admitted they couldn't think of anything. "And what's your opinion of China's military buildup?" I wanted to know. They claimed not to be aware of it.

I thought they were nice, but naive. They were young, and living in Nanjing, one could be forgiven for thinking that China was all peaches and cream. As Chinese cities went, it wasn't at all bad. Moreover, it was pleasant on its own terms, not because of some lingering Western architectural influence.

I had hoped to interview some Chinese students, but when I approached a group of them, they began to point and laugh. "Oh, my god!" they repeated, cackling.

I couldn't find a taxi driver that knew where Taiping North Road was, never mind that it was almost certainly named after the famous rebellion. I walked back to my hotel, which took quite a long time, but at least the walk was agreeable.

That night, on CCTV, I watched an English-language documentary on the Japanese occupation of Manchuria, news which reprimanded "Taiwan province" for "downplaying the Rape of Nanjing" in its textbooks, and a show on China's "8,000-year-old jade culture." After showing some early examples of jade ware, the narrator explained that because jade was considered 'good' and 'pure,' the word 'jade' was a synonym for 'goodliness.' In the Chinese language, there was a plethora of idioms containing the word 'jade,' all of which were resoundingly positive. Jade's association with all things good was the reason why a jade circle with a star in the middle had been chosen runner-up in the national contest to select an emblem for the Chinese Communist Party.

Chapter Twenty-One

In the queue for the check-in counter at the airport, four people took the foot of space between me and the person in front of me to be their own. In each instance, I asked, "Do you think you could please line up?" For each answer, I got an "Oh," the standard apology. Once seated, I was handed a copy of the *China Daily* so that I might have my Two Minutes Hate.

The president of Taiwan, Chen Shui-bian (routinely accused of splitting the motherland) was slammed for ordering the removal of the words 'China' or 'Chinese' from various government offices and state-run enterprises in the "province of Taiwan." This was what happened when a political party's sole objective was to benefit itself, the article moralized. Turning to sports, the national soccer team had apologized for its role in a brawl that occurred during a friendly with the London club, Queens Park Rangers. However, the Chinese media was disgruntled by the gesture as it was tantamount to an admission of guilt.

Admitting guilt is something you must do your utmost to avoid in Chinese society. Not only could it cause an enormous loss of face, but there is every chance it will only serve to embolden your accuser. And because you will never be forgiven anyway, there is little reason to express regret. Defiance and refutation are deemed vital, and therefore automatic responses. This is a defence mechanism akin to the one exhibited by Bo Yang's TB patient. It is no coincidence that Bo Yang's discourse on what ails Chinese culture begins and ends with vehement, white-knuckled denial.

One of the chief obstacles I encountered in teaching high school students in Taiwan was trying to impress upon them that it was all right to say they were sorry, at least to me and other members of the foreign staff. With new students, it took me months to prove to them that I really would forgive and forget and that by conveying a sincere apology they would not only garner my respect, but illustrate that they had taken a step toward the world of adulthood. This was a difficult concept to process, especially for the younger ones. Generally speaking, maturity is not viewed as a goal.

Once, as I was teaching a class, I heard a commotion in the hallway and opened the door to find a rare sight: two boys boxing each others' heads in. Naturally, I broke them up and marched them to the office. Their defence was that I had snagged the wrong guys. Two other boys had been fighting, not them; never mind that there was no one else in the hall, they were supposed to be in class, they had disrupted my class, etc., etc.

What happened next was what happened often: the director was impressed by their lying and denial, and by their ability to withstand her interrogation. Surely, these young scholars were slated for careers in law or politics. The onus was then on me to prove it had been them, but because I had no evidence or witnesses, they were let go with a light, almost respectful warning. As the foreign staff knew, there was never any point in suggesting to the local staff that they had things the wrong way round; it would only have been denied. Besides, suggestion is really just a form of criticism, and criticism only flows in one direction.

From a gleaming new airport, I rode on a bus through a sweeping, treeless countryside marked by smokestacks, grassy fields, erratically shaped hills, and loess soil. Approaching the city, the vehicle melded into a glutinous jumble of honking cars, tour buses, green taxis, and farm equipment. Haloed in a yellowish grey haze, the city of Xian proved to be an unbeautiful metropolis of cranes, overdone hotels, soulless side streets, dirt, and an ungodly amount of noise. It was surrounded by a very large and very impressive wall.

As I stood on a corner waiting for one of the city's green cabs, I was accosted by begging children, a pretty woman who gave me her English business card ('Are you like the special romance massage night? Yes? Quickly come this telephone!'), a cheery Muslim selling a kind of sweet snack (which I bought and enjoyed), a man peddling live rabbits from a cardboard box, and a screaming, bent-backed grandma who urgently wanted me to buy a map. "Inkylish! Inkylish!" she bellowed, waving it in my face. After half an hour, an auto-rickshaw pulled up, and the driver, a man with one leg, asked, "Where to?"

We manoeuvred down a long, grey, polluted boulevard toward the foreigner-friendly Ludao Hotel. After a steamy and refreshing shower, I headed to the ticket counter to book a trip to see the Terracotta Warriors. The female clerk was gorgeous.

"Is it really worth seeing?" I asked, as she wrote out the receipt.

"Sure," she said.

"And how many times have you been there?"

"Oh… well… none."

"You're telling me you live in Xian, but you've never been to see the Terracotta Warriors?"

"No, I haven't," she replied. "To tell you the truth, I don't think they're that interesting." And then in a lowered voice, she added, "They're just something that foreigners like. I don't really know why."

The following day was *Chuxi*, or Chinese New Year's Eve, and as I was the only person to have booked a tour, the receptionist called early to see if I would kindly cancel. "No problem," I said, and went back to bed.

Later, I took a walk through the city, making my way toward its restored Bell Tower and Drum Tower before backtracking to the Muslim Quarter. Along the way, I passed through a park and had a conversation in English with a man headed in the same direction.

"Hello," he said. "How are you?"

"Not bad, yourself?"

"I'm okay. I imagine you're a tourist."

"Yes, that's right."

"Well, welcome to Xian. Where are you from?"

"Canada."

"Oh, Canada. I see. Well, I imagine that it's a very nice country, although I wouldn't know because I've never been abroad. I imagine you've come here to see the Terracotta Army."

"Yes."

"Well, it's pretty interesting. I'm sure you'll enjoy it. Anyway, I'm going this way, so take care and enjoy your time in Xian."

"Thank you. I will."

When travelling in China, you reach a point where you become somewhat leery of people, and on this leg of my journey I had reached that point in Beijing. When the man failed to harass, solicit, or insult me, I wasn't just relieved; I was amazed.

A short while later, I was eating lunch in a half-full restaurant when a woman asked if she could join me. I said, "Sure," and she sat down. I kept waiting for the, 'Here's my card. Call me if you need a massage,' but it never came. She told me she was in the publishing business, we chatted about what that entailed, she asked me what I was doing in China, we talked casually about that for a while, we said it was nice to meet each other, and then went our separate ways. It was completely normal, and it confused me to no end.

I found Xian's Muslim Quarter to be rather fascinating and rather filthy. A cramped district that coalesced around a large mosque, which resembled a Chinese temple, scores of white-capped people sauntered between its open-fronted shops and stands. A medley of foodstuffs was on offer, everything from sizzling kebabs to coloured sweet cakes to grinning goats' heads. I peered into a kitchen; a cream-walled room in a grey-bricked building filled with Muslim women standing around vats of bubbling soup, flames licking the sides of the great containers. Across the street was a shop selling boiled-mutton-dumpling soup. A pair of men stood behind billowing pots while ladling their product into imitation china bowls. Another man smoked as he sat beside his bicycle. The attached cart was spanned by a board with a tablecloth over it. Holding it in place was a scale and a large round cake filled with peaches and walnuts. Shoppers filled cellophane bags with water chestnuts, pistachios, dates, and peanuts that were displayed in oval baskets that rested on battered tables in front of rudimentary stores. Others bought slabs of meat from *roudian*, or butcher shops: rooms of stains, dangling light bulbs, and rust-coloured hooked carcasses. Shop signs were written mainly in Chinese, although some were done in Arabic. One man sold decks of playing cards, which featured images of the top 52 most-wanted Iraqi war criminals and the top 52 Communist Party heroes. I saw Great China cigarettes, which had an image of Sun Yat-sen on the front, and *San Min Zhu Yi* cigarettes (Three Principles of the People), which used the Nationalist flag as its logo. The maker of the patriotic smokes was a company called Long Life.

In another lane, I came across a Han Chinese man doing calligraphy with heady gold ink on strips of red paper. People lined up to buy them and crowded around to watch. There were birds in cages, miniature Terracotta Warriors, embroidered silk slippers, and heaps of other curios. It was remarkably quiet and the only person who solicited me was a woman who said, "Pee boy" as I walked by. She poured water into the head of a figurine that "peed" past my elbow and onto the street. Perhaps it was because the quarter was Muslim that it was so sedate. Absent were the speakers and the 'Come on Barbie, let's go party,' dance tracks often found in rival Chinese areas.

These Muslims were the Hui, 50,000 of which live among Xian's 8 million Han Chinese. Habitually described as ethnically and linguistically indistinguishable from the Han (the two groups intermarried during the days of the Ming Dynasty), the Hui comprise roughly half of China's 20 million Muslims. Other Muslim groups include the Bonan, the Chinese Tatars, the Dongxiang, the Kazaks, the Kyrgyz, the Salar, the Tajiks, the Tibetan Muslims, the Uighurs, and the Uzbeks.

I asked a man who I guessed was Han Chinese (he wasn't wearing a cap) if the Chinese got along with the Muslims. He said, "Sure, no problems. They have delicious food and are good at business."

"What about in the past?" I asked.

"No problems," he replied.

No problems, except for a long and tumultuous relationship: one characterized by friction, repression, discrimination, unfair taxation, land seizures, settlement bans, violence, rioting, widespread and prolonged uprisings (which spread to Xian), jihads, Chinese attacks, Muslim counter attacks, open warfare, and, naturally, the deaths of millions of people. Most of this occurred during the Qing Dynasty (at one point, Qing officials were mulling over a Muslim extermination campaign), but was rooted in the distant past. Largely owing to the Silk Road, the Muslims had begun settling in China ever since the Tang Dynasty (618-907 CE). During the Yuan Dynasty (1271-1368 CE), the ruling Mongols gave Arab, Persian, and Uighur immigrants leverage over the Han by employing them as administrators, scholars, and architects. Han resentment was mammoth and the Muslims were made to pay in the centuries to come.

Although hushed, the Hui neighbourhood was exceedingly unhygienic. Its public toilets made for recurrent olfactory assaults and there was an endless supply of dirt. As I was debating another circumambulation, a woman swept a dead rat out of her door. It skimmed across the pavement and landed at my feet. 'Time to go,' I thought.

At the base of a stone ramp, I bought a ticket to the city walls and walked atop them for an hour or so. It was like walking along an elevated road, and I gazed through the parapets at all the smog, rooftops, and construction sites. The sun was represented by a long white fissure in an otherwise lugubrious grey sky. Underneath it, in a neighbourhood of grey houses and leafless trees, grown-ups sold New Year's couplets of brilliant red while kids lit the fuses of large firecrackers and then darted off, hands over ears. 'TSSSSSS – BOOOOOOOOM!!!!!' They were as loud as bombs; the sound recoiling off the sturdy walls and reverberating throughout the town.

That night was like World War III. The window in my room and, indeed, the walls of the hotel itself, shook until dawn. All the guests gathered in the lobby and attached restaurant to drink beer and dart outside for an occasional photo. In addition to the fireworks, people were lighting *crates* of firecrackers. A warning on one read, 'Caution – This Box Contains 100,000 Explosives.' It was unbelievable. People would fling lit matches at the containers, which were placed on sidewalks or streets, and then sprint indoors. The phosphorescence-bathed roads morphed into rivers of singed crimson paper.

I'll never understand the Chinese fascination with noise, but the Lunar-New-Year tradition is rooted in it. The reason why the Chinese explode firecrackers and paste couplets around their doors is to frighten off the beast Nian, who is afraid of loud sounds and the colour red. Nian lives under the sea or under the mountains and emerges during *Chuxi* to devour people, especially children. On New Year's Day, people greet each other by saying, "*Gongxi*!" or "Congratulations!" for having survived the night.

The next morning ("*Gongxi*!"), I got on a minibus with a very friendly and very funny Canadian named Nick and an equally convivial Dutchman travelling with his teenaged son and daughter. After visiting two sites that were so uninteresting that I willfully forgot what they were, we headed to the Huaqing Pool: hot springs that were first exploited some 3,000 years ago. Other than its neglect, my cohorts and I soon began to wonder what we were supposed to be noticing. In an adjacent building, I noticed a pair of bullet holes; one in a wall and one in a pane of glass. I peered through the cracked glass to see a well-preserved bedroom. This, I suddenly realized, was the site of the famous Xian Incident, a 13-day ordeal which helped to shape world history.

At dawn, December 12, 1936, Chiang Kai-shek was inside this room in his nightshirt doing his morning exercises when he heard gunshots followed by a full-blown gun battle. After climbing out the back window, the 53-year-old managed to scale a wall, but then slipped and plummeted to the other side, injuring his waste and groin in the process.

Without his shoes, uniform, or false teeth, the leader of Free China lay there dazed for three minutes before getting to his feet and scrambling up a steep slope as bullets whizzed and thudded all around him. Up through the snow, he cut his feet on rocks and hurt his knee and back after tripping on branches. He found a cave secreted by a slab of stone and hid inside it. Coincidentally, Chiang's given name, Jieshi (Chiang Kai-shek's full name in Mandarin is Jiang Jieshi), means "Between Rocks."

The men searching for Chiang failed to find him, but in the end – injured, exhausted, and freezing – he gave himself up. Arrogantly, he asked for a horse, but wasn't given one. Most of his body guards had been shot dead and his generals in Xian were being rounded up and placed under arrest. One was dragged from a brothel.

It was not a *coup*, but a kidnapping; an idea conceived by a marshal named Zhang Xueliang (or Chang Hsueh-liang). A former Manchurian warlord with a drug addiction and a playboy reputation, Zhang had lent the generalissimo vital support during the Northern Expedition and

as a reward he had been given control of Manchuria, all 793,300 km²
of it. However, when the Japanese invaded and turned his domain into
Manchukuo, the militarist and his Northeastern China Army fled. Not
surprisingly, this caused him a great deal of shame and resentment. It also
made him fiercely anti-Japanese, a sentiment his overlord did not seem to
share.

Zhang Xueliang spent the next several years tracking the Communists.
However, without much in the way of material support from Chiang
Kai-shek, his forces sustained more casualties than they should have.
Eventually, the marshal was relocated here to Shaanxi where he worked
with a former Northeastern China Army general (and current Nationalist
general) named Yang Hucheng. Both men believed they were about
to be marginalized once more as Chiang Kai-shek was bringing in his
best troops to eradicate the rebels hiding out in the caves of Yanan,
an operation which the generalissimo was referring to as the "last five
minutes." With this in mind, Zhang began to conduct secret negotiations
with the Communists, something that he did for months. Eventually, it
was decided to abduct the Nationalist leader and force him to commit to
a non-aggression pact with the Yanan faction and to rekindle the United
Front.

As it happened, capturing Chiang Kai-shek had been a reasonably
simple affair. Getting him to co-operate was anything but. Chiang scoffed
at Zhang and his list of demands. Then, he declined to take food or
drink or even to talk to his captor. To be certain, Zhang was in a bind.
His troops refused to attack a Xian airbase controlled by men supportive
of Chiang, and troops from Nanjing had been mobilized to move
against him. After a great deal of wrangling and indecision regarding
Chiang's fate (on behalf of all those involved; many wanted him hung),
the prisoner eventually agreed to a sit-down with Zhang Xueliang,
Yang Hucheng, and a Communist panel headed by Zhou Enlai. The
meeting was dominated by reciprocal flowery statements and tributes
and culminated in Chiang Kai-shek's verbal agreement to end hostilities
against the Communists and resume the United Front. The following
day, Christmas Day, Chiang Kai-shek was released whereupon he flew
back to Nanjing with Zhang Xueliang in tow. News of the agreement was
released to the public.

Chiang Kai-shek swiftly published a statement in which he insisted
he'd made no promises whatsoever. Moreover, he admonished Zhang and
Yang and ordered that they obey the orders of the central government so
as to "turn a national calamity into a national blessing." It was blessing,
all right – for the Communists. Because news of the pact had spread

so quickly, and because it was met with such enthusiasm, it would have been political suicide for Chiang Kai-shek to follow through with his extermination campaign. When one of his advisors urged for an immediate attack on Yanan, the freed Nationalist leader bowed his head and refused to answer.

In Nanjing, Zhang Xueliang was promptly arrested and put on trial. He received a 10-year sentence that was later commuted to detention at Chiang Kai-shek's discretion. The Manchurian marshal spent the next half century under house arrest, first in China, and then in Taiwan. He wasn't released until 1991. General Yang Hucheng was also placed under house arrest. His wife protested by conducting a hunger strike and died. Yang carried her ashes around in a box.

Thirteen years later, just before Chiang Kai-shek made his escape to Taiwan, he ordered that all political prisoners be shot. Then he gave a special order. Police paid a visit to General Yang's house where they shot one of his sons. Then they shot him, one of his daughters, six members of his staff, and their families. The bodies were drenched in acid and buried. Yang was buried in a flower box.

Zhang Xueliang is considered yet another shining Communist hero, as a sign near the bullet holes explained:

> 'In February, 1982, Five-Room House was listed as a major cultural and historic site under state protection and has been used for on-site patriotic education. Since 2005 it has become a tourist attraction for revolutionary education.'

I relayed a short version of the Xian Incident to Nick and the Dutch family. The father looked shocked. When our tour guide returned to fetch us, he asked her, "Did something important happen here in history?" "Oh, yes," she said. "I forgot to tell you the story about the emperor and his favourite concubine…"

It was how the Chinese preferred their history: in the form of fairy tales. Either that or it was enough to proudly parrot the phrase "Five thousand years of history!" without ever even alluding to what that history entailed. Surely, a darker or more tragic history cannot exist. Chinese history is thousands of years of tyranny, treachery, brutality, conflict, warfare, upheaval, and chaos. It makes Russian history, also extremely bleak, appear rather cheery by comparison.

We ate lunch in a restaurant that resembled a bunker. We were the only customers there and when the owner saw us, she shouted, "Hawlo, chicken? Hawlo, rice?" As we picked at oil-soaked cubes of meat and vegetables, people came in with large watercolour paintings, which they displayed silently as we talked. Then, they shuffled off. Historically, Shaanxi province has been a place of profound poverty.

Sated, it was off to see the Terracotta Warriors. Because it is the second most visited tourist site in the country, we were made to run a gauntlet of shops and stands pushing everything from warrior replicas to wolves' pelts. After inspecting a museum, we filed into Pit One. It reminded me of a sports arena. We strolled around the walkway, peering down at the columns of figures and fragments. With no temperature control, the air was cool and chalky and the walkway contained as many soldiers as it did tourists. They were being shepherded about by their squad leaders and given their daily dose of patriotic education ("You see!? We've *always* been a nation of warriors!"). Methodically, I made my way around to the southeast corner where I paused for moment. It was here where the discovery was made.

In the spring of 1974, Shaanxi suffered from a drought. The Yang brothers, all six of them; all farmers, decided they had to dig a well. When they had gotten a metre down, they struck a rock-hard layer of earth that they took to be the roof of an ancient kiln, something they knew the area possessed. It took them two days to get through this thin but solid stratum whereupon the soil became soft again. Then, they began to shovel up pieces of pottery, which confirmed that it was a kiln, but they remained unimpressed as their goal was water. Next, they uncovered what they thought was a pot, which pleased them because a pot was something they could use. Unfortunately, it wasn't a pot, but rather a ceramic torso, which they examined and cast aside. After that, they unearthed the corresponding head along with a set of arms and legs. As they continued to dig, all the debris started to attract attention and locals came to sift through it. Some bronze arrowheads that had been brought up were carted off and sold as scrap. Children carried away the torso and made it into a scarecrow. An old woman who fancied the head took it home, lit some joss sticks, and prayed to it.

What the Yang brothers had discovered was an adjunct of the First Emperor's tomb, an event which may have gone unnoticed had the chief of the agricultural cadre not come by to check up on them. He reported the finding to a local archaeologist and museum official who, after some hesitation (he had been struggled against by the Red Guards – accused of his connection with "old things"), reported it to the capital, whose leaders were still embroiled in their so-called revolution. It was fortunate that he chose that particular moment to do so. The deranged Jiang Qing and her disturbed coterie hoped that this news of "pottery figures unearthed near the First Emperor's mausoleum" would bolster their status as Legalists (like the despotic First Emperor had been) and aid in their struggle against the "Confucians" or "feudalists." In fact, a phone call from Jiang Qing is what got the excavation started. No sooner had the discovery of the Terracotta Warriors been made than it was utilized as a political tool, one to justify violence and oppression.

The premise behind such a tomb (located one and a half kilometres away from the pits of warriors, and only partially excavated) was by no means original. Kings and members of the aristocracy had been buried in elaborate and well-protected graves for thousands of years. As it was held that the afterlife reflected this one, it followed that the dead would require various articles to serve them once they entered it. These tended to include vessels of ceramic and bronze as well as items of jade, gold, and so on. Eventually, perhaps because of grave robbing or as a cost-saving measure, it was deemed that such items needn't be the genuine article; it was enough for them to merely represent an object. Materials like porcelain and bronze were substituted with clay. Some items were represented in miniature. Servants and concubines, who were customarily added to the sepulcher by being killed or buried alive, were replaced, or at least supplemented, by figures of wood and other materials.

Obviously, the man who united the seven Warring States would require something luxurious and highly realistic in order to impress the governors of the next realm. His tomb would have to be modelled after an entire imperial city, and seeing as how his unification and power had been achieved and maintained through the use of his armed forces, it was only logical that it should be protected by a spirit army.

A book I own claims that each warrior was made with an "individually crafted expression," which is not untrue, but not entirely accurate either. In actual fact, the army (of which some 8,000 figures have been discovered) was produced using a modular system, which is to say: they were assembled from prefabricated parts, almost certainly by a relatively small number of artisans. There were 80 primary molds, another 10 for the heads, 4 for the boots, 3 for the shoes, and 2 for the legs. It also appears that there were molds for the accessories, such as hair, ears, and mustaches. Indeed, hair, beards, and mustaches appear to have been very important in Qin society. There are infantrymen with flat-haired buns, round-haired buns, and pointed-hair buns. In Pit Number One, some mustaches are turned up, others are turned down; some are big; some are small – only one of the figures doesn't have one.

Once a warrior was assembled, it was then styled somewhat (with a scraper or a knife) to lend it a certain degree of individuality. The soldiers were also elaborately (some might say, 'gaudily') painted. Atop a base of lacquer (so much of which was used that it is believed whole forests were felled) went faces of pink, hair of black, uniforms of purple, green, blue, and red, and leather armour of white, orange, green, and yellow. After all of the figures (officers, archers, infantrymen, cavalrymen, horses, chariots, charioteers, etc.) had been assembled, styled, fired, varnished, and coloured, they were stored away to await the day when the progressively erratic and paranoid First Emperor shuffled off this mortal coil. Coincidentally, that day came while he was on a quest for an elixir for immortality.

As it wasn't known what the First Emperor's realm would ultimately encompass, and, by extension, what his tomb would need to possess, its construction, along with that of the warrior pit, was put on hold. It was resumed after a messenger returned to the emperor's palace (in the Qin capital of Xianyang) with the news of his death.

Atop a floor comprised of more than a quarter million bricks, the 6,000 warriors were placed, according to military formation, in the 11 corridors of the 260-metre-long, 62-metre-wide, and 9-metre-deep pit. At some point, the idea was expanded and three more warrior pits were built. In the adjacent Pit Two, archaeologists have identified another 1,300 figures, mainly archers, horses, and chariots. Pit Three is much smaller and believed to be a sort of command centre. There are 68 figures along with a 4-horse chariot. Pit Four is also tiny and a total mystery. It was left unfinished and unfilled.

At some undetermined point in time, a timber ceiling and system of support beams were added, another forest-felling endeavour. Something like 4,000 tonnes of lumber was transported by wagons from woodlands to the south. Once in place, the roof beams were covered by reed mats and clay for waterproofing. Next came three metres of land fill and a layer of topsoil. Down below, the colourful spirit army stood drenched in darkness and poised for battle – for all of four years. After the First Emperor's death, his kingdom relapsed into chaos and conflict and the pits were plundered for their weapons, all of which were very real and very useful. During the raid, a fire somehow broke out, apparently igniting the roof, which smouldered until it collapsed. The upshot was that not even one of the figures stayed intact. Hence, a restored figure is by no means the restructured version of the original.

Since the Yangs' accidental discovery (the hard layer of earth they encountered was, of course, the ceiling), archaeologists have cracked open hundreds of other pits, which contain tombs of the remains of those who followed the emperor (either willingly or otherwise – they were dismembered), a graveyard of crouching convict labourers, horse skeletons (hundreds of them), bird skeletons (in clay coffins), a giant-sized workshop, inexplicable stone armour, a "water garden" containing 46 bronze birds (cranes, geese, swans), dozens of gates and rooms, and a treasure trove of gold, silver, bronze, jade, porcelain, and much else.

Much more is sure to come. Archaeologists have been given the go-ahead to survey the entire area and a massive 57-km² museum complex is being planned. The tomb itself (350 square metres, with a 50- to 75-metre-high, pyramid-shaped mound) is now known to contain a walled structure, but besides that, what we know of it comes almost exclusively from an ancient historian named Sima Qian, who describes it as being filled with "wonderful objects," crossbows "rigged so they would immediately shoot down anyone attempting to break in," 'rivers and seas of mercury,' 'features of the heavenly bodies above' and 'of the earth below.' It may sound fantastical (indeed, the writings of Sima Qian seem to be as much legend as history), but mercury has been detected and may have been used to preserve the First Emperor's body. Excavation of the tomb is certain to prove a thorny affair. As the archaeologists learned with the Terracotta Army, the instant artifacts are unearthed they begin to decay. Mould is such a problem that in Pit Two, mushrooms were found. Carbon dioxide emitted from tourists and swarms of soldiers receiving patriotic education poses another threat. So does air pollution.

I thought the Terracotta Warriors were remarkable... to read about. Historian John Man's *The Terracotta Army* is unquestionably the best source. Seeing the clay soldiers, however, left a little to be desired. Still, I was glad that I'd visited China's ancient capital, situated near the Yellow River and the cradle of Chinese civilization.

The staff at the Ludao Hotel was extremely friendly and helpful. 'Obviously,' I thought, 'someone had had the good judgment to train them to be that way.' It turned out that that someone was the owner, a local man named (honestly) Jim Beam. I was glad I stayed there and not at some "authentic" hotel, where I would have been treated with suspicion, told it was impossible to use the telephone, and then solicited for sex. I spent my last evening in Xian in the hotel lobby and restaurant sipping beer and chatting with other travellers, including the quick-witted and humourous Canadian, Nick. He told me about his six-month stint in Africa working for Doctors Without Borders as a logistician.

"We were building a hospital," he explained, "so we needed cement. I was in charge of logistics, so I had to go to the local cement factory. Things move slowly in Africa, and I was there for something like five hours. Because the factory had been built by the Chinese, there were all these soldiers standing around barking orders at the workers and dressed in their combat fatigues. It was ridiculous. This was in the Congo, but they didn't speak a word of French. In fact, they never *spoke* to anyone, they just shouted. It was really strange. And the Chinese are all over Africa. But I guess it makes sense. African countries are so corrupt, it's only natural that the Chinese would want to do business with them."

Nick said he had come to China with the idea of living and teaching for a year or two, but had changed his mind.

"I don't know much about China, but from what I've seen it looks like it's stuck in a time warp. It feels like nineteen seventy-five."

At another table, I spotted a woman who I had run into that day while sightseeing. She had been on an identical tour with a different company and had wanted to know how much I paid for my ticket. We had paid the same price, about $26, for an excursion that included entrance to the Terracotta Warriors. She had fumed that she was being cheated, and then went off to take a photo in front of a large sign that said, 'Photos – 1 *Yuan*.' When someone tried to collect that *yuan* (about 13 cents), she started screaming. "No! No! I'm not paying! You didn't tell me! You didn't tell me!" Of course, having to pay for a photo was absurd, but I was positive that she did it on purpose. She had been looking for a confrontation. Now, she was asking me to join her and her husband.

"What did you think of the Terracotta Warriors?" she asked.

"I liked it well enough."

She twisted up her features and replied, "No! You are wrong! It was horrible! And people here… they only want your money!"

At China's second largest tourist attraction? Gee. Imagine that. Pleadingly, I glanced at her husband, whose eyes said, 'You don't have to tell me. *I'm* married to her.'

"Where ya from?" he asked.

"I'm from Canada."

"Well, *we* are from Croatia," his wife declared. "Have you been there?"

"No, I've never been to Europe."

"Never been to…? Never to been to Europe?" she stammered. She then looked me up and down with an expression that fell somewhere between awe and abhorrence.

"What? It's just churches and beer halls," I deadpanned.

"Churches and beer halls? Europe is *culture*. Ever since we have gotten here, we have been telling ourselves, '*Thank god we are European. Thank god we are European.*'" She pounded her fist rhythmically on the table as she said this, gritting her teeth. Then she said something I didn't quite catch. "Oh, well *please* pardon my poor English," she said dramatically. "But, in any case, it is *much* better than your Croatian."

I tried to excuse myself, but she petitioned me with questions before embarking on a lengthy tirade about how awful China was. India and Thailand had been "paradise," but not China. It had no culture, except for Beijing, which was "modern," and Chinese people were uncouth and only out to swindle you.

"You should try Sichuan," I said, but she failed to detect my low-brow North American irony.

"Really? Is it nice?" she asked, face suddenly alight with interest.

"Oh, it's *very* nice," I lied, "and very cultural."

She asked if I could recommend a city. "Chongqing," I said, and got out my map. "From there, you can take a Yangtze River boat tour. I did, and it was excellent. That river has so much culture and history, it's hard to describe really. In fact, you can probably book a trip right here from the ticket office. The price is very reasonable. Just go with the cheapest one. No need to pay extra."

She and her husband exchanged glances and nods. I reckoned that she would hurl herself over one of the underwear-draped railings after the umpteenth horn blast and the third swindle – sometime during the second day – thus doing the staff, other tourists, her husband, and doubtlessly several hundred Croatian citizens a great service.

CHAPTER TWENTY-TWO

I got up before dawn and caught a plane to Hangzhou, a city celebrated for its beauty. Hangzhou was Mao's favourite retreat, and his doctor, Li Zhishui, wrote that its West Lake was the most stunning place he had ever seen, and he had studied medicine in Australia. It must have been beautiful in the past, or perhaps it was meant to be visited in the summer. In any case, it wasn't beautiful at all when I went there.

I checked into a guest house on the lake and then went to the hospital. I had what I guessed was a urinary tract infection. Using the internet, I had diagnosed myself and bought what I believed to be the correct antibiotic. The hospital came recommended by my almost-always-reliable guidebook, but it was closed for the holidays. Luckily, its emergency room was still open.

After relaying the symptoms to the female receptionist, she diagnosed me with having a *xing bing*, or sexually transmitted disease, which she relayed to the staff by way of hollering. She then told me that the doctor had gone home, but that she would call him and ask him to come back.

"So, there's no doctor on duty right now?" I asked.

"Of course not," she replied. "It's Chinese New Year."

Hangzhou has a population of 8.1 million people.

I was given a plastic cup with, and I am not embellishing, a tiny hole in its side. The bathroom doubled as a public toilet. People walked in off the street to use it. Its floor was a lacquer of excrement, urine, and cigarette butts, and its window faced the road so that pedestrians could (and did) watch me producing a specimen. I turned my back on them and put some tissue over the hole. I brought it to the lab and then returned to the lobby to wait. And watch. The nurses' uniforms were brown with dirt; the walls had footprints on them. The place was dimly lit and effectively a shambles. The doctor was not happy to see me.

"Your urine test is fine," he barked. "Why are you here?"

"Well, I'm in quite a bit of pain."

We went into the next room to do a physical exam, but the light didn't work. He cursed and ushered me over to the door in order to utilize the light from the hall. When he went to put on a rubber glove, he dropped it and spent the next minute searching for it, swearing. When he found it, instead of putting it in the garbage, he angrily kicked it under a desk.

"You just have a slight infection," he concluded after feeling around. He was clearly annoyed.

"Is it a 'urinary tract' infection?" I asked, as we moved to another room.

"I don't know what it's called in English," he growled and then he flailed an arm, indicating that I could sit down. He prescribed some antibiotics and said, "There. Are you satisfied now? Take them three times a day. Don't eat spicy food or bananas. Drink plenty of warm water."

When I showed him the capsules I had bought at a drug store, he said, "Those are pretty much the same thing; same class. So, what did you come in here for!?"

But the antibiotics didn't work, and the discomfort didn't go away until I visited a hospital in Taiwan, where I got a full battery of tests, a proper diagnosis (it was a urinary tract infection; probably from drinking bad water), antibiotics that worked, and an English-speaking doctor with a professional demeanour. When I told him I'd just returned from China, he grimaced a little and said, "We'd better give you a thorough exam."

Incidentally, to the Chinese way of thinking, warm water is the cure for just about everything. By extension, cold water, and cold beverages in general, are to be avoided as they might adversely affect your health. This is widely believed, even by educated people. An influential nonprofit organization in Taiwan recently warned against "addiction(s) to cold bottled drinks on hot days." A doctor at the Taipei City Hospital supported the announcement by adding that although "gulping icy drinks probably cools people down and delights them," they could cause skin rashes, black eyes, nasal problems, diarrhea, and an ominous-sounding condition called dydroncus, which, it turns out, doesn't exist.

I went back to the lake and tried to walk around it, but gave up after about half an hour. The paths were overflowing with plodding tourists, trolleys with elderly passengers, megaphone-clutching tour guides, and parents straight from the countryside who actively encouraged their children to gawp and snicker at foreigners. I wasn't the only one targeted. I noticed a French-speaking couple that appeared quite distressed.

As for the lake itself, it was just a lake; steel grey and surrounded by dim brooding hills that were marked by pagodas. Having grown up minutes from a whole host of lakes that were much finer, not to mention free of man-made objects, I failed to see what the all the fuss was about.

Chinese people will flock by the tens of thousands in order to view something that is entirely commonplace in other countries. It wasn't that Hangzhou's West Lake was extraordinary, but rather that it was *said* to be extraordinary; testimony to the powerful influence of the oral tradition. "Above is heaven, below are Suzhou and Hangzhou," went the ancient maxim. So it had to be true. There was an ancient maxim. But its popularity was also evidence of the need to experience something collectively. It may be a loathsome generalization, but it is generally true: nothing frightens the Chinese quite like the prospect of isolation.

There's a lesson I recently taught to a class of adult students about New Zealand, where that country is described as beautiful, mountainous, full of farms, and ideal for swimming, skiing, boating, and other outdoor activities. It's accompanied by a picture of the snow-crested Mount Cook and shows a nicely built, empty highway snaking through fields of gold and patches of pine. When I said to my 17 students, almost all of whom were in their thirties, "It sounds great, don't you think? It makes me want to go there," there was a rare silence during which I swore I could hear a collective mental scream. An impromptu survey revealed that no one would be willing to go there; the photo contained no people.

Interestingly, during the cinematic success of the *The Lord of the Rings* trilogy, which was filmed in New Zealand several years earlier, nearly *all* of my students claimed they wanted to travel to that country to see its beauty. But that collective thought had been replaced by another one. Currently, the destination of choice was New York City because it was "modern" and "fashionable," or so every single member of another adult class I recently taught told me. After all, that was how it was portrayed in the new movie *Sex and the City*. When I politely informed my students that New York City was not entirely modern, less fashionable than they might think, not altogether safe, nor even very clean, many appeared quite shaken. Two or three were visibly upset. But I figured I was doing them a favour. The shock and disappointment wasn't nearly as large as the one they would have gotten had they travelled there. I have had two people tell me that the quietude of New Zealand and the United States nearly drove them mad. It was "so frightening," they both said. Left alone with their thoughts, they realized that, beyond a desire to be entertained, go shopping, or have a bite to eat, they didn't have any.

My guest house had a homey eating area, so I went there to sip tea and read. I got to talking with a meaty, self-effacing, happy-go-lucky American named Ryan who taught English conversation and literature at a university near the city of Jinan in Shandong. He'd just finished his first semester. I asked him what that was like.

"Well, it was certainly interesting. Probably the most interesting thing that happened this semester was that one of my students had a mental breakdown. After two months of being asked for his opinion and to interpret literary passages, he had an epiphany: he realized he didn't know anything. He said he knew a lot of facts, but that he didn't have any real knowledge or informed opinions; no one had ever asked him what he thought before and the facts he knew were all useless. It was kind of hard for him to take, and he was pretty depressed for a while, but he'll get over it I think."

I asked him what Jinan was like.

"Oh, it's *polluted*," he said. "It's a coal mine and cement factory town. They say America is more polluted than China, but it can't be. Not even Michigan, where I'm from, even comes close to some of the stuff I've seen here. One night, I literally could not see my hand in front of my face. I swear to god. *Literally*. My students always tell me that it's fog, but it's not fog. Fog doesn't make you choke. Basically, China's about a hundred years behind when it comes to pollution and environmental protection."

He went on to relay a story about being on a bus one day when he noticed that the top of a mountain was on fire.

"When I said, 'Hey, everybody! Look at that!' to the other commuters, *nobody* batted an eyelash; *nobody*. And I mean *the whole mountaintop* was in flames. It was serious, but no one seemed to care."

He said that his students often asked him questions about politics, but that he always tried to dodge them.

"Like, they always ask me about Taiwan, but I just lie and tell them I don't know anything about it. But they always say, 'But that's the most important political issue on Earth!' Of course it's not, but they think China *is* the Earth. They don't know very much," he added quietly, "but they *are* really nice."

I hung around Hangzhou for another day, but really shouldn't have. There wasn't anything to see or do. It was damp and foggy, and there were no shadows. It was as if I were existing within a Tupperware container.

I went to the bank again to change money, and of course they were showing an episode of Mr. Bean. Mr. Bean was trying to console a crying baby by tying a balloon to its carriage. When that didn't work, he bought a bunch of balloons and tied those to the carriage. As you will have guessed, the carriage became airborne. The 20 or so people watching this erupted into laughter. Then, they began expressing concern for the baby's safety. "*Na hen weixian,*" someone said. "That's so dangerous." "How are they going to get it back down?" "Oh, it's so frightening."

Good god.

At the counter, I wrote in all the usual smart-ass answers on the form. (Accommodation: igloos, wigwams, tree houses. Tickets: bus, train, Italian opera. Remarks: It's cool out this morning.) It was often impossible to know what information they wanted and no one could read it anyhow, so what did it matter? When I handed the sheet to the teller, she began to giggle. I thought she had spotted the 'I've a thing for dumplings' remark in the 'Reason for Visiting to PRC' box, but I was wrong.

"In your country," she asked, "telephone numbers only have seven digits?" When I said 'yes,' she went off to show her colleagues, who all tittered and tee-heed. In China, phone numbers contain eight digits. It reminded me of the part in *The True Story of Ah-Q* where the peasant protagonist ventures into another village and jeers at the locals for calling a "long bench" a "straight bench."

I gave the lake another try at night, and, admittedly, it was much more pleasant without the droves of cattle-like tourists. But it was still just a lake. I returned via the main road and saw three car dealerships all next to each other: Porsche, Ferrari, and Maserati. Besides being a status symbol, I wondered what the point would be in owning such a car in China. No sooner had I thought this than a tow truck rushed by pulling a half-demolished taxi.

The taxi driver I got the next day to the train station was a complete maniac. He cut people off, he wove in and out of traffic, and he tailgated, seemingly for the fun of it. I fumbled with the seat belt, but he ordered me not to put it on, citing that it was too dirty. I just got it fastened when we nearly rear-ended a bus.

From the outside, the train station looked like a refugee camp: hundreds of dishevelled-looking people were crouching and milling about. They ate, smoked, spat, stared…. I figured they'd gotten caught out in the holiday demand for tickets. I was about to enter the place when I heard an enormous row coming from some attached offices. There were violent crashing noises, shouts, shrieks, and more crashing noises. It lasted for several minutes and was so vicious-sounding that I fully expected to see a body come crashing through one of the windows. When it was over, I walked up the stairs and by all the gawks and blank expressions and found my platform.

On the train, I ran into a Liverpudlian named Paul who I had met at my guest house. He was in the dining car with four empty beer bottles sitting in front of him. He told me that he was travelling around the world and that he thought China sucked. It was the worst place he'd been to so far.

"Ever' body I meet, they're like, 'China this n' China that,' an' now I'm thinkin', 'Whuh the fuck were they talkin' about?' Like, ya take Hangzhou fer instance," he said, pronouncing it as though it were French, "Whuh the fuck was that then, eh? A fuckin' lake is whuh i' was. Thas all. So whuh? It's got a lake. I mean, it's nothin' compared ta whuh ya see in England. Give me the Lake District any day. An' I imagine ya got some pretty nice lakes in Canada."

I said we had thousands of them and he began to tell me about his Yangtze River boat tour.

"Aye, I tell ya, I've never seen anythin' like it in my life. *Never* in my life. T'was a fuckin' disaster. I mean, t'was hell – absolute hell. The boat was freezin', the beer was warm, n' first-class my arse! I've not seen a transport ferry that was that dirty in England. China," he said, lighting up a smoke, "is not all it's cracked up to be. An' I'll tell ya somethin' else: the people here are bloody savages. I was in the train station usin' the toilet an' I heard this big fuck-off racket comin' from upstairs. It sounded like bloody fuckin' World War Three, like the fuckin' bloody end o' the world."

"I heard that, too."

"Did ya hear that? I'm tellin' ya, if I had a pound fer every argument I seen here, I'd be a rich fuckin' man."

I met up with Paul later in the dining car. He had spent the afternoon drinking, something I gathered he did often in light of his robust constitution. We were joined by a girl from Auckland and another from Montreal who both taught English in Korea. Later, the four of us went to the girls' compartment. There, Paul and I were introduced to a smallish fellow sitting on the lower berth named Mr. Tang. Mr. Tang had large gold-rimmed glasses and an oily comb-over. He was a travelling salesman who managed a few halting English phrases with the aid of an electronic dictionary. He seemed happy to see us.

"This guy is like *so* funny," said the New Zealander. "We don't know what he's saying half the time, but he's always smiling." She asked him some simple questions, but he just grinned and said, "Okay, I know. I will to check my *dikensiali*." Before long, Mr. Tang wanted to discuss history.

"The hwapiam hwal," he said. "You should to know the hwapiam hwal."

"What?" said the Canadian girl.

I looked at his dictionary. It said, 'opium.' He was trying to talk about the Opium Wars.

"One day," he said, smiling, "we will to take revenge. China will to take revenge."

"What the hell is he talking about?" the girl from New Zealand asked, looking at me and pulling a face.

"I have no idea," I lied.

That night, the train shuttled southwest through Zhejiang province into Jiangxi province before swinging east into Fujian province. Because of the mountains, we were zigzagging our way to our destination. The trip ended up taking 26 hours.

In the morning, I went to the dining car to drink bottled tea and slurp instant noodles. The only customer there, I sat at a table in the middle, but was ordered by the waitress to sit in the corner. I could have predicted it.

"Why?"

"Because the staff is going to have breakfast and we need to sit together," the waitress said.

The staff came in and took up two tables. The cigarettes came out and everyone shovelled food into their gobs and yakked at top decibel. There were still two tables between them and the one I had been at. There had been no reason to move me, unless perhaps to exert authority. But I guessed it had more to do with the Chinese obsession with control, one of the many manifestations of their profound insecurity.

Rain swept against the window like falling gravel and the absence of sunlight caused the verdant and dramatic mountains of Fujian to appear as enormous piles of charcoal. Clouds of silver kneaded their craggy summits while crude cement homes lay scattered like dice at their feet. We clacked alongside a hulking, turgid river marked by bamboo piers and clusters of soaked skiffs. Its tawny waters stopped just short of flooding the horizon, above which rested a thick stratum of yellowish coral brush-stroked with grey rain. Later, the atmosphere turned cream and the rugged versants and ravines appeared less sombre and more handsome. The foliage was the colour of boiled spinach. Rain-battered palms were eyelashed to the tops of distant hills. The province of Fujian looked exactly as I thought it would: like the countryside of Taiwan, only much poorer. Only five percent of this province isn't made up of hills or mountains.

The train was not at all clean. It had the air-conditioned stench of ten thousand smoked cigarettes and the gangways were beset by packaging and grunge. In one such area, there was a sign above a black gooey floor ring where a trash can had obviously once been. Fittingly, it said, 'Rubbish Heap.' The bathrooms were equally horrid, as usual. I had become expert at using them while not touching a single surface. I couldn't wait to alight.

I went back to my compartment and read. The berth below mine was being shared by a couple in their early twenties. They were university students returning to school for the spring semester. He was as effeminate as she was and wore a T-shirt that said, 'Witch Notice.' Hers said, 'Panda Jamboree.' The pair blabbed, giggled, cuddled, wrestled, pinched each others' cheeks, tonsil swabbed, and dry humped – for hours. When she got up to go to the toilet, he would put in his ear phones, listen to speed metal at full volume, and violently shake his head. When he went to the toilet, she would play a game on her cell phone and talk encouragingly to the tiny screen.

I arrived in Xiamen (or Amoy, as English speakers used to call the place) to find that it was a civilized and healthy city. At least that's what the large-character sign said outside the train station. Xiamen means "The Gate of the Grand Mansion."

I traversed an overpass in order to get a taxi and was solicited by vendors with conical hats and fists full of fruit who spoke in the dialect known as *Minnanyu*, or Southern Min, which to my ear sounded identical to *Taiwanhua*, or Taiwanese, which is a form of Southern Min. Having lived for so long in Taiwan, this seemed very strange to me, although it shouldn't have.

I caught a ferry to Gulang Yu, or Drum Wave Islet, just a short hop from Xiamen. My guidebook described the tiny isle as "an enchanting retreat of meandering lanes and shaded backstreets, set in an architectural twilight of colonial villas and crumbling remains." The colonial villas and crumbling remains had to do with the 38 British gunboats that sailed into the harbour in 1841 demanding that the port open for trade. Once that happened, Gulang Yu became a foreign enclave.

After checking into a hostel, I walked around in the light drizzle. A tinkling of piano emanated from a white-washed, Western-style conservatory. I ambled around rain-swept lanes of shops and banyan trees until I came to a traditional market: people selling fruits and vegetables from metal trays resting on overturned baskets and cinder blocks.

After a terrible sleep, I called Xiamen Airlines to reconfirm my ticket to Hong Kong. I spoke to three people and was informed in the end that I didn't have a ticket to Hong Kong.

"So, why would I call to reconfirm a ticket that I didn't have?" I asked.

"Oh."

"Are you going to confirm it or not?"

"We need your telephone number."

I had already told them the confirmation number and wanted to know what my telephone number had to do with anything.

"We need it so we can call you if there's a delay or a problem," the woman said brightly. She didn't seem to understand that there was a delay or problem now. In the end, she determined that finding my reservation was a matter of *meiyou banfa*: "There's nothing that can be done."

Certainly, if this rising superpower, this fearsome dragon, this nation that was supposedly shaking or on the cusp of shaking the world, had a slogan, this would be it: *meiyou banfa*. There's nothing that can be done. You can actually see people mentally working toward it. It's like a goal that, once attained, alleviates one from all responsibility. You don't meet some arbitrary, unreasonable, or totally irrelevant requirement, so too bad for you. And as for your being a paying customer, well, there are plenty of those. Haven't you seen all the people walking around outside? In the end, my reservation was found and reconfirmed, but only after I got angry and asked to speak to a manager. As I saw it, I was left with no other choice.

Luckily, the beautiful sunny weather brightened my mood, and not even the multitudes of Chinese tourists, with their idiot grins and derisive greetings, could dampen it, although they definitely tried.

I walked to a beach: a stretch of sand half covered in white plastic tables skewered by blue umbrellas practically rubbing against one another. The other half was covered by hundreds of tourists bundled up in wool sweaters and winter jackets. They were standing and staring at the water, a narrow and unspectacular channel filled with boats. There were so many people, in fact, that I could scarcely see the sand. Why they were dressed for arctic weather was anyone's guess; it must have been 20 degrees Celsius.

From the beach, I walked to the Sunlight Rock Park, which cost nearly 60 *yuan* to enter, a steep fee in China. A sign said, in Chinese, 'This is a Civilized Scenic Spot, Be a Civilized Tourist.' I climbed up the steps and saw another sign in English saying, 'Caution! Cliff!' It had a picture of a man plummeting head first to certain doom. Two other English signs said, 'No Striding' and 'No Tossing.'

The view was arresting. Drum Wave Islet featured a marmalade jumble of orange-roofed houses, some of them falling apart, others well-composed timepieces. The plant life was pretty too, and the sunshine sharpened all the island's edges. Across the blue channel there stood the recently built glass towers of Xiamen, which, from this distance, almost looked pleasing. However, I hadn't paid eight bucks for the privilege of climbing a rock to look at some skyscrapers. Rather, I was hoping to catch a glimpse of Jinmen, which I knew was only two kilometres away. As it was, I was looking southeast, when Jinmen was actually due east. But it wouldn't have mattered anyway as a bluish murk made it impossible to see anything other than the faint outlines of oil tankers just a few hundred metres away.

I saw two stubbly faced soldiers smoking and leaning against a rail, so I walked over to them and said hello. They looked startled.

"Where's Jinmen?" I asked them. They deliberated, scratched their heads, examined the haze and concluded they didn't know. "So, when do you think China is going to attack Taiwan?" I casually followed up.

"N-n-no! No!" one began nervously ("*B-b-bu! Bu!*")."We're not going to attack Taiwan." A group of people immediately stopped to eavesdrop, so I moved on to talk to someone else. I spotted a couple who looked to be in their late twenties. They were both wearing identical sweaters: powder blue with the American flag. They explained by saying they had gotten them from their company, which was based in the United States.

"We work with Americans," she explained in English. "Actually, they are very nice to us. It's much better than working for a Chinese company."

"Why's that?"

"Well," the man began, "they almost never make us work overtime. We finish work at five o'clock. If they ask us to work overtime, they pay us extra. Our friends can't believe it. Everyone wants to work for that company."

"That's good," I said, and, unfairly perhaps, changed the subject. "Do you know how many missiles China has aimed at Taiwan?" They didn't. "More than eight hundred, and your government has been adding something like one hundred every year. What's your opinion about that?"

They reflected for a moment and then the woman broke into a wide smile. "I think it's very great!"

"What do you mean?"

"Well, we hope we won't have to use them," she said.

"There won't be a war between Taiwan and China," interjected her boyfriend.

"Then why all the missiles?" I asked, but they didn't have an answer. "Why should Taiwan become part of China?" I then wanted to know.

Still beaming, the woman said, "Because China is greater than Taiwan. Taiwan is just a tiny island and China is becoming more and more powerful."

"But what about the people living on Taiwan? Most of them don't want to unite with China. Why do you think that is?"

"It's the same as Hong Kong," she explained. "They became part of China and they're happier now. They've gotten used to it. Taiwan will get used to it, too."

"But Taiwan is democratic," I pressed. "People there have the right to vote. They have the right to protest. They have freedom of expression. The government doesn't control the media. People can…"

But I was cut short. I had used the d-word. I was informed that democracy was just a trend and that it wouldn't last. But I was undeterred.

"Let me ask you this," I said. "How would *you* feel if you lived in Taiwan and there were more than eight hundred missiles pointed at *you*? How would that make you feel?"

The answer was exactly as I had expected. They didn't know. They had never thought about it before. I asked them one more question. I wanted to know who China's friends were.

"Everybody is China's friend – besides Japan," the man declared in an *Everybody*-knows-that manner. When I asked if that included Taiwan, his girlfriend replied, "Of course! Taiwan is China's good friend!"

I thanked them and then made my way down the stairs, past dozens of winter-dressed tourists.

When I had said that most Taiwanese didn't want to have anything to do with China, the two had glanced at each other in veiled surprise. In China, people have been told that something to the tune of 90 percent of Taiwanese people want reunification, but according to various independent surveys in Taiwan, that number is more like 10 percent.[1]

This was yet another recurring theme that I'd noticed while living in Chinese society. Rather than simply lie, why not tell the exact opposite of what was true? What better way to cast doubt on whomever it was you wished to discredit? It was effectively perverse, but perversely effective.

Business experts have outlined a number of global developments that will help shape the office place of tomorrow. Empowerment is one, and a flattened management hierarchy is another. As its name suggests, this entails fewer managerial echelons and employees becoming more self-directed and more involved in the management process. It allows for project teams, whole departments effectively being run by groups of peers, and so on. How Chinese companies based on the Confucian model (which, for want of a better word, revolves around fear) will adapt if the potential benefits of such a system are ever widely realized should prove interesting. I reckoned the reason that "everyone" wanted to work for

---

1   According to Taiwan's Mainland Affairs Council, it's 11 percent: 2 who want immediate reunification and 9 who wish it to proceed gradually.

that American company wasn't solely because of paid overtime.

I walked back down the hill and strolled around for a bit. It really was a pretty island, bursting with attractive plants and flowers. And the footpaths were charming too, at least the ones away from the masses. A sign I passed summed up the island's beauty and history as thus:

Keep in mind the old drum wave island have local humanities special features. Keep in mind the old address that the old building is also 19 centuries "the German ecord foreign firm" Still have the foreigner paradise: Foreign consulate; International building; Ocean girl's bathroom; keep in mind the oldÿ be like; Piano island transportation; German foreign firm; Overseas Chinese club is several thousand history delicacies in your front. The foreigner seizes the beautiful drum wave island to print to record, establishing on the international rent boundary, 13 consulates and work department bureau bully an our country people long few decades, most after drive islander the people drive out of the whole history process of go abroad the door, the fulfills a hundred years mulberry. It can take you to cross a timespace letting your grasp the emotional stirrings that is among them really can let you feel and don't waste a this trip.

I tried to visit the Koxinga Memorial Hall, but for some reason it was closed. My guidebook described it as "an exhibition partly dedicated to the Dutch in Taiwan, and partly to Koxinga's throwing them out." Near my hostel, atop a cliff, there stood a huge white-washed statue of the famous figure. At night, it was illuminated by spotlights, making it visible from Xiamen. It resembled a truncated version of the Christ the Redeemer statue in Rio de Janeiro.

Koxinga, or Zheng Chenggong (1624–1662; Koxinga is a European corruption of his honorific name as pronounced in Fujianese), was an extremely wealthy merchant, naval strategist, and Ming loyalist who battled the Qing throughout the 1650s along China's southern coast. During the period his base of operations was here in Xiamen, the Qing regime decreed that all coastal settlements be moved inland so as to deny the rebel logistical support. After failing to seize the inland city of Nanjing in 1661, Koxinga and his enormous army retreated to Tainan, Taiwan where they laid siege on a Dutch garrison known as Casteel Zeelandia. Consequently, the Europeans were forced to renounce their claim on the island, which Koxinga then used to establish a government fashioned on that of the Ming. Koxinga died the same year, but it would be more than two decades before the Qing subdued his forces and brought Taiwan under its own tenuous influence.

For his many years devoted to the anti-foreigner cause, Koxinga was awarded a spot in the pantheon of national heroes, by both the Communists and the Nationalists. Indeed, the latter have compared him to Chiang Kai-shek, which is fitting in a way: Koxinga was half Japanese.

I walked back to the crowded central quarter and went into a restaurant for lunch. I ordered a beef dish with rice and a bowl of chicken soup. I don't usually have Chinese soup as it tends to be watery, but this stuff looked hearty and the owner claimed it was a local delicacy. He ladled it out of a ceramic jug and I sat down and tried it. I noticed something large at the bottom and fished it out with my chopsticks. It was a chicken's head complete with eyeballs and half a beak. I ate (the beef and rice) quickly and then went to the bathroom. I heard someone come in and yell to the owner, "Hey, owner! I heard there was a foreigner in here! What did he order, anyway!?"

The next day, at 7:20 a.m., I was jolted awake by a tour guide with a megaphone right outside my hostel. I peered out the window to see a group of heavily dressed people standing beneath the aerial roots of a banyan tree that was obscuring an ochre colonial building. The guide was imparting vital information: the tree's height, diameter, age…. The mustard-coloured building was "very old" and "built by foreigners." The troupe moved on, but was quickly replaced by another. "This building was constructed by Westerners a long time ago. And just take a look at this tree for a moment…." I got up and took a shower.

During a pleasant breakfast taken on the balcony, I noticed that the recommended places of interest on the map I had picked up at the local tourist office (yet another proud recipient of the 'Civilized Work Unit' distinction) were three medical facilities. There was the Army Sanatorium, the Navy Sanatorium, and the Cadre Sanatorium. Were they really open to the public? I didn't want to know, and headed to the ferry in order to have a look at Xiamen itself.

I started with the Overseas Chinese Museum, housed in a large Western-style building with a rooftop of ceramic tiles and flying eaves. I got out of the cab at the main gate, walked through the courtyard, and noted the houses and trees on my left and the line of cars on the road to my right. At the building's entrance, just outside the ticket counter, three young toughs were sitting on the steps. "Hawlo!" one yelled confrontationally, springing to his feet. Another bellowed a derisive, "How do you do?" and grinned. I paused to glare at them, but it had no effect. One, weasel-faced and wearing a fake leather jacket with lots of tawdry studs and zippers, flashed me a big contemptuous smile. His teeth were the colour of pine bark. I bought a ticket from two mousey middle-aged women behind the counter and went inside. As I did so, a man exited and shouted, "Hawlo America!" and began to laugh. So did the three punks. My patience, thinning for some time now, had just about run out.

No sooner had foreigners arrived in China than the Chinese began calling them "foreign devils" and "barbarians from across the sea." Everything about the intruders seemed grotesque and absurd. The men sported tight trousers (how could they walk?) and the women wore flowing gowns whose chief purpose appeared to be collecting dirt. One Chinese scholar commented that both the men and the women seemed more like "prancing Manchu ponies" and "water buffaloes" than human beings, while another official opined that the savages appeared to be playing "the parts of foxes, hares, and other such animals upon the stage." What was more, he stated, foreigners really *did* look like devils, so when people called them that it was "no mere empty term of abuse."

An early British interpreter in China by the name of Thomas Taylor Meadows remarked that the Chinese were "always surprised, not to say astonished, to learn that we have surnames, and understand the family distinctions of father, brother, wife, sister, etc.; in short, that we live otherwise than as a herd of cattle." But of course, when it came to dismissing outsiders as bizarre, the Chinese couldn't claim to hold a monopoly.

The first recorded Chinese female in America was a girl by the name of Afong Moy. In 1834, Moy travelled to New York City in order to take part in a cultural exhibit, which is to say that she was displayed in a human-scale diorama in a museum in Brooklyn. The 16-year-old donned a *cheongsam* and covered her crippled feet with matching silk slippers so that Americans could gawk at her as she ate with chopsticks, performed calculations on an abacus, and counted in Chinese. But Moy, along with the (ethnically Chinese) Siamese twins, who also went to America, were lucky. This was an age when the United States was still fairly awestruck by the numinous and inscrutable Orient; it was the time just prior to when the Chinese started to show up on American soil in large numbers.

Chinese emigration to the United States, as I learned from reading Iris Chang's *The Chinese in America*, has consisted of three main waves spanning nearly 160 years. The first wave, which occurred in the mid-nineteenth century, was an immense exodus involving millions of labourers, 100,000 of which went to San Francisco (or "Old Gold Mountain" as it's called in Chinese) to seek their fortune in the 1849 California gold rush. This mass departure occurred in a spite of a government ban on emigration, one concretized by the death penalty.

The second wave swelled a hundred years after this one, the direct outcome of the Communists' coming to power. But unlike the first group, this one contained a large percentage of elites: those with the wherewithal to leave the country (they often fled to Hong Kong or Taiwan first), or those (mainly students) who found themselves stranded in America after the Nationalists were expelled from China. This wave also included some 70,000 Guangdong residents who were permitted to leave that province in order to help ease the famine caused by Mao's Great Leap Forward. As Iris Chang observes in her book, "the arrival of these two disparate contingents in the 1950s and 1960s created a bipolar community in America, sharply divided by wealth, education, and class." Indeed, while wealthy and educated Chinese made their way to America's suburbs, political refugees tended to end up in Chinatowns only to be fleeced by unscrupulous business owners.

The third wave has occurred in the last four decades and has consisted of Chinese from a range of Asian countries and socio-economic backgrounds.

But that wasn't the story presented by Xiamen's privately funded Overseas Chinese Museum. According to it, the Opium Wars and the "unprecedented humiliations" they entailed constituted the starting point of Chinese migration. With the establishment of the PRC, this movement effectively came to a halt. Undeterred by the poor treatment they received in their new countries, the immigrants, once "coolies, cooks, barbers, and tailors" rose through the ranks to become "bosses, teachers, doctors, and lawyers." They also became the patriotic leaders of their adopted homelands while never losing their identities or loyalty to the motherland. Their success was the result of their ethnicity and work ethic, not their new environment, or their wealth, or education. And that was it, more or less. Like with so many Chinese museums, the take-home message was seldom complex.

The museum placed a considerable amount of emphasis on discrimination, and although this was typically one-sided, there could be no denying that such a claim was very, very true. In the United States, for example, the Chinese were subjected to a mind-boggling measure of injustice and prejudice. As for the initial wave – the Chinese gold rushers – they were extorted by immigration officials, subjected to unfair taxation laws, beaten and even killed by tax collectors, and barred from hospitals, just to name a few things. As the 1790 Naturalization Act prohibited Chinese and other non-whites from applying for citizenship, not only did the Chinese have little in the way of legal recourse, but they also had virtually no defence against coercion and persecution, elements which became systematized and officially sanctioned in America during that era; and it was all fuelled by barefaced racism.

The California state legislature Committee on Mines and Mining proclaimed the Chinese presence to be "a great moral and social evil – a disgusting scab upon the fair face of society – a putrefying sore upon the body politic – in short, a nuisance," a sentiment that was echoed throughout the subsequent decades by various influential people. In the 1880s, California senator John F. Miller (the man who introduced what came to be known as the Chinese Exclusion Act) likened the Chinese to a herd of beasts and the "inhabitants of another planet." A lawmaker from Colorado, who supported Miller, declared that white people had the right to discriminate against "every other branch of the human family" given their superior "intellectual force and mental vigor." The San Francisco school board once referred to the Chinese as "baboons" and "monkeys," and even President Cleveland stated that the incorporation of the Chinese into American society was "unwise, impolitic, and injurious." In spite of the Declaration of Independence's explicit denunciation of racism, it was high noon for ignorance and bigotry in the United States.

The Chinese were effectively forced out of the gold mining business and thousands turned to the construction of the transcontinental railway where they often handled nitroglycerin and dynamite. The railway never recorded how many died in accidental blasts, but two thousand Chinese died in total. During the ordeal, they were harassed by white workers who detested them for their sobriety and superior work ethic. On top of that, they were exploited by railroad executives and made to work longer hours and for far less pay than the Irish and Germans. They were also beaten and whipped and commonly treated as beasts of burden.

The first wave of Chinese spread out across the country. They found employment in canneries on the Pacific coast, on plantations in the South (after the end of the American Civil War), and as launderers and servants just about everywhere. White people accused them of refusing to assimilate even as they feared the consequences of assimilation. Caucasians despised the Chinese for their poverty and then later despised them for their wealth. As the Chinese population grew, so did white fear and antagonism.

More and more discriminatory restrictions were drawn up. In San Francisco, there was the "sidewalk ordinance," which made it illegal to carry a pole through town if it had baskets hung at each end. And then there was the Cubic Air law, so called because houses were to supply a minimum of 500 cubic feet of open space for each adult resident. The upshot was that Chinese labourers were carted off to prison and stuck in cells with 20 cubic feet of air while slum-dwelling whites went practically unmolested.

After the Chinese Exclusion Act came into effect, it was interpreted as a licence for violence. Instead of appeasing the American xenophobes, the new restrictions only served to inflame them. "Having succeeded in barring the majority of new Chinese immigrants from American shores," Iris Chang writes, "the anti-Chinese bloc began a campaign to expel the remaining Chinese from the United States." And so it went. The Chinese were ordered out of Washington Territory. There were ferocious raids on several Chinatowns, including one in Wyoming which saw 28 Chinese deaths. In Oregon, 31 Chinese miners were "robbed, killed, and mutilated by a group of white ranchers and schoolboys intent on stealing their gold and cleansing the region of their presence." There were three arrests, but no convictions. Reportedly, "a Chinese skull fashioned into a sugar bowl graced the kitchen table of one ranch home for many years." Yet, later, when a Chinese man killed a Caucasian ex-lover in New York, just about every "Oriental" in the country came under suspicion.

Although it is beleaguered with jaw-dropping examples of discrimination and hostility (more than a century's worth, as a matter of fact), the history of the Chinese in America is, like any history, long and complex: infinitely more so than the 'us good, them bad' version supplied by this museum.

For example, the Chinese in the United States weren't always honest or law-abiding. There were crime syndicates, there were youth gangs, there were gambling houses, and there were prostitution and smuggling rackets – just for starters. The money remitted to families back home often had a profoundly negative effect on local communities, often drawing attention from criminals or recklessly spent on things like servants, opium, and concubines.

Additionally, immigrants were not always 'loyal to the motherland' or 'proud of their identity.' After the second wave, young people identified much more with American culture and values than those of their typically controlling parents. They were apt to despise Mandarin classes and yawned at stories of the old country. Even some of those in the first wave who returned to China (none of the gold rushers had intended on staying in America permanently) found it impossible to reintegrate. Living in the United States had changed them, and China now seemed severe, lawless, and barbaric. One man described how he returned to Guangdong only to find himself at the tail end of a massacre where government soldiers had beheaded thousands of insurgents. The fields, he observed, were crimson with blood.

The Overseas Chinese Museum had one exhibit dedicated to Chinatowns. A wall-sized photo from the early twentieth century showed a squalid row of dilapidated houses cemented to a vehicle-jammed street filled with people. Long bamboo poles, like the ones I had seen in Shanghai, poked out of windows to provide the sidewalks with awnings of undergarments. A shot from the 1970s depicted another street filled with people sitting around tables and slurping noodles. No one appeared to be conversing and the tables were ringed with debris. I didn't understand what I was supposed to be looking at. Was I supposed to feel pity for the poor émigrés? Was this the glorification of a ghetto? Were the pictures meant to make for a contrast?

Chinatowns, of course, have never had much of a reputation. In your typical late-nineteenth-century American Chinatown dwelling, it was not always easy to determine where the sweatshop left off and where the living space began. Indeed, such places were dubbed tenement factories, and conditions were customarily horrendous. In the 1950s, the New York State Housing Survey of New York City Chinatown discovered that nearly one third of all homes lacked flush toilets. Nearly half had no showers or bathtubs and something like three fourths did not have central heating. By the 1960s, American Chinatown factories had become so notorious that they were frequently subjected to government inspections. The San Francisco Human Rights Commission found that female garment workers received no overtime pay, no vacation time, and no sick leave. Because of the more or less steady influx of new immigrants, there was always someone willing to work harder and for less pay. As one inspector noted, "It's really amazing how the Chinese exploit themselves."

Another exhibit was dedicated to the "Elite of the Times," which equated to successful businessmen. An entire wall was devoted to Jerry Yang, the founder of Yahoo! Inc., even though he was born in Taiwan and moved to the United States when he was 10.

Where were the writers Ma Jian, Gao Xingjian, and Jung Chang? They didn't exist. They were troublemakers whose works had been banned and whose presence abroad was an embarrassment.

As it happened, I was the museum's only visitor. That is, until the three hoodlums from outside bounded up the stairs to harass me. I knew there was going to be trouble the instant I heard footsteps.

"Hawlo! Fuck you!" one began, and started to cackle. The one with the rotten teeth said he wanted his picture taken with me and handed his camera to his mate. He walked over and tried to put his arm around me. I suddenly felt like a character in an Asiatic version of *A Clockwork Orange*.

I told them directly that if they took my picture I would smash their camera into a million pieces, and I meant it. To solidify my objection, I added a few choice lexical items that I'd picked up from teenagers in Taiwan, and strengthened them with a bit of international sign language and Neanderthal posing. They retreated, shocked and sulking. Of course, the female clerks had let them in without a ticket. I thought about complaining, but thought better of it. They were doubtlessly just simple women from the neighbourhood who sat around knitting all day and didn't know what the young men were up to. I left after making sure the punks were no longer around, and then I walked to Xiamen University.

After poking around the campus for a while, I popped into a McDonald's that was filled with gabbing students. I sat with three very polite engineering majors and we began to talk in Mandarin. I wanted to know if the twenty-first century were going to be China's.

"Yes," said one.

Another replied, "I think it'll be the world's century, but China is certainly going to play a very large part."

I asked him how.

"In terms of culture."

"What does Chinese culture have to offer the world?" I asked politely. The walk had calmed me down.

"Confucianism," he answered.

"As in the *Analects of Confucius*?"

"Yes."

"Have you actually read the *Analects*?"

"Of course."

"And Western people ought to study it?"

"Yes, it's very deep."

"Give me an example."

He struggled with this before telling me that people ought to obey their superiors.

"Always?"

"Of course."

"What if one's superiors don't treat them well?" I wanted to know. "What if one's superiors are bad people?"

He reflected for a moment and said, "We must obey our elders, otherwise there'll be chaos."

He was, of course, only echoing what the *Analects* said. He wasn't thinking about it at all.

"Will the Chinese language become the next world language?" I wanted to know.

"Possibly."

"Will China rule the world one day?"

"Possibly."

"When do you think China will become a democracy?"

There ensued a pause that blossomed into a long and uncomfortable silence. One fellow finally broke it. "You foreigners," he began slowly, "you think that democracy is so important, but it isn't. It's just a trend. It will disappear some day."

"That's right, and no two democracies are alike," added another.

A trend. It was the second time I'd heard it. No doubt millions believed it.

I readily conceded that no two democratic *nations* were alike and that democracy had its limitations, but I was only referring to the right to vote. I happened to believe that democracy was overrated. The choice you had was often not much of a choice at all. Democracy could be extremely divisive, rife with partisan grandstanding; a facade for capitalism, a tool of malevolent interest groups, a disguise to garner diplomatic recognition, monetary aid, military support, and much else. Furthermore, benevolent, non-democratic states did exist (although there was the problem of succession) and it was easy to argue that some cultures or nation-states were not ready for or even suited to the democratic process. But, despite democracy's many flaws, certainly – incontestably – it was preferable to a single-party system, and that was the argument I essentially pitched to them.

"Perhaps China will become democratic sometime this century," one said, but I got the feeling he was only telling me that because he thought it was what I wanted to hear.

"We can vote now," said the third fellow, who hadn't spoken until that moment, but the other two just stared at him.

I changed the subject, and we talked for a while about sports, girls, what it was like to be a student, and then I thanked them and took my leave.

Once again, I thought of *Nineteen Eighty-Four*, specifically Orwell's description of doublethink. "To know and not to know," he writes, "to be conscious of complete truthfulness while telling carefully-constructed lies, to hold simultaneously two opinions that cancelled out, knowing them to be contradictory and believing in both of them; to use logic against logic, to repudiate morality while laying claim to it, to believe that democracy was impossible and that the Party was the guardian of democracy...."

However, it wasn't only the Chinese who believed the Communist

Party to be the sentinel of suffrage. It was often argued – by foreign journalists, academics, and even heads of state – that democracy in China would inevitably spring from the existence of a free-market economy; that consumer choice would automatically engender a demand for political choice, and that China's Leninist administration would inevitably grant it. In argumentative logic, this is known as the domino fallacy, whereby a particular trend or event is considered one step (usually the first) in a series of steps that will inexorably lead to a specific (desired or undesired) result.

Of course, it was entirely possible for China to become democratic one day, but so far there wasn't so much as a scintilla of evidence to suggest even a modicum of political liberalization, let alone full-blown egalitarianism. China was, purely and simply, a totalitarian state, and those who advocated an alternative tended to deny the obvious: communism fit China like a glove. It was Legalism, Confucianism, feudalism, and the teachings of Lao Tzu all wrapped up into one, which is to say it represented a potent and frequently lethal blend of a number of native ideologies that were in and of themselves highly toxic and remedies for disaster.

From Legalism, the Chinese Communist Party derived the Law as spelled out in *The Book of Lord Shang*, the document that spoke to the heart of the First Emperor and Mao Zedong. "A weak people," declares its author, "means a strong state, a strong state means a weak people." As for Confucianism, the Party saw to it (after Mao died) that loyalty and obedience to one's family was replaced by loyalty and obedience to one's government. Indeed, the Confucian paradigm was deemed useful; however, it would have to contain fewer echelons, ones that were sharply defined. As for feudalism, the Party can be said to represent the nation's sole landlord. China's 800 million serfs (or peasants) are still legally bound to the land. Concerning Lao Tzu, his *Tao Te Ching* has served as a prescription for governance ever since it came into circulation. Of particular relevance is its third chapter, which reads:

If we stop looking for 'persons of superior morality' to put in power, there will be no more jealousies among the people. If we cease to set store by products that are hard to get, there will be no more thieves. If the people never see such things as excite desire, their hearts will remain placid and undisturbed. Therefore the Sage rules

By emptying their hearts

And filling their bellies
Weakening their intelligence
And toughening their sinews
Ever striving to make the people knowledgeless and desireless

Indeed he sees to it that if there be any who have knowledge, they dare not interfere. Yet through his actionless activity all things are duly regulated.

The second most persuasive argument I have heard vis-à-vis why China will not become a democratic nation in the foreseeable future comes from author James Mann and his relentlessly logical book, *The China Fantasy*. Mann asks why China's middle and upper classes should favour giving the vote to 800 million peasants in exchange for the stability offered by single-party rule; stability that allows them to make money and provide for their families. The *most* persuasive argument I have heard as to why China won't be switching to the ballot box anytime soon is the one that has come from the Chinese Communist Party itself: China will not be ready for democracy for another one hundred years. Full stop.

Writing in the early 1820s, German philosopher Georg Wilhelm Friedrich Hegel criticized the Chinese for failing to emancipate themselves from the tyranny of their emperors and for remaining isolated both physically and metaphysically from the outside world. This, he opined, consigned China to a place outside both the *spiritus mundi* and world history, realms which could only be accessed by embracing freedom and exploration. Of the Chinese people, Hegel lamented, "… it appears nothing terrible to them to sell themselves as slaves, and to eat the bitter bread of slavery." Certainly, time has proven the thinker correct; nearly two centuries on, and people in China still haven't liberated themselves.

Presently, there is much speculation about China's future, but the thing to bear in mind is that China's past will define its future. The Chinese do not possess a linear construct of history. To their way of thinking, the past, the present, and the future are all intertwined. This, along with the fundamental immutability of their culture and national psyche is something that Hegel (and countless others before and after him) failed to see or heed. For example, Hegel believed that there *was* a way to drag China into the orbit of global consciousness, and that was to seek it out and investigate it. Change in China, he theorized, could be realized through exploring and understanding it. However, this is precisely what everyone from the Jesuits to the subsequent groups of Catholic and Protestant missionaries to foreign doctors to foreign aid workers to foreign engineers to foreign advisors to foreign investors to foreign leaders has tried to do, only to realize – after a considerable amount of time and effort – that China does not want change, at least not beyond the superficial; and it assuredly doesn't want change at the behest of arrogant outsiders.

Nowhere is this better illustrated than in Jonathan Spence's *To Change China: Western Advisors in China*. A series of vignettes which read like a sequence of tragicomedies, the volume chronicles one ambitious and morally superior Westerner after another who gallops off to the Middle Kingdom convinced that he will be the one to succeed (in educating the Chinese, in converting the Chinese, in advising the Chinese, etc.) where so many others before him failed. In the end, the usually intellectually gifted and well-meaning individual finds himself being used by his hosts for his expertise before being icily discarded, and usually despised.

As a teacher who taught in Chinese schools and language institutes in Taiwan for more than 10 years, I could relate to many of the figures in Spence's book, at least to an extent, for I am no crusader. The problems that I regularly had to deal with were almost always of a cultural nature. For example, schools would often ask that Western norms and standards, along with lessons on Western culture, be incorporated into classes. Yet, what constituted Western practices and culture wasn't understood beyond the hypothetical, which is to say it wasn't understood at all. Although never stated, instructors were to utilize Western methodology within a Chinese context. They were to encourage creative thinking by assigning heaps of homework and following punishing testing schedules that rewarded rote memorization and the ability to recognize a correct answer, but not to produce one. Teachers were to promote discussion and a free exchange of ideas while cramming two hours of technical material into a one-hour class. They were to take a no-nonsense approach toward cheating and discipline issues by sending delinquent students to the director's office so it might be assessed how adroit they were at refutation, or how influential their parents were.

In essence, foreign educators were only to go through the motions and put on a good show. They were to take a page from Sun Tzu's *The Art of War* and practise the art of deception. They were not to attempt to make a genuine difference and they were absolutely not to ask questions, express criticism, or even offer serious suggestions. But they did anyway because foreigners were a perennially problematic lot. They had ideas. They had opinions. They had propositions. They had requests. They had complaints. They had integrity. They were impossibly proud and didn't understand their place. Not only did they disregard the Confucian paradigm, the majority wasn't even aware of its existence.

Instead of simply cheering on China's so-called great rise, I thought that Sinophiles and optimists ought to be asking themselves just how China was going to integrate into a world that was, for better or worse, Western-led. How was a culture predicated on coercion and disinformation, and preoccupied, as it was, with revenge, deceit, and distrust ever going to enter into a sincere relationship with the global community? How was China going to strike up a permanent partnership with the West while steadfastly maintaining that the West was the source of all its problems? Integration would demand transparency, which would in turn leave Chinese practices open to perpetual scrutiny. Given the enormous (and enormously puerile) emphasis on maintaining face, how could China ever possibly deal with that? Integration would also necessitate co-operation, which would entail a high degree of equality, a concept that the Chinese were rarely comfortable with.

In *The China Fantasy*, James Mann challenges America's China policy, or what it calls "the strategy of integration," which holds that by working to incorporate China into the global fold, the nature of its government will inevitably change. Mann asks: "If the world ends up thirty years from now with a Chinese regime that is still a deeply repressive one-party state but is nevertheless a member of the international community in good standing, will that have been a success for the US policy of integration?" He goes on to hypothesize: "If so, that same China will serve as a model for dictators, juntas, and other undemocratic governments throughout the world – and, in all likelihood, a leading supporter of these regimes. China is already serving that function with respect to a number of dictatorships, from Burma to Zimbabwe."

I saw much of the current interest in China as the embodiment of a collective wish: a wish to see one of the world's oldest societies open up, liberalize, and become free. After all, theoretically, that would be good for the Chinese people and good for all of humanity. But it was a wish fuelled by an abyss of naivety and a canyon-sized lack of understanding as to China's true nature.

The 2008 Reith Lectures were entitled *Chinese Vistas* and were given by Jonathan Spence. His first talk, 'Confucian Ways,' was delivered at the British Library in London. The master of ceremonies began by saying that China's "breathtaking economic growth" had transformed it into a "great power" and that there could be "no doubt that it (was) a country that (would) have a significant influence over all our lives in the years to come." How and why this was going to transpire (or why it should) was never articulated. It never is.

During the first speech's question period, it was hypothesized that the Confucian *renaissance* was being endorsed by the government so as to prevent a "moral vacuum" from being filled by "less desirable ideologies," i.e. Christianity. A double question was then asked of Mr. Spence: 'What was the Confucian understanding of religious freedom? And what was the government's view on it?' This was followed by a question from the Archbishop of Westminster, who spoke of Pope Benedict's hope for "a space within the great China for religious liberty, especially for Christians…"

It is doubtful whether anyone who had ever read Chinese history, specifically about the spectacular failures of the Jesuits and subsequent missionaries, let alone movements such as those of the Boxers and Taipings, would ever have broached the subject. The Christianity queries may have been well intended, but they underscored the Western-centric viewpoint which often prevails when it comes to analyzing China: 'Yes, yes. We know about Confucius. Now, tell me: when do you foresee the Chinese being permitted to worship the right god?' Such questions were also highly ironic given that conversion was near top priority when Westerners first began to arrive in the Middle Kingdom *nearly five centuries ago*. Although inadvertent, the Pope's wish smacked of the colonial mentality; a mindset that the Chinese are unendingly reminded of.

China has always represented different things to different people. It is a vast and vague entity onto which one is free to project one's own fears and desires. To the pious, it symbolizes a sea of prospective converts. To businessmen and industrialists, it is an immense pool of cheap labour. To neoconservatives, it is a concern. To me, it represents a fascinating subject, but it is also the epitome of George Orwell's most famous novel. It is '*Nineteen-Eighty Four* with Chinese characteristics.'

The parallels were ever-present: the lack of colour "except (for) the posters that were plastered everywhere," the "rubbishy newspapers," the "poorer quarters swarm(ing) with women who were ready to sell themselves," the Victory cigarettes (Great China cigarettes) and Victory gin (Red Star *baijiu*), the stall keepers and their "tired looking vegetables," the slogans, the censorship, the portraits of Big Brother, the Two Minutes Hate (found in *China Daily*, on CCTV, and on the ubiquitous tourist-site placards reminding you not to forget the foreign-perpetrated injustices of the past), the "primitive patriotism which could be appealed to whenever it was necessary," doublethink, Comrade Ogilvy, Newspeak (simplified characters introduced by the Party ostensibly to promote literacy), the Ministry of Truth ("which concerned itself with news, education, entertainment and the fine arts"), the Ministry of Love ("which maintained law and order"), "the mutability of the past" (as evidenced by the frequently closed Museum of Chinese History and the Museum of the Revolution), the Thought Police, and, of course, the place you went after it was judged you had gone too far: Room 101.

"*If there is hope,*" Winston wrote, "*it lies in the proles.*"

Perhaps.

But I was more inclined to believe that this was one of the few places where Orwell's fiction and China's reality deviated.

One of the more bizarre books I've read on China is called *Nine Commentaries on the Communist Party*, written by at least one anonymous dissenter (it's impossible to tell how many writers contributed) and published through the New-York-City-based newspaper, *The Epoch Times*. Described as a "conversation," the tone of the anti-government critiques often mirrors the sort of venomous rhetoric that the government itself has become celebrated for. Moreover, it is incredibly subjective, brimming over with begging-the-question type reasoning, and generally wanting in logic and linear thought. Although it naturally makes sense in places (and I sympathize with and greatly respect whoever was brave enough to write it) it is packed with sentences, headings, and sentiments like the following:

> "The rectification movement in Yanan was the largest, darkest and most ferocious power game ever played out in the human world."

> 'The Hunan Peasant Rebellion – Inciting the Scum of Society to Revolt'

> "Human nature universally repels violence. Violence makes people ruthless and tyrannical. Thus, in all places and all times, humanity has fundamentally rejected the premises of the Communist Party's theory of violence, a theory that has no antecedent in any earlier systems of thought, philosophy or tradition. The communist system of terror fell upon the earth as if from nowhere."

Again and again, the Chinese Communist Party is characterized as an entity that has absolutely nothing to do with China's history, culture, or people. It is instead characterized as a body that is utterly alien – an "evil spectre" foisted upon the wise, civilized, cultured, and peace-loving masses of the Middle Kingdom by some unseen, nameless evil – or perhaps the Soviet Union, depending on the section or author.

The Communist Party is described as "anti-human," "anti-heaven," and even "anti-universe," whereas Chinese civilization is depicted as "splendid," having been "nurtured by the Yellow River and the Yangtze

River." Similarly, China's history is "grand and moving" in addition to being the world's "longest and most complete." Repeated attempts to discredit the Party are made by claiming that it bears no connection with China's "harmonious" and "glorious" past. The argument is put forth that if only the people could find a way to return to the days of traditional culture, all would be well again. At one point, it's suggested that clocks be wound back to the Song Dynasty (970–1270 CE). Apparently, it was after this epoch when things began to unravel.

Never is it suggested that the Chinese ought to make a break with their past and invent a new future. Never is it asked why China has this "satanic" form of government. Never is it questioned how this form of government sprang from Chinese civilization, culture, or tradition. Never is a connection made between authoritarianism and Confucianism, or the teachings of Lao Tzu, or thousands of years of repressive and feudalistic dynastic rule. Never is the question raised why so many countries do not have such a repressive governmental system. Never is a comparison drawn between another country. Never are any tough, introspective questions asked. Never is any *bona fide* soul searching done.

Traditional Chinese culture is a shackle, and Chinese history is a dungeon from which it is impossible to escape.

Bo Yang says, "The pernicious influence of thousands of years of feudal and authoritarian government which has kept the Chinese people pickling away in the soy paste vat has crippled our thinking, hampered our judgment, perverted our world view, and kept us bottled up inside a thick set of walls. This influence has also impaired our ability to make moral judgments and deprived us of the courage to act on principle. As a result, we can only react to the world through our emotions and our intuition. In sum, we have lost the ability to think straight."[2]

Now that China has begun to prosper, modernize, and physically resemble the West, a cursory inspection has led many non-Chinese to believe that not only is China on the rise, but that it is on its way to global

---

2   On *The Epoch Times* website, there is an article entitled 'Over half of all Chinese have read *Nine Commentaries...*' At least that's the claim of a Chinese human rights activist seeking political asylum in Taiwan. The man, a Mr. Wu, supported his statement by saying, "According to what I know, more than half of the people in China have read it. In addition, the people who read it all comment that, 'This is true.'" Wu added that the book was "openly spread overseas, but in Mainland China, it is very precious and ... very difficult to obtain a copy." On the book's cover, it claims to have "shocked all Chinese around the world" and to be "disintegrating the Communist Party." It should be noted that *The Epoch Times* was founded by members of Falun Gong and often features favourable articles about that group. The broadsheet has been criticized by various US academics for its lack of journalistic standards and objectivity.

hegemony, a slippery slope argument if there ever was one. China's great rise is a great illusion. Modernization in Chinese society is little more than window-dressing, the welding of superficial constructs – Pepsi signs, department stores, state-of-the-art production methods – onto an antique mindset. To say that China is rising is exceedingly vague. To say that it is already great or slated for greatness is a mindless mantra at best and a cheap marketing ploy at worst. To argue that China is on the cusp of ruling the world is to engage in intellectual dishonesty. Non-Chinese people may need to learn a few facts about the economic giant, but what they don't need are far-fetched theories. Unless it attempts to do so by force, China is *never* going to shape the world. It is just another backward, bitter, idiosyncratic, xenophobic, despotic, intellectually impoverished nation-state; one effectively devoid of tact, charm, grace, creativity, or emotional intelligence, and to that end, it is definitely not unique. Why not herald Turkmenistan, Burma, or Iran as the next big-man-on-campus? Minus the economic vigor, any one of them seemed to meet the basic requirements. The reason couldn't be because those countries weren't as physically large as China because when it comes to cultural influence and appeal, size doesn't matter. One need look no further than Great Britain, France, Greece, or Japan to see that. Did it all revolve around China's population? That was the argument the Chinese often made. But by 2050, India is scheduled to surpass China in that capacity, never mind that it's a fallacious 'appeal to numbers' argument in the first place.

Is it all based solely on economics, then? China's economic advances are certainly impressive, although it's important to remember that foreign companies are responsible for roughly 60 percent of all Chinese exports and 85 percent of all high-tech exports. However, in all likelihood, it wouldn't matter if those numbers were 100 percent, and that's because China's ascension is perpetually contextualized as a phenomenon that transcends the world of business and finance; it is political, cultural, social, historical – astronomical. But, politically, culturally, socially, and historically, China has practically nothing to offer the Western world – or the Arab world, or the African world, or the Hispanic world, or any non-Confucian country or culture. The "Chinese way," as it pertains to the People's Republic of China, especially, is patently incompatible with the "Western way," and although proponents of China's hegemony often subscribe to the parallel theory of "the end of the Western world," this is yet more crystal-ball projection. What does it mean to say that the Western world is going to end? In this era of technology and globalization, the West is arguably more relevant and influential than ever. However, even if there were a waning of Western global influence (a possibility) that does not equate to or provide for China's global domination. China does not even meet the definition of a developed nation. As of 2009, it was listed on the United Nations Human Development Index as being in 92nd spot. How, then, is it going to mentor the 91 countries above it? Above all, how is it going to reverse the river of paradigms that flows from the West?

Apart from being outstandingly unsophisticated, the China-set-to-rule-the-world argument is also very distracting. It brings us no closer to understanding what China really is or where it is really headed. There is a surfeit of hard questions that need to be asked about China, its nature, its intentions, and its place in the world, and although there are some who are asking those questions, they tend to get crowded out by the mythomaniacs and propagandists, especially when some reporter needs a sound bite. But not all the sound bites or hocus pocus in the universe can belie China's lagging far behind. It is nowhere near as advanced as the West; it is not nearly as mature, either. But then, it is not as advanced or mature as many of its Asian neighbours. It has become unpopular to speak with such candor in this sorry era of cultural relativism and so-called political correctness, but it is indubitably true. At least, it is for me.

As I walked back to the ferry that would take me back to Drum Wave Islet, I thought about the last time China had been accepted into the big boy's club – by the Allies during World War II. At that time, American propaganda worked for a while, but in the end it was finally realized that such a relationship was not only unsustainable, but deeply embarrassing. The Republic of China was brutal, corrupt, and exceedingly dysfunctional, something the Americans only recognized when it was much too late.

My original intention had been to return to China and explore its rugged northwest. So far, I had been to or through 17 of the country's 22 provinces and the idea was to get to all of them. The rough plan was to start the third leg by beginning in the island-province of Hainan after which I would make my way to the industrial city of Lanzhou, the capital of Gansu. From there, I would take a train to Urumqi, the capital of Xinjiang. With stops along the way, I would investigate Buddhist grottoes, drive along the Silk Road, and chat with the Uighurs in the territory known before 1949 as Eastern Turkistan. I wanted to see what a terrorist, or at least an ungrateful Chinese citizen, looked like up close. I would take in "the end" of the "Great Wall" at Jiayuguan, marvel at the dramatic landscape near Dunhuang, visit the oasis town of Turpan, and much else. At least, that was the idea. But from Xiamen, I flew to Hong Kong and then to Taiwan, vowing never to return.

Without question, I had met some nice people and had experienced a few gratifying travel moments, but I was weary of the constant harassment and annoyances. The encounter with the hoodlums in the museum had been the last straw. Two months in China had been enough to cure me of whatever curiosity I had had about seeing it. Travel can cure you of many things. There was no need to return. To round out my account, then, I abruptly decided to journey around and write about the other China, the one I had been living in for the past decade, the one the world had forgotten.

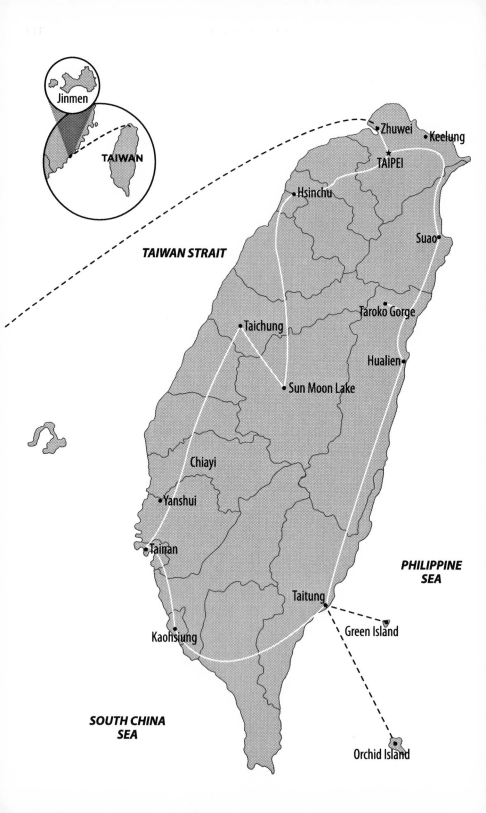

PART THREE

FROM
BAMBOO ENCIRCLEMENT
TO THE GOLDEN GATE

CHAPTER TWENTY-THREE

I had gotten into the habit of going on a leg-stretcher prior to embarking on a journey, so one sun-soaked morning in July, I arose early and headed out of my apartment building in Zhuwei, which means "Bamboo Encirclement," to go on a hike. Zhuwei is a smallish borough northwest of Taipei proper, pegged along that city's grey Danshui River.

My neighbourhood looked like any other in Taiwan: a tangle of high-rises with prison windows and tiles of coral and cream climbing out of a band of alluvial soil set between the river and the foothills of a collection of nearby mountains. The bulk of the district couldn't have been more than 1.5 km^2, yet it contained everything any self-respecting Taiwanese neighbourhood would: McDonald's, KFC, Starbucks, Starbucks knock-offs, a Subway, a Subway knock-off, Carrefour, a pair of local alternatives, no less than four 7-Elevens, four 7-Eleven rivals, a string of car dealerships, three video stores, four or five seedy karaokes, two Chinese medicine clinics, a handful of gaudy all-you-can-eat restaurants, an unkempt temple, a street market (where hawkers sold foodstuffs, a few of which were still unidentifiable to me), two fruit markets, a hospital (named after the legendary Canadian Presbyterian missionary, George Leslie MacKay; inside, there were oversized photos of him extracting teeth from cue-wearing locals during the 1870s), scores of other businesses, about a dozen signs written in bad English, and loads of friendly people.

Like most districts in Taipei, Zhuwei was, as the locals were fond of saying, "very convenient." You could get whatever you wanted, whenever you wanted it, and it was all more or less at your doorstep. The options at 7-Eleven alone were dizzying. In addition to all the items you would find at a convenience store anywhere, you could pick up a book or even a food item that you had ordered online – deep fried chickens' feet from the city of Tainan, for example. You could get insurance, you could pay all your bills, you could make photocopies and send faxes, you could send a package by courier, you could get a hot meal, you could pick up a bottle of wine, you could purchase paper underwear for those long and sweaty road trips; you could do just about everything except get married and divorced. It all made for extremely easy living. The notion of convenience is paramount in Taiwan.

I walked down a street of modest three-storey buildings, the ground floors of which served as both living room and family factory. This one stitched and punched handles into women's handbags; that one assembled pens. During the day, you could see an entire extended family operating machinery or packing their wares into boxes for delivery. At night, you could see them again, lounging in the glow of their television set and family shrine. I passed the office of the local fortune teller and then the local office of the Nationalist Party. Two workers loading a refrigerator onto a truck smiled and gave me a nod.

The grey and brown warren of houses and cottage industries tapered to a line of fortress-like white homes, and I entered a tiny valley of vegetable plots and makeshift fences. Some kids were hoping to catch frogs in a shallow pond. "Where'd they all go?" I heard one say. I was now halfway up the hill and standing in front of an ancient-looking brick house with a brand-new, cherry red Ford Focus parked in its courtyard. A black dog was chained to a bathtub (of all things) and barking. I turned to observe Zhuwei and the saw-toothed, tomb-strewn Guanyinshan[1] beyond it, on the other side of the river.

At the top of the hill, near a fine-arts college, I cast my gaze in the opposite direction, toward Taipei. The metro line hugged the mountains' hem all the way into the capital, piercing bunches of buildings and sprawling communities. Marshes and rice paddies marched away from the development in the direction of the unruffled waterway. Some 25 kilometres away, the 508-metre Taipei 101 building was wedged between a blanket of cloud and a pewter-hued blur of buildings and bridges. I stared at Taipei – its landmarks now miniature – as it quivered, mirage-like, in a silvery film of pollution.

I backtracked and looped around the rim of the small valley. The foliage here was glorious, especially the bougainvillea. There were a few proud houses with jagged bits of green glass topping their solid fences. I passed a temple, a tiny duck farm (the ducks were waddling all over the road), and a house that was once a Falun Gong activity centre. It used to

---

1   Guanyin, usually translated as the Goddess of Mercy, is the bodhisattva associated with compassion. There are several mountains in Taiwan called Guanyinshan, *shan* meaning 'mountain.' The one next to the Danshui River is said to resemble the goddess, and, with a bit of imagination, it does.

have a billboard showing two very small children meditating along with the slogan, 'Falun Gong is Good!' Presently, the home's proprietor was in the business of amassing compilations of bent nails and broken pallets.

I continued through a canopied corridor of buzzing cicadas, caught a whiff of a nearby pig farm, ambled past a golf course, and entered a neighbourhood of neat hedges and stucco walls. It was incredibly sultry, as it almost always is in Taiwan. I passed the hospital, a couple of graves, and a single-car garage attached to my building. The garage had been built out of odds and ends, and always disintegrated during typhoons. Across from it, an aging prostitute in a brown dress sat on her motor scooter and spoke Taiwanese into her cell phone. She catered to the old boys in the neighbourhood, who could occasionally be seen staggering to and from the place around midnight. Eying the woman was an egret, which stood on a blackened brick wall that spanned a fetid waterway, a tumult of froth feeding the river. A tropical storm had recently blown through and the empty street was speckled with little red lumps of paper, the lanterns overhead having been stripped to the wires by the wind. I went into to my apartment, got cleaned and packed, and headed to the metro station across the street.

In front of my apartment building, there are two betel-nut stands, a phenomenon as Taiwanese as the motor scooter, the yellow taxi, and the legislative brouhaha. A betel-nut stand is a glass booth within which a young and underdressed woman sells soft drinks, energy drinks, cigarettes, and betel nut to male customers, typically motorists. Betel nut is a lime-packed, leaf-wrapped drupe that provides chewers with a buzz and the need to spit. It has been linked to oral cancer.

The women who sell it are called "betel-nut princesses" or "betel-nut beauties," but a closer look often reveals a hardened character: chain smokers with tattoos and worry lines. Like many men, I initially assumed that the women were prostitutes, but in reality, peddling betel nut offers a viable alternative to that profession. In a new collection of Taiwan-themed, fold-out postcards, "betel-nut princesses" were featured as integral to Taiwan's unique culture. So were families on motor scooters, hectic temples, sign-addled congested streets, and the phallic Taipei 101 building.

I caught the metro to Taipei Main Station on a ride I had taken literally thousands of times. I could, with my eyes closed and with a pair of earphones in, identify exactly where I was at any given moment based on the arc of the train or the time between stations. Through the window, I observed one of Taipei's older neighbourhoods: a potpourri of tiles, bars, and patios crammed with plants and junk. The Taiwanese are not in the habit of throwing things away; that weekend edition of the newspaper could be worth millions one day.

It was Monday and the start of summer vacation, so there were mainly senior citizens and high school students onboard. The former hobbled to priority seats while the latter hopped up and down. The elderly men wore baseball caps and sunglasses; their wives wore frizzy hair, jade bracelets, and costume jewellry. Teenaged boys swung from handles as the girls giggled and covered their teeth. All the young people were cheerful and good-natured. They spoke to each other at such a decibel, it was a wonder the glass didn't shatter.

Sitting across from me was a kittenish, vacant-looking woman in a skirt and blouse applying makeup. She had set her Takashimaya Department Store bag on the spot next to her so no one else would occupy it. She pouted into her compact and frequently meshed her false eyelashes together in what was clearly a rehearsal. Her phone rang and she answered it sulkily. "*Wei?*" It was ornamented with fuzzy little trinkets and the plastic head of Hello Kitty.

A pair of engineers focused on their laptops. I knew they were engineers because of their clothes: jeans, name-brand shoes, plaid shirts with pockets stuffed with pens and folded papers. There was a Buddhist nun who held a string of prayer beads and mouthed the boxed characters in her vinyl-bound book. A Japanese couple alighted at Beitou in order to go to the hot springs. They must have spent the morning in Danshui. When the couple returned from the hot springs, they would have a lustre about them. Couples returning from hot springs usually do.

Droves of Japanese tourists come to Taiwan. It's close, it's safe, it's inexpensive, and it has oodles of shopping and good food. Like many long-term expatriates, I could spot a Japanese citizen on the streets of Taipei from two blocks away.

The train I got on in Taipei Main Station was old and slow, but it was comfortable and clean. It rollicked through a half-residential, half-industrialized section of the city's perimeter that I was largely unfamiliar with. There were warehouses and neighbourhoods of stunning unsightliness: blackened concrete, caged-up terraces, sooty wall tiles, smears and stains, glinting rooftop water tanks, corrugated roofs, and roofs of battered black tile, a few of which were held in place by tires, loose bricks, planks, or bags of rocks. There were garish signs: 'Ah-Fang's Kitchen,' 'Gold Mountain Enterprises,' 'The Chen Family Restaurant,' 'Hardware Store,' 'New Ray of Light Protestant Church,' 'Fortune Teller,' 'Big Slice Steak House.' Sidewalks were consummately crammed with rows of parked motor scooters.

As we left the city, the landscape changed and offered up pretty hills and patches of dramatic greenery, but everything man-made was really just an eyesore. I was travelling clockwise around the island, which was the norm given that the country's east coast is dramatically less developed and infinitely more picturesque than its overdeveloped western plains.

Because Taiwan is so much smaller than China, it is easier to quantify. It is comprised of the main island and several outlying islands. The islands in the Taiwan Strait include Penghu (the Pescadores), Jinmen (or Kinmen or Quemoy), and the Matsu islands (or Mazu islands – just off of Fuzhou, the capital of Fujian province) whereas those in the Pacific consist of Green Island and Orchid Island. The amount of water that separates Taiwan from China ranges from 160 kilometres to 240. The main island of Taiwan is 384 kilometres long, 136 kilometres wide, and approximately 36,000 km², just a fraction smaller than the Netherlands. Dividing the east coast from the western plains is the commanding Central Mountain Range. In fact, mountains or hills make up the bulk of Taiwan, meaning that most of the country's 23 million inhabitants are forced to reside in the densely crowded lowlands. Taiwan has a population density of just about 640/km².

More than 98 percent of that population falls under the nebulous classification of Han Chinese. Something like 70 percent is of Fujian ancestry (the first wave of Chinese settlers), 10 to 15 percent are Hakka (who followed the Fujianese), and the remaining 12 to 15 percent are the newcomers: Chinese who absconded to Taiwan mainly as a result of the Chinese Civil War.

Satellite photos of Taiwan resemble a tobacco leaf that has had its western section, eastern edge, and northern portion painted grey. The image could double as a poster for environmental degradation, yet it is a screen-saver favourite and widely considered to be "beautiful." The present view from the train window was anything but.

My plan was to alight at Suao, where I would catch a bus to the coastal town of Hualien. The Suao-Hualien Highway was said to be one of the world's most scenic – and risky. Photos depict a thin grey line etched into mountainside hundreds of metres above the brooding Pacific. In one section, the way reaches an elevation of a thousand metres, yet it is said that buses are barely able to get past one another. Typhoons, earthquakes, and mudslides play havoc with the path, and accidents and deaths are not infrequent.

The drive was supposed to be exhilarating, but I never got to do it. In the community of Suao, I was informed that it was impossible to board a bus to Hualien. A taxi was out of the question; it was

a 118-kilometre haul. I might have considered hitchhiking, only a
thunderstorm blew up and assaulted the coastline, which may have been
a blessing in disguise. My guidebook warned that even for experienced
drivers, the route could be "frightening" and "perilous" due to its
"hairpin bends, blind curves, narrow roads and insane drivers."

Bolts of lightning ripped through the humidity in search of
surrounding hilltops. The downpour welded the township to the tempest
without so much as a seam. I took refuge in a fried-chicken joint run by
an impossibly jovial owner who gave me a free bowl of ice cream with
my meal. "It's free, it's free," he said, waving his hand and chuckling.
"Welcome, welcome." As I ate, I watched him as he worked; he never
stopped smiling.

The Taiwanese have to be *the* friendliest people in all of Asia, if not
the entire world. And it's a genuine friendliness, not something contrived.
It's often said that they are more convivial to foreigners than they are
to each other, and there is some truth in that. However, they are also,
as a general rule, kindly among themselves as well. Heaven forbid you
should have to work for one of them, mind you (then the Confucian
paradigm would come into effect), or have contrary political leanings (the
Taiwanese can be fiercely passionate about politics, as we shall see), or get
on one's bad side (again, revenge is a powerful element in Chinese culture;
forgiveness is rare), but in regular day-to-day encounters, you would be
hard pressed to find people who are more cordial, even in the big cities.
The Taiwanese concept of civic mindedness may be relatively infantile
(people think nothing of watching the elevator door as it closes in your
face), but they are – and I'm being sincere – extremely nice, almost all of
the time.

And cordiality isn't even their finest trait. That would be tolerance,
a byproduct perhaps of living in such proximity. Like any nationality, the
Taiwanese possess more than a few shortcomings (as we shall also see),
but it is my belief that they are commendably live and let live.

The storm subsided and I went back to the station and caught
the next train to Hualien. From the window, I spied a perfect rainbow
touching down along a line of palm trees and vague grey buildings. The
view from the other window revealed a chunk of the island's fetching
Central Mountain Range, clouds crawling about its fissures and forms.
The train arrived in Hualien at 5:30 p.m. and I checked into a hotel that
had a lobby decorated with aboriginal art: carvings and wall hangings of
warriors in thongs. More than 433,500 (or about 2 percent) of Taiwanese
are indigenous.

A box on the registration form asked for my 'Firearm Registration

Number,' which threw me because it's illegal to own a firearm in Taiwan. When I asked the receptionist about it, she laughed nervously and snatched the paper out of my hand. As Paul Theroux observed in his *Riding the Iron Rooster: By Train Through China*, "The Chinese laugh is seldom a response to something funny – it is usually *Ha-ha, we're in deep shit* or *Ha-ha, I wish you hadn't said that* or *Ha-ha, I've never felt so miserable in my life…*"

That night, I supped at that archetypal Taiwanese dining establishment: Kentucky Fried Chicken. Without question, fast food restaurants were meant for a place like Taiwan, a place where people like their food quick and dripping with grease. KFC and all the other fast food chains (in Taipei, you could throw a stone and hit one) were just a variation of the local *lubiantan*, or roadside stall, only there were napkins, bathrooms, and air conditioning.

I took a second-floor seat next to a window that overlooked an intersection and I watched. I watched as a teenaged boy drove along with his dog standing on the scooter's footrest. I watched a woman on a scooter do a U-turn in the middle of the juncture with a toddler on her lap that had a soother in its mouth. Pedestrians kept getting stranded in the middle of the crosswalk because motorists making right turns wouldn't let them go. The light would turn yellow and a torrent of vehicles would increase in speed. Always, three or four scooters ran the red light. Then the pedestrians would get stranded again. Only when the group was large enough would it venture across the painted lines. The goings-on could have made for a television program or even an entire channel: *At a Crossroads in Taiwan – Live 24-Hour Chaos.*

The next morning, I rented a scooter (despite not having a local driver's licence) and headed out of town toward Taroko Gorge National Park, Taiwan's preeminent tourist site. I drove past a stretch of pretty farms and views of the mountains and passed through the park's *pailou*, or decorative archway. Inside, I made my way to a charming, butterfly-filled viewpoint where I stood and admired.

It was magnificent. The now-docile, boulder-strewn Liwu River had spent eons whittling a twisting corridor of marble through mountains of almost inconceivable lushness. In places, the massifs were so ambitious (one tops out at 3,700 metres) that I had to look more or less straight up to see the sky. The versants' gold-and-crimson pagodas completed the scene with that unmistakable seal of Chineseness. A wooden sign at the viewpoint said, 'What a spectacle except for the dam.' Another one said, 'Lich-like lichens on the bark.' I drove back down to the main road and hastened on.

Irrefutably, Taiwan's Taroko Gorge is a place of intense beauty and awe, and it's a good thing that it is situated here because if it existed in a country that cared an ounce for public safety, it would be sealed off completely and viewable only from a helicopter. The road, one segment of Taiwan's Central Cross-Island Highway, is an engineering miracle that bores through the base of the mountains. There are long, echoing, nerve-racking tunnels and much shorter ones with walls of rough-hewn rock. Some of the latter were cut by hand.

In places, the way is extremely narrow, but buses barrel along (there used to be two "competing" tour bus companies working the gorge), and people drive almost as recklessly here as they do everywhere else. Signs say, 'Do Not Linger,' and 'Beware of Falling Rocks! Please Pass Quickly,' as if acceleration will ward off disaster. In segments, written warnings have been traded in for symbols: triangle-bound exclamation marks appearing on the asphalt in succession. Approximately 450 labourers lost their lives constructing the highway. A tour bus once plunged into the chasm with tragic results, and earthquakes have caused it to close. On this day, a selection of pebbles bounced down the slopes and struck me on the helmet and legs.

I had been here once before (just after I moved to Taiwan), and when I exited the gorge on that occasion, there was a huge, weekend-ruining slab of rock in the road that hadn't been there on my way in. I also fell off my scooter, scraped my hands rather badly, and came fairly close to sliding over the edge after a run in with a tour bus whose driver saw me go down, but didn't stop to see how I faired. After passing back through the *pailou* on that day, I saw a dead body lying in the middle of the road. An angry bull that had been tethered to a telephone pole was standing in the highway. A man and woman had been driving a scooter toward the gorge when, apparently, they had an encounter with it. She died. He was beside himself with grief. There were police all around snapping photos and urging bystanders like me to move on, yet the irritated beast was still challenging oncoming vehicles and backing up traffic. It only backed down when tour buses drove straight at it, blasting their horns. I tucked in behind one and sped by it. I was passed by an oncoming ambulance a short while later.

This day was much hotter than that one, and I went into the gorge's Grand Formosa Hotel[2] to borrow some cool air. Outside, there was a large picture of the inn in the 1950s when it was called the Tienhsiang Lodge. Chiang Kai-shek was striding up to its front entrance with his

---

2   Not long after my visit, the Grand Formosa Hotel, a five-star affair, changed its name to Silks Place Taroko.

coterie.

On the drive out, I saw bands of local tourists doing cutesy poses near a bit of tunnel that had collapsed in dramatic fashion since my last visit. Signs ordered people to move on, but when it came to an opportunity to act cute, not even the prospect of being squashed like an insect was going to discourage that.

I spied some hiking trails, but decided against a trek given the temperature. I knew from my reading that many of these trails were formed by the park's earliest residents, the Atayal, one of Taiwan's main indigenous tribes.[3] Nowadays, the Atayal are known for their facial tattoos and weaving talents, although they were once known for something entirely different: headhunting. Indeed, three of Taiwan's tribes had once been reasonably addicted to the taking of enemy heads: the Atayal, the Bunun, and the Paiwan, although the Atayal were far and away the most ferocious.

For the Qing government, which only managed to annex Taiwan in 1683, the divide between the western plains, with their taxpaying Han settlers and "tame savages," and the Central Mountain Range and east coast, with their wild or "raw savages," was so pronounced that from 1739 to 1875, Chinese settlers were barred from entering what was considered barbarian territory. In 1871, when a boat from Okinawa got shipwrecked on the southern tip of Taiwan, the entire 54-member crew was beheaded by members of the Paiwan tribe, although, in the tribe's defence, this was not only a tradition, but a security measure; ships had landed and carted off members of their faction in the past.

When the Japanese petitioned the Qing court for compensation, the Qing claimed they held no authority over Taiwan's "savage territory" (half of its total area), thus prompting a Japanese invasion. After the Japanese took control of Taiwan in 1895 (the result of the First Sino-Japanese War, 1894-95, not the just-mentioned invasion), it took 50 years, a great deal of brutality, and the lives of thousands of imperial soldiers and police officers to subjugate the island's savages. In point of fact, the practice of headhunting on Taiwan was not eradicated until the 1920s.

In Janet B. Montgomery McGovern's *Among the Headhunters of Formosa*, the intrepid author and anthropologist documents headhunting practices on Taiwan (formerly Formosa) between 1916 and 1918. With regard to the Atayal, she describes headhunting as their chief social custom, explaining how it was "interwoven with the fabric of their whole social organization," and that it regulated "the social and political standing

---

3   It should be noted that the branch of the Atayal located in Taroko Park are now officially recognized as a separate group, called the Truku.

of the men in the tribe." McGovern also notes how there were allusions to headhunting in Atayal games, songs, and dances. It was the national pastime, as it were.

After a successful headhunting expedition, a great feast would be held. During the merriment, the victim's head would be placed on the village skull rack and food and millet wine would be set in front of it or "inserted into its mouth." The village chief or priestess would then utter an invocation urging the severed head to partake in the festivities and ask its brothers to come and join it. Although the Atayal constituted a single ethnic group, they were divided into some 16 splinter groups that regularly engaged in headhunting missions against one another.

As *the* predominant social custom, headhunting was naturally bound up with other rituals, such as marriage. As Mrs. McGovern concisely notes in her book, "No head, no wife." Indeed, the closing segment of an Atayal wedding ceremony consisted of the bride and groom drinking together from a skull, "preferably one which (had) been taken from an enemy by the bridegroom himself…" The author goes on to explain how other tribes started to substitute deer and monkey skulls for human ones, thus provoking Atayal contempt. The Atayal deemed drinking blood from the heads of deer and monkeys to be effete.

Mrs. McGovern explains how when foreigners came across skulls and skull racks (there are photos), they automatically assumed that the relevant clans were cannibalistic, but she didn't believe this to be so. This sentiment is echoed by many, including other experts, but evidence suggests that it is wrong.

As the aforementioned Canadian missionary, George Leslie MacKay, reported in his *From Far Formosa*, he was presented with human brains as a "rare treat" by members of the Atayal. Another Presbyterian missionary, a Scotsman by the name of Robert Campbell, was traversing the mountains one day when he came upon what he called a "headhunting-kit" containing "brain-glue tablets." He explained by saying, "Some of the Formosan tribes boil down every head brought in to a thick jelly, from which thin oblong cakes are made, for being nibbled to inspire fresh courage when another murderous attack is to be made upon the invaders of their country." Campbell sent the so-called brain-glue tablets to Berlin's Imperial Museum of Ethnology for study.

There is also evidence of Sino-cannibalism, indicating that the episode during the Cultural Revolution is not an isolated one. Writing in 1903 in his book, *The Island of Formosa*, James Davidson, Taiwan's first American consul, stated that part and parcel of the campaign against the aboriginals was the sale of their flesh in Chinese markets.

"After killing a savage," Davidson writes, "the head was commonly severed from the body and exhibited to those who were not on hand to witness the prior display of slaughter and mutilation. The body was then either divided among its captors and eaten, or sold to wealthy Chinese and even to high officials, who disposed of it in a similar manner. The kidney, liver, heart, and soles of the feet were considered the most desirable portions, and were ordinarily cut up into very small pieces, boiled and eaten somewhat in the form of soup. The flesh and bones were boiled, and the former made into a sort of jelly. The Chinese profess to believe, in accordance with an old superstition, that the eating of savage flesh will give them strength and courage…. During the outbreak of 1891, savage flesh was brought in – in baskets – the same as pork, and sold like pork in the open markets… before the eyes of all, foreigners included; some of the flesh was even sent to Amoy (Xiamen) to be placed on sale there. It was frequently on sale in the small Chinese villages near the border…."

This is corroborated by MacKay, who described a Chinese crowd waiting for an aboriginal warrior to be put to death. "Scores were there on purpose to get parts of the body for food and medicine… the heart is eaten, flesh taken off in strips, and bones boiled to a jelly and preserved as a specific for malarial fever."

In all my time in Taiwan, I never once heard headhunting mentioned by a local.

The Taiwanese and the aboriginals may have stopped murdering and boiling each other into tablets and jellies, but their relationship is still quite strained. Indigenous people in Taiwan suffer from generational poverty and discrimination. Typically, whenever I heard one of my students use the word 'aboriginal' (including my adult students), it was followed by a snicker; usually a group snicker. Even with affirmative action policies, few indigenous people attend university. The aboriginal unemployment rate is three times the national average and their life expectancy is fifteen years short of it. A good many drink themselves to death.

That evening, I walked around Hualien and concluded that it was a countrified conurbation of shops, signs, dubious-looking karaokes, and brothels. According to the *Taipei Times*, Taiwan has approximately 100,000 prostitutes.

After eating at a popular dumpling restaurant, I ambled down a street and came upon a brand-new section of sidewalk featuring nifty blue lights. There was a stylized cement bench and a bronze plate screwed into the ground that said, 'English welcome.' I looked around for a school, but didn't see one. There was just an old brick wall with peeling advertisements. I kept walking, but the sidewalk was blocked by a dozen large natural gas canisters. I walked around them, only to find the way blocked again by two parked trucks. I passed by a roadside stall with a family sitting on plastic stools, shovelling noodles into their mouths. Just a few metres away, a man was kneeling and welding – with no mask or goggles on. I sauntered past two stray dogs, a section of sidewalk with shattered tiles, a newly built and brilliantly lit church, and finally a Playboy store. A woman of 40 was inside feeling the merchandise. Playboy garments and accessories are popular with Taiwanese women as they have no idea that Playboy is associated with adult entertainment. Che Guevara iconography is also big, and no one has a clue who he is either. More popular still is the marijuana leaf. Children, students, grandmothers; no one is above sporting a 'Get High on Mexican Bud!' cotton top. Everyone seems to think it's the Canadian flag. In Taiwan, there are marijuana hats, bags, pencil cases…. Most Taiwanese (even college students) are revolted by the very thought of narcotics.

One emblem that the Taiwanese *can* identify, and absolutely adore, is that of Hello Kitty. Truly, Taiwan's obsession with things cute borders on the insane. Above and beyond an extensive list of stationery items and fashion accessories, there are Hello Kitty cafés, Hello Kitty cars, Hello Kitty motor scooters, and even – as I witnessed with my own two eyes – Hello Kitty dump trucks. Taiwan's EVA Airways unveiled a Hello Kitty airplane (complete with female flight attendants who donned Hello Kitty outfits), and there were riots in Taiwan's McDonald's when limited-edition Hello Kitty dolls were sold with meals. The latest Hello Kitty product to cause a stir was *Beaujolais Nouveau*, sold at a 7-Eleven near you. On the bottle, it said, 'Let people all over the world drink delicious wine and live their dreams in happiness – Hello Kitty.' Chiang Kai-shek and Sun Yat-sen may be on the money, and their images, names, and portraits may still abound, but it's the cat that everyone venerates.

Although there is little sign of her popularity waning, these days, Taiwan's best-loved kitten has competition. There's My Melody (a doe-eyed rabbit that wears a red hood), Pikachu (one of the Pokémon characters), Snoopy (who we all know), Puki (the dancing pig), Doraemon (a blue cat that can travel through time), Kiki & Lala (Kiki is 'a curious and cheeky boy who can fly by utilizing a star on his back.' Lala is a girl who is 'a little timid and cries easily'), and last but not least: Miffy, another female rabbit that looks suspiciously like My Melody and Hello Kitty.

It isn't just kids who like this sort of thing. Grown-ups get all slushy when confronted with such factory-fabricated lovability, saying,

'*Hao keai*' meaning "So cute!" or "So adorable!" '*Hao keai*' is a phrase you could easily hear 10 times a day in Taiwan, cutesy culture being a critical component of the island's brand of Chinese culture. Your typical Taiwanese office worker is bound to have at least one cutesy doll or figurine on their desk and it would be a challenge to find a motor scooter or helmet lacking a cutesy sticker. Even the armed forces adopted perky little doll-like icons (a soldier, a sailor, and a pilot) as a public relations measure, which is quite a contrast with some of the images utilized by the PLA, such as one of three Chinese soldiers standing atop China while thrusting their bayonets toward Taiwan.

Silliness exists everywhere, of course, just in different forms. In Taiwan, it exists in the fascination with schmaltz, chiefly with a mindless kitty-cat that has no mouth and consequently no voice. Hello Kitty might be the perfect symbol for Taiwan.

Naturally, Taiwan's *hao keai* culture has a dark side, abandoned pets being a prime example. Fido was so cute when he was a puppy.... In 1996, Disney released a remake of the film *101 Dalmatians*, resulting in a huge demand for the spotted dog. A year later, the same animals could be seen wandering Taiwanese streets.

From Hualien, I caught another train to the coastal city of Taitung late the following afternoon. It chewed through the East Rift Valley, a lengthy and fertile stretch of land set between the Central Mountain Range and the much smaller Coastal Mountain Range, a narrow buffer of summits that arose from the ocean. Testimony to my lack of Taiwan travel, I had never heard of the East Rift Valley before, and this was something I couldn't believe as I marvelled at it out the window in the dying light. It was green and gorgeous and its verdure made me happy. Of course, it was fairly impoverished; cement houses and betel-nut trees, but I selfishly ignored the poorness for my own jollification.

The train, with its mustard-coloured walls and moss green seats and curtains, stopped often – at odd little stations with odd little names. Most of the passengers were uniformed high school students with dark skin and round eyes. I guessed that they were either from the Amis or the Bunun group, but it wasn't the type of thing one asked. People ate boxed lunches from a trolley (fatty pork chops, sticky white rice, pickled vegetables) and gabbed as they scooped food to their mouths. All the passengers spoke Taiwanese and they were even more clamourous than Mandarin-speaking metro commuters in Taipei, which I didn't think possible.

Even after a decade in Taiwan, I only knew a handful of Taiwanese words and phrases. If Mandarin sounded like Taiwanese, doubtless I would never have attempted to learn it. When Mandarin is spoken clearly, that is: by an educated person, and by someone from Taiwan or southern China, I think it sounds quite pleasant. Taiwanese, on the other hand, sounds rustic and uncouth: ear-splitting honks and squawks made with the roof of the mouth and the nose. Linguists hold that no language is inferior, and in terms of function, that may be so. But language is like music, subject to personal taste, and Taiwanese didn't suit mine. Incidentally, something like 30 percent of Taiwanese people don't know how to speak Taiwanese. Reasons for this include being Hakka, being a "mainlander," and living in Taipei.

I got to the station after sundown and walked toward the exit. A large sign said, 'Welcome to Taitung!' and had a picture of a stout, heavily made-up female farmer in a conical hat proudly holding up a custard apple. I walked in the direction the city should have been, but I only saw a row of restaurants, tall grass, darkness, and a few distant lights. The sound of cicadas was electric and deafening, and I thought, 'This is Taitung?' I had read that it was a backwater and my students could never tell me what it was famous for besides marble and pineapple, but I hadn't been expecting this.

I walked down a street with no name and tried to find the guest house on my map. A taxi driver slowed down and asked me where I wanted to go. "Guangming Road!" I shouted. He shouted back, "It's ten kilometres away! The station here is the old one, not the new one!" I hopped in the cab and noted the betel-nut breeze and the shrine on the dash. Patiently, I put up with the awful Taiwanese love songs all the way to "the real Taitung."

CHAPTER TWENTY-FOUR

I awoke to the sound of gongs, firecrackers, horns, and keyboard; an eerie dissonance which passes for religious music in Taiwan. I pulled back the drapes to see a procession of blue work trucks inching down the road. They were garlanded in tints of orange, yellow, and white, and were flanked by people donning neon yellow baseball caps. Perhaps it was a funeral cortege. Or maybe they were drumming up business for a local temple. Or possibly they were just driving the evil spirits away. I didn't know. I only knew this was the wrong country to be a surgeon or an airline pilot or a member of any profession that required regular and uninterrupted sleep.

Today, I was heading to Green Island, a volcanic outcrop 30 kilometres off the coast. I bought a ticket at a travel agency that had a smiling and helpful staff, and then I caught a cab to the pier; another dash shrine; more plastic-sounding Taiwanese love songs; a laminated image of the Laughing Buddha hanging from the mirror.

The eggshell-tinted vessel secured to the dock had two passageways. People were shoving their way on and off by using both of them. I thought, 'Now, what's a way to solve this problem?'

Fifty minutes later, and we were docking. I rented a scooter and sped down one of Green Island's three roads. The isle was certainly appropriately named. The leafy protrusion possessed such an incredible hue of green that it gave the impression it had been plugged in. And where there wasn't this emerald iridescence, there were slabs of brilliant black volcanic rock violently cast hither and thither. There were pretty little inlets and ocean waves frothing on the dark stone shore. Green Island was the proud owner of a near ineffable splendour. From certain angles, it resembled the cover of a Yes album.

I drove past an exquisite but vacant campground (it was too hot for camping), went for a hike up a charming, lizard-predominant trail, and then checked out an unimpressive, tourist-clogged cave.

I drove around to a village dotted with bunker-like dwellings and dark-skinned, dejected-looking inhabitants. I saw a deer tied to a house and lots of people sitting on lawn chairs drinking, smoking, chewing betel nut, and spitting. Twice, when I made eye contact with someone, they turned their heads and discharged a streak of ruby red spittle onto the ground. I took it to be a local custom. I kept driving until I got to a place known as the Green Island Lodge, Taiwan's most infamous martial-law-era prison.

Critical to Taiwan's history is its 50 years as a Japanese colonial territory, from 1895 to 1945. In theory, as subjects of the Japanese Empire, the Taiwanese possessed all the rights and privileges of any Japanese national, but in reality the island was run as a military dictatorship with special privileges going only to *bona fide* Japanese citizens. For the Han Taiwanese, and especially for the aboriginals, this era of colonization was no picnic. Japanese interests in Taiwan were just those. True, the Japanese were not nearly as cruel as they were in other parts of Asia, but they were cruel nonetheless. Steeped in their totalitarian political tradition, Taiwan's new overlords – despite allowing some Taiwanese to vote – forbade dissent, dealt harshly with law breakers, and made liberal use of the death penalty. Moreover, the Taiwanese faced more or less constant racial discrimination and exploitation, not to mention cultural suffocation. The use of their language was discouraged and non-Japanese radio broadcasts and newspapers were banned. Taoism was smothered, too, and every household on the island was obliged to maintain a shrine dedicated to Shinto, Japan's national religion.[1] The Taiwanese were inculcated in Japanese customs, language, and culture to the point where they were encouraged to adopt Japanese names. Every school week began with students bowing toward Tokyo and the Japanese emperor, and students were funnelled into areas of technical study and dissuaded from fanciful forays into social sciences. No matter how intelligent, educated, or capable they were, it was all but impossible for them to attain positions of significance in government or business.

During World War II, the Japanese intensified production efforts on Taiwan and used it as a jumping-off point for their aggressive campaign of expansion. The Japanese dubbed the island their "unsinkable aircraft carrier." More than 80,000 Taiwanese served in the Japanese Imperial Army and Navy whereas another 125,000 played supporting roles. Aboriginals, for example, were often used as porters. Interestingly, most of the Taiwanese volunteered for service; Japan's influence was that substantial and its propaganda that effective.

---

1   With the end of World War II, Shinto ceased to be Japan's national religion.

As self-seeking, domineering, and militaristic as the Japanese were, the Taiwanese still benefited from their presence. In essence, Japan brought the backward and semiferal island of Formosa kicking and screaming into the twentieth century. In endeavouring to eliminate old customs and superstitions, the Japanese did away with such traditions as headhunting, foot binding, and indentured servitude. Taiwan underwent massive modernization efforts that saw the Japanese construct thousands of kilometres of proper road, railway lines, hospitals, harbours, irrigation systems, sewage systems, and hydroelectric plants. Crime, corruption, and disease dropped off while there were notable improvements in public order and education. Two hundred elementary schools were erected and literacy rates climbed. The Japanese even provided training and job opportunities to the aboriginals, even if they were brutally suppressing them and crushing their culture at the same time.

True, the Japanese siphoned off most of what they gained from Taiwan, but socioeconomic gains for the colony's citizens were substantial nevertheless. Agricultural yields more than tripled. Foreign trade swelled more than 15-fold, and Taiwan's standard of living exceeded that of any province in China.

As George H. Kerr, vice-consul of the American consulate from 1945 to 1947, recorded in his book, *Formosa Betrayed*, "The island is extremely productive in coal, rice, sugar, cement, fruits, and tea. Both hydro and thermal power are abundant. The Japanese (have) efficiently electrified even remote areas and (have) also established excellent railway lines and highways. Eighty percent of the people can read and write, the (very) antithesis of conditions prevailing in the mainland...."

Author Denny Roy, in his excellent *Taiwan: A Political History*, argues that Japan's most consequential contribution to Taiwan was allowing for the Taiwanese to develop a taste for the democratic process. By the end of the 1930s, there were about 3,000 Taiwanese holding seats in various assemblies, even if their power was largely symbolic (less than four percent of Taiwanese were eligible to vote, for example). Yet, in spite of such tokenism, allowing for *any* degree of elected representation may well have whetted their appetite for the practice.

Notably, after the Taiwanese first learned of their pending cession to Japan, back in 1895, an independent state known as the Republic of Formosa was declared. Six days later, the Japanese landed and the Taiwanese put up some pretty fierce resistance. The short-lived republic's Declaration of Independence included a statement which read, "If we, the people of Taiwan, permit the Japanese to land, Taiwan will become the land of savages and barbarians." But that wouldn't happen until after the Japanese left.

Given that Chiang Kai-shek and his Nationalists considered places other than Chongqing to be politically tainted and treasonous at war's end (never mind that he lived and studied in Japan, served in the Japanese Army, had an adopted son who was born in Japan, took six years to even face the Japanese in battle, refused in some instances to even remove the packaging from his Allied-supplied equipment, kept his hotline to Tokyo open, and oversaw an organization beleaguered with collusion), how his government handled Taiwan's so-called return is not surprising. Incidentally, Taiwan's "return" was approved by Roosevelt and Churchill at a 1943 summit in Cairo after Chiang argued that Taiwan had been stolen by the Japanese.

To the Nationalists, the situation on Taiwan was simple. In addition to having become Nipponified, the Taiwanese had obviously assisted Japan in its struggle against China. Even if one overlooked Taiwanese military involvement, the people's monetary and sociopolitical gains screamed complicity. There was a whole class of Taiwanese elites as well as a middle class. Why would the Japanese have rewarded these *Taibazi* (Taiwanese rednecks) if they hadn't been their accomplices? Taiwan would have to be punished for what it was: a conquered enemy territory.

It didn't take long for the trouble to start. During a speech at the handover ceremony, a prominent Nationalist general made the claim that the Taiwanese were a "degraded people" residing in a "degraded territory." Taiwan, he articulated, was "beyond the passes," meaning it was beyond the pale of Chinese civilization. An article in a Nationalist publication declared that the Taiwanese had been "poisoned intellectually" and what they required was "re-educating."

Apparently, this re-education was to be directed by the 48,000-strong, press-ganged rabble of Nationalist soldiers that arrived on Taiwan in the year that followed the Japanese surrender. The first 12,000 travelled to Taiwan via US transport. According to George H. Kerr, "They flatly refused to go ashore. At Keelung (a port city in the northeast) Chinese officers begged the astonished Americans to send an advanced unit overland – an American unit, of course – through the narrow valleys leading to Taipei…. The Chinese officers had heard that vengeful Japanese suicide squads lurked in the hills. Only a rancorous argument forced the Chinese to accept their fate and go ashore. At Kaohsiung (a port city in the southwest) the Americans, eager to empty their transports, had to threaten bodily ejection of the Chinese troops before their reluctant passengers would venture (onto land)."

As it happened, thousands of Taiwanese turned out to greet the soldiers, but were soon laughing at them. It was an inauspicious start. As Denny Roy notes, "There were abundant anecdotes illustrating the prevailing Taiwanese view that these troops were (hicks): crowds of soldiers staring in amazement at an elevator in a downtown Taipei department store, soldiers walking along the roads carrying stolen bicycles strapped to their backs, signals corpsmen laying telephone wires across railroad tracks."

The Chinese called themselves "liberators," but the Taiwanese knew that if they had been liberated at all, they had the Americans to thank. In fact, American military presence only made the Chinese look worse. The Americans were well disciplined, polite, easygoing, and fond of spending money. The Taiwanese thought they were terrific. Chinese officers began calling them "troublemakers." But only one uniform on the island of Taiwan signified trouble.

As was customary, the Nationalist soldiers were paid a pittance and therefore expected to supplement their income in the time-honoured tradition of carpetbagging. Public buildings (including hospitals) and private homes were made into barracks and stripped right down to the nuts and bolts. Soldiers would tear out doors, banisters, and window frames and use them for cooking fires. Looting became commonplace and was often orchestrated by officers. An initiative was undertaken whereby Japanese possessions were to be appropriated for redistribution, meaning the homes of some 330,000 Japanese citizens were seized, pillaged, and occupied. Next came the homes of the moneyed Taiwanese. Things only got worse when the new administration arrived on the scene.

For his first governor-general of Taiwan's new military regime, Chiang Kai-shek appointed his crony, Chen Yi. Like Chiang, Chen was born in Zhejiang province and had been one of the generalissimo's men ever since the all-important Northern Expedition, when he double dealt his warlord boss to cross over to the Nationalist camp. Chen Yi graduated from a Japanese military academy, spoke fluent Japanese, and had a Japanese mistress, whom he brought to Taiwan. According to Denny Roy, Chen Yi possessed "substantial Japanese connections and co-operated with Japanese officials and military officers on several occasions" during the years of Japan's occupation. Before the war, he had actually congratulated Japan on having brought Taiwan under its control. Of course, he also had Green Gang connections. He was, in Chiang's eyes, the perfect man for the job.

Under Chen Yi's mainlander-packed administration, extortion and carpetbagging were practically passed into law. It was a facsimile of what was going on in China; it was what the Nationalists did; what they had always done. If an officer or official desired a piece of property, all he need do was accuse the owner of being a collaborator, a phenomenon which became routine in Taiwan. Anyone who resisted was soon wishing they hadn't. Whatever the newcomers had no personal use for (fire hydrants, factories) they ripped up and sent to Shanghai to be sold on the black market. And they ripped up just about everything. George H. Kerr writes, "Several serious railway crossing accidents occurred before the public realized that the 'liberators' were carrying off automatic switch and signal equipment to be sold as scrap metal." To hurry scrap metal and other items to Taiwan's ports, every garbage truck in Taipei was commandeered, resulting in street-corner mountains of trash. Infrastructure that wasn't confiscated or exported was simply left to rot. Plundering became so endemic and so profitable that boatloads of Chinese began arriving to partake.

Meanwhile, the government churned out the propaganda. The administration wasn't looting, but rather transferring vital instruments to China in order to aid in reconstruction and assist in crucial anti-Communist campaigns. Paradoxically, government monopolies were introduced, ostensibly to benefit the masses, and 90 percent of Taiwan's economy came under state control. With little to no technical background or market understanding, one factory after another was run into the ground. Goods were hoarded and prices driven up. Then, Chinese officials moved their wares on the black market where they made a pretty penny. And they *were* Chinese. The Taiwanese were all but locked out of government jobs. Around 36,000 Taiwanese civil servants were laid off after the Chinese influx, and of the first 23 mayors and magistrates in Taiwan, only 3 were Taiwanese.

Taiwan's new police force was also comprised of Chinese, and like the military, its members were expected to augment their paltry pay cheques in creative ways. Precisely where law enforcement left off and the activities of the recently imported underworld began was difficult to determine. Crime exploded, and disease, such as bubonic plague and cholera, which had been eradicated under Japanese rule, resurfaced. Inflation soared, agricultural output tumbled, and anyone who dared criticize the new rulers found themselves facing harassment or incarceration.

But the Taiwanese still refused to show the illiterate pack of ransackers any respect. In fact, they openly derided the Chinese. Posters emerged of Chen Yi looking like a big fat pig. On city walls, people wrote, 'Dogs go and pigs come!' The dogs represented the Japanese: terrifying but protective; pigs had only insatiable appetites. The phrase 'Dogs go and pigs come' practically became a greeting among the Taiwanese.

On February 27, 1947, the situation reached the breaking point. A widow with the surname Lin was selling cigarettes in a Taipei park when a pair of agents from the Monopoly Bureau confiscated her goods and her cash. She resisted and was struck on the head with the butt of a pistol. She fell. A mob gathered whereupon it surrounded and threatened. To clear a path, one of the agents fired at them, mortally wounding one. The agents escaped to a nearby police station, so the crowd searched out their vehicle and torched it. The following day, a protest was organized and 2,000 people marched to Chen Yi's office. When they drew near, they were fired upon. Two were killed and many more were wounded. Hearing of the incident on local radio, the citizens of Taipei took to the streets, and protests spread across the island like wildfire. Within two days, the demonstrators had overwhelmed every major city on the island. Out of the original 48,000 Nationalist troops, only 11,000 remained as forces had returned to China to battle the Communists. That wasn't a sufficient number, and mobs of livid Taiwanese had little trouble targeting the soldiers, killing or injuring about 1,000 in total.

From his position of weakness, the usually hard-line Chen Yi had little choice but to negotiate. He publicly agreed to the Taiwanese demands, which included punishment for the two Monopoly Bureau agents and compensation for the victims. However, Taiwan's governor-general was then petitioned with a long list of additional demands, ones of a political nature designed to level the playing field between the Taiwanese and the Chinese. These called for, among other things, freedom of the press, freedom of speech and assembly, and guaranteed equal rights for aboriginals. Such demands Chen Yi could not accept – not if he wanted to save face.

Using the resumption of the Chinese Civil War in China as a pretext, Chen Yi opted to characterize the circumstances on Taiwan as tantamount to a major anti-government uprising rather than negotiate any further. He petitioned Chiang Kai-shek for reinforcements, a request the Nationalist leader was only too willing to comply with. Chinese armed police disembarked at Keelung and Kaohsiung, and this time there were no surrendered Japanese troops to frighten them. Immediately, the Chinese set about shooting, bayoneting, robbing, and raping anyone unfortunate enough to be caught outdoors. Initially, the killings were random. People were beheaded. Homes were ransacked. Corpses were defiled and left in the streets as a warning.

After the cities were retaken, the retribution became more systematic. The KMT embarked on an island-wide mop-up campaign which it labelled 'exterminating traitors.' Organizers, demonstrators, dissenters, and even individuals who were judged to have slighted a Chinese were tracked down and snuffed out. A large number of those killed were students.

The Nationalist answer to Taiwan's simmering discontent was a calculated massacre that took the lives of up to 28,000 people. Officially, it is known as the February 28th Incident, but colloquially it is called (in both English and Chinese) 2-28, pronounced 'two-two-eight.' The government blamed the revolt on Japanese imperialists, Communist agitators, and the unpatriotic, unappreciative Taiwanese. Only about 300 people died, they said, 100 of whom were soldiers.

Such a response brought Taiwanese political demands to an abrupt and bloody end. By the time Chiang and his entourage of cronies, gangsters, bumpkin soldiers (of which there were 600,000), and Chinese refugees (of which there were upwards of 2 million), beat their hurried retreat to Taiwan, local officials were still in the process of wiping out rebels, i.e. remnants of the Taiwanese leadership. Martial law was imposed and would last for another 38 years. During that time, it was not permitted to even discuss 2-28.

Although Chiang's Taiwan lacked the totalitarianism of Mao's China, in many ways it was a miniature mirror image. The Nationalists' chief obsessions were eliminating dissent and retaking "the mainland." Publicly, the KMT maintained that it was still guided by Sun Yat-sen's Three Principles of the People, one of which, you'll recall, called for democracy. However, although people possessed the right to vote, they did not possess the right to form political parties, and existing parties backed the KMT to the hilt. True democracy would have to be shelved until the clear and present danger of communism no longer menaced. Banners in the street read, 'Communist spies, turn yourselves in.' Civilians were charged with sedition and made to stand trial in front of military courts. Books were banned. Songs were banned. Freedom of speech was practically banned.

One of Chiang's first orders of business was to shake up his top brass by carrying out a purge that saw about 100 people die. A personality cult was then created. Propaganda posters from that era look almost identical to those of Mao Zedong and Kim Il-sung. Chiang was exempted from the constitutional clause that limited presidents to two terms in office. A sham election was held and the Nationalists won. The rival parties were phonies. Rival parties were then banned. As an "emergency measure," the constitution was suspended and all powers were handed over to the generalissimo, who presided over a government with virtually no Taiwanese representation and a thousand Chinese representing constituencies from all over China, hence helping to perpetuate the illusion that the ROC, and not the PRC, was China's legitimate ruler. A special law was passed to allow for the politicians from China to retain their titles for life. Meanwhile, Taiwanese who drew attention to themselves by, say, petitioning the administration for the right to form new political parties or requesting greater representation, were silenced, customarily by way of blackmail, torture, imprisonment, and firing squad. The Nationalists utilized well over half a million informants to keep tabs on the population, and keep tabs they did. In order to maintain his authority and be at the ready to launch an attack on his lost China, Chiang Kai-shek squashed Taiwanese nationalism by turning the island into a police state. Owing to his failure to bring China under his control, this must have been, in a sense, a dream come true for the old dictator.

Obviously, the situation on Taiwan wasn't especially conducive to being an intellectual, and one of the many to get snared up in the state's security apparatus was Bo Yang, who, like Kafka's Josef K, was prosecuted without ever having been told what crime he had committed. Instead, he was branded a "communist sympathizer" and given eighteen years (nine of which he ended up serving); forget that he was known for his anti-communist writings and had even been associated with an anti-communist association headed by Chiang Ching-kuo, Chiang Kai-shek's son. (Forget, too, that Chiang Ching-kuo had studied in Moscow.) What *really* landed the teacher *cum* journalist *cum* writer in hot water, as has been touched upon, was a Popeye cartoon that poked fun of President Chiang and his son. Having obtained the rights to publish the comic strip in Taiwan, Bo Yang created a version where Popeye buys a deserted island and goes to visit it with his boy, Junior. Here is the translation:

Popeye: "What a beautiful kingdom. I am king. I am president. I can be anything I want to be."

Junior: "What about me?"

Popeye: "Oh, you can be crown prince."

Junior: "If I am going to be anything at all, I am going to be president."

Popeye: "Your tone of voice is rather bold for one who is just a baby."

Junior: "But there are just (the) two of us in the whole country..."

Popeye: "My country is a democratic country. Everyone has the right to vote."

Junior: "Everyone? But there are just the two of us. Wait.
          Let me think. I'll run for election too."
Popeye: "Let me first make my election speech. Fellow
          countrymen…"
Junior: "Not a bad beginning!"
Popeye: "You must not, under any circumstances, vote
          for Junior!"
Junior: "Hey! What's the big idea?"

In March, 1968, Bo Yang was sent here to the Green Island Lodge to commence his sentence. He confessed to being a communist, although he was deprived of sleep and had one of his legs broken beforehand. He was told that signing a confession would reduce his term. This was during the era known as White Terror, which lasted from the 1950s until the 1980s. Virtually anyone, no matter whether Taiwanese or Chinese, viewed as a potential leader or threat was accused of communist plotting and locked up. Roughly 90,000 were arrested with something like 45,000 executed. Many of them were shot here, on this prison ground, which I walked toward after parking my scooter in a roasting-hot, sun-drenched parking lot.

Inside the main gate, there was a Nationalist flag (or Taiwanese flag; they are virtually identical) painted on the wall. On one side it said, 'I Love My Country,' on the other, 'I Love My Flag.'

In front of the crumbling old prison was something called the Human Rights Memorial, a museum which featured pictures and biographies of some of the more notable "troublemakers" that the regime incarcerated and executed. I couldn't help notice that many of them were writers.

As usual, the museum wasn't especially well done, but it got the point across. The memorial was established by the DPP, or Democratic Progressive Party, in 2000, the year it defeated the KMT to come to power. I walked through a vacant cell block (green doors now ajar, white-washed hallways bathed in natural light, dust) and imagined Bo Yang huddled in a cubicle, contemplating his fate.

After his release, Bo Yang wrote about his experience, saying that, for someone like him, incarceration was inevitable 'no matter whether in Taiwan or mainland China' because he had spoken the truth. "Why must Chinese people who have the guts to speak the truth suffer so terribly?" he asks. "I have asked a number of people from the mainland why they ended up in prison. Their answer was, 'Because I said a few things that happened to be true.' And that's the way it is."

Many people in Taiwan still haven't faced up to the truth about Chiang and his regime. At the time of writing, the KMT, or Nationalist Party, was back in power – *having been democratically elected*. Mind you, February 28 is now a public holiday, and there is a monument that stands in Taipei's 2-28 Park, but it is hideous and situated just down the street from what was, until very recently, Chiang Kai-shek Memorial Hall. Now known as National Taiwan Democracy Memorial Hall, the name change was part of an only partially successful (not to mention controversial and probably impermanent) name rectification campaign initiated by the DPP shortly before it became apparent it would most likely get voted out of office. Although the building itself has been renamed, and the plaza, too (it's now called Liberty Square), the name of the corresponding metro stop remains Chiang Kai-shek Memorial Hall Station. Chiang's huge bronze statue still sits inside the extravagant landmark. The Chinese characters for 'democracy' and 'ethics' are still etched into the wall behind the likeness. Chiang's Cadillacs can still be viewed in the basement. Signs tell of his government as having been a friend to all Chinese people and the entire world, and everything from Chiang Kai-shek lapel pins to Chiang Kai-shek coffee mugs to Chiang Kai-shek playing cards can be purchased in its gift shop. On any given day, the place is filled with visitors. In fact, it probably receives as many tourists as Taroko Gorge does. Parenthetically, and in case you missed it, the name National Taiwan Democracy Memorial Hall implies that democracy in Taiwan is dead.

The generalissimo's personality cult continues in Taiwan. As mentioned, Chiang's face still appears on the New Taiwan Dollar. Op-ed pieces in the hopelessly partisan (pro-KMT) English-language newspaper, *China Post*, defend him as a hero who united the country with his Northern Expedition before going on to fight – and defeat – the Japanese. Once ensconced in Taipei, Chiang set about to improve the little island via his beneficial policy of land reform and his ambitious reconstruction projects. Besides, if it weren't for him, every man, woman, and child would be a no-good, dirty commie.

Students are taught similar things. I used to teach at an all-girls Catholic high school where a picture of Chiang Kai-shek and another of Sun Yat-sen hung in every classroom in the building. At lunch, the girls would put down their Hello Kitty pencil cases and pick up their dummy rifles to practise marching around the courtyard. At my latest school, a group of razor-sharp grade-eight kids I taught told me that in history class they learned Chiang was a hero and that he lost China because of "icy weather." In an interview in 1997, Bo Yang blamed Chinese education for "continuing to foster a culture of dishonesty."

When the boat got to within 20 kilometres of the coast, it became clear to me why, in 1544, the Portuguese named Taiwan *Ilha Formosa* (Beautiful Island) without actually dropping anchor. They probably figured there wasn't a square foot flat enough to stand on. It looked incredible: a dark, spiky-spined leviathan rising up, out of the sea. Its summits were one, two, and three kilometres high, and an elephant's trunk of cloud wound its way along the tops of them. It was overcast, and so the mass was shadowy and contemplative and no man-made objects were visible.

Back in Taitung, I hopped in a taxi and handed the driver a card with my hotel's name and address on it. He read the details out loud, flipped it over, and scrutinized the little map on the back. "*Yeah!*" he said angrily, pointing to the representative little red square, "It's right *here!*" I told him that I knew it was right there; that's why I had given him the card. He shook his head and drove off muttering to himself. I figured the part of the conversation where I said, "No, *that's* not it," occurred somewhere between the time I left the ferry and the time I spotted his cab.

I was in the mood to explore Taitung, but quickly realized there wasn't much to see or do. When one of the top attractions in your guidebook is a fruit market (there are fruit markets all over Taiwan), that's a pretty clear signal that you are going to have to be inventive. I thought about going to an aboriginal museum just outside town, but decided against it when I saw an aboriginal woman with no helmet on weaving down the street on her scooter. She had her two daughters with her (they didn't have helmets on either), and was screeching out some song in her native tongue. I was quite confident she wouldn't have passed a breathalyzer test.

Taitung, which means "East Terrace," was most definitely not Taipei, or "North Terrace." Like almost any Taiwanese city or town, it was chaotic, loud, brassy, and generally unattractive, but it was also uniformly rustic. A lot of people wore sandals or even went barefoot. There were black feet, charcoal toenails, conical hats, leopard-skin-print shirts, wife beaters, dangling cigarettes, and sidewalks adorned with betel-nut-spittle stains. People tended to speak loudly and gesture operatically.

Physically, at least, Taiwan has developed so quickly. In the old days, farmers made up more than 90 percent of the population. In 1975, that number stood at around 50. More recently, it's about 8. A picture of Taiwan from the mid-1970s from a *World Book Encyclopedia* I own shows a farmer in a rice field drying his crops. In the bushy distance, there is a factory and a hazy mountain range, but none of the soaring tile-and-cage tenement blocks that are all-pervading nowadays.

Generation gaps are vast. Taiwanese kids grow up watching HBO, syncing their iPods, and playing Sony PlayStation and Nintendo Wii. By contrast, their grandparents, who take care of them, are mystified by things like touch-screen ticket dispensers and even older innovations such as elevators and escalators. I have seen elderly people stop at the bottom of escalators and stare. I have seen them grip the moveable railing for dear life, only to fall over. I have seen whole *groups* of them grip the moveable railing for dear life, only to fall over. I have seen metro employees politely explaining that the large, red, lit-up X at the turnstile indicates that you cannot enter, whereas the big, bright green check mark signifies that you can. And this was in Taipei, the country's capital and most urbane metroplex. During the 2002-2003 SARS epidemic, Taipei's metro system flashed the message, 'Please Do Not Bring Your Chickens on the Train,' on its electronic announcement boards. The buses, with their Samsung flat-panel plasma TVs, declared, 'No Ducks.'

CHAPTER TWENTY-FIVE

The next morning, I caught another cab to the pier. The two and a half hour jaunt to Orchid Island, or Lanyu, was exceptionally rough going. According to my guidebook, even Orchid Island residents balk at the idea of taking a boat through these waters. It warns, "If you have a weak stomach, the trip will be quite an ordeal."

The vessel would lurch forward, pitch to port, level out, stagger on, reel to starboard, become even again, hurl ahead, *ad nauseam*. Quite literally. All the seats came with barf bags and the woman behind me made use of hers. To combat seasickness, I chewed on a piece of ginger, focused on the television set, and tried to imagine I was somewhere else. But with the sickly stench of vomit in the air, that was hard to do. I was very happy when we docked.

After checking into a hotel, I rented a scooter and drove off. It was a pleasant experience. Like Green Island, Orchid Island was volcanic (a riot of vegetation and fantastic black rock), but it was even more mesmeric and about three times as large. It had winsome views in almost any direction you ventured to stare: grassy fields, lush and ambitious hills, wild bunches of stone, turquoise bays, and a white-capped, cobalt Pacific. I drove around for hours, exploring and exploring.

Most of the island's 3,000 inhabitants are members of the Tao, a tribe of Polynesian origin who are farmers and fishermen.[1] One of the first Tao I saw was a man with long salt-and-pepper hair tottering down the road with a liquor bottle in his hand and a toothy grin chiselled onto his face. The shops behind him were well stocked with shells, fish-shaped wind chimes, and other marine-themed baubles, but there wasn't a single tourist in sight. I thought of McGovern, who described the Tao as "gentle" and "ever-smiling," and that they seemed "to know nothing of either the making or drinking of wine – one of the few primitive peoples of whom this is true."

---

1   The Tao were previously known as the Yami. In fact, they were known as the Yami when I was there. The tribe had its name changed to Tao sometime after my visit.

Whole sections of the island's principal village were a shambles; I hadn't known such poverty existed in Taiwan. In addition to the sad, cinder-block buildings, there were hovels crafted out of driftwood, pipes, rocks, rope, tarpaulins – whatever people had gotten their hands on. In the dusty, junk-filled lanes, there were battered scooters, broken hoses, plastic basins, sleeping dogs, wandering chickens, statue-like goats, and the Tao themselves; smoking, drinking, brooding, forlorn…. None of them made eye contact with me. On Green Island, the thing to do upon spotting an outsider was to spit. On Orchid Island, it was to disregard. Among the penury, there stood a charming little wooden church painted in Tao symbols and colours: white with red and black trim. Obviously, it had been decorated by the same artisans who crafted the tribe's canoes, the painted canoes on either side of the doors being the clue. Canoe-making is one of the Tao's principal traditions; the stylized boats are really quite striking.

After a chocolate-box sunset and dinner on the balcony of a cute little restaurant called The Epicurean, I drove around again, stopping at this roadside bar and that one for a beer. You could just pull over, hop on a bench, have a Corona, and keep driving. Everyone did it; no one seemed to care. That was my justification.

Vespertine entertainment consisted largely of sitting at tables near the road and drinking without talking. Along a row of karaokes, fast-fry restaurants, and vacant souvenir shops, I went into a pub playing Eric Clapton. After the bartender silently served me, he pulled a chair up to the window, folded his arms, and sat staring toward the blackness that had swallowed the sea. There were two dark-skinned women sitting on the patio, and they too were hypnotized by the void. I desperately wanted to speak to someone, but sensed that no one on the island was much fond of dialogue. Perhaps they were taking solace in the sound of the ocean. Or conceivably they were wondering what lay beyond it. I couldn't tell if their sea-gazing was consoling or disconcerting. In the end, I concluded that it was just part of their culture. The Tao believe that their people "came up out of the sea," or least they did until their Sea God was replaced by the Christian one.

Interestingly, the Japanese saw no need to try and tame the Tao, and, except for a police station and school they set up, determined it was best to leave them alone. To the Nationalists, however, it was evident that the primitives would require a liberal dollop of Sinicization. They would have to take the cure. The KMT began relocating large numbers of Chinese to the island in the hopes that the Tao would become assimilated through intermarriage. The Tao, the most close-knit and family oriented of

Taiwan's tribes, wouldn't stand for it, and years of conflict and resentment ensued.

To protect themselves from typhoons, the Tao had learned to build sturdy wooden houses below ground. The only part above ground was a tiny, angled bit of roof. The houses were strong, practical, and aesthetically pleasing (I would see a few the following day), but the KMT ordered that they be demolished and replaced with concrete ones, which were poorly built and not fit for stormy weather.[2] After this, the tourists and missionaries arrived with their cameras and crosses. But the worst example of interference was yet to come. It was, of course, government orchestrated.

In 1982, the Lanyu Nuclear Waste Disposal Facility was established on Orchid Island and used to store some 100,000 barrels of radioactive waste. The Tao's head chief signed the relevant contract believing he was agreeing to the construction of a cannery. He was illiterate. Reportedly, the cement trenches that house the barrels have cracked (there are frequent earthquakes off of Taiwan's east coast) and as many as a fifth of the barrels have begun to leak. The government, naturally, has denied this. I wondered if anyone would tell me what the truth was.

The following day, I drove down a battered stretch of road and was passed by a World Vision van. I went for a short distance more and pulled into the parking lot of the Taiwan Power Company. When I walked in the front door, two of the three male clerks – none of whom was Tao – lifted their newspapers in front of their faces and hid. The third, a corpulent fellow with glasses, smiled nervously, frozen.

"Hi, I was wondering where I could find the nuclear waste disposal facility," I said.

"Oh? Why do you want to go there?"

"I'd like to learn more about nuclear waste."

One of the other men lowered a corner of his newspaper. "Are you a journalist?"

---

2   Chinese people tend to believe that building houses out of wood is foolish if not downright absurd. I have had several people tell me this and ask me why homes in the West are constructed with that material. The argument is that concrete is strong and wood isn't. Also, wood catches fire and concrete doesn't. A newspaper article I have from 2000 says that Taiwan had an average of 43 fires per day that year (down almost 15 percent from the year before) along with a spike in fire-related deaths: up to nearly 1,000, a statistic that authorities attributed to barred-up windows. In all my years in Taiwan, I never once participated in or even heard tell of a fire drill, yet one company I worked for asked me to pose for a photo with an extinguisher and sign a document stating I had received fire training. Once, when a building caught fire just outside of Taipei, fire engines couldn't reach it because the street was too narrow and jammed with parked scooters. People were shocked even though similar streets are in abundance.

"No, just a tourist," I said, and I looked it: sunscreen, shorts, and the tacky hat with the grinning orange squid on it. He appraised me for a moment and nodded to the big man, who cheerily introduced himself as Jack. Jack said that he'd take me there. We got on our scooters and sped away.

At the gate, I had to leave a piece of identification and sign in. I received a guest pass and was led inside by Jack, who seemed a very chipper fellow. "I hope I can get a transfer to a branch on Taiwan," he said, smiling. "It's too hot here and there are no good restaurants!"

Inside, I met a technician in a lab coat who looked decidedly tense. He stiffly shook my hand and introduced himself as Mr. Kuo, although he provided no job title. He and Jack then stepped into another room where they shared a heated moment of whispering. I heard Jack say, "Don't worry. He's a just a tourist."

I was shown into a conference room. The air conditioning was switched on and a film was shown. It was offered in Chinese, Japanese, and English. Mr. Kuo sat next to me. Two other lab-coated men came in and sat down next to him. They too looked nervous. Jack offered me tea. The film began, and I took out my notebook and tried to keep up.

The short started by focusing on Orchid Island's physical beauty. The island was dotted with orchids, hence its name. It was the only place in Taiwan with a rainforest. It had beautiful mountains and rock formations, etc., etc. Mr. Kuo attempted to overdub: "Oh! Look! So beautiful! You should go there!" I ignored him and kept scribbling.

According to the narrator, the island's 3,000 Tao inhabitants hadn't been assimilated in any way. In fact, most of them were Catholic or Protestant. Stills showed the men constructing their canoes and prancing around in their jock straps. The women wore skirts and smiled sheepishly. Because of the Taiwan Power Company, the narrator explained, the Tao had received scholarships, cash, and care for the elderly. The company had also hosted parties and other events. The film showed a large group of people singing karaoke at a banquet. Every single one of them was beaming with delight. Certain "modern additions" had been made to the island. There was now a clinic, a post office, a school, and, of course, the Lanyu Nuclear Waste Disposal Facility. After a brief overview of what the facility did, it was stated – four times – that it was in tip-top shape. There were "no problems" and "no negative effects." The trenches that held the barrels were "properly built" with thick concrete that was "secured with a waterproof agent." Moreover, the staff and local residents received annual check-ups and there hadn't been any disturbing discoveries. There was no abnormal radioactivity. This was also repeated four times. Even a smiling inspector from Japan had concluded that everything was above board. The film ended by saying that the Taiwan Power Company was "a good neighbour," dedicated to preserving Tao heritage and "this clean Shangri-La."

The lights came on and I put down my pen. Then, I asked ask Mr. Kuo a question in English. "But it's leaking, isn't it?"

"Leaking? No! Where did you hear that?"

"I read it in a book."

"Really?"

"Yes, and in the newspaper."

"Really?"

"Yes, and on the internet."

He did his best to appear amazed, which wasn't at all convincing. I thought of all the amateurish Chinese television dramas and movies I had seen. The other two men didn't look surprised at all. How could they have been? When the Tao finally figured out what was going on, they responded with protests. For a while, the story had received media attention. Even Greenpeace had gotten involved.

One of the employees said to me, "It's not leaking, but some barrels have opened and some waste has come out. But the trenches are fine." This was a rather different message from the one in the film. Incredibly, Mr. Kuo was still pretending that this was the first time he'd heard such a thing. He looked over at the other man in a My-goodness!-I-didn't-get-*that*-memo! manner.

"How thick are the trench floors?" I asked the man – who never introduced himself.

"Twenty centimetres."

"That's all?"

"We use a kind of sealant."

"Okay, but how old is the facility?"

"Twenty years."

"Really? I read 'twenty-five years.'"

There was an awkward pause during which the men exchanged glances. They never gave me an answer.

I'm no engineer, but to have a floor that was only twenty centimetres thick seemed, to say the least, inadequate. That was only two thirds the length of a common ruler. The sealant would be useless if the concrete were to crack, something bound to occur given the island's seismological circumstances. The Eurasian and Philippine plates meet under Taiwan and there are 51 active fault lines on the island-nation.

"The Tao looked pretty happy in the film," I said. "But they don't seem too happy in real life."

"The local people… don't really understand the situation," Mr. Kuo said, contorting his features into an aspect of disdain. The other men made faces, too. Jack, who didn't appear to understand English, just sat there, contentedly sipping his tea. The technicians and I stopped talking and looked at him. He grinned gingerly.

I was asked if I had any more questions or wanted anything else to drink, at which point I was handed a brochure with all the plant's specifications. I thanked them and stood up. As a bit of parting advice, the now-happy-looking Mr. Kuo said, "Don't believe everything you read!"

'Or hear,' I thought.

On the way back to the parking lot, Jack said that the government was planning on moving the plant somewhere else, but I knew they had been saying that for something like 15 years. Foot-dragging is universal, of course, but this method of dealing with problems and complaints in the Chinese world seemed to me to be formulaic: say you'll look into it; that you're very concerned; that you'll do whatever it takes to make the situation better, but, unless it's something that's going to cost you money or face, don't so much as lift a finger, except of course to churn out a bit of propaganda. Never mind corporate social responsibility; not even state-run enterprises would budge.

The Taiwan Power Company had wagered on the Tao's lack of resolve. They had also wagered on the fickle Taiwanese and their racism and penchant for forgetting. They had wagered correctly. But at least I was allowed into the place. I was even given tea. That really impressed me. In China, I would likely have been arrested and put on an airplane. A local would likely have been arrested and put in a death van. Once again, it must be said that the Taiwanese are a mild and gracious lot, even when they are (in all likelihood) poisoning the Pacific while steadfastly maintaining that they aren't.

I spent the rest of the day driving around and doing little walks. The island was gorgeous. *Lost* gorgeous. Although there were just 3,000 residents (very few of whom were outdoors), I encountered three traffic jams despite only meeting an oncoming vehicle (usually a scooter) once every 30 seconds or so.

Troupes of Taiwanese tourists would park their scooters *on* the road and take pictures of some rock formation or each other, wholly oblivious to their having created a situation. In one case, traffic was held up because a man in his twenties had a nosebleed and had to be attended to by six or seven of his friends. Even the goats knew enough to get out of the way, but not the Taiwanese; they could generate traffic congestion and chaos with just a dozen people in the middle of absolutely nowhere.

At a couple of spots near the water, people had built what the locals called *fadai tai*, or 'space-out platforms,' because you could sit on them and just space out. I did this for a while, and then I chanced upon a village with traditional houses. Dried fish hung on wooden racks; yard fires chased plumes of smoke into the air; chickens and pigs strolled about, and goats stood on roofs. I walked up and down people's paths and was incredibly nosey, yet no one paid the slightest bit of attention to me. It dawned on me why the Japanese had decided to leave the Tao alone: doubtless the Tao had never acknowledged their presence.

The Sea God was merciful the following morning, and the waters between Orchid Island and Taiwan were placid. On the boat's TV, I saw what I honestly thought was the scene of a mosh pit at some Japanese rock concert. Then I noticed that the moshers were wearing suits and ties. The camera pulled back, revealing the outsized portrait of Sun Yat-sen. It was yet another brawl in Taiwan's national legislature, this one involving approximately 120 lawmakers.

Customarily, when Taiwanese legislators contest a bill, they do so by taking to the floor (usually *en masse*) in order to wave banners and placards that read "Opposed!" so as to prove to their constituents they are really doing something. In 2006, a female legislator representing the DPP had a more original idea. Before the disputed document could be signed, she stuffed it in her mouth and attempted to eat it. However, before it could be swallowed, members of the KMT forced her to spit it out – by violently pulling her hair.

Interestingly, the majority of Taiwanese has no idea that their homeland is arguably most famous for its governmental ruckuses. They simply aren't aware that those incidents tend to make international news because, overwhelmingly, they aren't concerned with or aware of international news. Most Taiwanese are under the impression that Taiwan is best-known for its food, night markets, temples, and the Taipei 101 building. If you tell someone the truth: that most Western people have little to no idea where or what Taiwan is (and often confuse it with Thailand), or know only that it's a manufacturing hub, has a strained political relationship with China, and has policymakers who spend an immoderate amount of time slapping the holy snot out of one another, you're likely to be met with an expression of dismay. I once saw a Taiwanese TV show where a Korean soap opera star said, to be honest, Korean people knew very little about Taiwan, including its location, and that Taiwan was almost never featured in Korean news. The hostess couldn't believe it.

It was a divine day and the train pulled away from the Taitung station and moved at a leisurely pace through some lovely countryside. Before this trip, I had only taken the train in Taiwan on four short excursions. I realized now that I should have used it more. It was a great way to travel. The stations were a bit primitive perhaps, but the trains were clean, comfortable, and prompt. The government had recently completed a high-speed railway from Taipei to Kaohsiung, but what was the point of seeing everything as a blur? The old trains didn't rush; you could relax and take everything in. There were no dining cars, but if there had been, rest assured they would have been smoke-free, devoid of peasant security squadrons, and non-Chinese like myself wouldn't have been barked at to change seats or leave.

The train clacked along the east coast to the town of Tawu, whereupon it swung inland, passing theatrical hills, suspension towers, and boulder-strewn riverbeds. After just 25 kilometres, it turned northward, and just like that, I was on Taiwan's west coast. Near a place called Fangliao, things started to go from green to grey. The neat rows of betel-nut trees couldn't compete with the ash grey cubicles and cement fish-hatcheries, and things got uglier and more industrial as the minutes passed. I alighted at Kaohsiung and went to buy an onward ticket. Taiwan's second largest city was not part of my itinerary.

A few years back, I had flown to Kaohsiung for a week-long work assignment. The city was horrid – even from the airplane. Mind you, the people were even warmer and friendlier than they were in Taipei (and people in Taipei are pretty darned friendly), but Kaohsiung's pollution and brutalized appearance were just jaw-dropping.

I had read that, in the four or five years since my visit, Kaohsiung had been cleaned up, but of course that was just propaganda. People were saying the city's Love River was clean when I was there, yet it smelled. Efforts might have been underway to begin a clean up, but to say it was completed, or even well on its way, couldn't possibly have been true. A prerequisite for cleaning Kaohsiung would have been levelling it.

Kaohsiung was now clean because its municipal government had begun telling people it was now clean. Taipei's municipal government did something similar when it launched a campaign called 'Taipei – Healthy City' which consisted more or less exclusively of adding logos to brochures and posters saying, 'Taipei – Healthy City.'

A couple of years earlier, I had read a report in a local newspaper about Kaohsiung's water supply having been utterly and completely poisoned. Someone had dumped enough chemicals into its reservoir to warrant an entire page of journalistic scorn and alarm. It was the type of story that would stop many nations in their tracks. There would be regular updates. The head of the government would make a determined statement. A state-of-emergency would be declared. There would be criminal investigations followed by arrests and resignations. Temporary water stations would be set up, perhaps by the military. Donations would be made. The media, the public, and the elected opposition would all weigh in on the matter, and the debacle would be assigned a proper name, archived, and referred to for years to come. But mysteriously, this story promptly vanished. I waited and searched for a follow-up, but never found it.

Later, another pollution horror story emerged and then hastily disappeared. A survey on the environmental sustainability of 146 countries conducted by Yale University concluded that Taiwan ranked 145th, 11 places behind China, and even behind Iraq, a country then in the middle of a war. The only country to rank lower than Taiwan was North Korea. A story that was clearly front-page news featured on the back page of the hopelessly partisan (pro-DPP) English-language newspaper, *Taipei Times*, and subsequently went off the radar. (The DPP is fond of holding itself out as Taiwan's green party.) Taiwan's Environmental Protection Administration dismissed the report as "unfair and biased" and that was that. I scanned the papers for updates, but never heard tell of the matter again.

Even Kaohsiung's train station was a mess; a mélange of patches, stains and unpleasant smells. My train departed right on time, however, revealing a crumbling line of tenement blocks, bars, and laundry under a nuclear-fallout sky.

I arrived in Tainan, which means "South Terrace," at twilight and found accommodation just a short walk from the train station. The hotel was delightfully tinsel, the type of place where you bargained for a room and made a mental note of where the fire extinguisher was. The staff must have known I was coming because there was a tube of Whitemen toothpaste waiting for me in the bathroom. Whitemen is a cheap alternative to Black Man, Taiwan's best-loved brand. On the Black Man package, the Chinese name Black Man is offset by the English name Darlie. The original English name was Darkie. Its logo was, and still is, a pearly toothed African in a tuxedo and top hat.

My hotel was stuffed into a dense row of bustling shops along a sidewalk piled high with synthetic clothing and accessories. Teenaged clerks handed out flyers while megaphones laid out on tables competed for customers. 'Today only! Buy one pizza, get another for free! Buy

one, get one free!' The Taiwanese love megaphones, which are set out
in front of stores to repeat the same screeching, static-filled sales pitch
again and again and again. Trucks drive around with ad banners on their
sides and between one and four megaphones attached to their roofs. The
announcements are incredibly loud, often shrill, and they reverberate
down lanes and off tall buildings. Recordings often promote "European-
style" apartments (Taiwanese-style apartments with mansard roofs), but
they could also be used to sell pineapple or fresh crabs. During elections,
politicians hire similar trucks to blast their campaign messages throughout
neighbourhoods.

I woke up the next morning and walked until I found a place to have
breakfast. Past streams of shops and parked scooters I went. Periodically,
the scooters were interrupted by bicycles, the baskets of which had
been used as trash cans. Finding a real trash can in Taiwan is like finding
the proverbial needle in a haystack. Stores often hide them, apartments
convert them into pot holders for plants, and in places where it's
impossible to do this (metro stations, for example) the slots are miniscule.
Signs on trash cans specify that they are not to be used for refuse from
one's home.

I walked down a narrow lane of tiled buildings and patio plants, past
a shop with a sign that said, 'Inside – inside perhaps you'll find what you
want inside.' Tainan may have been a major city, but it had a rambling,
small-town feel about it. On the whole, I found it to be a bit more human
than Taipei.

Tainan had once been Taiwan's capital, having been settled by the
Dutch between the years 1624 and 1663. Originally, the Dutch had
established their base on Penghu, a windy archipelago in the Taiwan
Strait, but the Ming Dynasty insisted on their leaving, urging them instead
to withdraw to Taiwan. Penghu, you see, belonged to China.

The Dutch, *not the Chinese*, were the first people to attempt to develop
Taiwan and to establish governmental controls. Before their arrival, only
the aboriginals and a few thousand Chinese farming families lived on the
island. The Dutch promoted immigration by offering settlers things like
seeds, tools, and oxen, and thousands of landless peasants from Fujian
turned up to work the island's new plantations and mines even though
immigration to Taiwan was expressly prohibited by the Qing authorities.

The population soared and business boomed. The Dutch sold dried
fish, deer meat, deer skins, deer antlers (to be ground into an aphrodisiac),
sugar, and camphor to China and Japan while squeezing money out of
its newfound refugee labour pool. For the migrant Chinese, Taiwan
represented an opportunity, but one that came at a cost. They were

heavily taxed and forbidden from purchasing land, even the parcels that they worked. This era wasn't without co-operation, but there was an ample amount of resentment, which degenerated into rebellion. Chinese revolts were answered with brutal Dutch responses. The Dutch faired much better with the aboriginals, yet there was also friction and fighting there. Luckily for the Chinese, the Dutch were sent on their way by the Ming loyalist Koxinga. If the Chinese were going to be subjugated, better it was done by one of their own.

Remnants of Tainan's past exist in its present, hidden in corners of the city among the apartment blocks and gimcrack shops. I set out on a walking tour to inspect some of them, starting from a roundabout marked by a cream-coloured statue of Chiang Kai-shek. The interior of Tainan's Confucius Temple was pleasantly modest and curiously tasteful. The Great South Gate (Tainan was once a walled city) was also charming and contained slabs of stone that had been gathered from around town. In the old days, these were often used to communicate decrees. One from the eighteenth century declared that beggars were not to display cadavers when canvassing for alms. I spent a couple of hours locating and snooping around other altars, temples, and shrines, and I found them to be interesting enough.

Unlike China (including Hong Kong) or Singapore, religion thrives in Taiwan; a passionate medley of Taoism, Buddhism, ancestor worship, folk custom, geomancy, and voodoo. Only seven percent of the Taiwanese have been baptized in spite of three and a half centuries of missionary work, and the Mormons, who are out in full force in Taiwan (they have nearly 100 centres island-wide), make a mere 50 converts a month.

Because it served as a shortcut, I walked through the grungy temple grounds near my apartment building nearly every single day. I have been to temples with my Taiwanese friends and have watched them pray for riches and good grades. I have even gone to a place colloquially known as the Money Temple located on a mountain somewhere in Taiwan's northeast. There, I dropped three prognostication blocks on the floor, and they divined that I should receive three $NT-100 notes, worth about three dollars apiece. All I had to do to get the money was show some identification. My name and personal information were then entered into the temple's computer. The crisp red bills were placed in a red envelope. I was to deposit them into my bank account and keep a special piece of gold-and-crimson paper in my wallet. Within two or three years, I would become wealthy (all three prognostication blocks had fallen the right way, you see), at which point I was to return to the temple and make a

donation. As part of the ritual, we were required to dust ourselves off
with *qi*-infused ostrich feathers, bow to the God of Money, and make
our way to an outdoor platform that was level with the roof. We also had
to follow a special route: we weren't to skip floors and we had to inspect
each floor in a certain way. The final step was to burn a few bundles of
ghost money on the platform and send a heady plume of smoke into the
atmosphere. This experience was strange, but not nearly as strange as a
temple exorcism I once witnessed.

Like churches, I appreciated temples for their aesthetic value, but
many were filthy (the one near my house was a hangout for drunks and
stray dogs) and I couldn't help dismiss the rituals that went on in them as
pure superstition. The Money Temple ritual reminded me of the kinds of
games I played as a child: the carpet is lava, the sofas are islands, touching
the lamp in the corner will enable you to walk on the lava for three
seconds, the first one to touch the TV wins half a cherry Popsicle.

Invariably, religious ceremonies involve pollution of one variety
or another, the burning of joss sticks and ghost money being prime
examples. On the first and fifteenth day of every lunar month, and during
the entire seventh lunar month, or Ghost Month, the Taiwanese burn
ghost money in stainless steel furnaces and canisters in order to appease
the deceased. My apartment building even has a designated burning
area: a row of ovens next to the pool with all the flues pointing into the
parking lot of the aforementioned hospital – named after a man who
found Taiwanese folk customs and beliefs exasperating.[3]

Businesses burn ghost money, too, in addition to laying tables
out with edible offerings: usually fruit, crackers, potato chips, and soft
drinks. On the designated days, you can see sharply dressed opticians
and real-estate agents feeding bundles of gold-and-crimson paper into
smoke-billowing sidewalk containers. Schoolchildren trundle through
carcinogenic clouds while vendors sell clothes and fresh food just metres
away. The only people I have ever heard complain about this are other
foreigners.

Once, when I questioned a class of adult students about the potential
dangers and health effects of having smallish bonfires in front of every
fifth shop in the nation, I was given an interesting answer. First, I asked
if the smoke bothered anyone, and only one student raised their hand.
I then asked how many thought the practice should be banned. No one
raised their hand. Next, I wanted to know if they might feel differently if
they were blind, allergic to smoke, or asthmatic. There was a hush, broken

---

3   George Leslie MacKay described Taiwanese religion as "the same kind and quality as the
heathenism of China. It is the same poisonous mixture, the same dark, damning nightmare."

when one woman said, "If those people don't like it, they can move!" Everyone (business people, university students, engineers, housewives) thought this was hilarious, thus the debate was concluded.

But then, the Taiwanese have a serious inclination toward setting things on fire. It's part of their culture. Every year, a temple near my house launches hundreds of lit lanterns into the air. Once, one touched down in the hospital parking lot next to my apartment building causing a cluster of bushes to burst into flame. I watched this happen. The thing could just as easily have landed on (or under) a car, or a child, or someone in a wheelchair. A couple of years later, one of the lanterns made it all the way to Chiang Kai-shek International Airport, where it caused a grass fire so large that arrivals were disrupted. I was on one of the delayed planes.

One of Taiwan's most famous festivals (it is even featured in a popular English textbook published by Cambridge University Press) is called the Plague Expulsion Festival. Held in the town of Yanshui, about 40 kilometres north of where I was now, the event involves fireworks being discharged into throngs of willing participants who don motorcycle helmets, protective visors, and fire-resistant clothing. The ceremony is, in part, a tribute to the God of War, whose image is believed to have ended a cholera epidemic 200 years ago. Every year, dozens of people wind up in the hospital with serious burns and lost eyes, although no mention of that is made in the textbook.

In addition to ghost money, the Taiwanese also burn an assortment of paper and cardboard funerary articles, such as houses, cars, and furniture, so that their ancestors don't go without. And if it's not ghost money, or funerary items, or firecrackers, or fireworks, or lanterns the people of Taiwan will be sure to find something else to set alight. Farmers are forever burning brush, and I once had a neighbour who tried to burn 20 bags of rubbish on the lawn of my rooftop apartment. He only stopped when I threatened to call the police. Interestingly, I read two nearly identical accounts from other foreign residents in Taiwan. It's rare to go a whole day on the island formerly known as Formosa without smelling smoke. I don't know how many times I have had to change my clothes because of it.

A young Taiwanese politician once suggested enacting a law that would make the denomination of ghost money much higher, thus forcing people to burn only one or two notes at a time. His notion came to naught, and he was criticized for being "too practical." In the early 1990s, a group of Taiwanese succeeded in erecting the world's largest ever Lego-made building, which they hoped to have listed in *The Guinness Book of World Records*. To celebrate, fireworks were launched and the structure promptly caught fire and burned to the ground.

Although largely dismissive of Taiwanese religious beliefs and associated practices, there was one facet that I greatly admired: no one ever tried to convert you. Whatever shrine or temple you prayed at (or didn't) was a non-issue. In my more than 10 years in Taiwan, I have never once heard religion come up in the office place, except in passing, or when a Falun Gong member told me that if I signed up and practised, I would have so much energy I would never require sleep again.

I walked and walked through the sweltering lanes of Tainan, and eventually I found Koxinga's Shrine. The architecture and scarlet-heavy colour scheme were striking, and like many of Tainan's historical relics, the structure was surrounded by a pleasant little park. I saw a youthful couple poking around, which sort of surprised me. I didn't think young people would be interested in a man revered for battling the Qing and banishing the Dutch. It is rare to meet a Taiwanese person with an interest in history, so I stopped to talk.

"Yes, we think Koxinga is a hero," the man explained. "He gave Taiwan back to Chinese people." They were tourists from Taipei.

"Do you think Taiwan might have done better for itself had the Dutch not been expelled?" I asked.

"No."

"Why not? The Netherlands has a very high standard of living, one of the highest in the world."

The man said, "Okay, but we want to be ruled by someone Chinese, not someone Western."

"Someone like Chiang Kai-shek?" I asked. I couldn't help myself.

They admitted that I had a point, and admitted too that their reasoning was rooted in emotion, not logic. Fair enough. I then asked politely (because they were very polite) if either of them knew what the man's orange shirt said. She looked over and he looked down and together they attempted to make sense of the Romanized word printed across his chest before conceding that they didn't understand. I translated. It said, 'Nederland,' and on the back, there was the number 9 and the name Van Nistlerooy, the famous soccer player. Here was a fellow who had come to pay his respects to the figure who had kicked out the Dutch whilst unknowingly sporting the Dutch national soccer jersey.

Even though I believed much of Chinese historical interpretation to be incredibly biased and selective, I wasn't usually one to defend colonialism. I had always been quick to recognize the colonial mentality in my fellow expatriates, and judged it to be an antiquated if not wholly ignorant mode of thinking. However, as a student of history, I knew that colonialism was often a mixed bag of things detrimental and beneficial.

It was impossible to say what might have happened had the Dutch stayed on in Taiwan. The Dutch East India Company was here first and foremost to make a profit, not to enlighten and civilize the Chinese workforce. Having said that, the Dutch organized labour, introduced the Roman alphabet to the aboriginals (who had no script of their own), and significantly raised the island's standard of living, health, and security. The Chinese hero who expelled them turned the island into a dictatorship before going insane. Even cutting down bamboo was punishable by death under the rule of Koxinga, and like another hero nearly three centuries later, the Ming loyalist was preoccupied with rescuing "the mainland" from an illegitimate government.

After Koxinga's Ming-modelled Taiwan dynasty was dismantled, the Qing actually asked the Dutch if they wanted to buy the uncultured and problematic island back. They didn't, so, the Qing, after toying with the idea of removing all Han settlers and abandoning Taiwan altogether, decided to annex it as a prefecture so it wouldn't fall into the hands of more foreigners or other hostile elements. Under this arrangement, Taiwan was, as Qing authorities admitted it was, governed only partially – not to mention ineffectively and corruptly – until it was handed over to the Japanese in 1895. It didn't become an actual province until 1885. Bear in mind once again that the Qing were ethnically Manchu and considered by Han Chinese to be foreigners.

That night I went to a bar to cool off with a few drinks. I met some nice locals and chatted and had fun. Cities in Taiwan have very healthy night lives and prices for food and drink are very reasonable. After midnight, I hailed a cab and told the driver I wanted to go to the train station. He asked me, in genuine mystification, where that was.

"Turn right at the third set of lights and go straight for half a kilometre," I said.

"Wow! You really know your way around!" he replied. "How long have you been living in Tainan?"

CHAPTER TWENTY-SIX

The back-alley breakfast shop had peeling paint, handwritten taped-to-the-wall menus, plastic stools, flimsy tables, and one partially hidden package of napkins for common use. It smelled of mould and bacon. A Republic of China calendar had been thumb tacked next to a glossy poster spotlighting the shop's spicy chicken sandwich; Chinese characters brushed in flame-like strokes. I noted the calendar's year: 96. Year 1 was 1912 CE, the year the republic was founded – the year after "Sun Yat-sen's" "revolution." Thus, this year, 2007, was 96. Oddly, the days and months of the ROC calendar followed the Gregorian system. Every time I saw a calendar in Taiwan, I imagined the commanding officer of the great uprising hiding under his bed.

I ordered a *peigen jishi sanmingzhi* [a transliteration: '(a) bacon (and) cheese sandwich'], an omelet, and a milk tea. Then I grabbed a stack of complimentary newspapers and searched for something to read.

Chinese-language newspapers in Taiwan are really quite remarkable. They are extraordinarily thick and made up of countless sections that consist of just about everything except insightful news. The detail that goes into them, however, is astounding; they are jam-packed with photos, artwork, colour, and design. Anything involving death or injury is sure to get liberal coverage. Two entire pages of computer-generated images could be used for a "re-enactment" of, say, a drunken domestic squabble resulting in a pair of fatal stabbings, the final frame containing pixilated figures lying on the kitchen floor in a pool of ruby ooze. Real blood-soaked corpses are shown on front covers, and the rest of the paper is largely given over to gossip, fashion, local politics, restaurant reviews, recipes, entertainment, and sports.

I examined an easy-to-read article about a local woman who had moved to Israel after meeting her Israeli husband in Taiwan. The woman noted that, although a Jew, her spouse wasn't a "darkie," unlike a lot of Middle Easterners, and certainly unlike anyone hailing from Africa. He looked Caucasian, so the reader needn't worry. The food in Israel didn't

compare with food in Taiwan (that was what she missed most), but it was
pretty good nonetheless. She then described the food she liked in great
detail in paragraph after perky paragraph. There was no commentary on
what life in Israel was like or how it differed from life in Taiwan. There was
no mention of politics, economics, education, religion, culture, architecture,
history, or climate; not even an amusing anecdote; just a racist remark and
comments like, 'It's so crispy *luo*!' and 'It tastes too good *luo*!' The particles
luo and *la* are used copiously in Taiwan Mandarin, adding a dimension
of softness or cuteness to the language. The font in the article was white
and the background was pink. The background was adorned with cutesy-
wootsey pictures of bunnies, flowers, and hearts.

There are 12 major Chinese-language dailies in Taiwan and more
than 2,000 newspapers in total. There are more than 7,000 magazines,
172 radio stations, and almost 12,000 publishing companies. There are 63
cable television operators and 8 twenty-four-hour news channels. The most
popular news channel is TVBS. No kidding.

Taiwanese news channels engage in fierce competition to provide
viewers with the latest scandal or disaster. Sensationalistic reportage in
America, for example, doesn't even come close. News crews in Taiwan walk
straight up to moaning, gurney-ridden accident victims in public hospitals,
stick microphones under their noses, and casually ask, "So, how do you
feel?"[1] Doctors take time-outs to answer questions, and distraught friends
and relatives are filmed sobbing and wailing. There is also an emphasis on
filming accident scenes (more corpses), and reporting on suicides and fires.
Human tragedy aside, television news is more or less a constant pageant of
fracases, scandals, scam warnings, and political bickering.

For a while, I found Taiwanese news (as reported in the island's three
English-language dailies) so absorbing that I began to amass a file. I would
say that, on average, I was clipping out five stories per week. Here is a
sample of some of the headlines and quotes I collected: 'Two Taiwan men
pull truck by their penises,' 'Thousands gather at gang leader's funeral,'
'Taxi drivers, Taipei Mass Rapid Transit System workers in huge brawl,'
'Prisoners turn down freedom for New Year due to poor economy,'
'Taipei cracks down on drunk driving with new equipment (breathalyzers;
previously, officers used Styrofoam cups, which they sniffed), 'Coastguard
nabs smuggler ship full of rooster testicles ('"This was not the first time

---

1   I was under the impression that this only occurred in Taiwan, but one day I saw on
CCTV (it used to be aired in Taiwan until someone decided to cancel it) a report on a female
member of Falun Gong who attempted a self-immolation, but lived. Badly burned, the
woman lay in a hospital bed sobbing miserably when a reporter – in the exact same laid-back
manner adopted in Taiwan – asked her, 'So, how do you feel?'

we have seized smuggled rooster testicles," a spokesman said.'),' 'Customs hopes to sell unclaimed MiG-21 fighter jet to military,' 'Taiwanese airlines record large number of 'abnormal' acts ("Passengers attempted to open exit doors while airborne, quarrelled, complained loudly, and tried to sleep on the floor."),' 'Taiwan has highest rate of accidents in the world,' 'Illegal companies exceed legal ones, study shows,' 'Yellow lights don't mean stop ("according to new traffic rules enacted by the Ministry of Transportation and Communications."),' 'Taichung lawmaker-elect enjoys taste of freedom ("Under Taiwan's constitution, he will now not have to serve any jail time as long as he can keep getting himself re-elected to office."),' 'Cadaver adds unexpected twist to river inspection (then Taipei mayor and current Taiwan president Ma Ying-jeou declared the Danshui River much improved just before a corpse was spotted floating by; he performed the water-quality test by dipping a Styrofoam cup into the waterway and sniffing it), 'Whale explodes in Tainan street,' 'Parliament brawl fails to unfreeze budget,' 'High-speed train billows smoke ("Three delays in one day; operator forgets to let passengers off."),' and so on. There was also a clipping I somehow lost. It showed lines of kids with cellophane bags over their heads – being taught what to do in the event of a fire.

There are, of course, recurring themes: shoddy construction, drunk driving, fires, unruly lawmakers, KMT corruption, DPP incompetence, inebriated police, corrupt police, inept police, company executives fleeing to Guangdong with suitcases of cash, jail breaks, disturbed bus drivers, outlandish court rulings ('Oral sex not a form of adultery,' 'Attempted assault not a crime'), ghost stories, stories about superstition, the wily antics of runaway orangutans (yes, it's a recurring theme), and accounts of teachers administering cruel and unusual punishments. Most unusual, perchance, is the persistent theme of Nazism.

Taiwan is big on theme restaurants: there is the toilet restaurant (where dishes come in the shape and appearance of toilet bowls), the hospital restaurant (where customers order "medicine" served by waitresses dressed as nurses), the airplane restaurant (where food is served by pretty "flight attendants"), and finally there was The Jail restaurant, which featured Nazi death-camp photos of ovens and emaciated captives along with a large sign over the doorway to its pipe- and gauge-adorned bathrooms that read, 'Gas Chamber.' The Jail closed after protestations from the foreign community.

Nazi iconography and images of Adolf Hitler have been used in Taiwan to sell everything from athletic shoes to heaters to cars. Taiwan actually has its own National Socialism Association, a thousand-member group of mainly college students whose stated aims are to strengthen national unity, return to traditional Chinese values, and promote Hitler's "good points." The former German consul to Taiwan once stated that when he told people he was from Germany, people would often respond with something like, 'Oh, Hitler was from Germany. He was very powerful.'

The DPP once deemed it would be a good idea to use Hitler in a TV ad in order to attract new recruits. Their commercial began with a 10-second clip of the *Führer* thumping his chest, banging his podium, and rolling his eyes into the back of his head during one of the Third Reich's legendary rallies. The ad went on to show images of Fidel Castro, John F. Kennedy, and Lee Teng-hui, Taiwan's first democratically elected president. When asked why Adolf Hitler was chosen as one of the four leaders, a party spokesman explained that it was because he had "dared to speak his mind," and that the idea was to encourage youth to "express their views boldly."

After being condemned by the Israeli government, the German government, a host of Jewish groups, and the New-York-City-based Anti-Defamation League, the DPP (then Taiwan's ruling party and symbol of its new democratic identity) refused to pull the ad, saying that, "humanity does not have to be so heavy, but can be expressed with ease and a sense of humour." After the outcry that this comment caused, the DPP altered the ad, inserting the phrase "dictatorship spawns disasters" into the Hitler segment and "democracy requires public participation" into the Kennedy clip. This, they explained, was a "goodwill response." Finally, after further remonstration, the ad was taken off the air.

Never one to be outdone by the use of dictators, the KMT ran an ad campaign of its own during the 2004 presidential election where it compared the DPP leader and incumbent president, Chen Shui-bian, to Adolf Hitler, describing his rule as a dictatorship. (Chen Shui-bian won the 2000 election, thus bringing 55 years of uninterrupted KMT rule on Taiwan to an end.) After yet another round of foreign derision, the Nationalists refused to pull their ad, choosing instead to replace the image of Hitler with that of a Buddhist monk.

In the same election, the DPP ran an Uncle-Sam-style ad campaign where the bearded American icon was replaced by a sultry teenaged girl wearing a high school uniform. Its slogan said, "It's my first time, and the whole world is watching." Because you must be 20 years of age to vote in Taiwan, and passing students graduate by the age of 18, it could only be reasonably deduced that Taiwan's ruling party was either attempting to garner the vote of the nation's perverts or promote sex with its teenaged girls.

Unquestionably, these were odd stories, but the oddest story to come out of the 2004 presidential election had to do with the assassination attempt on Chen Shui-bian's life.

It happened here in Tainan, the day before voters were supposed to go to the polls. President Chen Shui-bian and his running mate, Vice-President Annette Lu, were campaigning from the back seat of a convertible Jeep when each was struck by a bullet. He was grazed across the abdomen whereas she was struck in the knee. Luckily for her, the bullet hit a cast she was wearing. They were both taken to a nearby hospital, treated, and released. The following day, their party was re-elected by a razor-thin margin. Many thought they had won by obtaining the sympathy vote.

KMT supporters went wild with rage. They organized demonstrations and took out a full-page ad in *The New York Times* claiming election fraud. Conspiracy theories were hatched: the event had been staged, Chen Shui-bian had been treated at a DPP hospital, etc. One Nationalist Party lawmaker went so far as to build a homemade gun with a curved barrel, thus illustrating how it was entirely possible for the president to have shot himself. Experts were called in, including Dr. Henry Lee of O.J. Simpson-trial fame. He claimed he wasn't there to draw any conclusions, although in the end he drew a rather peculiar one: the shooting couldn't possibly have been premeditated because the weapon, which was homemade, wasn't powerful enough. About a year and a half after the incident, the police closed the case, having determined that the shooter was one Chen Yi-hsiung, a man found dead shortly after the assassination attempt.

A pro-KMT businessman I was tutoring when Chen was shot cancelled classes that week in order to join in the huge and unruly Chen-stole-the-election protests in downtown Taipei. When we resumed, he asked me, "Do you really think someone could have shot him with all that security around?" In point of fact, the sidewalks were so packed with people lighting off firecrackers that a decent-sized field gun could have been pulled up to the road, fired, reloaded, fired again, and hauled away without anyone having been any the wiser. At the office in which I was working at the time, my very sensible South African director decreed that the local staff could no longer discuss politics while on duty because it was interfering with normal working relations.

Appeal though they did, the Nationalists failed to overturn the result. Halfway through his second term, President Chen embarked on his name rectification campaign, where he attempted to remove the word 'China' or 'Chinese' from government offices and state-run enterprises. Chiang Kai-shek International Airport became Taiwan Taoyuan International Airport. As mentioned, President Chen also succeeded in changing the name of the Chiang Kai-shek Memorial Hall and was temporarily victorious in turning the space surrounding Chiang's statue into what resembled a junk store.

Chen Shui-bian described Taipei-Washington relations as being analogous to the homosexual love portrayed in the Oscar-winning film, *Brokeback Mountain*, and he decided to celebrate the twentieth anniversary of the lifting of martial law by initiating a commutation bill that resulted in the immediate release of 9,597 inmates, including convicted murderers. Every vote counts. The Tainan-area-born leader, who had grown up poor, been a model student, and become Taiwan's youngest lawyer, urged tolerance and explained that the addition of the detainees to Taiwanese society ought to be viewed as "an asset rather than a liability." In just a little over two weeks, these assets had committed crimes in just about every major city and county in the country. Twenty-one died from drug overdoses and one attacked and killed a university professor as he was riding his bicycle through a Taipei park, something he was doing because he considered Taipei's roads to be too dangerous.

Prior to this state-spawned crime spree, Chen Shui-bian's wife and son-in-law had their own problems with the law. She was indicted on corruption charges while he was jailed for insider trading and embezzlement. Chen Shui-bian himself was accused of corruption, and with the aim of forcing his resignation, a series of large-scale and frequently disorderly protests ensued, including a "siege" of the Presidential Building.

Donning red T-shirts and bandanas, the anti-Chen-Shui-bian bloc adopted the English word 'depose' as its motto and what resembled a pair of Vs as its symbol. A spokesperson explained that the emblem represented "Taiwan's Nazca Lines," an allusion to Peru's Nazca Lines, renderings of gargantuan animals carved into a plateau in that country some two millennia ago by the native Indians. Viewable only from altitude, it is believed that the pictures were meant to facilitate communication with the gods. Anti-Chen-Shui-bian demonstrators were to assemble in imitation of the lines so as to communicate with their own gods, hence summoning the transcendental oomph required to oust the scandal-tainted president, which never occurred. Demonstrators were triumphant in hindering ambulances from getting to and from Taiwan's foremost hospital, however.

Some time later, another group of red-shirted, anti-Chen-Shui-bian activists assembled in front of the Presidential Building with the aim of illustrating their discontent by using 30,000 candles to form a single Chinese character. The character they chose was *pi*, or 'fart,' which is slang for 'rubbish' or 'nonsense.'[2]

---

2   This is not a one off; not exactly, anyway. Once, in order to protest the ever-growing number of Chinese missiles pointed at Taiwan, a man set up a cement penis at some point along the Taiwanese coastline and "aimed it" at China. When asked why he had chosen a penis, the man said it was because he could think of nothing more offensive.

After his party lost in the 2008 election, Chen Shui-bian admitted that he had funnelled funds into overseas accounts. He was indicted for money-laundering and the misuse of public funds. So were his wife, son, and daughter-in-law, along with other relatives, friends, and various assistants.

Too many Taiwanese news stories look as though they've been swiped from *The Onion*. There was one about a primary school educator, who, after discovering a natural spring on the grounds of her school, decided to take action. Viewing it as an educational opportunity, the teacher helped turn the wetland area into an ecological park, replete with frogs, fish, butterflies, and egrets. She even erected a pavilion that featured solar-powered lamps. Impressed with the woman's efforts, the Ministry of Education awarded her school a quarter-million-dollar grant in order to expand the park. Unfortunately, it was discovered that the spring was no more than a broken water pipe that had lost an estimated 45,000 tonnes of water.

Many news stories in Taiwan play out like soap operas; you tune in daily for the latest installment. Like soap operas, these stories have the ability to invoke an entire spectrum of emotion. One such account had to do with a group of construction workers who were building an embankment in a river when a flash flood occurred. Four got out, but another four got stranded. Their foreman called 911. The local fire department, which received the call, passed the message on to the local police department, which in turn got in contact with the air force, which claimed that, technically, it was only responsible for emergencies occurring higher than 2.5 kilometres above sea level. The air force then suggested that the local police contact the airborne squad of a more substantial police department located in a city nearby. The city police informed the local police that they ought to get back in touch with the air force given that they were closer to the situation. But the air force hadn't been kidding about its 2.5-kilometre contract clause, so the airborne squad of the city police had to scramble a chopper to try and rescue the men, who had drowned by this point as it was two hours after the initial call from the foreman. Ironically, a news chopper was promptly on the scene, televising a grainy image of the four men holding on to each other as the river raged all around them. In fact, units from no fewer than four fire departments had turned up, but unfortunately they experienced some technical difficulties. What they required was a rope gun, but the first two crews forgot to bring theirs, the third brought a broken one, and the fourth arrived too late.

Keen to wipe the egg off its face, the government held a training exercise the following month, inviting news crews to come and film it. In one scenario, flare and rope guns were used, but none worked. Next, a cameraman was pitched into a river when two police boats crashed into each other. A month after this performance, a demonstration was orchestrated to show the public how a similar situation would be handled in the future. The rescue helicopter on this day crashed next to the river, leaving the pilot in a coma and injuring five others.

For weeks, the fire department, the two branches of the police force, and the air force all heaped blame on one another in the press, with none of them admitting to so much as a particle of wrongdoing. In the end, when the government found all parties culpable, the fire department took it especially badly. Firefighters drove to Taipei, where they protested by burning their uniforms.

But of all the bizarre and twisted Taiwan tales, the one that takes the cake is the Chen Chin-hsing saga. Hold on to your seat.

On the afternoon of April 14, 1997, in a suburb outside of Taipei, three ruffians named Chen Chin-hsing, Lin Chun-sheng, and Kao Tien-min kidnapped 17-year-old Pai Hsiao-yen, the daughter of a famous singer and television personality named Pai Ping-ping. After telephoning Mrs. Pai to demand $5 million in ransom, the kidnappers used the next three days to repeatedly alter the drop-off point. On April 17, Pai Ping-ping went to the latest drop-off point, but to no avail. The hostage takers failed to show, supposedly because they had spotted members of the press shadowing her. A new drop-off point was selected, but again the kidnappers did not materialize.

On April 23, the trio cut one of Pai Hsiao-yen's fingers off and sent it to her mother along with a note instructing her not to go to the police. A day later, the thugs outlined several new drop-off points, but failed to appear in each and every instance as they were convinced Mrs. Pai was being tailed. Angry that she had refused to heed their warning, the abductors beat their captive so badly that she died of internal bleeding. They drove her corpse to another district and dumped it in a drainage ditch.

As it turns out, Mrs. Pai had contacted the police, although, supposedly, they hadn't leaked any information to the press. On April 25, the police arrived at Chen Chin-hsing's apartment to arrest him, but he managed to escape after his wife saw them coming. She was arrested along with two of Chen's friends. The next day, the police found Chen and cornered him. There was a fire fight, but the fugitive escaped once more. At this point, the police made a public statement about the situation and launched an immense manhunt in the mountains west of Taipei. On April 28, Pai Hsiao-yen's body was discovered.

The police spent the month of May searching for the three suspects. Wanted posters covered the island. The public became incensed and there eventuated three large public protests. There had been a dramatic escalation of crime in Taiwan, one unhindered by arrests. In an apparent attempt to compensate, the police apprehended 17 of the trio's friends and relatives as possible accomplices.[3]

On May 28, Chen, Lin, and Kao wrote a letter to the authorities admitting that they had indeed kidnapped and murdered Pai Hsiao-yen. However, they vehemently denied that any of the suspects the police put behind bars had anything to do with it. The police wouldn't be swayed, though, and two months later (two months during which the three men were still at large) the police handed the detainees over to the prosecutors to await trial.

On August 8, the three fugitives kidnapped and extorted a businessman for the equivalent of $150,000 before promptly disappearing. The public grew angrier. Parents started driving their kids to and from school. The rich began taking holidays abroad. In the areas where the hoodlums had been spotted, property prices plummeted. Chen Chin-hsing quickly struck again: he robbed a house, temporarily abducted three inhabitants, and shot and wounded a police officer who tried to intervene. As you will have predicted, he escaped yet again.

Finally, the police got a lucky break. Lin Chun-sheng and Kao Tien-min were spotted in a building in downtown Taipei. Two hundred police officers hastily secured the area. Lin was chased down a dead-end lane and a gun battle erupted. Rather than surrender, he shot himself in the head and died. Meanwhile, Kao slipped through the ring of police officers and got away. Because of a reward system specially created for this case, more than 50 police officers received promotions for their part in Lin's demise. The public remained unimpressed.

On September 18, Chen raped a high school student near Taipei. On September 22, a pair of traffic cops ran into him in an alley, but because they were frightened, they allowed him to drive away on his motor scooter. One month later, Chen and Kao popped into a plastic surgery clinic to have some work done. Kao had his eyelids altered before he and his associate brutally ended the lives of the doctor, his wife, and a young nurse raped beforehand.

Public discontent was now near fever pitch. There were checkpoints all over Taipei manned by police officers with rifles. They looked into every

---

3 In his *From Far Formosa*, George Leslie MacKay, in describing how impossibly corrupt the legal system was on Taiwan during the nineteenth century, talks about the concept of punishing criminals by proxy. Once, MacKay was asked to make an appearance at the local courthouse because the thief who had stolen something from one of his chapels had been apprehended. But it wasn't the right man. When MacKay pointed this out, a court official replied that he was aware that it wasn't the right man, but that "by punishing this man the real culprit would be so afraid that the moral influence would be quite as salutary."

car. Scooter drivers weren't supposed to wear visors. Every officer of the law in Taiwan was issued a shoot-to-kill order.

On November 3, Kao was seen in Taipei's Shilin district. Shots were exchanged and the criminal fled toward Yangmingshan. A dragnet comprised of *thousands* of police was cast, but nothing was netted. The following day, a local newspaper received a letter from Chen chastising the police for failing to catch him. After all, it had been more than half a year. The fugitive pointed out that finding him would have been much easier if all the people who knew him hadn't been rounded up and thrown in jail. He also reiterated his claim that those people had been framed. The only way someone like his wife would have confessed, Chen said, was if she had been tortured. If the so-called accomplices didn't receive a fair trial, he warned, he would go on to commit more brutal acts.

It was after this that the police caught another lucky break. Kao was spotted in a brothel in Shipai district. The police turned up and began firing. Prostitutes jumped out of windows to escape. Two civilians and one police officer were wounded. Like Lin, Kao turned his weapon on himself and committed suicide. Reportedly, after that happened, the media stormed the building before the police did.

By this point, Chen Chin-hsing was clearly feeling unloved. He was also feeling ignored. His charge against the police had gone unregistered, and he wasn't about to let the matter go. He needed to have his message taken seriously, so he hatched a brilliant plan: he would kidnap a couple of Americans.

On the evening of November 18, a heavily armed Chen broke into a house in Taipei's Beitou district, but much to his irritation, the American husband and wife who lived there were not at home. Not knowing what to do, the dejected criminal sauntered back to the street where he saw a Caucasian man driving his car into the garage next door. Chen Chin-hsing couldn't believe his luck.

The house next door was occupied by the Alexander family. McGill Alexander, the man in the car, was the South African military attaché to Taiwan. When he returned home that evening, he was met by his wife, Anne, his two daughters, Melanie and Christine, and their adopted Taiwanese baby, Zachary. It was just another evening in the Alexander household. Anne was preparing spaghetti. Melanie was practising her scales on the piano. Suddenly, Taiwan's most-wanted criminal was standing beside Melanie and pointing a gun at her head. McGill was handcuffed and the family was ushered into the living room. Someone telephoned for one of the daughters and the kidnapper handed her the phone. That's how the police were notified.

No sooner had the police turned up than they began taunting Chen. He fired at a shadow through the front window. Insanely, the police fired back. He used Melanie as a shield and took a few more shots. He yelled at the police not to return fire or make any move toward the house, informing them that there was now someone between him and them.

The police, however, ignored both of his commands and attempted to shoot their way through the home's aluminum double-door. In his mesmerizing account of the ordeal, *Hostage in Taipei*, McGill Alexander recalls what was going through his mind at that moment: "Had the police gone completely mad? Had (they) decided to sacrifice our lives in their insane desire to kill this man at all costs?" "I realized," he writes, "that the arrival of the police signalled danger rather than deliverance." Alexander screamed at them, "You idiots! What do you think you're doing!? Stop shooting!" In fact, the whole family shouted at the police to stop shooting, but English isn't widely understood in Taiwan, and it is unlikely that the police would have listened anyway.

A foreign witness standing outside the home with a growing mob of onlookers and reporters described what happened next: "A motley bunch of very young-looking policemen came bolting down the road heading towards the house and bristling with guns, shields, and body armor. No one seemed to be in charge of them; and several of the men managed to drop bits of the equipment that bounced around them as they ran."

This witness, a friend of the family, phoned the Alexanders and managed to get Chen on the line. When he tried to get the police to talk to him, they wouldn't, at least not until he became physical with the officer who claimed to be in charge. After a brief and apparently pointless conversation, the officer (who identified himself only as Scott) performed a vanishing act. It became obvious that the police were not very intent on pursuing mediation.

The police then penetrated the house, but Chen was ready for them. They stormed up the stairs only to be obstructed by a table he had placed there. They stalled; he fired. McGill Alexander writes, "The police faltered. In the dark I glimpsed them falling over one another on the narrow stairs." Chen continued to fire, and accidentally shot McGill Alexander through the leg. His daughter, Melanie, was hit in the wrist and back. Chen shouted to the police to tell them what had happened. He asked that they send up a doctor.

The police sent up one of their own, and although the man was highly trained in his own right (a division chief, he was the real man in charge and would later facilitate dialogue with Chen), he was not a doctor, nor did he speak English. McGill Alexander was dragged from the house and plopped onto an awaiting wheeled stretcher. His daughter was carried out, too, but only after the officer further injured her wrist.

Outside, the police attempted to clear a path to the awaiting ambulances, but a ravenous pack of reporters collapsed their lines and completely impeded McGill's and Melanie's movement. McGill Alexander writes, "I became aware of microphones shoved in front of my face, cameras flashing in my eyes, and Chinese accents shouting questions at me in English. 'How do you feel?'" The media only backed off enough for the father and daughter to move forward after Alexander threw a proper fit. Still, the two were hounded and hindered all the way, and the police and stretcher attendants were powerless to do anything about it.

Although at least 400 police officers and half of Taipei had converged on the Alexander house, there were no physicians or paramedics on hand. The young stretcher attendants (who McGill Alexander describes as "excited and enthusiastic, but totally untrained") eventually got Melanie into the first ambulance, but the second ambulance, which McGill was placed in, was half a kilometre away and totally surrounded by unmoving cars. When he got in it, the attendants refused to examine him. He noted that his daughter's attendants seemed wholly oblivious to the fact that she was even wounded, even though she was screaming out in pain. Parenthetically, a Taiwanese ambulance is just a painted-up minivan with lights and a two-way radio. There is no medical equipment to speak of inside it.[4]

Meanwhile, inside the house, Chen made Christine into a shield, and the standoff continued. Ignoring the lesson learned from the first storming-of-the-fort, the authorities sent an entire SWAT team into the house, although once inside they were smart enough not to attempt any heroics. They probably wouldn't have been able to anyway as their constant noise-making alerted Chen to their presence.

The national government held an emergency cabinet meeting after which they ordered the police to cease shooting, and the tension subsided. The remains of the evening and all of the night passed as a sort of press conference with Taiwan's arch felon talking to various members of the media on the phone. The content of the conversations was broadcast live nationwide. Chen demanded the release of his wife, brother-in-law, and others who had been rounded up, and he sang a popular children's song. Because he was busy speaking to a string of media outlets (at least seven), there was no way for the police to contact him. But that was fine with

---

4   There was a news story in Taiwan about a fake ambulance service. The imitators would pick up calls on the radio and then rush to the scene to retrieve the patients before the genuine article arrived. They did this in order to receive a bounty which some private hospitals offered.

Chen. What he wanted most was a bit of publicity. Although he admitted to and apologized for many of his crimes, he also played on the public's emotions and presented himself as a victim of society. The competing television stations had a field day drawing him out so that he might add more and more dimensions to the story.

Negotiations didn't get under way until sometime after dawn. A few hours later, Chen's wife, who had received a 12-year sentence as an accomplice, arrived on the scene with her close friend, a fortune teller who went by the name of Madame Chen. Noticing that Anne Alexander was a bundle of nerves, the two women offered to give her a massage.

Throughout the day, negotiations continued, with authorities promising to re-examine the cases of Chen's wife and the others who had been incarcerated. Allegations of police torture would also be looked into. Chen's wife claimed she had been kicked in the vagina, beaten, given electrical shocks, forced to sit naked on a block of ice, and made to sit on a chair of nails.

Twenty-four hours after Chen appeared in the Alexander home, the last of the family members was released, and Chen was taken into custody.

In the hospital, the recovering South African military attaché received a multitude of visitors and well-wishers. Among them were Vice-Premier John H. Chang and Director General of the National Police Administration, Ting Yuan-chin. After apologizing, both men (the two came on separate visits) assured McGill Alexander that the police had not fired a single shot at his house, although the latter did state that Chen Chin-hsing had fired 160 shots from inside it. The house was in fact badly shot up by police, but when McGill Alexander, a lifelong military man, lividly brought this to the director general's attention, he was ignored. Incidentally (and something which McGill Alexander failed to note in his book), John H. Chang, also known as John Chiang, is Chiang Kai-shek's grandson.

McGill and Melanie were successfully treated for their wounds and would each go on to make a full recovery. Aware that they were in need of psychological counselling, hospital staff gave them each an American IQ test to fill in.[5]

Public debate simmered and many heaped scorn on the police and legal system. It was clear from police techniques that the days of martial law were far from gone. They appeared to be employing time-honoured interrogation tactics honed during the era of White Terror. Cracking cases or even exercising discretion was beyond them. Others came to view Chen

---

5   I used to live just down the street from this hospital, and from where the Alexanders lived. One afternoon, I was taking the bus home when I noticed the hospital was holding a large event on its front lawn. It was a rock concert.

Chin-hsing as something of a folk hero, and people came forward to defend him as such.

From the day after the standoff ended, the Alexander house was transformed into a tourist attraction. People would bring lawn chairs and sit in the street looking at it, and when one of the family's friends went there to assess the damage, she discovered a Taiwanese family inside posing for photos in front of bullet holes.

Forensic experts appeared and went through the house with a fine-toothed comb. Later, the Alexanders found enough undiscovered shells, cartridge cases, and unfired rounds to fill an entire bag.

After Chen accidentally shot the pair of South Africans, and after the police stopped shooting at him, he softened toward Christine and Anne, and, under the circumstances, treated them rather well. A major newspaper ran a story with the headline: 'Melanie: Chen tried to rape me.' The only thing that prevented him from doing so, according to the Chinese-language daily, was the police arriving minutes after the crisis began and firing on the culprit in order to distract him. Naturally, the Alexander family was stunned and incensed by the paper's dishonesty, and they were certain that the police had concocted the story and then leaked it, but when they attempted to complain about this, and about the way the police handled the situation from the beginning, they were summarily disregarded.

In spite of this, the Alexanders were pestered by the press right up until the moment they returned to South Africa. Members of the media somehow managed to get past customs and into the passengers-only area at Chiang Kai-shek International Airport. As they were waiting to board, they found themselves surrounded by cameras and microphones.[6]

Before they left Taiwan, McGill Alexander and his wife, Anne, both devout Christians, actually met with the detained Chen Chin-hsing in order to "bring him the gospel." They took him a Chinese version of the Bible, told him they had exonerated him, and urged him to find forgiveness in the Lord. Chen claimed to have been incredibly touched by their compassion and eventually became a born-again Christian. However, during a press conference he was permitted from prison, Chen brandished a small blade and slashed at his own throat, shouting that he now refuted God. His injuries were not serious, and he later claimed that he underwent

6   Elton John, one of the few big-name entertainers to ever come to Taiwan, was mobbed by the media the instant he stepped off the airplane – and the police did nothing to restrain them. He got upset and called the press "rude, vile pigs" before one reporter suggested that he "get out of Taiwan." At his concert, he cheerily greeted the crowd before politely saying he had been to more than 60 countries and had never been harassed like that, and that people ought to be ashamed of that sort of reception as it makes for a very bad impression. On the news, only the greeting was shown; the admonishment was cut.

a momentary lapse of reason; he still believed Jesus Christ to be his saviour. Chen was counselled by a pastor, and two months after the neck-slashing incident, he was baptized behind bars. He wrote a letter to the Alexanders in South Africa asking them to adopt his two sons. After much consideration, they declined.

Meanwhile, it was discovered that a serial rapist who had been on the loose the same time Chen and his two cronies had been on the loose was in fact Chen himself. Chen was charged with committing 10 rapes, although he admitted to committing twice as many. Furthermore, DNA testing showed that he was the one who had raped the young nurse at the plastic surgery clinic before she was stabbed and shot.

The legal proceedings turned out to be something of a rollercoaster ride. Sentences were passed, appealed, and dramatically overturned. Chen's brother-in-law was acquitted, given a life sentence, and then acquitted again. Other "accomplices" were acquitted as well. Some received significantly reduced terms; some didn't. Chen's wife had her sentence overturned. Chen himself received two life terms and three death sentences. It would have been five death sentences, only the charge for the murder of Pai Hsiao-yen didn't stick. Neither did the charge for the kidnapping of the Alexander family. The reason cited was – wait for it – "a lack of conclusive evidence."

Chen Chin-hsing was executed under the Republic of China's bandit law, passed by the Nationalists in 1944 – when they were still in China. At the time he was put to death (with a bullet to the back of the head), seven other felons around Taiwan were disposed of in the same way and under the same law.

The media knew that Chen had been killed when they saw people leave the pertinent building in order to go outside and burn ghost money. His body was rushed to a nearby hospital where his organs were removed so that they could be given to waiting patients. Newspapers showed whole-page photos of the stretcher-bound corpse, its head wrapped in a blood-soaked bandage.

Allegedly, the kidnapping of Pai Ping-ping's daughter had to do with her mob connections. Chen, Lin, and Kao were also believed to have been in the pay of the mob, the incredible amount of arms and ammunition they possessed being an indication.

Taiwan, Republic of China is a perennially weird place and for quite some time its frequent bouts of nuttiness punctuated, as they are, by recurrent episodes of sheer lunacy had held me in a state of more or less perpetual rapt attention. I've never seen a reality show that could compete with Taiwan's television news, and it is unusual not to see at least one oddball news article or witness at least one peculiar public event every day. Naturally, there exists a healthy amount of normalcy as well, but just when you've convinced yourself that Taiwan is only mildly idiosyncratic and not outright schizophrenic, something will occur to cause you to readjust that point of view. Observing Taiwanese society is akin to surveying the site of a vehicular accident; you know you shouldn't stare, but you just can't help yourself.

In almost no time, my file became huge, but then I left it to neglect as I just didn't find things so amusing or peculiar anymore. Sometimes I found myself becoming immune to the strangeness; at other times I merely felt disappointed or simply dismayed. More recently, I had become saddened.

Although I had never subscribed to the view that Chinese people were of superior intellect, or mystical, or in possession of some knowledge or secret that had managed to elude people elsewhere, I had believed that they were generally intelligent and erudite. But I have seen little evidence of that. Without question, there are some smart people walking around; I have met some of them and have had more than a few bright students. But their intelligence existed in spite of Chinese culture and education, not because of it. They were anomalies, and they weren't hard to spot. They were the one in twenty-five who didn't have the same opinion as everyone else. They read – for pleasure. They were thoughtful and quietly sceptical. They didn't list sleeping as a hobby (nearly everyone does) and they didn't describe themselves or Taiwanese people overall as "clever" as people grinningly tend to do.

I knew too, from having taught adults for so many years, that if the education system didn't eventually asphyxiate young people's passion, creativity, and desire to learn and discover, it would be a small miracle. For the most part, the system would stream them into an area they had no interest in. Education was test-based and focused almost solely on rote memorization. That's commonly known, but to *see* it in action; to witness high school students who only know how to memorize and take multiple-choice tests; to encounter university graduates who have never read a novel or written an essay; to watch "educated" adults fail to locate their own country on a map; it was astonishing and profoundly disturbing. The Taiwanese study longer and harder than almost anyone else on Earth with the upshot of having virtually no idea where they are in either space or time.

Chinese education is an eclectic mix of cruelty and coddling, and to that end, it is also responsible for fostering a tradition of immaturity. If students fail, teachers are to blame, and maniacal parents ensure that there will be blame. Consequently, instructors threaten and mollycoddle poor performers; whatever it takes to promote memorization and better scores. In fact, students often want teachers to be strict. It's expected. A survey carried out by National Taiwan Normal University found that 80 percent of students believed that corporal punishment was apt as long as it didn't result in physical injury; 85 percent of parents agreed.

Perpetually treated like infants, students behave like infants, and the pressure and pampering at school is often mirrored at home. It starts at a young age. In parks you can see parents chasing their kids around and shouting, "Be careful! Be careful! Be careful!" and on the Taipei Metro, it's possible to witness children as old as 10 being forced by parents to sit in priority seats. Middle-aged people stand up to accommodate them. The Japanese have a saying: 'Fall down seven times, get up eight.' The Chinese have an easy answer for that: never let anyone fall down.

All those things that kids and teens in the West are supposed to do – climb trees, fall in love – are discouraged to the extent that they never occur. Whenever I asked my teenaged students what their hobbies were, they usually mumbled that they used to enjoy badminton, or hiking, or reading Harry Potter novels, before dejectedly imparting they weren't allowed to have hobbies anymore. School-aged children are not even accorded chores for fear that it will interfere with their studies. The outcome is wave after wave of young people who have virtually no life experience and who don't know how to cope in the world of adults. Without having learned to take any of life's bumps or knocks (people typically live with their parents until they are in their thirties), those who haven't yet reached middle age tend to be thin-skinned, lacking in emotional intelligence, and in possession of colossally inflated egos. Borderline personality disorders abound. But people are numerate, technologically adept, and experts at choosing A, B, C, or D, I will readily concede.

Bo Yang says, "On my visits to the United States and Europe, I've especially enjoyed watching children playing in the parks. They seem so happy, uninhibited and well adjusted…. In Taiwan, on the other hand, every child who goes to school has to wear glasses to correct their myopia, and in order to cope with the pressure of schoolwork, many children grow aloof and arrogant. A woman faints and collapses at home, but when her son tries to help her, she shouts at him, 'Let me die! Don't bother with me! Do your homework! Do your homework!'"

Surveys and government studies habitually indicate that not only is Taiwan's education system not working, but students are suffering physically because of it. It seems that sitting in cramped classrooms 10 hours a day while staring at complex characters is bad for your health. Myopia is pervasive as is limited mobility and stunted physical development.

Perhaps the oddest thing about Chinese education is that many people, including educators, are entirely aware of its numerous deficiencies. People know, for example, that there is a scarcity of critical thinking and that memorization and constant test-taking are largely to blame. People realize that Western education is superior, but a dramatic change would represent a break with traditional culture, and that is unfeasible.

Just about every kid in Taiwan crams like mad for a decade and a half in the hopes of attending National Taiwan University, the country's most prestigious centre for higher learning. Doctors, lawyers, and other professionals use their graduated-from-NTU status to wow prospective clients. Just mentioning that you attended garners instant respect. In 2010, National Taiwan University had a Times Higher Education World University Ranking of 115.

Having played a part in the Chinese education system for so many years, I can say, with some measure of confidence, and in all sincerity, that if Chinese education were ever adopted by a Western country, it would soon find itself coming under attack as a form of child abuse.

Its myriad idiosyncrasies and predicaments notwithstanding, Taiwan, for an expatriate, really isn't such a bad place to live – once you get used to it. It is reasonably interesting, the people are almost always pleasant and accommodating, it has low taxes, a pretty good health care system (markedly more accessible than the one in my own country), super public transportation, an efficient postal system (again, as good as or better than the one in Canada), good food, reasonable prices, and, except for motorists, typhoons, earthquakes, the spectre of a Chinese invasion, and the odd serial killer/rapist who the Keystone Kops can't catch, is generally quite safe. Above all, Taiwan possesses a degree of civility that is all but absent in China. Even with its oddness, Taiwan, Republic of China is considerably more normal than the People's Republic of China, and its citizens are visibly happier; living in a free and open society seems to have that effect on people.

Without question, Taiwan is more advanced than China in almost every regard, yet in terms of cultural influence vis-à-vis the West and the rest of the world, it is on a road to nowhere; and culturally, Taiwan and China are, to borrow a Chinese expression, as close as lips and teeth. For someone like me, who lived in "the other China" for such duration, the China-set-to-shake-the-world argument didn't just come across as highly improbable; it was categorically delusional.

I made my way to Casteel Zeelandia, where I inspected some Qing Dynasty artifacts along with some Dutch helmets, swords, and pole arms. As a timepiece, the fort was second-rate, but it had a pleasant yard full of glorious banyan trees. I sat under one for the better part of two hours reading Mark Twain's *The Innocents Abroad.*

That evening, I hoped to spot one of Tainan's garbage trucks, but didn't. In Taipei, garbage trucks played Beethoven's 'Für Elise' on an endless track to prompt people to take their garbage out. (Up until the 1980s, people used to drop it out their windows.) Here in Tainan, sanitation trucks weren't musical, but rather linguistic, offering daily lessons in English.

"Hello. How are you today?"

"I'm fine. Thank you."

The idea was hatched by the mayor's wife.

CHAPTER TWENTY-SEVEN

Again, the train left the station right on time, and again I whiled
away the minutes reading, dozing, and gazing out the window at all the
bleak cement. I arrived in Taichung, which means "Central Terrace," at
around noon and checked into a hotel near the Japanese-built railway
station. [Guidebook: The third-largest city in Taiwan, Taichung is often
considered the most liveable. It has the mildest weather, the least air
pollution, and probably the best laid out city centre (you can thank the
Japanese for the latter).]

I headed to a place called Qingming Street, listed in my guidebook
as the first attraction and described as "Taichung's first attempt at a
pedestrian-only commercial zone." I ordered a coffee and sat down to
relax. The street was altogether unimpressive, unique only in that it had
been blocked off. It's a bit of a pastime in Taiwan to build pedestrian-
only areas and then allow vehicles to drive on them.

On my map, there was a coffee-shop-dotted block labelled Little
Europe, which turned out to be a spruced-up neighbourhood with better
sidewalks and nicer signs. Still, there were betel-nut stands and whizzing
work trucks and places with names like 'Let's Coffee.' The only thing
vaguely European about it was a Second Empire building that had so
many bars on it that it resembled a French jail. Not for the first time on
my journey through the two Chinas, I very nearly went back to the station
to hop on the next train.

For lack of a plan, I carried on to the Fengle Sculpture Park, where
I discovered bronze statues of kids with exposed genitals like the sort
I had seen in China. Taiwan and China had been separated (if it can be
said they were ever together), for more than 110 years, yet artisans in each
territory had arrived at the same conclusion, as it were. I had the same
reaction I often had: I was amazed, but only for a second or two. Then,
it seemed to make perfect sense. Finally, I forgot all about it. Like the
narrator in Gore Vidal's *Creation* says while travelling through Cathay (a
medieval name for China), "I have found that if one travels far enough,

left becomes right, up down, north south."

That evening, I finally found something I enjoyed: a coffee shop *cum* private movie theatre *cum* video store that specialized in foreign films and classic movies. The selection was salient, with the complete catalogue of practically every famous director who ever lived and obscure films from just about every corner of the globe. There was a remarkable cinematic assortment, for example, from Hungary; there was a larger one still from Iran. As I picked out films by Stanley Kubrick, Woody Allen, Terry Gilliam, Alfred Hitchcock, Federico Fellini, and the Coen brothers, it struck me that this place would never have been allowed to exist in China. The movie theatre in the basement was showing *Anna Karenina*. I reckoned that even that would have been too patrician or at least too foreign for those on the other side of the strait.[1]

In the mood to see a movie (I had recently read and watched *Anna Karenina*, coincidentally), I hailed a cab to a theatre complex located in Taichung's flashy centre. The driver, who took me straight there, was pretty much the only one I'd had since I left Taipei who knew where he was going. He was also the only one who didn't appear to be in any way deranged. I had to settle for the latest Harry Potter film, which wasn't so bad. There was an earthquake halfway through, but you get used to them. On the way back to my hotel, I passed by two palatial, neon-decorated bordellos, or "barber shops."

"They're huge," I said to the driver.

"They're a waste of money," he replied caustically.

In addition to its immodest brothels, Taichung is legendary for its gangsters. It isn't uncommon to spot headlines in the English dailies like 'Marvin "Tiger" Wang blows away Vincent "Snake-fist" Chen in Taichung tea house,' and wherever there are gangsters in Taiwan, there are sure to be politicians. Although members of the KMT aren't the only ones tainted by "black gold," the local term for collusion between government and crime, they do tend to dominate. Mobsters use their pull to get candidates elected. Once in office, politicians then pay the mob off or endorse their businesses. Each of Taiwan's major gangs runs a construction operation, and bid-rigging is common when government projects are put out to tender. Such an arrangement can have fatal consequences: companies are notorious for skimping on material. There have been post-earthquake discoveries of apartment building walls filled

---

1   Three Chinese movies that I would classify as excellent are Chen Kaige's *Farewell My Concubine*, Zhang Yimou's *Raise the Red Lantern*, and *To Live*, also directed by Zhang Yimou. Anyone wishing to understand more about Chinese culture and twentieth-century Chinese history would certainly benefit from watching them.

with pop bottles and plastic pails, and some of Taipei's metro stations were found to have walls that were hollow. According to *The Economist*, nearly a third of all infrastructure development in Taiwan is lost in kickbacks.

One day in Taichung was enough. It wasn't as claustrophobic as Taipei, and it *was* cleaner and better organized, but culturally, I couldn't see what it had to offer. There was a science museum that everyone said was excellent, but I felt I had had my fill of the lowlands. At noon the next day, I bought a bus ticket to Sun Moon Lake and was one of only three passengers to be transported inland past construction sites and over undulating hills toward the dead centre of the island.

I was rolling through the heart of betel-nut country: slope after slope of ramrod-straight palm trees. Ordinarily, forests in Taiwan are incredibly dense, the trees having been lashed together by creepers. Here, the original tangle of forest had been chopped down and replanted, and without deep roots or adequate shade the result was soil erosion and mudslides. After rice, betel nut is Taiwan's most lucrative crop. Something like 1.5 million Taiwanese chew it. Among the working poor, it's a way of life.

At Sun Moon Lake, I got a fine hotel room for a steal. It was a weekday, and there were few tourists, so you could bargain. As storm clouds loomed, I headed out for a stroll. After moseying along a lakeside path for a few minutes, I came across a sign that said, 'No padding – crack down on that if you are against the regulation.' Another one written mainly in Chinese asked that people take responsibility for any mess left by their dog. In English, it asked, 'Whose dog-shit?'

I then discovered something much more interesting: a small, freshly painted boat that Chiang Kai-shek had fished from immediately after he fled to Taiwan. I examined the craft for a moment and then gazed past it toward the palm-edged, turquoise waters. On the far side of the pool, mist-fringed knolls of green were being erased by a mass of grey. I could hear peals of delicate thunder.

With China in a state of pandemonium and momentum firmly on the side of the Communists, Chiang Kai-shek made plans for his "strategic retreat." He reckoned that with his air force and navy, neither of which the Reds possessed, Taiwan would be a cinch to defend. Besides, not only did it have zero Communist presence, but the locals had only recently been subdued.

On January 21, 1949, Chiang arose to do his morning exercises. Then he went to church. After that, he called a cabinet meeting and bequeathed authority to his vice-president before being driven in one of his Cadillacs to Nanjing's Purple Mountain in order to pay homage to Sun Yat-sen. With the help of a cane, the 62-year-old climbed the 392 steps leading to the doctor's mausoleum whereupon he thrice bowed to his marble likeness. Emerging from the hall, Chiang stood in the sunlight for a moment and gazed upon his capital. He descended between the pine trees and security guards after which he was driven to the airport and flown to Hangzhou.

The vaults of Shanghai's banks were emptied by members of the Green Gang, and the nation's gold and silver reserves were shipped across the Taiwan Strait. China's national treasury would be transferred to Taiwan. The national collection of historical relics and art, which had followed Chiang around from capital to capital, would also be transferred. These days, China's imperial treasures are not found in Beijing, but rather in the National Palace Museum, in a suburb of Taipei. It is always said that even with all the years of transport and near misses in Japanese bombing raids, not one of the 650,000 artifacts was damaged or lost. Because this is always said, it couldn't possibly be true.

With Mao's troops headed south, there was talk of an American air and naval blockade along the Yangtze, an event which could have divided China and altered the course of history. However, Harry Truman wouldn't agree to it as he had come to the same conclusion Winston Churchill had several years earlier: China didn't matter.[2]

One by one, the KMT-held cities fell. Just before they did, there was always massive rioting, looting, and disorder. In Nanjing, for example, government offices were stripped to the bone. When it came time for Chongqing to go, there was similar chaos. Deng Xiaoping became the mayor and political commissar of the former wartime capital. A week later, the Nationalists voted to move their own capital to Taiwan. Two days after that, on December 10, 1949, nearly 13 years to the day he was about to embark on his "last five minutes" against the Communists from his base in Xian, the generalissimo boarded a plane from Xian and took off for Taipei. As it happened, there were no radio stations to provide assistance and the pilot had to fly using his intuition. It was overcast, and only a temporary break in the cloud allowed him to spot an island off of Fujian, which enabled him to set a course for Taiwan. When a major delivered this message to Chiang, all he could do was nod.

---

2   Shortly before Pearl Harbour, a mission from London had reported that the government in Chongqing was largely inept and that its leader "did not have an intelligent grasp on the situation." Winston Churchill was perennially surprised by the importance America placed on China during the war. Speaking to Roosevelt at one point, the British prime minister casually dismissed China as "four hundred and twenty five million pigtails."

From Taipei, Chiang Kai-shek went to Sun Moon Lake with his son, Chiang Ching-kuo. At his hotel, he received word that the province of Yunnan had fallen. Chiang and his protégé took a walk and decided to go fishing. Upon finding an old man with a boat, Chiang Kai-shek offered him money for it. Then he caught a five-footer, which he took to be a good omen, or so one hagiographer has claimed. Meanwhile, in China, autumn was about to succumb to winter. During the previous winter, there had been starvation and reports of cannibalism; cadaverous civilians wore winter coats made out of the furs of dogs and cats they had eaten. As I stared at the lake, I imagined Chiang contentedly casting his line. I imagined dull-eyed Communist soldiers with their sneakers, green cotton uniforms, and emergency rations of crushed locusts still strapped to their backs marching into cities that had been gutted by his goons.

I continued on. I walked through a small village and wound my way around the other side of the lake. At one point, I slipped and fell on a slick bit of path and tried to break my fall by grabbing onto a pipe. It broke and water pooled all around me. I imagined a man with shampoo-lathered hair confusedly adjusting his shower nozzle.

I thought about telling someone about this, but knew it was a bad idea. I would never have been forgiven and might have been extorted, or worse.

The sky cracked open and buckets of rain fell. It just wouldn't let up. I hid for a long while in a long, pitch black tunnel before giving up and attempting to hitchhike back. After what seemed like forever, a cab stopped and I got in.

The next day, I rented a scooter and explored the gorgeous countryside before doing a few laps around Sun Moon Lake. The turquoise tarn was beautiful and much nicer than it appeared in photos. The area around it was also peaceful and short on people, so I stayed for a couple more days. I read, I walked, I explored. I was 762 metres above sea level and happy because of it. Evenings were cool and I could sit under the starred darkness with a book and a cup of tea. On the lowlands, it is rare to see even a single star.

I awoke early one morning and waited outside my hotel for the bus. It was a four-hour jaunt to Taipei and I wanted to watch the scenery go from green to grey. But while rolling between sun-dappled rice fields, I fell asleep and failed to watch anything except the insides of my eyelids. When I awoke, we were in Taipei: buildings of tile, barred-up windows, scooter-lined sidewalks, convenience stores galore, and processions of brassy signs. We passed a Mister Donut, a Dunkin' Donuts, a Häagen-Dazs, and two Starbucks. Doughnut shops are all the rage in Taipei.

When the first one opened, people lined up for an hour to get in – for more than a year. I got out at a major intersection and watched as the light changed to green and a torrent of scooters, taxis, buses, BMWs, and Mercedes-Benzes surged by.

Even in Taipei, cars seldom signal, and scooter drivers almost never look before rocketing out of side streets. Scooters sometimes race (occasionally in packs) and often weave in and out of traffic. Because they park on the sidewalks, they have to drive on them. Pedestrians, by contrast, often walk on the roads.

There is little to no respect for pedestrians in Taiwan. As touched upon, right turns on red lights trump walk indicators, even if those walking are children, the elderly, or women with strollers. I don't know how many times I have seen mothers jerk their strollers out of the path of a speeding work truck or taxi; hundreds probably. And it never seems to matter whether intersections have traffic cops or not. There are so many infractions; where would you even start?

Not only is the concept of law a touch sketchy in Chinese society, but it is steeped in Confucianism. It isn't that motorists should drive properly so as to be within the limits of the law; it's that they should drive properly in order to be morally upstanding citizens.

Here are some example questions taken from the English version of Taiwan's driving test handbook. They have been copied verbatim.

a.) The driver follows traffic rules because… 1. he is afraid of being punished. 2. he has the sense of responsibility, honour for personal and other people's safety. 3. there is someone to supervise him.

b.) If drivers want to be honoured, happy, safe on traffic, they should 1. have a sense of morality and follow the laws. 2. have good driving skills. 3. not drink and smoke.

c.) To ensure the safety of oneself and other people, the driver should always make an effort on cultivating his morality and 1. control himself and help others. 2. control others from flaunting other's physical superiority. 3. Find ways to deal with others.

d.) How does the driver think about his clothes and appearance? 1. There are no restrictions. 2. He should be clean and dignified. 3. It is not important.

e.) True or False: Politeness and tolerance are the best virtues of showing driving morals.

Bo Yang says, "The terrible traffic congestion in Taipei is a problem that should and could have been solved a long time ago. If penalties for driving offences were stiff enough, the chaos on the island's public roads would be reduced immediately. But there are a number of people who advocate teaching traffic offenders the rudiments of 'road etiquette,' as this is 'more Chinese.' This sort of etiquette has been taken too far. We painted zebra-stripe crossings on the street to aid pedestrians. But then people started getting run over when they walked on them."

Incidentally, it bothered Bo Yang to comment on the dark side of Chinese culture, but he felt it to be something that couldn't be ignored. If a foreigner had written such a book, they would have been branded a bigot, even though racism has nothing to do with it. Culture and mindset are everything; race is incidental. I had hoped to interview Bo Yang at his home in Taipei, but was informed that he was unwell and not accepting visitors. He died shortly afterward and his ashes were scattered off of Green Island, where he had been imprisoned.

The plan was to head back to my apartment in Zhuwei and then spend a couple of days roaming the streets of Taipei. I would go to National Taiwan Democracy Memorial Hall[3], Sun Yat-sen Memorial Hall, 2-28 Park, the Taipei 101 building, the splendidly slapdash Shilin Night Market (which the Taiwanese believe to be internationally renowned, like the Hermitage or the Louvre), the National Palace Museum, one of Chiang Kai-shek's former residences, and the iniquitous and tasteless Snake Alley. But I couldn't get motivated to tour a city I had lived in for the past 10 years. It wasn't that I didn't like Taipei; I did. It was an incredibly easy city to live and work in and it had a fair amount to see and do. I didn't subscribe to the local view that it was "beautiful," but I did agree that it was "very convenient." There were great restaurants, decent cafés, excellent bookstores, fine music stores, lots of museums…. In many ways, it was akin to Paris. Well, in one: there was dog shit everywhere.

From Taiwan's busiest intersection, I headed straight for the nearby Songshan Airport and bought a ticket to the island of Jinmen. Or Kinmen. Or Quemoy.

Of course, I was well aware that Jinmen was, at its closest, only two kilometres from China. After all, at Drum Wave Islet, just off of Xiamen, I had fruitlessly attempted to spot it. But to fly to Jinmen from Taipei and land on the tawny and green, bow-tie shaped Taiwanese island while observing the coast of China contract to a line on the horizon was really

---

3   In 2008, the Nationalist-led government voted successfully to restore the site to its original name, Chiang Kai-shek Memorial Hall. The original signage was reinstalled in 2009.

quite an experience.

In Jincheng (or Kincheng), the island's main town, it took me a while to find a hotel. The one I decided on was located on a main drag that was so subdued that shirtless old men played Chinese chess while standing along its tree-lined meridian. What cars there were made lazy arcs around them.

I rented a scooter and zipped out of town. Jinmen was much prettier and much more pastoral than I had imagined. I had read that Koxinga had cut down all the island's trees to build his armada, and that the locals were still annoyed about it, but there were plenty of trees. There were also delightfully expansive fields with flowers and large, well-built homes. There were old brick homes, too, topped with saddle-style roofs, an architectural hallmark of Fujian. These were angled this way and that in rambling villages that dated back to the Qing and Ming dynasties. Their yards were filled with clutter and dust and weeds and everyone living in them appeared to be very old.

It was blazing-hot and more than once I got hopelessly lost. The roads ran in all directions and they all looked the same to me. What I needed was a compass. I pulled over often to drink water, apply sunscreen, and consult my map.

There was evidence of the military everywhere. I passed by several service roads blocked by barbed wire and notices marked by bold red characters and fat exclamation marks. Thin, despondent-looking soldiers fulfilling their obligatory national duty idled about with their guns. I saw heavy equipment under camouflage nets, and one or two hills which were obviously man-made. There were towers and antennae and various installations, but then it's no secret that Jinmen is heavily fortified. (Guidebook: Locals joke that Jinmen is hollow inside – beneath all the grass and pretty flowers are mazes of bomb shelters, tunnels, and military storage units.)

With some difficulty, I managed to find the Kuningtou battlefield, where Nationalist forces, in an impressive and rare victory, fended off three Red Army divisions, or 10,000 men, during an amphibious assault in 1949. More than 15,000 soldiers lost their lives in the fight. I drove by an old brick house that had borne witness and still bore the scars; it was riddled with bullet holes.

I drove to the Kuningtou War Museum, where I went inside and was grateful for the air conditioning. The museum was a propaganda piece heavy on artists' renditions of the illustrious clash: amateurish, wall-sized portraits of combat explained in tedious captions of broken English. Except for the pictures of Chiang Kai-shek and the fact that the good guys' uniforms were khaki and not olive, it was unerringly parallel to the type of thing you would see in China, right down to the megaphone-fortified tour guides, the hollow explanations, and the expressionless squadrons of gawping tourists.

With the Korean War, Mao had become distracted, but once an armistice was in place on that peninsula, he refocused his attention on "recovering" Taiwan. The problem was that the US Seventh Fleet was in his way, and America, as Mao finally realized, was not a "paper tiger," or empty threat, at all.

In August, 1954, China's state-run press began ratcheting up the rhetoric. It denounced the "American imperialists" for their sustained "occupation of Taiwan" and stated that the island would be "liberated" by force if required. To illustrate his seriousness, Mao moved 100,000 troops to the Fujian coast along with all manner of equipment.

The Americans wanted Chiang Kai-shek to discard Jinmen, Matsu, and its other small islands in the Taiwan Strait and focus on defending Taiwan proper, but old Chiang dug in his heels. Those islands were symbolic. By holding onto them, it proved he was sincere about retaking "the mainland." With a Soviet-supported China and an American-backed Taiwan, the situation was bound to come to blows.

On September 3, 1954, the PLA began shelling Jinmen. The Nationalists replied in kind, and it appeared that the final phase of the Chinese Civil War was on. Communist forces landed on one island of Taiwan's Dachen group and all 720 Nationalist soldiers stationed there died trying to defend it. The Americans helped citizens and soldiers on the other Dachen islands evacuate to "mainland" Taiwan. The fighting continued for another year and is known to history as the First Taiwan Strait Crisis. Things only came to a stop when the United States hinted at using nuclear weapons.

No sooner had peace broken out than Chiang ordered the deployment to Jinmen of 100,000 of his own men and a third of his equipment – against America's protestations. The crafty old devil was taunting Mao while trying to manoeuvre the cautious Eisenhower into an all-out war.

There were high-level negotiations, but they broke down, and the Second Taiwan Strait Crisis commenced on August 23, 1958. There was more shelling along with air battles. Most significantly, there was a blockade. China was endeavouring to choke Jinmen into submission.

This time, Eisenhower became annoyed, and he ordered a large amount of weaponry to be sent to Taiwan, including nuclear-capable missiles. No fewer than six aircraft carriers steamed into the area and US warships were ordered to escort a convoy of Nationalist supply boats into Jinmen's harbour in what proved to be a foreshadowing of the Cuban Missile Crisis. Mao blinked and the blockade was broken.

Shortly thereafter, the PRC announced an "even-day cease-fire," meaning that it would only shell Jinmen on odd-numbered days. When the smoke cleared, 3,000 of the island's civilians and 1,000 of its soldiers lay dead. The ordeal lasted for 44 days, and, according to the Nationalist government, saw upwards of 474,000 artillery rounds land on the island.

I left the museum and walked back to the parking lot to fetch my scooter. The environment was serene and a welcome breeze was causing the flora to fidget. Sunlight leaked through the tree-tops as butterflies flitted and danced among the evenly manicured hedges. There was almost no litter here. To keep them busy, soldiers on Jinmen are put to work doing landscaping and fixing up bits of infrastructure.

That evening, back in Jincheng, I walked into a restaurant and sat down. An anxious-looking waitress approached me and asked, in English, "Cheese pig?"

"Sorry?"

"Cheese pig?" she asked again, making the gesture to eat. Two other staff members stood staring at me from behind the counter, petrified. When I left, the woman escorted me to the door, bowed low, and said, "Good morning!" Unless they work in a Japanese restaurant or as an elevator attendant in one of Taiwan's big Japanese department stores, people in Taiwan never bow. Later, in a convenience store, I bought a bottle of water and couldn't help notice that the cashier appeared visibly frightened. When I set my purchase on the counter, he took a step back and yelled, "Internet!"

Martial law wasn't lifted on Jinmen until 1993. Before that, foreigners weren't permitted to travel here, nor were the local residents allowed to leave. For decades, they were stuck in limbo and didn't even use the New Taiwan Dollar as currency. Perhaps all of the isolation had had an effect on them.

Instilled with the charity of night, Jincheng was quite charming. I found a collection of wonderful old homes whose builders hadn't discriminated against construction material. The long-ago-fired tiles were fractured, the concrete mouldy, the ponderous wooden doors cracked, and the windows yellowed with age. I stuck my head into a beauty parlour with a list of services and prices painted on the wall above the mirrors. It could have been 1953. This was the part of travel I enjoyed the most: time travel.

I played tourist in the commercial district, sampling bits of locally made candy and snooping around a shop selling a locally produced alcohol called Kaoliang. Kaoliang is a potent spirit made from sorghum. It can be 63 percent alcohol by volume and it smells and tastes like petrol. Along the restored Mofan Street, I studied the Western-style buildings dating from the 1920s (brick archways, wooden doors) and noted a lovely looking café called Mao Zedong's Milk Tea. Through the window, I spotted a waiter wearing a Mao T-shirt. Here. In Jinmen. Of all places.

I saw young Taiwanese wearing T-shirts all the time with pictures of Bob Marley, Ho Chi Minh, and (as mentioned) Che Guevara; they had no idea who they were. But they must have known who Mao was. It would have been tempting to credit Mao Zedong's Milk Tea to Taiwanese tolerance and liberalization, but it would have been accurate to ascribe it to historical ignorance and a lack of education.

The next day, I set out on another drive. I drove past duck ponds and more fields, and down littoral roads walled with sublime flora and gaps that allowed for glimpses of the Taiwan Strait. Wherever there were little communities, everything (recreation centres, parks, streets) seemed to be named after Sun Yat-sen, Chiang Kai-shek, or Koxinga – the Nationalist pantheon of heroes.

Again, I wanted to go to a museum, and again I got disoriented. I asked three female street cleaners for help, only for each of them to simultaneously point in different directions. I saw a group of firemen outside a fire station and approached them with my map, but they started to giggle and make fun of me. Later, I would walk out of two different establishments after being treated like some sort of circus freak by the staff. The people of Jinmen were most obviously bored and did not appear to be in firm possession of all their faculties.

It was called the August 23rd Artillery War Museum, and it was meant to commemorate the Second Taiwan Strait Crisis. It was more interesting than the museum I had seen the day before, but it was also quite bizarre. But here, in the Chinese universe, bizarre was normal. What would have been truly out of the ordinary was if the subject matter had been given objective treatment and the museum had been properly put together.

There were some great old photos, however, and even some video of the fighting and devastation, but never once was the phrase 'civil war' invoked. The Nationalist-Communist conflict was instead characterized as something global and Taiwan was depicted as an innocent victim caught up in the power plays of the United States and the Soviet Union.

There was a fairly interesting exhibit on propaganda canisters that each side either shot at or sent by balloon to each other. The ones from China were called "propaganda" whereas the ones from Taiwan were labelled "messages," "leaflets," "gifts," and "rations." Although never explained in the exhibit, the canister phenomenon was spawned by China's "even-day cease-fire." The canisters commenced after the live rounds stopped. According to an old Taiwan Lonely Planet I own, "To avoid injuries, (the firing of the canisters) was done according to a regular schedule – Taiwan fired propaganda shells on Monday, Wednesday and Friday while the mainlanders launched theirs on Tuesday, Thursday and Saturday. The Cold War was put on hold during Sunday so everyone could enjoy a holiday." This went on right up until the 1990s. In fact, some people on "the mainland" almost assuredly learned of the "Tiananmen Square Massacre" via a note fired from Taiwan.

Here on Jinmen, the PRC canisters were collected and made into knives and meat cleavers, which were then sold to tourists. According to my old guidebook, when the shelling finally ceased, the knife-making industry collapsed. I had been in a store nearby Mao Zedong's Milk Tea that had been filled with canister-made knives and knife sets. I wondered if they were fakes.

At the time, Taiwan referred to its canister and balloon campaign as "psychological warfare." As my guidebook explains: "Balloons containing pamphlets and various top-secret 'psychological warfare apparatus' were regularly launched from (Jinmen and Matsu). One balloon drifted all the way to Israel, where its canister was opened and the world finally learned what type of 'psychological warfare apparatus' was being used – see through underwear."

It definitely wasn't the only oddball story to come out of the standoff. As Denny Roy explains in his *Taiwan: A Political History*, "During fishing season, (an) ROC fleet consisting of two landing ship tanks (LSTs) and several warships rounded up groups of Chinese fishing boats, sometimes after driving away PLA navy escort ships. The ROC sailors then moved the Chinese crews into the spacious LSTs. There the fisherman watched movies, heard anticommunist propaganda, enjoyed a banquet, and received gifts. Afterward they returned to their boats and went back to fishing. The crews of 370 Chinese fishing boats underwent this process."

For their part, Beijing organized what might be called a campaign of personal appeal. Nationalist leaders took delivery of letters that were published in newspapers or broadcast on the radio by friends, family, and former colleagues still in China. The letters urged them to work toward so-called reunification.

But there was much more going on between the two Chinas during the Cold War than propaganda games. During the 1950s and 1960s, there were all sorts of operations taking place – on land, at sea, and in the air. Taiwan sent commandos into China (with America's blessing) on numerous occasions, there were small-scale naval battles with ships lost on both sides, the ROC air force bombed targets along China's coast, and much else.

There was also the CIA-supported guerrilla war that smouldered along the Yunnan-Burma border. After Yunnan fell, some 12,000 KMT troops set up camp in Burma. From there, they recruited local bandit groups and swelled their ranks to over 18,000. They picked away at the morale of the PLA soldiers in commando raids and all-out battles. Chiang Kai-shek supplied the technical advisors while the US supplied the weapons. The general who led them not only received a pay cheque from Taipei, but was furnished with the title "Governor of Yunnan."

Burma complained to the UN and Eisenhower called on the Chiang administration to withdraw. Taipei denied it had any influence in the matter, thus prompting Eisenhower to write Chiang asking him to remedy the situation. An evacuation was staged – older troops were removed only to be covertly replaced by 1,200 new ones who were added to the thousands of younger ones that stayed behind. The area controlled by the Nationalists was within the Golden Triangle. To help raise funds, the local narcotics industry was exploited. Even after KMT incursions dropped off, its participation in the opium trade continued to thrive. Up until very recently, you couldn't buy bagels with poppy seeds on them in Taiwan. Anyone flying to the Republic of China these days will be reminded on their disembarkation card and by way of announcement that drug possession is punishable by death.

The strangest thing about the August 23rd Artillery War Museum was the war simulation room. People went inside and the room shook, flashed, and boomed with the recorded sound of explosions. There was a huge queue; mothers holding hands with their overexcited kids. I could see people within the cubicle shrieking and giggling.

On my third day on Jinmen, I caught a ferry to Liehyu Island, sometimes called Little Jinmen. Jinmen is actually an archipelago of 15 islands and islets, of which Taiwan controls only 12; China controls the other 3.

Once across, I retrieved my scooter and drove by a statue of Chiang Kai-shek. I was headed in the direction of yet another war museum. It was closed for renovations, fine with me because I had only come for the observation room.

It was here where the Taiwanese used to blast out propaganda messages over the world's loudest speakers. China used to counter. It was also here where an enormous neon sign was once erected. It read, 'Three Principles of the People – Reunify China!' The sign was so popular with tourists in Xiamen that when it was finally decommissioned, that city's municipal government lodged a formal complaint about it.

Past the construction workers I went, walking up a set of stairs and entering a door. Corridors of earthen walls and intermittent light bulbs lay beyond. I came to a cool room with photographs of Chiang and his chums. The room was actually a bunker and it offered a view of China's coastline. A number of high-powered binoculars were on hand. I looked across the water and saw thin stretches of sand, fishing boats, houses, and a dark line of trees. In the distance there stood an indistinct mountain. I failed to recognize anything I had seen when I was in Xiamen. The circular scene was hazy and the boats and homes rather pathetic. I was struck by how different it all looked from Taiwan.

I left and found a vacant pathway that mimicked the curve of the island. I raced down it, between a passageway of trembling firs and by a pasture of lounging cows until I came to a clearing and saw water. There was a small oatmeal-coloured beach, passage to which was stymied by a low, camouflaged parapet and a row of cacti. Down the way, next to the road, there were barracks: saddle-shaped rooftops poking above a wall with a freshly painted war mural on it. Valiant-looking soldiers dashed about a patch of sand beset with explosions and plumes of white smoke. The picture resembled an outsized comic book mail-order ad for plastic army men. And these were the only army men who appeared to be around.

Facing the water was a pillbox; I climbed inside and had a seat. There were cactus plants on its top. I looked again at the cacti planted along the parapet. It was then I spotted the English sign.

Military defence plants
Prickly plants such as Agaye
sisalana Perr. Ex Engelm.
and cactus are down on the
peripherals of barracks and
forts for defence.

And there you have it – defence against the world's largest military courtesy of prickly plants. Just for the record, there weren't even that prickly. I checked.

On my way back to the ferry, I stopped at a convenience store and bought a drink. The shop had a shaded parking lot and a couple of picnic tables, and some old folks were there gabbing and minding their grandchildren. I bought some penny-candy, gave it to the kids, and gave them all high fives. The old folks grinned. I pretended I couldn't understand Chinese.

One kid said, "He looks like a bird. Do all foreigners look like birds?"

"I dunno," said his friend, "but he sure is fat."

A third piped up. "My teacher said that foreigners are fat because they only eat fast food. Everything is fried. They don't eat healthily like we Taiwanese."

"And they aren't as smart as we Taiwanese," said the first. "Isn't that right grandpa?"

Grandpa nodded in confirmation.

It was something many Taiwanese (and Chinese) people believed. Whenever I asked my adult students to describe Taiwanese people, I almost always got the same answer: "Taiwanese people are hard-working, friendly, and clever." When I asked, "Clever how?" the response was usually, "Clever at business." I never had the heart to tell them that 'clever at business' and 'clever generally' were two entirely different things.

In June, 2001, Jinmen's deputy county commissioner, Yen Ta-jen, was quoted in the *Taipei Times* as saying, "Foreigners are just not as smart as we Chinese people."

I glanced around at the row of houses I assumed these people lived in. They were dreadful: dirty and decrepit; among the worst I'd seen in Taiwan.

From the ferry terminal, it was now possible for Taiwanese to travel to China. In the year 2000, the Chen Shui-bian government, rather than accept Beijing's One-China policy (there is but one China, and Taiwan, Macau, Hong Kong, and the mainland make up that China), decided to appease the red giant by lifting a ban on trade and direct travel between PRC- and ROC-held islands in the Taiwan Strait. In 2001, a boatload of Taiwanese bigwigs sailed from Jinmen to Xiamen in what was the first direct legal civilian voyage between the two Chinas in more than five decades. During the martial law period, and under the umbrella of Taiwan's "three-no's" policy (no contact, no negotiation, no comprise with the Communist regime), there wasn't even indirect travel between the two entities. Taiwan's travel ban wasn't lifted until 1987. Presently, an estimated 800,000 Taiwanese work in China and tour groups from "the mainland" are finally permitted to travel to Taiwan, even if they do tend to be comprised of septuagenarians. ROC passports are no good in the PRC and *vice versa*. A citizen of one China wishing to visit the other must apply for a special permit.

Back in "Big Jinmen," I ran into a Canadian friend nicknamed Big John. He was there with his Taiwanese wife and a local friend to participate in some sort of swimming event. I was actually thinking about him the very instant I saw him walking across the road, something I am forever doing. I hadn't known he was going to be here.

John's take on Taiwan was different from mine. Like many long-term, married expatriates, he thought it was great. Sure, it may have been a little quirky at times, but it wasn't outright weird. It was interesting, modern, and peaceful.

I agreed that it was interesting, but for me, Taiwan constantly redefined the concept of weird. This was, after all, a country that had erotic dancers at weddings – and funerals; a country where public bathrooms were practically never supplied with toilet paper or hot water, yet often came with signs saying, 'Please do not stand on the toilet;' a country whose government had asked me in a survey whether I thought cultural interaction between locals and foreigners could be enhanced through the "excavation of ancient remains;" a country where people drove on the sidewalks and walked on the streets.

But I respected John's opinion. Unlike many of the Taiwan faithful, he wasn't dogmatic. I'd encountered more than a few expatriates who were fanatically patriotic when it came to Taiwan, something I could never fully understand.

Outwardly, Taiwanese people are friendly, open, and cheerful, but they can also be deeply irritating, like a group of relatively bright adolescents bubbling over with enthusiasm and wanting everything done yesterday. But worse than their teen spirit, as it were, is their xenophobia. All told, foreigners are foreigners and are referred to as such. Go to a bank in Taiwan, and you could easily hear one teller shout to another, as I had countless times, "This foreigner wants to remit money! Are they allowed to do that!?"

The government itself tends to view foreign nationals as a necessary inconvenience and is often very bad at hiding this. Over the years, I had been treated with utter contempt at government offices on several occasions. I had tried to apply for permanent residency – something you can do after seven years of continual habitation – only to receive an icy reception at the relevant bureau. At around the same time, my friend from Britain applied. He worked for a prominent foreign publishing company and was planning on marrying a local woman. He was told that his tax records would have to be scrutinized as a condition for application. If any irregularities were found, he was informed, not only would he not be granted permanent residency, he would be deported. Indeed, the phrase, 'We will deport you,' was on the tip of the tongue of every single Taiwanese manager I ever worked for. Two Taiwanese managers I worked for did little to conceal their abhorrence for bigheaded Westerners and their lofty ideals, and I never encountered a single one who didn't have a fondness for dealing with non-native people dishonestly.

I was an oddity, and it was amazing I had survived as long as I had. The only way to acquire meaningful knowledge about Chinese culture and society was to become immersed in it for a protracted period of time. Yet that typically necessitated a large degree of acceptance and a certain amount of admiration. There was no question that my experience had made me more tolerant, but I would never become a cultural convert. As someone who has always harboured a deep-seated suspicion toward authority, Chinese society's paternalism perturbed me. So did its Philistine nature, its perennial miserliness, its myopia, its near total ignorance of the outside world, its quashing of creativity, its ruination of critical thinking, and its disregard for individualism. To counter Mao's Cultural Revolution, the Chiang regime launched a crusade called the Cultural Renaissance. In addition to glorifying Sun Yat-sen's Three Principles of the People, it belittled Western liberalism and its overarching emphasis on the individual. Definitely, things had gotten a lot better since the Chiang days, but if you asked me, they were by no means good.

In a culture that disdained truth, I sought it; I revelled in it. But it wasn't some Boy-Scout disposition that drew me to it. To my way of thinking, the truth may have been ugly, but it was almost always more interesting than the myth. And Chinese culture was sustained by myth. With such a sorrowful, tumultuous, and inglorious past, myth was imperative.

Coincidentally, it was myth that was helping to define China now – outside the Chinese realm. The Chinese word for 'crisis' is not a character comprised of 'danger' plus 'opportunity.' In fact, the word for 'crisis' is comprised of two characters, not one. The Chinese curse, 'May you live in interesting times,' isn't a Chinese curse or expression at all. Mandarin is not a monosyllabic language, nor is its script a collection of ideograms. Dowager Empress Cixi is not one of history's most wicked figures. The famous sign in Shanghai's former Public Garden, 'No Dogs or Chinese Allowed' is a figment of someone's imagination. The Tiananmen Square Massacre is an invention of the Western media. The Great Wall is largely an invention of the Western collective unconscious. The Terracotta Warriors speak more to superstition and despotism than they do to craftsmanship. Chinese society has never been a harmonious and peace-loving one. For thousands of years, China has been a land of tribalism, practically uninterrupted warfare, unimaginable tyranny, and indescribable upheaval. There isn't much that's spiritual or mystical involved in burning bundles of ghost money or praying to bug-eyed statues for good grades and winning lottery numbers, and Chinese classics like the *Analects of Confucius* and the *Tao Te Ching* are so profound as to be almost completely meaningless. What's more, they continue to lend legitimacy to authoritarianism and aid to perpetuate a culture in which genuine thought and direct questioning are effectively nullified.

Then, of course, there is the latest myth: the twenty-first century is going to be China's. Bo Yang says that this is "impossible," owing to the simple fact that Chinese culture and society are "too primitive." By making such grand statements, the writer says, Chinese people are displaying their tragic flaw: being "dishonest with themselves and others." On top of dishonesty, there is that other great Chinese defect: infighting. Bo Yang says, "Chinese people squabble among themselves in every situation, since their bodies lack those cells that enable most human beings to get along with each other. When non-Chinese criticize the Chinese for this weakness, I like to warn them, 'Chinese people are like this because God knows that with more than one billion of them, if they ever got their act together, the rest of the world wouldn't be able to handle them. God has been good to you foreigners by making it impossible for Chinese people to co-operate among themselves.' But it is very painful for me to say this."

I couldn't stop driving. The island was so bucolic and beautiful that I had to explore it once more. When it came time to return to Jincheng, I wasn't sure which way to go, so I stopped and asked two soldiers. They didn't know either. All they could do was scratch their heads and say they were sorry. Jincheng was to the west, the same direction China was in. I thought of the two stubbly faced soldiers I had spoken to in Xiamen, the ones who didn't know where Jinmen was. In November, 1994, an artillery unit on Jinmen accidentally bombed a village in China, injuring several people. I now understood how a mishap like that was possible.

That evening, I decided to go for a night drive. I rode past a line of old brick homes, their weed-choked courtyards awash in 90-watt glows. Their wrinkled inhabitants, some of whom I imagined were born during the death throws of the Qing Dynasty, sat outside fanning themselves and chatting – something they couldn't have done until fairly recently. During martial law, there was a curfew and all lights had to be switched off or hidden behind blinds.

I came to yet another beach where I sat all alone and watched the glow of Xiamen duplicated in the still water. I reckoned that I was among only a handful of people to be doing this at this particular moment in time: sitting on one China and looking at the other. Figuratively, I was also sitting at the crux of a political conundrum.

In the early 1970s, Taiwan was one of the most totalitarian places on the planet. The Nationalist regime exercised complete control over all branches of government, the economy, the press, and every organization except the Presbyterian church. In 1996, Taiwan held its first direct popular presidential election.

The road to political liberalization was a long and arduous one, the culmination of various factors and influences. The KMT itself deserves credit, even if it was doing what it had to in order to ensure its own political survival. The part Chiang Ching-kuo played was especially prominent. The United States acted in a supporting role by cautioning the Nationalists to safeguard civil liberties and by keeping the Communists at bay. Grass-roots activism was the prime mover, with Taiwanese dissent having been spurred on by the People Power movement in the Philippines and successful demonstrations in South Korea.[4]

Taiwan's democracy is not what you might call mature, but the fact that it exists at all is nothing short of incredible. Taiwan, one of the so-called Asian tigers, has often been dubbed an "economic miracle," but I didn't subscribe to that point of view. With the head start it got from having been a Japanese colony, the enormous influx of capital it received from the KMT, the protection, aid, and technical support it was provided by the United States, and a citizenry imbued with the work ethic, it would have been unusual if Taiwan hadn't risen to become an economic power. The Taiwanese work an average of 72 hours per week, longer than anyone else in the world – including the Japanese. They are reluctant to form unions, they seldom complain, and they don't earn half of what they ought to. But a culture of exploitation could hardly create conditions deserving of the word miraculous; if Taiwan is any sort of miracle, it is a political one.

Taiwan's democracy may be divisive, inchoate, and chaotic, but it contains enough substance to deeply annoy the other Chinese government to claim sovereignty over the island. Whereas the Nationalists showed remarkable restraint when its people finally decided

---

4   Because Taiwan has become democratic, some have made the argument that China will too. After all, both states are Chinese. But this proposition is extremely simplistic. Even if China were to become democratic, the pertinent circumstances couldn't possibly approximate those that occurred on Taiwan.

to stand up and demand that one of Dr. Sun's Three Principles of the People be made a reality, the Communists reacted to a similar request with machine guns and tanks. But then, crude responses are something of a PRC hallmark.

On the eve of Taiwan's first direct presidential election, China held military exercises where it simulated an invasion of one of its own islands. More significantly, it fired missiles at Taiwan, which landed just off its coast. China's bellicosity only subsided when Bill Clinton ordered two aircraft carrier battle groups into the Taiwan Strait. After the votes had been tallied, Taiwan's new president, Lee Teng-hui, called for "state-to-state" talks with Beijing only to be branded a traitor and reminded that China possessed the neutron bomb.

It was part of a pattern. Since its inception, the Chinese Communist Party has interceded in Korea, swallowed Tibet, attacked India, provoked border clashes with the Soviet Union, encouraged rebellion in Indonesia, and backed juntas in both Asia and Africa.

In terms of territorial claims, Communist China still has much on its agenda. In addition to Taiwan, it believes the Russian Far East, parts of Siberia, parts of Central Asia, all of Mongolia, and all of the rocks that make up the Spratlys and Paracels to be its own. Chinese tourists have informed citizens of Vladivostok, for example, that they are living on Chinese soil. Although the government in Beijing doesn't formally lay claim to any of these areas (except for the islands), that isn't to say that it won't, or that it won't resurrect previous claims. In Chinese culture, nothing is ever finalized; everything is open to endless negotiation. In any event, China, to the Chinese, is a nebulous concept; more an idea (or myth) than a clearly defined swath of soil.[5]

Given that China practises what author Steven W. Mosher has aptly termed "the politics of historical revenge," the *status quo* between the two Chinas cannot remain, even if there has been somewhat of a thaw in relations of late. Simply put, something has got to give. Taiwan is preventing China from fulfilling its destiny.

In 2005, the People's Republic of China passed its Anti-Secession Law. It was, in part, a counter to Taiwanese rumblings of independence. It is a short document comprised of 10 articles. Here are a few of its key points:

---

5   This is a fact that can, in part, be evidenced by the other China's territorial claims. In addition to holding itself out as the rightful ruler of that which is presently administered by the People's Republic of China, the government on Taiwan claims to reign over territory controlled by Afghanistan, Bhutan, Burma, India, Japan, Mongolia, Pakistan, Russia, and Tajikistan. In other words, despite the fact that it controls only Taiwan and a handful of outlying islets (or the "Free Area of the ROC," in Nationalist parlance) the Republic of China actually claims more territory than the People's Republic of China does.

- There is only one China in the world. Both the mainland and Taiwan belong to one China.
- Accomplishing the great task of reunifying the motherland is the sacred duty of all Chinese people, the Taiwan compatriots included.
- In the event that... possibilities for a peaceful reunification should be completely exhausted, the state shall employ non-peaceful means and other necessary measures....
- In the event that (non-peaceful means and/or other necessary measures are employed), the state shall exert its utmost to protect the lives, property and other legitimate rights and interests of Taiwanese civilians and foreign nationals in Taiwan, and to minimize losses.
- The Taiwan question is one that is left over from China's civil war of the late 1940s. Solving the Taiwan question and achieving national reunification is China's internal affair, subject to no interference from outside forces.

The Anti-Secession Law is essentially a carefully worded and toned-down codification of sentiments (read: threats) the PRC has been expressing for years. In the past, it has threatened military action if Taiwan declares independence, delays reunification, attempts to acquire nuclear weapons, allows for the presence of foreign soldiers, or experiences a breakdown in civil order. Incidentally, China's Anti-Secession Law was passed by its National People's Congress by a vote of 2,896 to 0.

No matter what China says, or what laws it enacts, the issue does not have anything to do with Taiwan having split the motherland. In fact, just prior to the end of World War Two, the Communist Party actually urged Taiwan to seek independence from Japan. In 1936, Mao Zedong himself was quoted as saying he didn't believe Taiwan to be one of China's so-called lost territories and that he favoured its independence.

What the issue really has to do with is the Chinese government repeatedly *saying* that Taiwan split the motherland, so it will be forced to maintain and act on those words. If the Chinese Communist Party were to renege on its Taiwan claim and allow the island to slip away, that would be indistinguishable from failing to protect the nation's political and territorial integrity. This, in turn, would equate to a colossal loss of face, and, although it may appear as a casual oversimplification, face is the essence to which this matter may be distilled.

To the People's Republic of China, the Republic of China's continued existence is an echo of the Chinese Civil War, that great symbol of Chinese disharmony laid out for the entire world to see.

Moreover, China's inability to do anything about it only underscores its weakness, and has done so every day for six long decades. Consequently, to right a long-standing wrong, Taiwan must be held up as some errant, obdurate child that deserves to be punished for having brought shame to the national family. China's position has virtually no basis in fact, but then it doesn't have to. Evidence takes a back seat to feelings in the Chinese world, and China *feels* very strongly about Taiwan. Feelings fuel myth and myth forms reality.

Besides the United States, which has been deeply and quietly committed to Taiwan for decades, China's most considerable obstacle to "reclaiming" "its" "precious island" is that there are *millions* of Taiwanese people who don't want anything to do with it. And it isn't just those who are descendents of early Fujianese or Hakka immigrants: those who tend to support the DPP; those who bristle at the thought of the misrule of that other Chinese political party, the KMT, and its record of sleaze, repression, and cultural suffocation. For the most part, KMT supporters themselves – those who came to Taiwan as a result of the Civil War, or Korean War, their offspring, or people who have converted through marriage or otherwise – don't wish to be ruled from Beijing either, at least not a communist Beijing; never mind that their party is committed to eventual quote-unquote reunification.

Because Taiwan isn't a member of the United Nations (it lost its seat in 1971), it isn't listed in that organization's Human Development Index. However, by utilizing the pertinent formula, it was calculated in 2005 that Taiwan would, theoretically, have ranked 23rd. Without getting into the nuts and bolts of the matter, that would appear to be about right. Presently, Hong Kong is ranked 22nd, South Korea 25th, and Singapore 28th. Even if Taiwan were 40th, that would be a far cry from China's sorry 92nd. All tallied, China has nothing to offer Taiwan, and "marry me or die" is the worst pick-up line of all time.

China interferes with Taiwan to the point where it must compete in international sporting events as Chinese Taipei. If Taiwan hosts a sporting event where China is a participant, Taiwan may not display its national flag. If Taiwanese businesspeople go abroad to represent Taiwan at a trade show, China will be sure to lodge a complaint with the event's organizers. In addition to routinely being denied a seat at the UN, Taiwan was refused entry into the World Health Organization 12 times, although in 2009 it finally gained observer status under the moniker Chinese Taipei. Taiwan is perpetually marginalized and only has 24 diplomatic allies, many of which sound more like rum cocktails than nation-states.

When China meddles and threatens, the Taiwanese temporarily

shelve their differences and their identity crisis and feel a sense of connectedness. And Taiwan does have an identity crisis. The KMT (or Pan-Blue Coalition, the bloc the KMT forms the majority of) wants so-called reunification or at least closer ties with China whereas the DPP (or Pan-Green Coalition, the bloc the DPP forms the majority of) hopes for independence or at least a moving away from China. Some Taiwanese want immediate "reunification" while others want immediate "secession." The majority – something like 70 percent – wishes to keep the *status quo*. Poll a group of Taiwanese citizens about whether they are Taiwanese or Chinese or both, or whether Taiwan is a country or a province, and you'll receive varying answers.

But certainly, whatever Taiwan is and whatever it will become is up to the Taiwanese people and the Taiwanese people alone to decide. As citizens of a free and democratic nation, they've earned the right.

I stood up, turned my back on the tacky radiance of Xiamen and walked through the darkness toward my rented scooter. The air was sultry and deathly still. The bushes whirred with insects. As I swiped sand from my pants, the atmosphere fizzled and split with a crack. There ensued an explosion so loud that I actually ducked. Hands raised around ears, I spun around to see the coast of China lit up like a bonfire. Fireworks. This time.

EPILOGUE

I broke the pledge I had made to myself and returned to China the following summer for one week in order to visit Meizhen. From Hong Kong I flew to Nanning, where I touched down on a rain-drenched airstrip one muggy, grey morning. It dumped rain every day, in fact, permitting me to do very little out of doors. During the mornings and afternoons, I would occupy a corner table of some coffee shop and read. At night, I would meet Meizhen for dinner and a movie. I spent the majority of my time holed up in my hotel room watching the European Cup and CCTV news.

This was only a week after the Sichuan earthquake, an event so powerful that it was felt in 10 other countries. Chinese television was saturated with images of searching helicopters, toiling soldiers, slogan-chanting rescue workers, and concerned officials addressing crowds with megaphones. The clips were arranged in a seemingly endless loop. I must have seen one of a dazed, stretcher-bound, young girl being whisked to safety by a dozen soldiers at least 30 times. Only twice did I see shots of actual wreckage, and these were extreme close-ups and only shown for an instant. There were no wide-angle pictures or views of devastated towns and no interviews with the bereaved. I knew that the situation had to be dire.

The most unsettling thing I saw was a piece on some "hospital" near Chengdu. A frowzled physician was in an ill-lit ward filled with injured children, most of which were sobbing pitiably. However, their open and evidently infected wounds were not being tended to. To be sure, there wasn't a nurse or a bandage in sight. Rather, the doctor was offhandedly leading the camera crew around to film the victims. "Look at this one," he said casually, pointing to a young girl. "Her feet will have to come off. What a shame. She's so cute." He then lifted up one of the girl's mashed and discoloured appendages before letting it fall. The girl shrieked and I shuddered. After the amputation, the girl was interviewed. She wailed hysterically and kept stammering how she had seen three of her classmates die. The female reporter kept repeating, "*Meiyou guanxi*," or "It's okay. Don't worry about it," in an affected, upbeat tone. This caused the girl to cry even louder. The reporter turned to the doctor and smiled. "Do you think she might experience depression?" she asked. "It's possible," he answered.

Meanwhile, out on the streets, vendors were making a killing hawking 'I Love China' bandanas, T-shirts, and flags, which *everyone* seemed to be buying or sporting. This was in connection with the upcoming Olympics. I enjoyed my time with Meizhen, but at the same time, I couldn't wait to leave.

Back in Taiwan, I read an article in *The Guardian* about how, behind the massive reconstruction efforts, the Chinese government was doing its utmost to silence the parents of children killed in the disaster because they were asking difficult questions. Chiefly, they wanted to know why 7,000 classrooms had collapsed and why, in some areas, schools were reduced to heaps of powder and folded metal while other buildings nearby remained largely intact.

Initially, the government allowed for such questions, not to mention complaints, protests, and even investigations into corruption and the resultant substandard construction. But when the movement got to be too large, cadres in the capital clamped down. Police were ordered in to guard demolished sites, bulldoze all the rubble, break up demonstrations, and warn vocal mothers and fathers not to talk to foreign reporters or even each other. When angry citizens attempted to buy train tickets to Beijing to protest, they were stopped by members of the Public Security Bureau. Other officials pressured parents into signing a document promising to "abide by the law and maintain social order." If they didn't, they were told, they wouldn't receive their compensation packages. Parents were isolated and told that everyone else had signed; if they didn't comply, they would be the only ones denied the government package. Thereafter, citizens found not to be "maintaining social order" in regard to this issue were sent to prison or re-education camps, or so said a Hong-Kong-based human rights group.

Reading this article in a coffee shop in downtown Taipei, I was reminded once more of how progressive Taiwan was in comparison with China. In addition to the three English-language dailies, I could easily buy a copy of the *International Herald Tribune* or just about every major news magazine in existence.

Still, a free press wasn't enough to sustain me, and I came to the realization that I had been living in Chinese society for far too long. It was indeed a social order "built upon a foundation of sand," and this was especially true for me. As an alien resident without a Taiwanese wife or child, I had virtually nothing in the way of legal recourse and was subject to the whims and fancies of anyone who might happen to take issue with me. But what bothered me more was that I would never be accepted as just another person; I would always be an outsider.

Such thoughts and frustrations finally congealed into a decision to move back to Canada to take a teaching position at a university. I spent the first few months of my homecoming in a state of more or less constant reverse culture shock.

It was interesting to view the two Chinas from such a distance after having been immersed in the culture for over a decade. The first related news piece I saw was on the CBC (Canadian Broadcasting Corporation) and came in the form of the 'the misplay of the week' award on a Sunday news show. It went to the people of Taiwan for venturing outside during a typhoon. A shaky camera showed people frantically gripping sign posts so as not to become human projectiles in the midst of ferocious winds and sideways sheets of rain. The following week's misplay nod went to China. The Xinhua News Agency had reported a successful space mission replete with astronaut discourse even though the astronauts were actually still on the ground. "Separatist" Uighurs made headlines when they allegedly attacked law-abiding Han citizens in Xinjiang, although the Uighurs insisted they were protesting peacefully when they were fired on by police. And, back to Taiwan, Chen Shui-bian, the man who vowed to end a lifetime of Nationalist Party corruption, was sentenced to life in prison for graft.

Canada's national newspaper, *The Globe and Mail*, reported that the Canadian prime minister, Stephen Harper, was rebuked during a trip to Beijing for not having visited China sooner. In a side room in the Great Hall of the People, Harper was scolded by Chinese premier, Wen Jiabao, who said, "Five years is too long a time for China-Canada relations and that's why there are comments in the media that your visit is one that should have taken place earlier." Of course, those comments in the media (read: the Xinhua News Agency) were ones supplied by Wen Jiabao's government. Harper had angered the Middle Kingdom by meeting with the Dalai Lama (an honourary citizen of Canada), not attending the Beijing games, and declaring he would not "sell out" on human rights when it came to China. For showing a bit of backbone, the Western leader was chastised by *The Globe and Mail*, which preached that he possessed a simplistic world view. Incidentally, my first trip to Beijing coincided with the previous visit by a Canadian prime minister to that city. When I tried to snap a photo of a guard standing in front of a

Canadian flag, an undercover police officer grabbed me roughly by the arm and told me to put my camera away and keep walking.

On an afternoon talk show, I watched a Canadian political commentator interviewing an ethnically Chinese author who'd written a biography about Chiang Kai-shek that cast the former dictator in a favourable light. The writer indicated that negative assessments of the generalissimo had been overblown. Chiang *was* strict, mind you. In those days, with the war on, you had to be. The Canadian nodded and agreed with every point. Nothing wrong with few austerity measures, he said. In the West, it seemed, practically anyone could be a China expert.

One evening, I noticed that the Chinese ambassador to the United States, Zhou Wenzhong, was being interviewed on the PBS talk show, *Charlie Rose*. After Mr. Zhou mentioned that there were some 90,000 Chinese students studying at universities in the United States, Mr. Rose asked what it was about the US that made China want to emulate it. China's ambassador answered that it was its emphasis on science and technology, its management skills, its enterprising mentality, and its creativity in relation to work. Mr. Rose then asked, "What should we learn from you?" a question that caused the sharp and otherwise articulate diplomat to falter. "Uhhhh, China, you know, ummm, Confucius's sort of philosophy... uh... being part of a tradition in China.... With influence of that tradition, we put more emphasis on the role of the collective rather than (the) individual, so we tend to emphasize more the role of the collective rather than the role of the individual...."

After that, it was all quite scripted. China had opened up (its citizens had Deng Xiaoping to thank for that), but still needed to adhere to the path of socialism with Chinese characteristics. Political reform was important, but had to be "suited to Chinese conditions" because so many people lacked a proper education. No, China was not on a collision course with the United States. In fact, China wasn't even a modern country. Besides, harmony was "the centre of Chinese philosophy" and it was China's greatest hope "to live in peace with everyone."

Later, I saw Tung Chee Hwa (the former chief executive of Hong Kong and current chairman of the China-United States Exchange Foundation) on the same program. Mr. Tung said that, unfortunately, there were quite a few "misperceptions" in America about China. For example, China was a "responsible player on the world stage," a "force for good," and a nation focused on "harmony." Its military budget wasn't really *that* big, and largely stemmed from an increase in soldiers' salaries. China was "very defensive in its military objectives." Moreover, China was "building a democratic system," and already had democratic institutions in place, its government fully aware of the importance of "social justice," "openness," and "accountability." China had "freedom of information" now, too, and human rights were moving forward as well. In fact, there were only a few "individual cases" when it came to human rights in China, and those tended to revolve around preserving national security. In short, China was "integrating with the world" and evolving at a rapid clip.

This gave me an idea.

A short while later, I hopped in my car after class one day and hit the highway. I sped between sloping fields dotted with hay bales and sweeping forests sprayed with autumnal red until I arrived in another city. I had arranged for an interview at one of Canada's six Confucius Institutes and was going to speak to a Mrs. Cai, the centre's executive director. As it happened, she was incredibly happy to see me.

Mrs. Cai explained that she had been living in Canada for three years. Before that, she worked at a university in Beijing helping to co-ordinate an overseas study program in addition to facilitating foreign students who came to China. This branch of the Confucius Institute was involved in various cultural events and had helped to establish the province's very first Mandarin program. Now, there were Mandarin programs at high schools all over the province and at one university. Mrs. Cai taught some of those classes. Small talk out of the way, I asked, "Why the Confucius Institute? Why not, say, The Chinese Council, or The Chinese Language and Culture Centre?"

She responded by saying that a group of professors in Beijing, where the institute had its headquarters, had come up with the idea.

"Do you consider Confucius to be China's greatest thinker?" I followed up.

"Yes," she said. "China's greatest thinker and China's greatest educator."

"Why?"

"Because we (knew) him since we were (children)," she replied cheerily. There was an awkward pause, and then, "Okay, maybe you take a walk with three people, and on that walk you discover one of those people is your teacher. Do you understand? He taught us that we should learn from others." She went on to explain that Confucianism had been very well received in other Asian countries, such as Korea.

"What does Confucius have to teach non-Chinese or non-Asian people?" I wanted to know.

Mrs. Cai searched for the answer for some time before concluding, "Harmony." That was the reason China had had such a long and peaceful history. When I asked if that was all – harmony – she repeated the three-

people-go-for-a-walk anecdote. Then she latched onto another idea
and paraphrased one of Confucius' sayings. Confucius says, "Is it not
a delight after all to have friends come from afar?" This taught us we
should embrace strangers, just as the Chinese had at the Beijing Olympics.

My next question was, "How does Confucianism compare with
Western philosophy?" She responded by saying she didn't know. When I
mentioned Socrates, she thought I was talking about Sartre. When I tried
to explain that Socrates had been born in Greece, and that the West had
been heavily influenced by him and other Greek thinkers, she had no idea
what I was talking about. To be fair, this may only have been a linguistic
problem. I gave her a brief outline by stating that whereas Socrates
teaches us that we must always ask questions in order to establish facts
and determine the truth, Confucius tells us that obedience is all and that
asking questions is a no-no. Mrs. Cai's cheeriness began to fade. She didn't
make any significant comment.

I took out my copy of the *Analects of Confucius* and asked her, politely,
what "The plague of heterodox theories can be eliminated by fierce
attack," meant. After admitting she hadn't read Confucius since high
school, she said, after some hesitation, that it meant, "When you criticize
something, you already know that it's bad." When I pointed out that this
wasn't what the English translation said (each quote was written in both
Chinese and perfect English), she claimed not to be able to read it, citing
that it was classical Chinese. "It's like Shakespeare," she said. "No one can
understand things Shakespeare wrote." I found this intriguing, especially
seeing as how she was a language teacher. A few days after our interview,
I asked a friend of mine from China if he could read the *Analects*. I
handed him my copy, and he looked at it and said, "Of course! It's in
Chinese!"

"And what does Western thinking have to teach Chinese people?" I
wanted to know. Mrs. Cai's reply was "individualism." The high school
students she taught "all (had) their own ideas," something that would
have been impossible in China. "In China," she explained, ominously,
"you must follow the way." When I asked if she *really* felt that China
needed Western-style individualism, she said that it needed some of it,
and I thought this was a reasonable response. However, she went on
to add that Canadians had too much individualism not to mention too
much freedom. She then intimated that this made them lazy. A few of
her high school students wanted to take a year off after they graduated.
Some wanted to travel. Others wanted to get a part-time job. She didn't
understand why they all didn't want to go on to university. Her daughter
studied every day from morning to midnight. Mrs. Cai said that when she

worked at her university in Beijing, she arrived at the office at 7:00 a.m. and went home at 9:00 p.m. But people didn't do that here. They weren't very fond of hard work. She couldn't understand why.

"Critics of Chinese culture, such as Bo Yang, have argued that Chinese people must abandon Confucianism and truly embrace the Western way of doing things if they are to advance," I said. "What do you think?"

"I disagree," she answered. "Of course, Chinese culture has many good points... and we should keep them... but we should also learn from the West."

I jotted down her answer and steered the exchange toward global influence. "Will Mandarin become a world language one day?" I asked, politely.

"As a language teacher, I have to say I hope so. Did you know there are more than one thousand Chinese teachers in Thailand? But Korea and America have the most Chinese learners. Chinese is very popular in Korea," she beamed.

"Will China become a global leader one day?"

"Actually, we don't want to be the leader. That is not important to us." She explained by saying there was no benefit to being a global leader, and I agreed that it certainly did entail a lot of responsibility before moving on to my next question.

"What do you think of Canadian politics and the Canadian democratic process? Do you think that such a system could ever work in China?"

"I don't know anything about Canadian politics," she conceded. "I'm not a citizen, so I think it's none of my business. About democracy... I don't think it's suitable for China," she said, frowningly. "You know, there are so many poor people in China and they don't have a very good education." As I was noting this down, she added, "In fact, we have democracy in China now. I know some foreigners say we don't, but (we do). There is more than one party. There are several parties."

I managed to stammer a, "I thought there was only one party in China, the Chinese Communist Party."

"No," she laughed. "There are many."

"Can you vote for them?"

"Of course! Take me for example: how do you think I got my position at the university I used to work for? I was elected." She then gave me a big grin.

I clarified by saying that I was referring to the right of all citizens to vote for their political leaders, not the manner in which various organizations decided on hiring or promotions, but she held firm. Contrary to what Western people believed, there was democracy in China.

"Many people are concerned with China's military build-up. Should they be?"

"Oh, we need it because China has so many countries around it," she said. She then got out a map of China to show me, but much to my surprise, she wasn't referring to border countries at all. Instead, she pointed out the provinces of Xinjiang, Tibet, and Inner Mongolia. "Like yesterday, there was a problem in Xinjiang," she said, pulling a face. "Maybe you heard about it." Actually, I hadn't.

"And have Tibet and Xinjiang always been part of China?"

"Of course."

"But many of the people living there say that isn't so."

"Oh, but we Chinese *believe* they are part of China."

"What about Taiwan? Has it always been a part of China?"

"Yes," she said. "It has always been a part of China because in nineteen forty-nine, a mainland government moved there after a civil war."

"Do the Taiwanese people believe they are living in China?"

"Oh, yes. *All* Taiwanese people believe that Taiwan and China are the same country. We are just like a big family. The new president of Taiwan believes that, too, and so does the Taiwan government."

"*All* Taiwanese people believe Taiwan is a part of China?" I asked.

"Before, no. But now, yes. Taiwanese students can go to China to study," she said, "and I even have a couple of Taiwanese students here."

"But if Taiwan is really a part of China, why does China have more than one thousand missiles pointed at it?" The number had continued to grow.

"Where did you hear that?" she wanted to know, insulted. When I told her, she indicated that Western news wasn't always very reliable. As a matter of fact, it was "very different" from Chinese news. Chinese news was much "happier," she said, and she didn't understand why Western news was "always so negative." "Let me give you an example," she went on. "Before the Olympics, some Western newspapers reported that shops in Beijing were too dirty, so they were forced to close by the government. That is not true. I am from Beijing, so I know that is not true. That's impossible."

I have rarely engaged in political discussion or debate with someone from the People's Republic of China, but when I have, it is always the same. If ever some event, news story, or historical reality is brought up, it will be shot down as propaganda, as if the entire world were engaged in a conspiracy to besmirch China's good name. That very morning, three of my Chinese students had vocally taken issue with a line in an article we were studying about William Golding and his theory about different classes of thinkers. According to Golding, the vast majority of people lack the ability to criticize or question. This type of individual is docile, cannot distinguish fact from fiction, and would have been "willing supporters of Hitler, Stalin, and Mao…." The word 'dictator' was one of our vocabulary items. I hadn't chosen the lesson. It was part of the curriculum.

Mao wasn't a dictator, I was informed. Rather he was "*just* a great leader," and "our hero." All Chinese people knew that. Why did foreigners always say he killed people? He didn't kill anybody. And what was so bad about Stalin, anyway?

I had known this was coming, so I directed the trio to the text's publisher, Oxford University Press, and suggested they write a letter of complaint. One student replied, "I will." The previous week, the same student had announced to a multiethnic class that Chinese people had the second highest IQs of anyone on Earth, second only to the Japanese. When I ignored him, he got upset. The following day, he brought proof – some printout from a Chinese website – but I ignored that, too; it had nothing to do with our lesson.

On *Charlie Rose*, Ambassador Zhou had told his American host that China was "singled out for whatever reason" in its dealings with Sudan, which was then being criticized for atrocities in the Darfur region. I asked Mrs. Cai if she ever watched the CBC news or read Canadian newspapers because I wanted to know if she believed the Canadian press ever singled China out. She answered by asking, "What's CBC?"

If the responses from the executive director of this Canadian-based branch of the Confucius Institute, an organization, by the way, that the Canadian Security Intelligence Service (CSIS) has raised concerns about, had been different, it is doubtful I would have asked her my final question. But as it was, I was deeply curious to know what her response would be.

"As you are doubtlessly aware," I began, "this is the twentieth anniversary of the Tiananmen Square Incident. I was wondering what your opinion of that event was, and I was also wondering what this image means to you." The image was a black-and-white photo of a lone man facing down four tanks. She looked at it, but didn't respond. "That picture is famous," I went on. "That man is probably one of the most famous Chinese people of all time, and many people would like to know who he was and what happened to him."

"We also want to know," she said, putting on a smile. "You know, just like you watched that on TV, well, we also watched it on TV, but nobody knows what happened to him. I think… you know… in China, like in the Qin Dynasty…. China is very big, so we (could not) let those people separate the country. We must have power."

"The people who demonstrated at Tiananmen Square in nineteen eighty-nine were separatists?" I asked. "They are seen in the West as having been pro-democracy demonstrators, mainly university students."

The question wasn't addressed. The comment after it was handled by saying the entire event had been orchestrated by a pair of professors. "Again, you know, I am from Beijing. I remember that time. For sure, some people died, but not as many as Western newspapers reported."

Technically, she was correct, but she was ignoring (or ignorant of) the massacre of workers and passersby that took place just down the road from Tiananmen Square after the crackdown. To restate, the Party admitted that 300 people died – substantially more than "some." But I knew there was no point in discussing this. I knew what I had known for a long time: there was no point in discussing anything.

Realizing that the interview had gone badly, Mrs. Cai attempted a bit of damage control. She asked that I submit whatever I wrote to her boss for approval. I remained silent. She had agreed to do the interview without any conditions. The silence continued. She smiled again and showed me a picture book about Confucius as well as pictures of the Chinese Ambassador to Canada meeting with the local mayor. The two were grinning and painting the eyes on a dragon costume. By adding a streak of red to the black eyeballs, she explained, the dragon would come alive. But the cultural attaché could see that I wasn't in any way taken by the dragon. Dragons, after all, do not exist. I thanked her for her time, got in my car, and headed for home.

SELECT BIBLIOGRAPHY

Alexander, McGill. *Hostage in Taipei* (Santa Rosa, CA: Cladach Publishing, 2000)

BBC News, World Edition. "China's Cigarette Threat," http://news.bbc. co.uk/2/hi/health/216988.stm

Becker, Jasper. *The Chinese* (New York: Oxford University Press, 2002)

Bender, Andrew, et al. *Taiwan: Lonely Planet* (Melbourne, Australia: Lonely Planet Publications, 2004)

Bloom, Allan. *The Closing of the American Mind* (New York: Simon & Schuster Paperbacks, 1987)

Bo, Yang. *The Ugly Chinaman and the Crisis of Chinese Culture*, trans. Don J. Cohn, Jing Qing (Sydney, Australia: Allen & Unwin Pty Ltd., 1992)

Chang, Jung, and Jon Halliday. *Mao: The Unknown Story* (London: Jonathan Cape, 2005)

Chang, Jung. *Wild Swans: Three Daughters of China* (New York: Touchstone, 2003)

Chang, Iris. *The Chinese in America* (New York: Penguin Books, 2004)

Chang, Iris. *The Rape of Nanking* (New York: Penguin Books, 1998)

China: Lonely Planet, 9th edn (Melbourne, Australia: Lonely Planet Publications, 2005)

Clissold, Tim. *Mr. China: A Memoir* (New York: Harper Paperbacks, 2006)

Confucius. *Analects of Confucius* (Beijing: Sinolingua, 2005)

Crook, Steven. *Keeping Up With the War God* (Brighton, UK: Yushan Publications, 2001)

Crook, Steven. *Taiwan: The Bradt Travel Guide* (Chalfont St. Peter, UK: Bradt Travel Guides, 2010)

Davidson, James W. *The Island of Formosa, Past and Present: History, People, Resources, and Commercial Prospects* (Taipei: SMC Publishing, 1992)

Dikötter, Frank, et al. *Narcotic Culture: A History of Drug Use in China* (Chicago: The University of Chicago Press, 2004)

Dong, Stella. *Shanghai: The Rise and Fall of a Decadent City* (New York: Perennial, 2001)

Fenby, Jonathan. *Chiang Kai-shek: China's Generalissimo and the Nation He Lost* (New York: Carroll & Graf Publishers, 2005)

Fenby, Jonathan. *The Penguin History of Modern China: The Fall and Rise of a Great Power, 1850–2008* (London: Allen Lane, 2008)

French, Patrick. *Tibet, Tibet: A Personal History of a Lost Land* (New York: Alfred A. Knopf, 2003)

Gifford, Rob. *The China Road: A Journey into the Future of a Rising Power* (New York: Random House, Inc., 2007)

Gottlieb, Anthony. *Socrates* (London: Phoenix, 1997)

Harrer, Heinrich. *Seven Years in Tibet*, trans. Richard Graves (New York: Jeremy R. Tarcher/Putnam, 1997)

Heller, Joseph. *Catch-22* (New York: Simon & Schuster, 1996)

Hessler, Peter. *River Town: Two Years on the Yangtze* (New York: HarperCollins Publishers, 2001)

Jacques, Martin. *When China Rules the World: The End of the Western World and the Birth of a New Global Order* (New York: The Penguin Press, 2009)

Johnson, Paul. *A History of the Jews* (New York: Harper Perennial, 1987)

Kerr, George H. *Formosa Betrayed* (Upland, CA: Taiwan Publishing Co., 1965)

Lao, Tzu. *Tao Te Ching* (Hertfordshire, UK: Wordsworth Editions Limited, 1997)

Larmer, Brook. "Manchurian Mandate," *National Geographic* (Washington, DC: Sept., 2006)

Lu, Hsun (Lu, Xun). *Selected Stories*, trans. Yang Hsien-yi, Gladys Yang (New York: W.W. Norton & Company, Inc., 2003)

Lu, Xun. *The True Story of Ah Q*, 3rd edn (Beijing: Foreign Language Press, 2003)

Lewis, Simon. *The Mini Rough Guide to Beijing* (London: Rough Guides Ltd., 2000)

Li, Zhishui. *The Private Life of Chairman Mao* (New York: Random House, Inc., 1994)

Ma, Jian. *Red Dust*, trans. Flora Drew (London: Vintage, 2002)

Ma, Jian. *Stick Out Your Tongue*, trans. Flora Drew (London: Vintage, 2007)

MacKay, George Leslie. *From Far Formosa* (Taipei: SMC Publishing, 1995)

Man, John. *The Great Wall* (London: Bantam Press, 2008)

Man, John. *The Terracotta Army* (London: Bantam Press, 2007)

Mann, James. *The China Fantasy* (New York: Viking Penguin, 2007)

Martin, Bradley K. *Under the Loving Care of the Fatherly Leader: North Korea and the Kim Dynasty* (New York: Thomas Dunne Books, 2004)

Mason, Richard. *The World of Suzie Wong* (New York: Pegasus Books, 1994)

Mathews, Jay. "The Myth of Tiananmen and the Price of a Passive Press" (Columbia Journalism Review, September/October, 1998)

McGovern, Janet B. Montgomery. *Among the Headhunters of Formosa* (Taipei: SMC Publishing, Inc., 1997)

Menzies, Gavin. *1421: The Year China Discovered the World* (New York: William Morrow, 2003)

Mitamura, Hose, et al. *China by Numbers 2008* (Hong Kong: China Economic Review Publishing, 2008)

Mosher, Steven W. *Hegemon: China's Plan to Dominate Asia and the World* (San Francisco: Encounter Books, 2002)

Nine Commentaries on the Communist Party (Gillette, NJ: Yih Chyun Book Corp., 2004)

Orwell, George. *Nineteen Eighty-Four* (London: Penguin Books, Ltd., 2003)

Parfitt, Troy. *Notes from the Other China* (New York: Algora Publishing, 2008)

Ross, John. *Formosan Odyssey* (Taiwan: Taiwan Adventure Publications, 2002)

Roy, Denny. *Taiwan: A Political History* (Ithaca, NY: Cornell University Press, 2003)

Seagrave, Sterling. *Dragon Lady: Life and Legend of the Last Empress of China* (New York: Vintage Books, 1993)

Seagrave, Sterling. *Lords of the Rim* (New York: G.P. Putnam's Sons, 1995)

Seagrave, Sterling. *The Soong Dynasty* (London: Corgi Books, 1996)

Spence, Jonathan D. *Mao Zedong: A Life* (New York: Penguin Books, 2006)

Spence, Jonathan D. *The Search for Modern China*, 2nd edn (New York: W.W. Norton & Company, Inc., 1999)

Spence, Jonathan D. *To Change China: Western Advisors in China* (New York: Penguin Books, 1980)

Stefan Landsberger's Chinese Propaganda Poster Page: Lei Feng. http://www.iisg.nl/landsberger/lf.html

Storey, Robert. *Taiwan (Travel Survival Kit)* 3rd edn (Hawthorn, Australia: Lonely Planet Publications, 1994)

Sun, Tzu. *The Art of War* (London: Oxford University Press, 1971)

Theroux, Paul. *Riding the Iron Rooster: By Train through China* (New York: Random House, Inc., 1989)

Thompson, Hugh, et al. *China: Eyewitness Travel Guides* (New York: DK Publishing, Inc., 2005)

Vidal, Gore. *Creation: A Novel* (New York: Vintage Books, 1981)

Wong, Jan. *Red China Blues: My Long March from Mao to Now* (New York: Random House, Inc., 1996)

Zheng Yi. *Scarlet Memorial: Tales of Cannibalism in Modern China* (Boulder, CO: Westview Press, 1996)

ABOUT THE AUTHOR

Troy Parfitt is the author of *Notes from the Other China*. Born in Saint John, New Brunswick, Canada in 1972, he lived for nearly two years in Seoul, South Korea and for more than ten in Taipei, Taiwan. He currently resides in Canada where he is writing a book about that country.

To learn more, visit www.troyparfitt.com.

Quick Order Form

Telephone orders: Call 1-506-639-9996. Have your credit card ready.

Email orders: west.hem.press@gmail.com

Postal orders: Western Hemisphere Press, 125 Rothesay Ave., PO Box 1401, Saint John, NB, Canada, E2L 4H8

Please send _____ copy/copies of *Why China Will Never Rule the World: Travels in the Two Chinas* to the following:

Name: _____

Address: _____

City: _____ State/Province: _____

Zip/Postal Code: _____

Telephone: _____

Email address: _____

Please send me free information on future books.

_____ Yes, please.   _____ No, thank you.

Shipping (estimate):
USA: $7.50 per copy.
Canada: NL: $12.75 per copy. NS, PE, NB: $9.25 per copy. QC: $10.25 per copy. ON: $11.00 per copy. MB, SK, AB, BC: $12.75 per copy. NU: $15.00 per copy. NT, YT: $11.85 per copy.

QUICK ORDER FORM

Telephone orders: Call 1-506-639-9996. Have your credit card ready.

Email orders: west.hem.press@gmail.com

Postal orders: Western Hemisphere Press, 125 Rothesay Ave., PO Box 1401, Saint John, NB, Canada, E2L 4H8

Please send _____ copy/copies of *Why China Will Never Rule the World: Travels in the Two Chinas* to the following:

Name: _____

Address: _____

City: _____ State/Province: _____

Zip/Postal Code: _____

Telephone: _____

Email address: _____

Please send me free information on future books.

_____ Yes, please.   _____ No, thank you.

Shipping (estimate):
USA: $7.50 per copy.
Canada: NL: $12.75 per copy. NS, PE, NB: $9.25 per copy. QC: $10.25 per copy. ON: $11.00 per copy. MB, SK, AB, BC: $12.75 per copy. NU: $15.00 per copy. NT, YT: $11.85 per copy.